Library of
Davidson College

The mystery plays of medieval England have traditionally been analysed in ways which centre on the texts and their religious significance. Hans-Jürgen Diller's major study, first published in German, seeks to recover their dramatic potential by focusing on the function of language, in conventional modes of speech, prayer, address and dialogue. His examination of speech and dramatic form in the plays yields new insights concerning spatial and temporal orientation, the expression of emotions, and the relationships between characters on stage, between actor and audience, and between the dramatic world and the ordinary world outside it. It offers new ways of understanding the relationship of vernacular drama to its liturgical antecedents, and new means of distinguishing stylistically between the cycles, and between the groups of plays they comprise.

European Studies in English Literature

The Middle English Mystery Play

European Studies in English Literature

SERIES EDITORS
Ulrich Broich, Professor of English, University of Munich
Herbert Grabes, Professor of English, University of Giessen
Dieter Mehl, Professor of English, University of Bonn

Roger Asselineau, Professor Emeritus of American Literature, University of Paris-Sorbonne
Paul-Gabriel Boucé, Professor of English, University of Sorbonne-Nouvelle
Robert Ellrodt, Professor of English, University of Sorbonne-Nouvelle
Sylvère Monod, Professor Emeritus of English, University of Sorbonne-Nouvelle

This series is devoted to publishing translations in English of the best works written in European languages on English literature. These may be first-rate books recently published in their original versions, or they may be classic studies which have influenced the course of scholarship in their world while never having been available in English before.

TRANSLATIONS PUBLISHED
Walter Pater: The Aesthetic Moment by Wolfgang Iser
The Symbolist Tradition in English Literature: A Study of Pre-Raphaelitism and 'Fin de Siècle' by Lothar Hönnighausen
The Theory and Analysis of Drama by Manfred Pfister
Oscar Wilde: The Works of a Conformist Rebel by Norbert Kohl
The Fall of Women in Early English Narrative Verse by Götz Schmitz
The Rise of the English Street Ballad 1550–1650 by Natascha Würzbach
Romantic Verse Narrative: The History of a Genre by Hermann Fischer
Shakespeare's Festive World by François Laroque
The Eighteenth-Century Mock Heroic Poem by Ulrich Broich
The Middle English Mystery Play: A Study in Dramatic Speech and Form by Hans-Jürgen Diller

TITLE UNDER CONTRACT FOR TRANSLATION
L'Etre et l'avoir dans les romans de Charles Dickens by Anny Sadrin

The Middle English Mystery Play

A Study in Dramatic Speech and Form

Hans-Jürgen Diller

Translated by Frances Wessels

Published by the Press Syndicate of the University of Cambridge
The Pitt Building, Trumpington Street, Cambridge CB2 1RP
40 West 20th Street, New York, NY 10011-4211, USA
10 Stamford Road, Oakleigh, Victoria 3166, Australia

Originally published in German as Redeformen des englischen
Misterienspiels by Hans-Jürgen Diller 1973 and © Wilhelm Fink Verlag,
Munich, Germany

First published in English by Cambridge University Press 1992 as
The Middle English Mystery Play: A Study in Dramatic Speech and Form

English translation © Cambridge University Press 1992

Printed in Great Britain at the University Press, Cambridge

A catalogue record for this book is available from the British Library

Library of Congress cataloguing in publication data
Diller, Hans-Jürgen.
[Redeformen des englischen Misterienspiels. English]
The Middle English mystery play: a study in dramatic speech and
form / Hans-Jürgen Diller; translated by Frances Wessels.
    p. cm. – (European studies in English literature)
Translation of: Redeformen des englischen Misterienspiels.
Includes bibliographical references and index.
ISBN 0 521 32062 3
1. Mysteries and miracle-plays, English – History and criticism.
2. English drama – To 1500 – History and criticism. 3. Speech in
literature. 4. Bible in literature. 5. Rhetoric, Medieval.
I. Title. II. Series.
PR643.M8D55 1992
822′.051609–dc20   91-16963 CIP

ISBN 0 521 32062 3 hardback

UP

To Audrey and Clifford Davidson for their
friendship, hospitality, and advice

Contents

Preface	*page* xi
Note on texts used	xiii
Abbreviations and special symbols	xiv
Introduction	1

Part I The foil: Latin church drama

1. Liturgy and drama 9
   Impersonation and representation 9
   The structure of the first situations to be represented mimetically 13
   The language of the Revelation dialogue 22

2. Liturgical point of view surrounding the dramatic core dialogue 25
   Lyrico-liturgical point of view after the core dialogue 25
   'Victimae paschali' as an intermediate stage between drama and liturgy 27
   Narrative point of view in the introductory responsories and processions 28
   Further manifestations of the liturgical perspective in the processional songs 29
   The interplay between dramatic and extradramatic elements in the early liturgical drama 30

3. 'World-containing' situations 33
   Origins and character of the new situation-type 33
   Interpersonal relationships 37
   Emotions 41
   Herod's wrath 41 Laments 45 Excursus: The Latin and Middle High German *planctus* in the Benediktbeuern Greater Passion Play 51

4. The dramatization of narrative sources 54
   The transposition of mental processes into the dramatic medium 54
   Rôle-type characterization 58
   Time and space 64

x   Contents

Part II The English Creation to Doom cycle

5. The origins of the Creation to Doom cycle and its stage   71

6. The representation of time and space in the cycles   79
   Sketch of a typology   79
   Time and space in the Chester cycle   80
   Time and space in the Yorkshire cycles   88
   Time and space in N-Town   99

7. Address to the audience   109
   General aspects   109
   Liturgical 'forerunners' 109 The significance of the audience-address for the vernacular drama 112 Recognizing the audience-addresses 113
   The audience-address in Chester   114
   Edificational audience-addresses 114 Open play-sphere and 'histrionic' audience-address 114 Speech-types resembling the audience-address 119
   The audience-address in the York and Towneley cycles   122
   Absence of separation between the two spheres, especially in the earlier strata 122 Later tendencies towards a closed play-sphere 128 'Popular' audience-addresses 128 The development of the bragging speech 132 Peculiarities of Towneley 135 Peculiarities of York 140
   The audience-address in the N-Town cycle   145
   Changing speaker perspective in the 'Proclamation thirteeners' and short octaves 145 The 'histrionic' audience-address in LC XIV, with a digression on the early history of the Vice 148 Other parts of N-Town 152 Speeches of tyrants and devils 152 Contemplacio 154 'The Assumption of the Virgin' 157

8. Intra-dramatic speeches   160
   Revelation speeches   161
   The opening prayer   169
   Chester 169 York and Towneley 171 Excursus: Coventry 174 N-Town 179
   The verbal presentation of mourning and grief   180
   Marian laments   182
   Other laments   194
   Towneley 194 York 197 Chester 203 Brome and Northampton (with a view to Ch IV) 206 N-Town 209
   Dialogues
   'Serial' dialogues 216 Dialogues of strife and insult 224 Devils' dialogue 226 Cain and Abel 227 The Torturing and the Crucifixion of Christ 232 The Shepherds 240

9. Conclusions   251
Notes   254
Bibliography   300
Indexes   323

Preface

The history of this book is such that most of it has to be told in the Introduction rather than the Preface. The German original was first written as a *Habilitationsschrift* and submitted to the Faculty of Philosophy of the University of Göttingen in 1968. In book form it appeared, with minor revisions, under the title *Redeformen des englischen Misterienspiels*, published by Wilhelm Fink Verlag, Munich, in 1973. When invited to prepare an English translation for the *European Studies in English Literature* series, I felt the double obligation of preserving the German background from which the book originated and taking note of scholarship which had appeared since the publication of the original. These two goals are not easily reconciled with the equally important one of reader-friendliness. Footnotes such as 'But see now X' and 'See now also Y' are required by intellectual honesty, but courtesy to the reader demands that they be kept to a minimum. Oversights and errors that were brought to my attention have been corrected and acknowledged. In this respect Dieter M. Schmidt's dissertation (Free University of Berlin) ought to be singled out for special mention.

During the lengthy process of translation and preparing for the press I enjoyed the help and advice of many collaborators and friends. First among them are my translator, Frances Wessels, and my student assistants. Mrs Wessels showed great resourcefulness in finding nearequivalents for my academic German, and even greater patience in discussing them with me. Petra Beste, Ulrike Bethlehem, Ulrike Borgmann, Carsten Breul, and Silvia König spent endless hours checking quotations, harmonizing citations and wrestling with the word processor. Together with Katrin Klaetke they were also engaged in the unexpectedly complex proofreading process. The staff of many libraries in Britain, the United States and Germany were invariably helpful. My university, Ruhr-Universität Bochum, granted me sabbatical leave for the summer term, 1987.

To Professors Audrey and Clifford Davidson this book owes more than a mere dedication can express. Their friendship and hospitality during part of my sabbatical, spent at Western Michigan University (Kalamazoo), gave me the leisure to familiarize myself with much scholarship which otherwise I might have been unable to assimilate. Together with their colleagues at Western Michigan's Medieval Institute and above all its director, Professor Otto Gründler, they made that period thoroughly enjoyable and extremely fruitful. Clifford Davidson read the translation in typescript, and his advice and criticism have been invaluable. The remaining shortcomings of the book are of course my own responsibility.

It seems fitting also to remember those scholars to whom the original version owes most. Theodor Wolpers acted as my *Habilitationsvater* in 1968 and gave advice and encouragement in the preceding years. His influence is much more pervasive than citations can indicate. Robert Weimann, of what was then East Berlin, generously allowed me to read chapters of his *Shakespeare und die Tradition des Volkstheaters* prior to publication. His readiness to exchange views freely, at a time when *Abgrenzung* was the order of the day between the two Germanies, has been one of the most heartening experiences of my academic existence.

Finally, I want to thank my wife who believed in the value of my work even when I was less sure.

Note on texts used

The English Creation to Doom cycles are cited from the following editions (for complete bibliographical information consult this study's Bibliography):

Chester [Ch] Lumiansky, R. M., and David Mills, eds. *The Chester Mystery Cycle*
Where necessary, the older edition by Deimling and Matthews is used:
Deimling, Hermann, ed. *The Chester Plays.* Part I
and Matthews, J., ed. *The Chester Plays.* Part II
N-Town [LC] Block, K. S., ed. *Ludus Coventriae, or The Plaie called Corpus Christi*
(*The N-Town Play*, ed. Stephen Spector [EETS, SS 11 and 12] (London, 1991) appeared too late for inclusion.)
Towneley [T] England, George, ed. *The Towneley Plays*
for the plays attributed to the 'Wakefield Master':
Cawley, A. C., ed. *The Wakefield Pageants in the Towneley Cycle*
York [Y] Beadle, Richard, ed. *The York Plays*

Unless otherwise stated, the Latin liturgical offices and plays are cited from:
Young, Karl *The Drama of the Medieval Church*

Abbreviations and special symbols

Abbreviations:

ABELL	*Annual Bibliography of English Language and Literature*
AH	Dreves and Blume, eds., *Analecta Hymnica*
App.	Appendix
Archiv	*Archiv für das Studium der neueren Sprachen und Literaturen*
AYL	Shakespeare, *As You Like It*
Br	Play of Abraham and Isaac from the commonplace book of the Brome family
CB	The play of Christ's Burial from MS e Museo 160, often called the 'Digby' Burial play
Ch	The Chester Plays
CR	The play of Christ's Resurrection from MS e Museo 160, often called the 'Digby' Resurrection play
DM	*The Chester Plays*, eds. Deimling and Matthews
DMC	Young, *The Drama of the Medieval Church*
DVjs	*Deutsche Vierteljahrschrift für Literaturwissenschaft und Geistesgeschichte*
EDAM	Early Drama, Art, and Music
EDD	*English Dialect Dictionary*, ed. Joseph Wright
EETS, ES	Early English Text Society, Extra Series
EETS, OS	Early English Text Society, Original Series
EETS, SS	Early English Text Society, Supplementary Series
ELH	*Journal of English Literary History*
ERD	Craig, *English Religious Drama of the Middle Ages*
F. f. a.	*Flete fideles animae*
FMLS	*Forum for Modern Language Studies*
Gen.	Genesis
GRM	*Germanisch-romanische Monatsschrift*
JEGP	*Journal of English and Germanic Philology*
LC	The N-Town Plays, formerly known as *Ludus Coventriae*

Lev.	Leviticus
LFGS	Stemmler, *Liturgische Feiern und Geistliche Spiele*
Lib.	Liber
LM	*The Chester Cycle*, eds. Lumiansky and Mills
LThK	*Lexikon für Theologie und Kirche*
Luke	The Gospel according to Saint Luke
MÆ	*Medium Ævum*
Mark	The Gospel according to Saint Mark
Matt.	The Gospel according to Saint Matthew
MED	*Middle English Dictionary*, 1954– , ed. Hans Kurath, Sherman M. Kuhn, *et al.*
METh	*Medieval English Theatre*
Mic.	Microfiche number of American dissertations
MLN	*Modern Language Notes*
MLR	*Modern Language Review*
MP	*Modern Philology*
MS	*Mediaeval Studies*
MS(S)	Manuscript(s)
NF	Neue Folge
Nh	The Northampton play of Abraham and Isaac, from a Dublin MS
Nic.	The Gospel of Nicodemus
NLH	*New Literary History*
NS	New Series
ob.	obiit
PBB	*Paul und Braunes Beiträge zur Geschichte der deutschen Sprache und Literatur*
PL	*Patrologia Latina*, ed. Jacques-Paul Migne (Paris, 1844–55)
Pl. a. n.	*Planctus ante nescia*
PMLA	*Publications of the Modern Language Association of America*
PQ	*Philological Quarterly*
Prot. J.	Protevangelium Jacobi
RDK	*Reallexikon der deutschen Kunstgeschichte*, ed. Otto Schmidt *et al.*
REED	*Records of Early English Drama*
RES	*Review of English Studies*
RORD	*Research Opportunities in Renaissance Drama*
Sc.	scene
SD	Stage Direction
Sh.-Jb.	*Shakespeare-Jahrbuch*

SITM	Société Internationale du Théâtre Médiéval
SPCK	Society for the Promotion of Christian Knowledge
Spec.	*Speculum - A Journal of Medieval Studies*
STCo	The Shearmen and Taylors' Pageant of the Coventry Corpus Christi Cycle
st(s).	stanza(s)
St. L.	*Stanzaic Life of Christ*
s.v.	*sub voce*
T	The Towneley Plays
TN	*Theatre Notebook*
WCo	The Weavers' Pageant of the Coventry Corpus Christi Cycle
Y	The York Plays
YWESt	*The Year's Work in English Studies*
ZAA	*Zeitschrift für Anglistik und Amerikanistik*
ZfdA	*Zeitschrift für deutsches Altertum*
ZRPh	*Zeitschrift für Romanische Philologie*

Special symbols:

x (between figures) designates a date between the two dates given, as opposed to a dash, which designates 'from ... to' (e.g. 'John of Hildesheim 1310x20–1375': John was born between 1310 and 1320, died in 1375)

+ (added to a figure) indicates an unnumbered line (usually a stage direction) following the line to which the given number belongs

Introduction

In the late 1960s and early 1970s, when the German original of this book was written and published, the study of medieval English drama was still largely text-centred, and this orientation implied certain tacit assumptions: that the four extant cycles were representative of the lost religious drama as well; that the manuscripts preserved gave a fairly accurate picture of the acted texts; that the Corpus Christi cycle was the dominant type of Middle English communal religious drama; and that the pageant-waggon was the typical stage for such a cycle. Of the many other dramatic activities and their socio-economic context, little was known that went beyond the famous Appendixes to Chambers' *The Mediaeval Stage*. The systematic search of archives for unpublished dramatic records was then just beginning.[1] Our knowledge of the iconography of the medieval theatre was still much more haphazard than it is today: the *Early Drama, Art, and Music* project started publishing in 1977.

The standard work to which everybody referred, even if it was mainly to criticize it, was Hardin Craig's *English Religious Drama of the Middle Ages*. Craig, whose book is still the last comprehensive monograph on the subject, epitomized more than half a century of criticism in his claim that the 'life-blood' of the religious drama of the Middle Ages was religion and that it represented 'the strange case of a drama that was not striving to be dramatic but to be religious'. Where Craig diverged from his predecessors, especially from E. K. Chambers, was in his evaluation; he asked critics to prefer the 'religious' to the 'dramatic', and he condemned earlier interest in 'raging tyrants, and clowns' as missing the ethos of the genre.[2]

Craig's apparent resignation before this 'strange case' provoked a new generation of scholars into re-arguing the relationship between 'drama' and 'religion'. While V. A. Kolve tried to explain the indubitable, long-lasting success of the cycle plays by recourse to the imaginative appeal of the feast of Corpus Christi and its religious message, Eleanor Prosser attempted to develop a standard by which the quality of a religious, didactic drama could be judged. While she gave us many insights into the techniques which made moral and religious messages dramatically effective, her view of the function of comic scenes remained severely limited by her insistence on a neo-classical unity of mood.³

My own criticism was sparked off by Craig's slighting reference to the 'simple' and 'crude' technique of the medieval playwrights (pp. 4, 6). I felt that a close analysis of the extant texts under recurrent criteria would demonstrate an accumulated expertise in acting and staging techniques and in the use of dramatic language which might well turn out not to be as simple as Craig made us believe.

At the same time I hoped that such an approach could help overcome the false dichotomy between 'religious' and 'secular' which was continued even by Prosser. Since the publication of her book so many records have come to light and have been quoted in the literature that it is now commonplace to say that the civic cycles were staged 'for the honour of God, and worship of the City'.⁴ Medieval gradualism certainly knew a contrast, even conflict, between lay and ecclesiastical interests. But it did not know that cleavage between two spheres of existence which is central to the *Lebensgefühl* of modern man. Paradoxically, Prosser even stresses the very point which should have saved her from misjudging the Passion plays: to the medieval public the events represented in the mystery plays had the same reality as their everyday lives or, perhaps, an even greater reality. The consequences which this fact has for the emotional impact of certain scenes are, however, ignored. The modern spectator will find the blasphemy of the Passion scenes disturbing precisely because he is less than certain of the existence of God and of the divinity of Christ. He cannot be sure that the blasphemers will receive their just punishment. To the medieval audience none of these points was in doubt. Blasphemy was indubitably blasphemy, the 'right' reaction to which could hardly be in question. It did not 'hurt religious feelings'; these begin to need protection only when they cease to be shared by the entire population.

I still believe that this example shows the dangers of judging the aesthetic character of medieval works by taking a short-cut via a timelessly conceived 'emotional effect'. Twenty years ago I was hardly less critical of V.A. Kolve's attempt to gauge the emotional impact of the Corpus Christi plays.⁵ The evidence on which Kolve draws includes the teaching of the medieval Church concerning laughter (ch. 6), the acting instructions of the post-Reformation Chester Banns (p. 138), the effect of modern productions of medieval plays (p. 139), and his own subjective responses. Today I am more inclined to accept his results; I believe, with him and against Rossiter and Weimann,⁶ that 'we are separate from' the *Tortores* of the Passion plays (p. 138). But I am still dissatisfied with the way by which he reaches these results, and they strike me as doing less than justice to the considerable differences that exist between the four cycles and between individual scenes within each of them. These can be brought out only by a systematic study of selected aspects.

I was also uncomfortably aware that there was still a tendency for scholars to find those things in the plays which appealed to them on ideological grounds. Profiting from discussion and correspondence with Robert Weimann, who was then writing the German original of *Shakespeare and the Popular Tradition in the Theater*, I was fascinated by the continuity of comic acting and speech which in Weimann's presentation linked, for instance, the N-Town Joseph with so many figures of the Shakespearean stage. Yet I was doubtful about the underground paganism which he assumed in much of medieval religious drama.[7] And while I accepted Weimann's (and Rossiter's) postulate that the official ideology does not automatically exhaust the legitimate responses to a performance, I remained unconvinced that, for instance, the irreverence of the Towneley Cain was meant to be shared by the audience. It was my hope that close textual analysis under recurrent aspects might resolve at least some of the disagreements under which the criticism of medieval drama laboured then, as it does now.

Such a study, I felt, would also help to refute Craig's sweeping claim that the difference between the liturgical and the vernacular drama was marked by 'no new and revolutionary elements' and 'no new motives' (p.1). Dissatisfaction with Craig made me preface the study of the English cycle plays with about a hundred pages on the liturgical drama. The choice of the recurrent aspects under which the plays were to be studied was also determined by this dissatisfaction. They had to be those where the difference between liturgical and vernacular drama promised to be most striking. Most of them are closely related to what Georg Lukács has called the 'world'-creating capacity of the work of art. An aesthetic creation ['Gebilde'] becomes a 'world' in Lukács' understanding when it is transformed into

ein wahrhaft selbständiges Gebilde, das dem Menschen als ein auf sich selbst gestelltes Ansich gegenübersteht

a truly independent creation which confronts ('stands opposite') man as a thing-by-itself resting on its own foundation.[8]

This independence is exactly what the liturgical drama largely lacks and what we find in varying degrees in the vernacular plays and the Latin saint plays. It is also the implicit basis for the distinction between *Feier* (liturgical ceremony) and *Spiel* (play) which Helmut de Boor and Theo Stemmler have drawn.[9]

The notion of 'world' determined the choice of categories under which the texts were to be studied. The two basic differences between liturgical and later drama concern time and space and the relationship between the 'play' and those who watch it. While the true play has to 'create' the time and place of the world represented in it, the liturgical ceremony finds them, as it were, ready-made by the liturgy: the altar suggests the sepulchre, Easter matins evoked the first morning after Christ's resurrection long before the first *Osterfeier* was even thought of. The play is also distinguished from the liturgical ceremony in that it presupposes an audience which it 'confronts'; the ceremony knows only a congregation consisting above all of participants; it may, but need not, include onlookers. This makes the audience-address and the relationships which it expresses into an essential aspect of the *Spiel*.[10] The other features treated in this book concern the inner aspects of the 'world' created in the play: the study of dialogue is made necessary by the importance which interpersonal relationships acquire for the construction of the dramatic world, while the inner world of the characters demands the study of the means by which emotions are expressed.

Looking back on my criticism of Craig twenty years ago, I must now admit that there is one assumption which I adopted from him and his predecessors without much questioning. Craig followed Greg and Chambers in the belief that the texts of the cycles which have been preserved allow us to distinguish various 'strata' or 'layers' and thus to trace stages in the development of dramatic style and technique. This belief has been largely discredited in recent years. The hard evidence gathered from archives and manuscripts, especially by the powerful teams of Toronto and Leeds, has made it increasingly clear that the plays as we have them are products of the fifteenth and the early sixteenth century; any hopes of uncovering earlier strata, which might take us back to the first beginnings of the cycles in the late fourteenth century or even earlier, must now be regarded as largely unfounded.

We have also learnt to be more cautious in ascribing a home to every cycle. *Ludus Coventriae*, certainly not from Coventry, is now being increasingly referred to as 'N-Town'. This designation, which appears in the 'Proclamation' of the cycle (line 527), is perhaps best explained as a variable name to be replaced by the name of the town where the next performance was to take place. In that case the cycle for which the 'Proclamation' was originally written[11] belonged not to a city but to a group of strolling players. Attempts to localize the cycle in Lincoln or Bury St Edmunds have found little acceptance.

Doubts multiply also concerning the Wakefield provenance of the Towneley cycle. A civic character can, therefore, be safely assumed for only two of the cycles that have come down to us in more or less complete form, i.e. for York and Chester. And of these two only York was connected with the feast of Corpus Christi.

In the field of medieval drama, as in so many other fields, progress in knowledge often leads to the loss of false certainties. The consequence for a stylistic study is that any attempt to compare 'early' or even 'original' parts with 'later revisions' must proceed with the greatest caution. Nor is it possible to derive far-reaching conclusions from the fact that many York plays are shared by the Towneley cycle, if the latter does not reflect the development of civic drama in Wakefield. I have taken pains to eliminate those of my former certainties which I no longer think warranted. But I cannot hide the fact that the subdivision of some chapters is largely determined by a belief in early, middle, and late strata which, however vague, was supported by the authority of W.W. Greg, E.K. Chambers, and countless others.

To change this would have meant the writing of an entirely new book, which would have been contrary to the purpose of a series called *European Studies in English Literature*. But even on less pragmatic grounds such a change was felt unnecessary. The putative strata of earlier scholars are largely based on metrical criteria. There is thus some independent reason for the grouping which I have retained. If an analysis using the criteria outlined above supports (or casts doubt on) groupings based on metre, this should be of some interest in itself. Stylistic and metrical differences may still contain clues to the composition of a cycle. The task that remains is to correlate the soft evidence which they provide with the, comparatively speaking, harder evidence of manuscripts and archives.

Part I

The foil: Latin church drama

1 Liturgy and drama

Impersonation and representation

The dramatic character of the Roman liturgy has been much discussed. It would be far beyond the scope of this study to recapitulate that discussion here, especially since it has suffered from a lack of agreement on the definition of 'drama' or 'the dramatic'. Instead of offering my own definition, I propose to discuss the merits of two definitions which have been influential in recent years. The first goes back to Eric Bentley: 'A impersonates B while C looks on.'[1] The other has gained currency through the well-known work of Keir Elam and has recourse to the semantics of possible worlds.[2] Elam distinguishes between 'theatre' and 'drama', where 'theatre' refers to the performer–audience transaction, while drama means 'the network of factors relating to the represented fiction' (p. 2).

The trouble with these definitions for our purposes is that the first includes too little, and the second too much. Bentley's definition leaves out the 'network' of relationships which Elam refers to and thereby makes the notion of 'looking on' questionable. Are the children merely 'looking on' when Uncle Jim 'impersonates' Santa Claus? 'Looking on' or 'watching' suggest a detachment which seems possible only if more than one person is being represented or embodied. This appears to leave us with Elam's description of drama as a network of factors. For a historical study, however, Elam's definition has the drawback that it is concerned not with texts but with the worlds represented by them. The text which the philologist or the theatre historian studies and classifies is only the score for the 'world' or 'fiction' which the reader or spectator creates in his mind. Moreover, the metaphor of 'dramatic world' suggests a self-containedness which would exclude practically all pre-classical drama if it were taken literally. Most of the texts which form the object of this study show none of that self-containedness.[3] Rather than opt for any one definition, the best course for a historical study is probably to accept a range of dramatic varieties which may extend between the poles indicated by our two definitions, knowing full well that neither of the two extremes will appear in our corpus.

While the one-man show that would be included under Bentley's definition has no importance for our study, the implications of the notion of 'dramatic world' deserve some closer scrutiny. A dramatic world that was truly self-contained would be incomprehensible to onlookers inhabiting the ordinary world. The signs of the dramatic world signify to those onlookers just as much as they do to the inhabitants of the dramatic world. This double layer of information can exist also in the ordinary world, but in the dramatic world it is a *sine qua non*.[4] We shall have more to say about this when we analyse the first liturgical 'dramas'. The distinction between two worlds – 'ordinary' vs. 'dramatic' or 'First' vs. 'Second' – will be used repeatedly in the course of this study.

Before we come to that, a few questions may be in order which will help us understand the difference between 'drama' and 'liturgy'. How do the time, place, and objects (including persons) of the ordinary world come to represent the time, place, and objects of the dramatic world? From the mystery plays to the theatre of the absurd the answer will be the same: there is a contract between spectators and performers that we are going to see 'a play' which will represent a world of its own. The here-and-now of the performance will not, as a rule, be identical with the there-and-then of the play; during the time of the performance Sir Laurence Olivier will 'not be' Sir Laurence Olivier but someone else. On this general premise more specific relations of representation can be built, the clues for which will usually be given in the play itself. Not so in the liturgy and the liturgical drama. When the first liturgical plays were performed around the altar on Easter morning, they could represent only the revelation of the Resurrection to the three Marys at the Sepulchre. Time and place had their liturgically regulated meaning before the first play was even conceived of.[5]

Until now we have used the word 'represent' rather glibly, although its meaning is not at all clear. Karl Young distinguishes between 'to represent' and 'to impersonate' – witness his frequent phrase 'the choir may be said to represent, though not to impersonate [e.g., the Disciples]'.[6] Although he does not define his two terms, it is clear that impersonation is a special case of representation. The relation between the impersonating 'actor' and the impersonated 'character' is more suggestive than in the case of mere representation.[7]

The evidence on which Young recognizes impersonation is largely that of the stage directions. He searches his texts carefully for hints concerning dress and attributes, such as palm branches in the hands of the angels.

When he finds such hints he assumes that impersonation was intended for the entire piece and thus classifies it as 'drama'.[8] Hereby Young creates a new difficulty: when he finds impersonating and non-impersonating features side by side, he is forced to regard the latter as 'dramatic improprieties' or 'ineptitudes'. This is particularly frequent when the represented persons refer to themselves in the third person or when a text shows conflicting statements concerning the number of *dramatis personae*.[9]

Three objections are to be raised against this rigid use of 'impersonation'. First, the double function of the performers and their attributes, which comprises both liturgy and representation, does not become sufficiently clear.[10] Underestimating the 'referring' symbolical features of the liturgy, Young is unable to recognize the true significance of the 'undramatic' elements within the larger whole of the liturgical drama, but considers them as mere relics of an earlier stage of the evolution of the genre. This results in occasional misinterpretation, which one example may illustrate: Young interprets the thuribles carried by the priests 'impersonating' the Marys as representing the spices which the biblical Women bought to anoint the body of the dead Jesus. But the performers employ the thuribles usually to cense the empty tomb. This is a merely sacral act which has no counterpart in the represented world and is thus 'undramatic' by Elam's definition of drama (see above). The thuribles, which are frequently hailed as a first step towards detailed scenic realism,[11] should rather be regarded as 'improprieties' in Young's sense of the term. In reality the thuribles are of course a liturgical symbol for the Women going to the sepulchre, which is much older than the Easter play.[12] Thus they belong to that liturgico-dramatic interface which slips through Young's conceptual grid, because the relationship between signifying and signified is established symbolically rather than iconically.

Secondly, impersonation becomes the characteristic of individual plays; its significance for the *genre* of the liturgical drama is thus missed. The specific relationship between representation and reality which, as we shall see, distinguishes the liturgical drama from the liturgy on the one hand and from the mystery play on the other, is not given its due.

Thirdly, Young is forced either to assume or to deny impersonation for an entire play. That this leads him into difficulties, especially with the rôle of the choir, has already been indicated. It also makes it impossible for him to analyse a scene in light of the fact that certain utterances are more embedded in their situation than others. The question of where 'improprieties' are more acceptable than elsewhere does not receive the weight which I believe it deserves.

But the concept of impersonation is not only too rigid; it is also too narrow. If one interprets it (as Young seems inclined to do) as a sub-type of 'representation', one is forced to call the sacrifice of the Mass undramatic, because it does not *represent* but *repeat* the sacrifice of Christ. That certainly has the advantage of a clear, unambiguous terminology, but it obscures those features of the Roman Catholic service which were the necessary prerequisites for the birth of the drama. These features are closely related to the symbolic-referring character of the liturgy, without, however, being exhausted by it. They are based primarily in that aspect of soteriological thinking which has been variously called 'typology' or 'figural interpretation'. In its most general definition a type is

eine Person, Sache, Handlung oder Einrichtung, die durch positive Bestimmung des die Geschichte vorausordnenden Gottes neben ihrer durchaus selbständigen Bedeutung als Tatsache ihrer Zeit noch eine zukünftige Person, Sache, Handlung oder Einrichtung (*antitypus*) vorherbildet.

a person, thing, action or institution, which, in addition to its independent significance as a fact of its own time, prefigures some future person, thing, action or institution (the *antitype*). This prefiguring function is given by God, who pre-ordains history.[13]

Typology, which was designed to make the Old Testament acceptable to the pagan converts of the first centuries AD,[14] is above all applied to Old Testament characters, who are viewed as prefigurations of Christ. In this interpretation, Abel's sacrifice and his murder by Cain, the sacrifice of Isaac, Melchisedek's bread and wine (Gen. 14.18) are repeated and elevated in Christ's Last Supper and Crucifixion. In analogy to this the Mass is a repetition of the sacrificial death of Christ and also includes its Old-Testament prefigurations. In that sense, even Holy Communion, which according to the dogma of the real presence is a salvific act in its own right, has a referring character. But the similarities to typologies are still more far-reaching: just as the antitype leaves the type in its own concrete historical context, so the 're-peating' service leaves both events, the signifying as well as the signified, in their respective contexts.[15] This is what distinguishes typology from allegory, which it resembles in that its signification is guaranteed by convention or authority rather than by mere similarity.

His narrow concept of impersonation also prevented Young from recognizing the importance of the allegoreses of the Mass, which, while not exhausted by typology, are nevertheless deeply rooted in typological and soteriological thinking. They demonstrate that a more-or-less of representation is quite possible. They carry the referring element of the divine service to greater lengths without, however, creating it. They interpret individual persons, gestures, and objects of the liturgy as referring to analogous elements in the history of Man's salvation.[16]

The most serious objection to Young is that he treats the difference between representation and impersonation as a matter of either-or. The fact that there are degrees of impersonation does not receive its due weight. But these degrees are most important. If an olive branch may be enough to 'impersonate' an angel, a Herod will soon require elaborate oriental dress, royal insignia, and an appropriately violent acting style. Moreover, many students of the liturgical drama would object to Young's implicit assumption that the relation between representer and represented is somehow more tenuous in the case of the Disciples than in that of the Marys or the Angel. This is especially true of those scholars who emphasize the 'ritual' quality of the liturgical drama. Following Mircea Eliade and others, Clifford Flanigan reminds us that ritual does not distinguish between actors and spectators.[17] Even if we do not wish to go this far, we will have to accept another point made by Flanigan: that the liturgy, like any other ritual, is an attempt 'to reactualize a past experience of encounter with the Other'. The analysis of the *Visitatio Sepulcri* of the *Regularis Concordia* will show that this function is particularly important in the case of the choir which, according to Young, merely 'represents' the Disciples.

The structure of the first situations to be represented mimetically

For the liturgical drama to originate it was therefore not necessary to create as many correspondences as possible between liturgical acts and biblical events. It was not the multitude of events that created the drama; one event which is particularly outstanding in the Christian history of salvation found a moment in the liturgy and a place in the church whose references, at first purely allegorical, coincided so that an event which had been evoked merely in the imagination came to be represented mimetically. The *Quem quaeritis* dialogue spoken at the altar in the Easter vigil or after the third responsory of the Easter matins was the first linguistic interchange at a represented place and a represented moment. Place and time, however, always remained the real place within the church and the real moment in the divine service. Their new functions did thus not replace the old ones but were merely added to them. And, what is even more important, their referring function existed prior to the acted text. In this respect they differ radically from theatrical place and time in the ordinary sense.

In defining the relationship between reality and representation it is perhaps best to begin by analysing the type of situation which is to be found in the earliest liturgical dramas. After that we have to enquire into the peculiarities of the language of the liturgy. In this way we shall attempt to define the intermediate position of the liturgical drama between real ceremony and represented reality.[18]

The earliest 'drama' of Western Christendom, the *Visitatio Sepulchri* of St Æthelwold's *Regularis Concordia* (c.970) constantly shuttles back and forth between the two Worlds. The shortness of the text permits extensive quotation:

Dum tertia recitatur lectio, quattuor fratres induant se, quorum unus, alba indutus ac si ad aliud agendum, ingrediatur atque latenter sepulcri locum adeat ibique, manu tenens palmam, quietus sedeat. Dumque tertium percelebratur responsorium residui tres succedant, omnes quidam cappis induti, turibula cum incensu manibus gestantes, ac pedetemptim ad similitudinem quaerentium quid, ueniant ante locum sepulcri. Aguntur enim haec ad imitationem angeli sedentis in monumento, atque mulierum cum aromatibus uenientium ut ungerent corpus Ihesu. Cum ergo ille residens tres, uelut erraneos ac aliquid quaerentes, uiderit sibi approximare incipiat mediocri uoce dulcisone cantare Quem quaeritis [in sepulchro, o Christicolae]? Quo decantato finetenus, respondeant hi tres, uno ore, Ihesum Nazarenum [crucifixum, o caelicola]. Quibus ille: Non est hic. Surrexit sicut praedixerat. Ite, nuntiate quia surrexit a mortuis. Cuius iussione uoce uertant se illi tres ad chorum, dicentes Alleluia. Resurrexit Dominus, [hodie resurrexit leo fortis, Christus, filius Dei]. Dicto hoc, rursus ille residens, uelut reuocans illos, dicat antiphonam: Venite et uidete locum [ubi positus erat Dominus, alleluia]. Haec vero dicens, surgat et erigat uelum ostendatque eis locum, cruce nudatum sed tantum linteamina posita quibus crux inuoluta erat; quo uiso deponant turibula et extendant contra clerum ac, ueluti ostendentes quod surrexerit Dominus et iam non sit illo inuolutus, hanc canant antiphonam: Surrexit Dominus de sepulcro, [qui pro nobis pependit in ligno, alleluia.] [S]uperponantque linteum altari. Finita antiphona prior, congaudens pro triumpho regis nostri quod deuicta morte surrexit, incipiat hymnum Te Deum laudamus. Quo incepto una pulsantur omnia signa.[19]

Clearly, this little production uses predominantly elements of a code which was not developed specifically for dramatic representation.[20] This is true already of the time and place of the performance. The time was between the nocturn and the matins of Easter Sunday. In the order of the church year it corresponds exactly to the moment when, according to the gospels, the women went to the sepulchre. The place also has its liturgical significance: it is the choir, i.e., that part of the church which is reserved for the clergy. As in all religions, the altar is 'the place of divine presence and of communication between Man and the deity' ('Ort göttlicher Präsenz und Kommunikation des Menschen mit der Gottheit'). Since the third century altars had been erected over the graves of saints and martyrs; in later periods relics had to suffice.[21] The connection between grave and altar was thus a very close one. It may be going too far to say that the actors themselves are part of the liturgical code; but it is certainly noteworthy that they are never designated by their 'rôles' but are always called 'the sitting one' or 'the three', respectively. The garments are clearly part of the liturgical code; they retain their liturgical names (*cappae*, *alba*), and they can hardly have lost their liturgical significance, certainly not that of their colours.[22] The *cappa* is the only priestly dress which can be worn by all clerics.[23] Equally liturgical are the thuribles which the three Women carry. Although they are said to be in imitation of the 'aromata' with which the Women intended to embalm Christ's body, they do not stand to them in that iconic relationship which we expect of scenic properties. Moreover, incense is not used to embalm a corpse but to surround a deity with mystic and agreeably smelling odours.[24] It is with good reason, therefore, that after the Revelation the thuribles are deposited in the 'Sepulchre'. The 'Sepulchre' is thus shown to be not merely a prop, but also an object of veneration. It can hardly have had the appropriate size, being erected on a part of the altar ('in una parte altaris qua uacuum fuerit').[25] In the vernacular drama this fact would merely be a defect in iconicity; here it fits the liturgical frame. Like the thuribles, the shroud assumes a double function that is part liturgical, part dramatic: until the Women take it out of the 'grave' it is part of the dramatic world. While they hold it up to the Disciples, it is ambivalent. When finally they deposit it on the altar, it becomes a liturgical object. This act re-transforms the altar into what to the Christian understanding it is throughout the church year and what it cannot be only during the time of Christ's death: a laid table.[26] The closing *Te Deum* is exclusively liturgical and therefore 'First-World', but at the same time it is a reaction to a piece of information which has its origin in the Second World.

Whether the palm branch in the hand of the 'angel' can be called liturgical may be a moot question. But more important than such borderline cases is the fact that there are also elements which decidedly do not belong to the liturgical code. There is above all the dialogue. The *Quem quaeritis* has never been part of the prescribed liturgy, and within the *Regularis Concordia* the *Depositio* and *Elevatio* ceremonies remained optional. The dialogue is a trope, i.e., an interpolation originating in antiphonal singing. Equally non-liturgical is of course the 'sepulchre', the erection of which was permitted – not decreed! – in the Good Friday chapter of the *Regularis Concordia*. Nevertheless, it becomes the object of something like cultic veneration, as we shall see later on.

If these last-mentioned elements are non-liturgical, are they, then, dramatic? The answer cannot be a simple 'yes' if the dramatic sign is defined as an icon of an object or a process that forms part of the imagined reality.[27] The 'imagined reality', as it is reported in the gospels and as it was of course known to the celebrating monks, is rather different from what appears in the ceremony. First, the dialogue itself finds no warrant in the gospels.[28] Secondly, the biblical Women do not pass on the news of the Resurrection directly to the Disciples, and still less are they immediately believed. Although the gospels diverge considerably on this point, they all agree that the Women reacted with fear and the Disciples with unbelief. Instantaneous jubilation is not in the gospels. And that the Women should report the Resurrection before looking into the grave is entirely without dramatic logic.[29] Even the going to the grave, which the 'play' describes as *pedetemptim ad similitudinem quaerentium quid*, bears no resemblance to anything in the represented world. It is a miming of the verb *quaerere* (without specified object!) rather than an icon of the action reported in the Gospels.[30] The Women had been present at the burial; hence there is no need for them to walk with halting steps and to 'seek' the grave. This manner of walking is thus no more than a way of conveying by gesture the action to which the angel refers in his question: it signals to the onlookers that the people represented are looking for something, it is not meant to be a true or 'faithful' imitation of the action which the biblical Marys would have performed. The lifting of the curtain which hides the inside of the 'grave' may stand for the removing of the biblical stone, whose weight worried the women on their way to the sepulchre (Mark 16.3). But in the gospels the grave is of course not opened in their presence. None of these signs is therefore what theatrical signs normally are: icons of the *signifié*, of the imagined reality. Since the elements of the imagined reality do not present insurmountable difficulties for iconic representation, this disregard for the iconic principle can be explained only by the wish to integrate all those elements which are not part of the liturgical code at least into the syntax of that code. That syntax requires the abrupt change from mourning to jubilation and adopts elements of the Second World only to the extent that they support this abrupt change.

Until now we have not distinguished systematically between actions and props. Actions are often grouped in pairs: if I take an object to hand, I have to deposit it sometime somewhere; an order has to be obeyed (or disobeyed), a message requires a comment, etc.[31] On investigating those pairs a little more closely, we discover that their first constituent belongs to the Second World, the second to the First. This is true not only of the dialogue, but also of the treatment of the thuribles and the shroud. The meaning of these actions is constituted by their syntax: precisely because the second constituents do not find a place in the Second World, they

Liturgy and drama 17

have to be interpreted in the First, i.e., the liturgical. In this manner they change from signs of mourning into signs of the Resurrection.

So far, we have left out one question which is important for the relation between First and Second World. In Keir Elam's words we can phrase it thus: 'How does one get there *from here*?'[32] Elam intends the question in the sense of possible-worlds semantics: by what formal operations can we generate the Second World from the First? I propose to give it a psychological meaning which in the context of the theatre is perhaps more natural: how is the audience (or the congregation) transferred from its First World into the Second? The *Visitatio Sepulchri* of the *Regularis Concordia* tries to manage this transition as imperceptibly as possible. The cleric acting the part of the angel is to enter the choir 'as if he were to do something else' and to approach the sepulchre 'secretly' (*latenter*). During this procedure the other monks must listen to the third *lectio*, and the entry of the Three Marys is similarly 'veiled' by a liturgical act, in this case the singing of the third responsory. All of this conspires to divert attention from the 'creation' of the Second World until the moment when the angel begins to sing. The function of the liturgical acts here is surprisingly similar to that of the curtain in the modern illusionist theatre: it conceals the arranging of the props and the actors moving into their starting positions. This 'sneaking' into the Second World is something which the liturgical drama and the naturalist stage have in common; it is utterly alien to the vernacular religious drama of the Middle Ages.

At the core of the earliest scenes – the Women at the Sepulchre, the Shepherds and the Magi at the Manger – there is always a revelation of the divine, a theophany.[33] But the divine is revealed only indirectly. The result is a 'Revelation scene', which knows two basic rôles: a 'Revealer' (or group of Revealers) facing the 'Recipients'. These rôles are not indissolubly tied to any one group of individuals: the Recipients of one scene may become Revealers in the next, as we shall see later in this chapter.

The Revealer facing the Recipients is the basic arrangement of most liturgical situations: the priest, proclaiming, faces the congregation. Situations of this structure will henceforth be called 'Revelation situations'. They will be distinguished from the 'world-containing' situations to be discussed later (e.g., Hortulanus, Herod).[34] Whenever the focus is on the relationship between the dialogue partners, we may also use such expressions as 'hierarchical situation' or 'hierarchical dialogue'. For what is common to all Revelation scenes is a marked hierarchical distance between the parties of the dialogue: the Revealers will be better informed than the Recipients, they will also normally initiate the dialogue and issue commands, while the Recipients tend merely to reply and obey. The Revealers will thus be in a position of authority over the Recipients. The physical position of the Revealers will tend to be fixed, while that of the Recipients can change during a scene or from one scene to the next.

Above all the Revelation situation is distinguished by the fact that the relationship between the parties is reduced to that between Revealers and Recipients. Their rôles exhaust their being. Any interpersonal relations that may have prevailed between the biblical or apocryphal originals of the speakers are rigorously excluded. To borrow a term coined by Hans Jantzen, we can describe the figures of these scenes as 'gestural' (*Gebärdefiguren*). They do not even permit the beholder 'to understand them in any other sense than the one symbolized by the gesture which characterizes them'.[35] Such reduction, necessary as it was to concentrate the attention of the believers on the mystery behind the visible 'stage' events, was bound to keep the development of the Revelation scenes within narrow limits. The period between *Regularis Concordia* and the first *Hortulanus* scenes, which appear in the twelfth century, seems to have been characterized by a production style which resembled the cultic representation image (*kultisches Repräsentationsbild*) in its rigid, hieratic transparency and which found a counterpart in the stylizing tendencies of Ottonian art.

Behind this parallelism of stylistic development there are more profound similarities which again concern the relationship between representation and reality. Neither the cult image nor the liturgical drama marks the boundary between their own world and that of the beholder. As far as medieval painting is concerned, H. Jantzen and W. Messerer have demonstrated that the beholder does not 'face' the painting, but that he must allow himself to become the addressee of the gesture represented in the picture. The reduction to few but significant gestures prevents the beholder from mere emotional empathy, for instance with the three Women at the Sepulchre. Rather, the beholder has to follow the gestural figure 'as a directed figure (*als gerichteter Gestalt*)' with his eye, 'in order to perceive the meaning which is enacted and produced anew in the gesture'.[36] And the beholder of the cult image as well as of the dramatic Revelation situation is part of the represented event, standing as it were in the continuation of that line of communication which leads from the Revealer to the (represented) Recipient, being present at the gestures of announcing and hearing and sharing their communicative effect.

Erwin Panofsky has described the 'unbridgeable difference of status (*unausgleichbarer Niveauunterschied*)' which exists between the person represented in the cult image and its beholder who is 'confined to the position of mere veneration'.[37] A similar difference exists between the Revealers and Recipients of the Revelation on the one hand and the audience of the *Visitatio Sepulchri* on the other. To bridge this difference of status, the *Quem quaeritis* dialogue developed in the only direction open to this gesturally stylized drama: the original Revelation was relayed by the Marys to further Recipients, whose 'status' was somewhat closer to that of the congregation. The hierarchical distance between the two sides of the dramatic experience became thus more finely graded.

The *Visitatio* itself shows this process. It is 'dramatic' merely because of it. The impersonators of the Marys are singled out from the choir and receive the message of the Resurrection which subsequently they pass on to the choir which in its turn represents the congregation as a whole. Further 'relays' are to be discovered in the Race of the Apostles and in the sequence *Victimae paschali*. Here the Apostles Peter and John on the one hand and Mary Magdalene on the other are inserted between the Marys and the choir. The choir now receives the message from these 'mediators'.

Panofsky mentions vellum-holding angels and prophets, who as it were 'present' or 'expose' the pictures of saints. Their function is fully comparable to the 'relayed Revelation' of the liturgical drama: Here, too, the aim is not

to draw the objects into the sphere of our own subjective experience, but on the contrary to draw the subjective experience out into the sphere of the object, not so much an assimilation of the represented object to the consciousness of the beholder as assimilation of his consciousness to the represented object.[38]

This comes very close to the spiritual attitude recommended in Pope Gregory's homily on Mark 16:

... this that they did, teaches what we, the members of the Church, should do ... if laden with the fragrance of virtue and the reputation of good works, we seek the Lord, we may truly be said to come to the sepulcher with sweet spices.[39]

The visit to the Sepulchre presents a model of how the Christian should act. He is not invited to empathize with the experience of the original visitors of the grave. There is as yet no intention of making the sacred events accessible to the human emotions. That intention is to be characteristic of the devotional image and of large parts of the mystery cycles.

The pattern of 'relayed revelation' serves to retain the hierarchic character of the original Revelation scene while at the same time bringing it closer to the congregation. The familiar medieval notion that Man needs a mediator between himself and the divine finds its expression here. What we normally call a 'dramatic' situation is characterized by an inner dynamism and a dissonance which tends toward resolution. The pure harmony of the Revelation situation has no use for this kind of drama. It even must avoid any conflict, since conflict would mean at least hypothetical equality between the two parties of the dialogue. And because of their close connection with the liturgy the Revelation scenes had also very little use for emotional and visual detail. The basic pattern of the Revelation situation had to be preserved: at the beginning the dialogue at the Sepulchre, at the end the reception of the message by the choir. Any additions had to be inserted between these two ends.

The structural principle of hierarchical relaying and its pre-eminence over dramatic mimesis are impressively confirmed by those offices which combine the Race of the Apostles and the Easter sequence. For *Victimae Paschali* is usually placed after, not before, the Race although according to John 20.2 the latter is really occasioned by Mary Magdalene's report which forms the nucleus of the sequence:

>   Dic nobis, Maria,   Angelicos testes,
>   quid vidisti in via?   sudarium et vestes.
>   'Sepulchrum Christi viventis,   Surrexit Christus, spes mea;
>   et gloriam vidi resurgentis;   præcedet suos in Galilæa.'
>
>   Credendum est magis soli
>   Mariæ veraci
>   quam Judæorum
>   turbæ fallaci.[40]

The situation in which Mary Magdalene answers the question of the Disciples is not defined with absolute unambiguousness. Theoretically it is also possible after her encounter with the risen Christ (John 20.11–18). But the dialogue of *Victimae paschali* is much more plausible immediately after the encounter between the three Marys and the Angels.[41] It is not for nothing that most of the plays which omit the Race are quite explicit about the Women coming (or even speaking) directly from the Sepulchre. If the plays which combine the two scenes place the sequence after the Race, they are once more tolerating 'dramatic ineptitudes'. They are not concerned with the correct chronology of biblical events. The liturgical office follows its own structural laws. These require, after the climax of the purely dramatic dialogue at the Sepulchre, a gradual return to the First World of the cult. *Victimae paschali*, unlike the Race of the Apostles, offered an opportunity to conclude the office with extensive choral singing. And the questions and answers of the sequence provided more intimate contact between 'actors' and chorus than did the antiphons which could at best be attached to, rather than integrated in, the Race.

Whatever the situation, the Recipients of the Revelation assume in part the rôle of the choir. At this stage, therefore, the unfolding of the liturgical drama means a hierarchical differentiation of the choir. That differentiation, which is also characteristic in the religious service as such, shows once more that the liturgy gave the early liturgical drama not only isolated formal features, but also its basic structural principle.

When the Christmas services were embellished by quasi-dramatic interpolations, they adopted not only the dialogue pattern of the *Quem quaeritis* but also the basic structure of the Revelation situation. The apocryphal *Obstetrices* appear in dialogue both with the *Pastores* and with the *Magi*. It has been rightly objected that the *Magi* arrive in Bethlehem at a time when the services of the *Obstetrices* are no longer required.[42] It could be added that there is no authority, not even apocryphal, for a meeting between Shepherds and Midwives. This neglect of plausibility and scriptural authority is due to the 'Revealing' function of the Midwives, which is of course patterned on that of the Angels. We here find further proof that the pragmatic *nexus* have to take second place after the hierarchical ones.

Here, too, the Revelation situation can be relayed again: in some offices the Shepherds returning from Bethlehem meet the Magi and inform them of what they have seen and heard at the Manger.[43] The constantly recurring process of relaying offers a better explanation of the origin of new scenes than those hypotheses which seek it in the narrative sources of these 'plays'. Anz, for instance, points out that the Midwives are mentioned in the Apocrypha; but he does not take into account the fact that the latter are silent on an encounter between the Midwives and either the Shepherds or the Magi; the encounter between Shepherds and Magi he attributes to the influence of the plastic arts, without offering evidence earlier than the sixteenth century.[44] In view of these hardly convincing hypotheses Young believes that the scene is an original growth of the liturgical drama.[45] If Young is right – and all the evidence suggests that he is – our theory of the hierarchical structure of the Revelation situation and of the principle of relaying is impressively confirmed. Liturgical structure and relayed Revelation are not only useful concepts to describe the liturgical drama, but they also have an explanatory power: in contrast to the vernacular religious plays (and some Latin plays as well), the liturgical office does not 'dramatize' events reported in the narrative sources, it 'creates' them according to its own needs and structural principles. The fact that the vernacular mystery cycles do not adopt the encounter between Shepherds and Magi shows how intimately the episode is connected with the liturgical drama.

The evolution of new rôles and scenes out of the liturgical ceremonial is especially clear here, since the question of the Magi is a modified antiphon: *Quem vidistis, pastores dicite? Annuntiate nobis in terris quis apparuit?*[46] In some plays and ceremonies this becomes *Pastores, dicite, quidnam vidistis, et annuntiate Christi nativitatem.*[47] The 'Magi' here are not Second World characters wanting to know but liturgical celebrants wanting to hear.

The language of the Revelation dialogue

The peculiarities of the hierarchical situation can best be seen in the dialogue. To bring the characteristic features of this dialogue into sharper focus it may be useful to compare it with other conversations. A 'normal' conversation, whether on stage or in our daily lives, always reveals more than its words express. A competent observer can gather from it information concerning the social position, the mood, and the intentions of the interlocutors, even if these subjects are not overtly mentioned. In every conversation we assume a tacit substratum which we may interpret correctly or incorrectly but which we cannot ignore if we want to grasp the meaning of the conversation.

Such a tacitly assumed substratum is largely absent from the liturgical and by implication from the 'hierarchical' dialogue. Relationships between interlocutors exist only to the extent that they are verbalized. This becomes evident in the formality of the addresses: *Christicolae, celicolae, socii, pastores*. Never do the sentences express anything beyond their overt function; they are always pure questions, pure answers, pure communications, pure commands. There is no room here for what Searle has called 'indirect speech acts'. Of course, exclamations do occur even in the simplest Easter offices, and, to use Bühler's terms, they express rather than present the joy at what was just heard.[48] But these exclamations are neatly separate from the dialogue at the Sepulchre *sensu stricto*. The rejoicing takes place only after the Women have told the choir of the Resurrection. Moreover, the rejoicing concerns only Christ the Redeemer and ignores Jesus the close relative and beloved teacher. The relationship to Christ which the Marys express here is one which they share with all believers. The rejoicing is that of the Christian congregation, not of the human beings who were close to Jesus during his lifetime. It is worth pointing out again that the gospels know nothing of the jubilation which forms so important a part of the liturgical Easter office.

There is only one place where the hierarchical dialogue psychologizes. In the later version of the dialogue at the Sepulchre, which is very widespread in the more comprehensive pieces, the Women are addressed not as *Christicolae* but as *mulieres ... plorantes* (or *gementes*).[49] But even here emotions are neither expressed nor described; it is merely their external symptoms which are noted by observers. The practice of the liturgical drama to convey external symptoms rather than the emotion itself will remain for a long time.[50]

Although the phrase *mulieres plorantes* must be interpreted as a symptom of an increased interest in the emotions, it is still faithful to the practice of the original hierarchical dialogue: it verbalizes everything that matters, it leaves nothing implicit. The *sepulcrum* and the *praesepe*, which figure so prominently in the hierarchical dialogue, never appear in direct speech in those biblical texts which conceivably might have served as 'sources' for the plays. This seemingly trivial fact is in reality highly indicative of the different ways in which narrative and drama render the relationship between human speech and the world in which it occurs. Narrative can give a truer, more 'realistic' reflection of human speech because the extra-linguistic context can be dealt with in the co-text which surrounds the dialogue. Drama has to seek ways to integrate the representation of the context into speech.[51] The question of how this is done will have to be discussed repeatedly in the following chapters.

The method of 'total verbalization' proper to the liturgical drama shows the absence of a substratum already mentioned in yet another light: like the relationships between the interlocutors, the objects represented exist only to the extent that they are verbalized. The physical structures representing the *sepulcrum* and the *praesepe* were often too unlike real graves or mangers to be recognizable, quite apart from a performance in the choir being invisible to large parts of the congregation.[52] The liturgical-hierarchical dialogue had, consequently, to 'create' its own situation, it could not tacitly assume anything as extra-linguistically given. An additional reason for this 'context-free-ness' of the liturgical dialogue is probably that the objects often retained their liturgical function beside their 'dramatic' one. The dualism of being and representing which characterizes the persons is apparent also in the 'props'.[53]

In comparison to the referential function the conative one is strongly reduced.[54] Dramatic, i.e. represented, action does not appear at all in the pure Revelation scenes. The two commands uttered by the Angels, *Ite et nuntiate* and *Venite et videte*, lead back from the dramatic world to the liturgical one. The first command is followed by the Women singing an antiphon which, as stated already, is directed at the community of all believers, not the biblical Disciples. The second command, going back to Matt. 28.6, appears to be fully embedded in the context of surrounding events, but it is precisely this command which shows how little such embedding matters. Earlier scholarship had always assumed that impersonation necessarily implies the intention of continuous representation of the other non-linguistic context. Young in particular criticizes this command and the action following it for coming after, rather than before, *Ite et nuntiate*. He can explain 'this inept arrangement' only 'from a reverent unwillingness to disturb the original simple structure of the trope *Quem quæritis* – and from a lack of dramatic resourcefulness'.[55] But this criticism misses the point just as much as Arnold Williams' attempt at a psychological explanation of the arrangement.[56] It is a misunderstanding to assume a consistent psychological substratum underlying the speeches and actions of the Revelation situation. Actions and speeches are gestures which symbolize the act of announcing and hearing ever anew and which receive their full effect only if they appear in a certain isolation from their context. The *Ite et nuntiate* of the Angels with the Women's following *Surrexit* or *Resurrexit* is one performance of this gesture, *Venite et videte* with the subsequent showing of the linen is another.[57]

2 Liturgical point of view surrounding the dramatic core dialogue

Lyrico-liturgical point of view after the core dialogue

The situation-bound and hence, in our sense, 'dramatic' *Quem quaeritis* dialogue never appears alone.[1] Even in the oldest texts of the *Visitatio Sepulcri* it is surrounded by 'non-dramatic' text. As a rule, it is at least accompanied by the antiphon *Surrexit* or *Resurrexit Dominus*, whereby the Women pass the message of the Resurrection on to the choir.[2] Young considers this a regrettable accident of textual transmission.[3] Apparently he assumes that the seed of the liturgical drama must have existed once in pure form, without any traces of the surrounding liturgical context. But this is exactly what is open to question. While David A. Bjork has produced impressive evidence that the *Quem quaeritis* trope 'is a self-contained little song',[4] it still seems to be the case that important dramatic features do not accrue to the original dialogue unless they are accompanied by certain non-dramatic ones. The 'dramatic features' in question all serve to make the Second World situation visible (as opposed to audible, which was of course done already by the unamplified *Quem quaeritis* dialogue). The 'non-dramatic' features lead us out of the Second World and back into the First World of the liturgical ceremony.

Since the compilers of these offices were primarily interested in heightening the effect of the liturgical Revelation and not in a scenic version of the biblical narrative, it is quite possible – and even probable, in view of the testimony of the texts – that the passing on of the message was an integral part of the scene from the very beginning.[5] If we regard the Easter dialogue as a Revelation situation, the testimony of the textual tradition is by no means odd. After all, it is only with the *Surrexit* that the chain of Revelations comes to a satisfactory end.

But this antiphon differs from the preceding dialogue in not carrying any hint as to the situation in which it is uttered or heard. It has been said already, in a different context, that Christ is here regarded as the Redeemer *qui pro nobis in ligno pependit*, not as the teacher or close relative. The antiphon thus is more appropriate from the point of view of the liturgical congregation than from that of the Nazarene's human contemporaries.[6] With the antiphon the priests representing the women have left the Second World and have returned to the First World of the congregation which is represented by the choir.

This interpretation is supported by a number of further observations. First, the censing, which normally takes place before the *Surrexit*,[7] marks a clear boundary between the 'dramatic' and the liturgical action. Other acts of purely liturgical significance are often inserted in places like this. In the Fritzlar *Visitatio*,[8] for instance, a crucifix is raised up during the *Surrexit*. At a corresponding point in the Fleury *Herod* the Shepherds call upon the congregation to join them in adoring the Christ child.[9] The showing of the grave linen, which is without biblical authority,[10] seems to have been primarily intended as a visible underlining of the liturgical Revelation. The *Te Deum*, the closing reaction of the choir to the message of the Resurrection, leads us conclusively back into the regular liturgy; and the choral antiphons between Revelation and *Te Deum* express above all the mood of the celebrating congregation. This mood is supported and heightened by the visual representation, but mood and representation belong of course to different worlds, as they would in any modern theatrical experience. The dialogue and the following jubilation both result from the general impulse to elaborate the liturgy and to increase its devotional impact. Strictly speaking, the jubilation itself does not represent an increase of the dramatic element. *Pace* Young, who believes that the choir represents, without impersonating, the disciples, the utterances of the choir take entirely the point of view of the real cultic situation. They contain nothing that would be explicable only as an utterance of the disciples.

Since these utterances are situationally neutral, they also lack that internal progression which usually characterizes dramatic dialogue and which even the tiny stretch of the *Quem quaeritis* dialogue reveals. The exchanges between Women and Angels which are inserted between the Revelation antiphon and the *Te Deum* are no longer a sequence of question and answer, but a loose series of exclamations of praise and joy which are not necessarily connected with one or the other party of the dialogue. In most cases the exchange was merely expanded by adding antiphons which were to be found in the rituals for convenient use.[11] The compilers proceeded on entirely liturgical considerations in order to heighten the devotional effect of the ceremony.

Because of their situational freedom the antiphons were capable of being sung by the choir as well as by the Marys. This is particularly true of those which occur only in the later, more comprehensive ceremonies and whose attribution to a 'speaker' never became quite settled, such as *Dicant nunc Iudaei*.[12] But even the *Surrexit* or its equivalents are occasionally given to the choir.[13] This, however, is possible only on one condition: either the choir merely repeats the antiphon sung by the Marys, or it replies to another form of Revelation. That a Revelation of some form has preceded the utterance of the choir is thus an absolute requirement. Never does the choir react immediately to the Revelation of the Angels.[14] The hierarchical situation, which demands that no link be missing from the chain of 'relayed' Revelations, demonstrates its structural importance once more.

'Victimae paschali' as an intermediate stage between drama and liturgy

The Easter sequence *Victimae paschali* replaced the 'lyrico-liturgical' antiphons in many ceremonies of the twelfth and especially the thirteenth century.[15] Because it combines elements of 'liturgy' and 'drama' it is of special interest to us. The dialogue of the sequence is hardly less situation-bound than the *Quem quaeritis*: it describes the encounter between Mary Magdalene and the disciples after her discovery of the empty grave (John 20.2). There was only one fact working against its full integration into a Second World situation: from the *Visitatio* there are still three Marys on the 'stage', whereas *Victimae paschali* explicitly refers to only one: *Soli Mariae*. As Young notes,[16] this inconsistency was recognized, and there were various attempts to remove it. These attempts are another indication that the prime motive of the compilers was not to come as close as possible to reality. The most 'natural' way would have been to allow two of the Women to leave and charge the third with the answers prescribed in the sequence. But this is precisely what does not happen. At the most, two of the Women are ignored by the choir.[17] Usually the answer is sung by the three Women in unison, or it is divided between them. In that case, the choir repeats its *Dic nobis, Maria, quid vidisti in via*. Since the syntactic unity of the answer is lost in the procedure, the result is anything but a coherent 'dramatic' dialogue. The text of the third Mary in particular is not really an answer to the question *quid vidisti*: her line (*Surrexit Christus, spes mea*) is an inference from the testimony of the first two; under the normal rules of conversational logic it loses its meaning when separated from the first two lines of the reply. Syntactical and logical coherence are disregarded here pretty much as they were in the *Quem quaeritis*.[18] But again the isolation of the sentence elevates it to the rank of a linguistic 'gesture'. The fact that the sentence 'Surrexit Christus' appeared as a personal and hence subjective inference from the evidence seen and heard was irrelevant for the liturgical Revelation, perhaps even irritating. For what is required here is not the personal conclusion of a *dramatis persona* but a fact of Christian belief spoken with authority.

That the triple *Dic nobis* does not have the function which Young wishes to ascribe to it becomes evident from those texts in which each of the three questions is answered by the three Women in unison. Here the two 'solutions' are combined in a way that destroys their effect. The aim here, clearly, was not to come close to the represented reality but to use as many scenic and musical effects as possible. The devices used saved the formal balance, which would have been disturbed by two of the Women standing idly about. Such 'divided speeches', which are frequent in the antiphonal singing of the liturgy, prove that, even at a fairly advanced stage of impersonation, the connection between rôle and linguistic utterance was still fairly loose and even inept from the point of view of dramatic mimesis. The utterances must have been regarded as quotations in the mouths of the 'actors'.[19] The fiction that they came into existence at the very moment of articulation was not even aimed at. Divided speech is typical of those ceremonies which have preserved their liturgical character. It disappears with increasing 'dramatization';[20] a mitigated form occurs in those hymns which the Women sing in later ceremonies on their way to the Sepulchre.[21]

Narrative point of view in the introductory responsories and processions

Because of their lyrical character, the Easter antiphons are usually situationally neutral. This saves them from colliding directly with the pragmatic context in which they are used, although most of them reflect the point of view of the Easter congregation rather than that of the disciples and relatives of Jesus. But there are also sentences which are meaningful only as spoken by the liturgist, not by the represented person. Prominent among these are the narrative responsories and antiphons which, forming part of the canonical liturgy, introduce the dramatic ceremony. These narrative introductions – and above all the so-called antiphon *Maria Magdalena*[22] – are often sung by the *dramatis personae* themselves. The same is true, though not quite so generally, of the antiphon *Currebant duo*, which occasionally is sung by the clerics representing Peter and John while they are in fact performing the Race to the Sepulchre. Those representing the Magi, too, sometimes refer to the Magi in the third person while on their way to the Manger.[23] These particularly obvious violations of the dramatic principle would have been too easy to avoid to be attributable to dramaturgical incompetence. Rather, we have to conclude that the will to dramatic consistency, which was fully active in the core dialogue, had no power in these parts of the

Liturgy and the drama 29

ceremonies. The violation is no more serious than the 'divided speech' of *Victimae paschali* which Young not only leaves uncriticized, but which he commends as a particularly apt dramatic solution.

We shall probably come closest to the intentions of these ceremonies if we regard the people appearing here not as *dramatis personae* but as participants in a procession who are approaching the place at which the Second World event is to take place. Many texts show that the occupying of the dramatic positions (*sedes*), while belonging unambiguously to the world of the real cult, was a ceremonial act which prepared rather than weakened the dramatic effect.[24]

It mattered a great deal where these 'dramatic improprieties' occurred. Third-person reference by the actor to his part is by no means tolerated everywhere: formulae introducing direct speech, for instance, are rare exceptions.[25] Apparently, the clash between report and representation was here felt to be an irritation. Consequently, we are not dealing with lack of insight into the requirements of the drama, but with a limited yet well-circumscribed inclination to honour them.

The label 'incongruity' is thus of little use. What is necessary is to find those standards which made apparent incongruities acceptable. To do this it is necessary to define the principles of the liturgical ceremonial and the area in which they cease to be in force. Since in the context of medieval aesthetics the individual phenomenon with its specific details was relevant only as a reflection and sign of a more general significance,[26] since moreover too much detail and realism were even suspect in the Middle Ages,[27] it is not the 'incongruities' which are surprising but the fact that the mimesis of the liturgical drama became at all possible. Aesthetic practice is here in advance of aesthetic theory.

Further manifestations of the liturgical perspective in the processional songs

The narrative character of the antiphons which introduce the Easter ceremonies is of course the most cogent proof that the processions belong to a different ontological plane than the dialogues at the *sedes*.[28] A closer look reveals the same perspective in other processional songs, too. The Magi, for instance, indulge in lengthy theological discourses on the birth and soteriological function of the Christ child. They also see themselves as carriers of a soteriological function, as the following hymn demonstrates:

> Nos respectu gratiæ
> gentium primitiæ
> spem totius veniæ
> vobis damus hodie.[29]

In other ceremonies, which carry the dramatization of events further, the Magi recognize themselves as those kings to whom the prophecies of the Old Testament refer: *qui scriptum didicimus: Adorabunt eum omnes reges...*[30] Or they address the Shepherds who are returning from Bethlehem with the words: *Pastores, dicite, quidnam vidistis, et annuntiate Christi nativitatem.*[31] They 'know' already what the Shepherds have seen, their request does not express the point of view of *dramatis personae* who want to know, but that of liturgists who want to hear.

'Liturgical point of view' means a knowledge which is not circumscribed by the Second World speech situation. In the liturgical drama speakers seem often familiar with those mysteries of the Christian religion which in the sacred narratives are still waiting to be revealed to them. The vernacular dramas, by contrast, show carefully how the Magi, for instance, have acquired their (often limited) knowledge. Final certitude is gained only after extended reflection; it is always emphasized that the events pass human understanding. All of this is uttered with the intention to instruct or at least to astonish. In the liturgical drama – and especially in the processions – the proclamation of such tenets of the faith serves merely the cultic end of proclaiming the glory of God.

In keeping with this tendency, the processional anthems do not show any tendency to realize the spatio-temporal medium in which the represented events took place[32] or to distinguish clearly between the ecclesiastical ceremony and the historical event. Thus it is not unusual for the Three Magi to refer to the *celebranda dies*, i.e. to the date in the church calendar.[33] This is almost as great a 'dramatic impropriety' as the Magi's referring to themselves in the third person, which was criticized by Young.[34] Taking all these 'improprieties' together (which occur exclusively in the processions), the impression is inescapable that dramatic representation was as little aimed at here as it was in the narrative responsories. Like those, the processions prepare for the Second World emerging in the dialogue at the *sedes*, without being already part of it.

The interplay between dramatic and extradramatic elements in the early liturgical drama

The use of non-dramatic elements has proved to be so consistent that it has already given rise to occasional polemics against Young's expression 'dramatic improprieties'. Before trying to give this polemic a positive turn we have to clarify our terminology. When we refer to 'non-dramatic elements' it is not merely to avoid the pejorative overtones of Young's term, but also to cover a wider area. The term 'impropriety' can be applied meaningfully only to those utterances which are clearly inappropriate to the represented situation, notably the narrative sentences at the beginning; these utterances are impossible in the mouths of the represented characters because they refer to the latter in the third person or use the wrong number etc. 'Non-dramatic', on the other hand, can be predicated also of the lyrical exclamations at the end of the ceremonies. The integration of these utterances into the surrounding situation is so weak that the question of 'propriety' does not arise. They are situationally neutral rather than 'improper'. Non-dramatic elements will occur in the drama of all ages;[35] the set speeches of the Elizabethans are an almost classic example. But as soon as the drama has become a genre in its own right with its own set of conventions and rules, it will deal with dramatic 'improprieties' in two ways: it will avoid them or confine them to a limited number of situations where their use is sanctioned by convention. Young's talk of 'impropriety' betrays a tacit teleology: it suggests that the writers of the early liturgical dramas were groping their way toward a drama whose rules already existed in an invisible heaven of norms. Of course the 'improprieties' prove that the drama had not yet come into its own; but the more important questions are: how do the non-dramatic elements relate to those which would be called 'dramatic' even by modern standards, and what is the effect of this fusion between the Second World of the drama and the First World of the cult?

These questions will be answered when we study more closely that consistency in the use of non-dramatic forms to which we have already referred several times. The different types of non-dramatic utterance which we have noted are always conditioned by the surrounding liturgy. To make this apparent, we must first of all study the points of contact between liturgy and dramatic representation. Since the interplay which interests us has developed above all in Easter matins, it is sufficient to study the liturgy of this service only.[36] Here the dialogue is inserted immediately before the end, i.e. between the third responsory and the *Te Deum*. As already mentioned, that responsory tells of the three Marys going to the Sepulchre, while the *Te Deum* is a general praise of God with no reference to the specific occasion. The non-dramatic edges of the *Visitatio* are thus adapted to the character of their liturgical environment. Never do the Revealers give up their dramatic point of view, never is the dialogue at the Sepulchre preceded by antiphonal singing between choir and 'actors' – and this applies to the 'core dialogues' of the other ceremonies as well. Never is the dramatic World broken in the core dialogue, and with a single exception the core dialogue is never followed by narrative utterances from the choir.[37] As we shall see, this very strict order is largely dissolved in the vernacular drama.

The 'dramatic improprieties' are thus not regrettable defects but well-justified formal features which alone enable the dramatic moment to contribute to the total effect of the cultic act. This effect, regarded as a whole, is of course not a dramatic one. The order of liturgical and dramatic utterances, which together shape the liturgical ceremony, does not imitate the curve of the emotions and tensions of a represented situation (as a drama would); but it follows and supports – from expectation to fulfilment to final jubilation – the mood of the celebrating congregation. The emotional curve of the ceremony, which rises to the altar and re-descends to the choir and congregation, integrates the events of the biblical Easter where it can benefit from them. The central event, the dialogue at the Sepulchre, is only a visualization of what would also 'happen' without it: the re-enactment of the Easter miracle through the ecclesiastical year.

Differences from, and similarities to, the vernacular drama become apparent here. The basic structure of 'ascent' to the Second World and 're-descent' to the First, which on occasion transforms the onlookers into participants, is also to be found in the mystery plays. But there the represented events have their own spatio-temporal extension and thus their own structure, which asserts itself within and against the framework of the First World. Since representation in the liturgical ceremonies is restricted, as it were, to points-in-time, such structures cannot develop here. For the mystery play the events exist independently of their representation, but they are no longer *present* without it: for the mystery play the openings into the world of the audience are occasional sallies; for the liturgical drama audience-time never ceases to provide the dominant structure. The liturgical ceremony does not know the *tabula rasa* of the 'plain' or 'place', on which the mysteries and moralities erect their Second Worlds. They are always performed in a space whose sacred function is never forgotten. Because of this, even the dialogue at the Sepulchre and the corresponding core dialogues at other *sedes* never produce the illusion of a Second World, although they do suggest that World.

3 'World-containing' situations

Origins and character of the new situation-type

In the scenes treated so far the basic liturgical structure was still recognizable. Notwithstanding their historical 'rôles', the 'actors' behaved as liturgist and congregation, as Revealers and Recipients. Between the two parties no relationship existed other than that established by the act of Revelation.

The type of the Revelation scene was left behind for the first time when the encounter between Herod and the Magi was included in the eleventh century.[1] Like the scenes previously discussed, this too has its liturgical forerunners, in this case the responsories:

Magi ueniunt ab oriente, Ierosolymam quaerentes, et dicentes: Ubi est qui natus est, cujus stellam vidimus, et venimus adorare Dominum

and

Interrogabat Magos Herodes: Quod signum vidistis super natum Regem? Stellam magnam fulgentem, cujus splendor illuminat mundum; et nos cognovimus et venimus adorare Dominum.[2]

These responsories accompany the Rouen *Officium Trium Regum*. They retain their narrative form and disregard the turn-taking of the speakers correspondingly. But the same office contains a completely 'dramatized' dialogue between the Magi and *duo de maiori sede cum dalmaticis* who have been introduced, as in other *Officia Stellæ*, in obvious analogy to the Midwives of the *Officia Pastorum*.

The Rouen texts which have come down to us do not go back beyond the thirteenth century,[3] but there are earlier texts from other cities which not only are fully dialogued but also show a remarkable independence of the liturgy. In the eleventh-century text from Freising (Young, *DMC*, vol. 2, pp. 92–7), the variety of spatio-temporal and interpersonal relationships in the encounter between Herod and the Magi, the raging of Herod, and the orthodox hexameters clearly suggest non-liturgical influence. The lively questions which Herod puts to the Magi, irrelevant as they are to the main action, are worlds apart from the severe gestures of the Revelation situations. The dialogue in which Herod enquires about the Magi's provenance is hardly less vivid than that of the most lively vernacular plays:

> Rex ad Magos. Ad i:
> Tv mihi responde, stans primus in ordine, fare.
> Respondet i:
> Impero Chaldeis dominans rex omnibus illis.
> Ad secundum:
> Tv ai, vnde es?
> Respondet ii:
> Tharsensis regio me rege nitet Zoroastro.
> Ad tercivm:
> Tv tertius, vnde es?
> Respondet iii:
> Me metuunt Arabes, mihi parent vsque fideles.

The elaboration which we can observe here affects not only the realistic details but also those parts of the play which still belong altogether to the liturgical world. The twelfth-century texts from Montpellier and Fleury emulate Freising with their raging Herods, but they also elaborate the *Processio Stellæ* with repetitions and additional explanations. In two twelfth-century texts[4] all three Magi point out the Star to each other (*baculis erectis* in the Montpellier MS) and exclaim three times 'Ecce Stella'. They also exchange the kiss of peace at the altar. In the Montpellier MS the encounter of the Three Magi is followed by a narrative 'antiphon'[5] whose extra-dramatic status is comparable to the *Currebant duo* of the Race of the Apostles. The gestural repetition of ceremonial acts will be encountered again in the 'world-containing' parts of the Herod plays, where it will frequently create inconsistencies in the pragmatic nexus.

The result is a peculiar ambiguity of the Herod plays: they remain within the framework of the liturgy and use liturgical or quasi-liturgical formal elements, but their development is no longer subject exclusively to those liturgical principles treated in the previous chapter.[6]

Unlike the Shepherds and the Magi, Herod was unable to retain a rigid liturgical posture vis-à-vis the message of the birth of the Christ child.[7] He is the first *dramatis persona* to stand outside that chain which extends from the first Revealers down to the choir and at times even to the lay congregation. As soon as he is introduced into it, the liturgical drama ceases to follow exclusively the principle of 'relayed Revelation'; from now on it develops by following the course of the Second World story. Until now, the introduction of new scenes and utterances depended on their position in the context of the liturgical ceremony; now such scenes and utterances are motivated by the mimetic nexus. It will be shown later that Herod becomes the starting-point of new 'relays' independent of the cultic ones.

In this respect the Herod plays form the transition between pure Revelation situations and the later liturgical plays which, more and more and in ever increasing detail, dramatize biblical material and adopt the representational devices of their models in the process. The transitional character of the Herod plays comes out above all in the fact that they combine new 'world-containing' aspects with traditional quasi-liturgical techniques. But quite apart from their transitional position, the Herod plays deserve our attention also for their wide dispersion and the great number of textual variants which they have to offer. In their comparatively free combination of dramatic and liturgical elements they stand in marked contrast to the Passion, Daniel, and St Nicholas, of which only a few examples exist, which moreover have largely left the context of the liturgy.

The new problems and attempts at solving them arose from the segments of reality which now became objects of scenic representation. One of the most important of these segments is the human psyche, which enters the medieval scene in the figure of Herod. It has often been said that Herod is the first stage villain in the history of European drama. The attention of scholars usually concentrated on the character features with which the authors had endowed their negative hero.[8] But the more basic question of how character features can be represented on stage was hardly ever posed. This omission led to numerous misinterpretations, often to anachronistic psychologizing.[9] Only if we correct this omission can we hope to identify the dramaturgical difference between the Revelation scene and the world-containing play. The person of Herod is of particular interest in this context because the biblical accounts show him in a number of stageworthy situations which the plays were able to exploit. Herod's actions are not dictated by the requirements of the religious ceremony, they spring from personal motives. His speeches are not merely acts of communication and command, they can also serve the ends of self-portrayal or represent psychological reactions. In Bühler's terms: the expressive function of speech now becomes as important as the appellative and presentational ones which dominated the Revelation scenes.[10] His character, moreover, does not move in a vacuum but in the social relationships of which he, as a ruler, forms a part. These relationships in their turn determine the selection of the other characters of the play. Herod can adapt to the psychology of these characters: he need not merely command, he can also flatter, promise and threaten. Thus a considerable number of perlocutionary speech acts enters the play with him. The messengers, soldiers, and scribes do not merely obey

Herod's orders, but in obeying they show fear, submissiveness, and anxiety. With this the wide field of interpersonal relationships becomes a necessary object of dramatic treatment. Such relationships we do not expect to be manifested in isolated utterances. Large chunks of dialogue have to be matched, thus creating, potentially, a continuous substratum of characters, moods, and reactions. This creates the further possibility of altering mood and tone in the course of the dialogue. The element of change endows the time factor with a new relevance: whether something happens suddenly or gradually may be decisive for its effect. While the liturgical Revelation situation maintained a steady, measured tempo, the world-containing situation can change tempi and thus approximate non-liturgical modes of presentation whose speed is determined by the course of the events staged. For the same reason, locality becomes dramatically – as opposed to liturgically – significant: it does make a difference whether, for instance, the Magi announce their intention of seeking the new-born king somewhere on their way to Jerusalem or in the presence of Herod the Jewish king.

We now have to study how and to what extent the world-containing scenes developed these situations. To do this, we have to find a compromise between chronological and systematic presentation. A purely chronological presentation would treat the scenes in the order in which they came into being, i.e. first the Herod scenes, then the Hortulanus ones, and after these the other scenes from the Bible and the legends. But such a procedure would run the risk of rather tiresome repetition. All the aspects of interest to us, from characterization and interpersonal relationships to the representation of space and time, would have to reappear in each section, even if a given scene-type has nothing new to offer. A strictly systematic order would presumably have to begin with the smallest unit, the individual character, and proceed from there to more comprehensive categories. Since the earlier scenes do not yield much with respect to the dramatic presentation of character, the inevitable consequence would be a distortion of historical perspective. We would be creating the impression that certain techniques of *Personenkonstellation* and partner relationships are the result of advanced characterization, while in reality the exact opposite is much nearer the truth.

For these reasons our presentation will be systematic in a way that is modified by chronology: each of the different aspects will be treated in the order in which it appears in the development of the world-containing liturgical drama. Each chapter will thus study the entire genre under one particular aspect. Because the earliest scene-type, the Herod play, is particularly rich in personnel, the problem of interpersonal relationships will be treated first. Emotions appear in the Herod plays, in the laments of Mary at the Cross and of the Women at the Sepulchre. Characterization will be treated last because it becomes a dramaturgical problem only in the later plays. This compromise between chronology and systematisation also promises the best strategy for making visible those historical relationships which exist between the various aspects.

Interpersonal relationships

The simplest *Magi* plays show the encounter between Herod and the Three Kings in a simple question–answer pattern which recalls the rigidity of the Revelation situation. The Kings appear only as a group, in this respect resembling the Women at the Sepulchre and the Shepherds at the Manger. They answer in *unison*. Only on one occasion do they speak singly in all plays: when they explain the significance of their gifts. But this does not make the connection between speaker and utterance truly dramatic. For instead of self-contained sentences, the Magi utter only parts of such sentences whose form and syntactic function is, moreover, determined by the preceding assertion which they made together:

> MAGI: Hunc regnare fatentes, cum misticis muneribus de terra longinqua adorare uenimus, trinum Deum uenerantes tribus in muneribus.
> PRIMUS: Auro regem.
> SECVNDUS: Ture sacerdotem.
> TERTIVS: Mirra mortalem.[11]

The undramatic character of this distribution becomes even more evident when we recall that it also occurs in the procession of the Three Kings at Besançon, which retains the narrative text of Matt. 2, dividing it between the *cantor* and the clerics cast in the rôle of the Kings, without – apart from this one passage – respecting the adequate connection between speaker and utterance.[12] The connection between speaker and utterance is still 'liturgical': while the drama rests on the fiction that the utterance originates in the speaker at the very moment of its being uttered, the liturgical utterance is overtly fixed in advance and is assigned to the speaker by the order of the ceremony which encloses it. That the contrast between these ceremonious utterances and the vehemence of Herod was felt, is to be inferred from the rubrics in the Montpellier manuscript, which has the Kings rise and genuflect while showing their gifts.[13] The 'divided speech', as we may call it, is a typical liturgical speech form, which we have found already in some arrangements of the Easter sequence *Victimæ paschali*. If the chronological order of the manuscripts provides reliable evidence here, 'divided speech' has found its way into the drama via the *Processio stellæ*, which we have touched upon already in connection with the extra-dramatic forms and which will claim our attention again when we discuss the treatment of space and time.

While this speech is 'divided' in all the plays, it remains the only instance of its type: the later additions do not show 'divided speech'.[14] But it is only in a few, usually late and rather diffuse plays that the Magi answer Herod's questions in self-contained individual speeches. Apart from the 'gibberish' in which the Secundus and Tertius Rex greet Herod in the Montpellier MS,[15] individual replies are to be found only in one scene which is peculiar to Bilsen and Freising:[16] after Herod has consulted his Scribes he repeats the questioning of the Magi (in a particularly threatening tone, according to the Bilsen rubrics), before he releases them with the usual *Ite et de puero diligenter investigate*. This freely invented episode, which can easily be detached from its context, has not found general acceptance. Individual replies by the Magi have never become typical of the Herod Play as a genre. For all its naturalism in gesture and even in some utterances, it retains the liturgical relationship between speech and speaker in which the speaker appears to be quoting rather than performing a situationally embedded speech act.[17]

The original sentences of the dialogue between Herod and the Three Kings resemble the Revelation dialogue not merely in form but also in content. In reply to the questions from Herod (and his messengers) the Three proclaim Christ king and explain the mystical significance of their gifts. They also point frequently to the Star as proof of their assertions. Pointing and naming are as characteristic of this dialogue as they are, for instance, of the showing of the linen in the *Visitatio Sepulcri*. Speech underlines and extols something which exists outside the speech situation. It is not integrated into the speech situation in the sense that it is modified by it stylistically or attempts to alter the situation.

The earliest expansions of the encounter between Herod and the Magi also reveal a marked similarity with the Revelation situations. A messenger is inserted between the two parties, just as the Apostles were inserted between the Marys and the choir. Although the apocryphal gospels contain a first hint of the messenger,[18] yet the use which the Herod plays make of the messengers resembles the Revelation scenes much more than it does the *Protevangelium*: with their help the pattern of 'relayed Revelation' which we found in the Easter scenes is repeated, even though the Revelation is now an indirect one since it cannot use Herod as one of its stages.

Since the following pages will be devoted to the 'liturgical' features of the messenger scenes, it is necessary to discuss the traditional thesis that they represent an early example of 'stage realism'.[19] It has been said that the messenger's language reveals him as a type of the self-important subaltern.²⁰ Whether this is justified is at least doubtful in view of the speech used by other members of the court. Verbose orders containing the exact details of their execution are used by all, including Herod himself. Bombast characterizes the entire court, not just the messenger. Finer distinctions such as Anz attempts must remain largely subjective.

On the other hand, the messenger is the first to embed the events staged into a social *milieu* dominated by such norms as prevail also in the real world. When he questions the Magi concerning the 'whence and whither' of their journey, a first element of courtly etiquette enters the play which can develop into long greeting ceremonies. In this respect the messenger contributes to the gradual overcoming of the liturgical style.

But often he does not really mediate between Herod's questions and the Magi's answers, he merely duplicates them. It is only in a few late plays, such as Freising and Benediktbeuern,²¹ that his appearance before Herod is really motivated by the Magi's request *Dicite nobis, o Hierosolimitani cives, vbi est expectatio gentium*...(after Matt. 2.2).²² It is only once that the Magi begin a genuine exchange with the messenger by asking counter-questions.²³ That the rôle of the messenger was but slightly integrated into the whole sequence is borne out by the fact that the number of messengers was often multiplied. Strassburg²⁴ and Freising²⁵ distinguish between an *Internuntius* and an *Armiger*, Compiègne²⁶ divides the messenger's part between a *Nuntius* and a group of *Legati*. Bilsen²⁷ and Fleury²⁸ have as many as three variously designated messenger parts.

It occurs only rarely²⁹ that the effect of these multiplications can be called realistic. More frequently a chain of question and information, as we find it for instance in Freising, loses its coherence by these expansions. Sometimes Herod, who has ordered his messenger to enquire about the provenance of the Magi and to bring them before him has to repeat his second command because the messenger has complied only with the first.³⁰ Even more marked is the disintegration of the dialogue in Bilsen. There, Herod is informed by three messengers of the arrival of the Magi, and although only the first has actually talked to them, the last appears to be the best informed.

This triple messengers' report shows such a conflict of stylistic tendencies that a more detailed study seems worthwhile. None of the three messengers has questioned the Kings on their provenance and destination. The first *Internuntius*, the only one shown in actual conversation with the Magi, has merely told them to appear before Herod. Interestingly, he had no specific orders for this request. Nevertheless, he can report that they are looking for a newborn king. The second one reports that that king has been born by a virgin. He is so excited that he addresses Herod three times (*Rex! Rex! Rex!*). His rubric carries the significant information 'cui tunc hec sunt patefacta'.[31] As so often, the audience is informed of events that have not been staged. The third messenger finally reports that the child will be a king of all kings to whom the Magi are bringing their gifts. After Herod has learnt all this, he still wants to hear directly from the Magi: *Qui sint, cur ueniant, quo nos rumore requirant*. This can hardly be called a 'logical composition'.[32] The fact that Herod's question is traditional[33] while the messages of the *Internuntii* occur nowhere else in this quantity explains to some degree the origin of this 'dialogue'. But it does not describe the stylistic tendency which made such insertions acceptable. Clearly, the function of the messengers is not to inform Herod as fully as possible; at least he gives no sign that he has taken cognizance of their reports. Nevertheless it would be wrong to dismiss the triple messengers' report as a senseless repetition. The number of messengers and the second one's excitement certainly provided welcome show effects; but that does not exhaust their function. The fact that each report is followed by one even more astonishing and that all of them give information about the new king and not about the Magi indicates that the news of Christ's birth is to be given a psychologically effective form. It is, moreover, interesting to observe that this effect works exclusively for the benefit of the supernatural character of Christ's kingship. Herod's mistaken notion that Christ is to become his political rival, which is central to the vernacular Herod plays, is merely marginal here and does not affect his subsequent course of action. The psychological effects thus appear to be meant not for a realistically conceived intra-dramatic character but for the extra-dramatic audience. Thus even the messengers of the evil king become instruments of the Christian message which in this 'world-containing' play is repeated and relayed in much the same fashion as in the Revelation situations.[34]

Another scene which at first sight seems to harbour a rich potential for the presentation of interpersonal relationships serves above all the revelation of a theological truth. The scribes who are ordered to find the scriptural passage predicting the Nativity at Bethlehem could easily be developed into king's counsellors. But in fact most plays even reduce their part by giving the relevant quotation (Micah 5.2) to the choir rather than to the Scribes: the intention is clearly to give the prophecy a truth-value which it would not have if it came merely from the mouths of Herod's underlings.[35] Since the Scribes never appear as Herod's advisors, they can be questioned in the Magi's presence without awkwardness. Sondheimer's criticism of this arrangement misses the point of the scene just as much as does Young's attempt to justify it.[36] This is not the hatching of a plan which would have to be kept secret from the Magi. Only in a few late plays is the *Scribae* scene followed by a consultation scene, and only in Benediktbeuern is the element of

Revelation definitively relegated to second place by the *Archisynagogus*' subtle advice.³⁷ The Scribes never act as Herod's advisors, although such a combination of rôles seems to suggest itself and does occur in the vernacular drama.³⁸ Instead of the Scribes, Herod consults his *Armiger* in Bilsen and Freising, his son in Fleury.³⁹ In the later liturgical drama, to say nothing of the mystery plays, such moments of advice show an interest in intrigue and psychology. Here they are mechanically attached to the reading of the Scriptures, without a fixed place in the drama.⁴⁰

The Herod play contains only the very first elements of the presentational forms of the later mystery plays, especially in its 'objective' speech style and in the creation of a real socially defined substratum for the action of the play. But this does not create that direct line of development from the expanded dialogues of the Latin Magi plays to the Herod plays of the vernacular stage which is naïvely assumed by evolutionist *simplificateurs*.⁴¹ While certain limited elements of the content may have been transferred directly, the forms of dramatic discourse and the much-talked-about 'realism' which characterize the mystery plays as a genre owe nothing to their liturgical 'predecessors'.

Notwithstanding many additions, the treatment of interpersonal relationships remains fairly constant in the liturgical drama. They are largely those between ruler and underling and manifest themselves in command and obedience.

This relationship is important throughout the liturgical drama, but since the manner of its presentation does not change significantly, its further treatment can be brief. As may be expected, it occurs chiefly in the Daniel plays with their long stretches of court ceremonial. The *conductus* of these plays serve a function which is similar to that of the messenger in the Herod plays: they announce the newcomers to the king. But the weight of ceremony has been transferred to lengthy eulogies which, as a rule, do not influence the action. Accompanying the entry of important personages, they function not so much within the World of the play as within the stage business which represents that World. In getting people from one place to the next they resemble the processional chants of the *Officia Stellæ*.

Emotions

Herod's wrath

Herod's anger made the liturgical drama receptive for human feelings and passions. His bursts of rage became one of the most popular comic attractions of the mystery stage. While these facts have been known for a long time, far less attention has been devoted to the problem of how these passions were presented to the audience. There seems to be no coherent account of the ways in which psychological processes are expressed or simply described.[42]

As soon as one approaches this question, one discovers that at first Herod's fury appears exclusively in the stage directions. In the Montpellier manuscript and in Bilsen he brandishes swords,[43] in Fleury and Freising he throws the prophetic books to the ground,[44] but in none of these plays does the dialogue betray any symptoms of emotional disturbance. Occasionally a line may become psychologically more plausible if it is uttered in a heightened tone. In the interrogation of the Magi, which is one of the earliest parts of the Herod play, Herod asks: *Regem quem quaeritis...* Having received a reply he asks again: *Si illum regnare creditis, dicite nobis.* This repetition, which has already been criticized by Anz,[45] is no doubt more readily understandable if in the second question the king is *ira tumens gladios sternens*, as he is in Bilsen.[46] In Freising on the other hand the dialogue gains nothing by such emotionalized gesturing, the Montpellier manuscript even creates a contradiction:[47] Having vented his anger against the book which prophesies the birth of Christ in the Magi's presence, he pretends to them that he, too, wants to adore the Christ child after their return to Jerusalem. It is hard to imagine how this ruse can succeed with the Magi after they have seen his previous behaviour. It seems that wrath and ruse, gesture and speech, were not conceived as links in one integrated chain of communicative events which were to cohere as a whole. They are elements which have to be staged because they appear in the narrative source, but become isolated stage occurrences in the process of transposition. In that process it can happen that dialogue and stage instruction each go their separate ways, the stage direction expressing an emotion which the dialogue does not require or even belies.

This form of emphasis, which often isolates individual emotional moments, appears also in the Saints' legend, and there again it is frequently used to portray the Saints' antagonists.[48] But what happens in the plays goes a little further: one single emotion dominates the scene even in those phases in which it disturbs rather than furthers the action.[49]

That Herod's wrath should erupt even in the presence of the Magi is not attested by the Bible. Matt. 2.3 and 2.7 merely state that he 'was troubled, and all Jerusalem with him' and that he called the wise men 'privily'. His behaviour is thus more indicative of cleverness than of an unbridled temper. Nor do the apocrypha and legends which may have served as sources for the plays show a raging Herod at this juncture.[50] Matters are different, however, in the plastic arts. The triumphal arch of Santa Maria Maggiore in Rome (fifth century) shows Herod on his throne accompanied by a devil who symbolizes his evil thoughts. And St Maurice in Vienne (twelfth century) shows him between two masks, one of which seems to give sage counsel to the Magi, while the other whispers malicious plans into Herod's ear.[51] The northern portal of Poitiers Cathedral also shows a devil advising the Jewish king.[52] From the tenth century onward we find an *armiger* behind Herod, armed with a huge unsheathed sword. He is probably to be identified with the *armiger* of the plays or even with Herod's son Archelaus.[53] The plastic arts may thus be said to have developed modes of representation which allowed them to reveal Herod's evil nature behind his friendly mask. Both art and drama allow the simultaneous representation of successive events, because they are not interested in the faithful depiction of a moment in time. Both represent 'within one figure the presentation of two activities which, to organic thinking, do not go together'.[54] While it is true that the fury of the dramatic Herod has more in common with the antics of the Boy Bishop[55] than with the static attributes[56] with which Herod is endowed in the plastic arts, the importance of the 'simultaneity principle' which drama shares with art should not be neglected.

In the light of these principles of representation it is not surprising that Herod's wrath should have left no noticeable effects on the other characters. If they did react to his outbursts at all, such reaction is traceable neither in the dialogue nor in the rubrics.[57] In reality, Herod's wrath is not directed against the Magi in his presence, it is merely an expression of his evil disposition which is directed against the newborn king. This disposition is always in him and has to be signalled above all to the audience.

Interaction between different emotions is not to be expected with this conception of the *Herodes iratus*. It appears only in the dialogue between Herod and his son in the Montpellier manuscript (after the flight of the Magi) and in Fleury (before their journey to Bethlehem).[58] But the very fact that this dialogue can appear in such different places demonstrates that the dramatic and psychological integration of the emotions was less important than their scenic effect. The rich stage directions of the Fleury Play Book[59] are most revealing as to the representation of conflicting emotions: Herod flings the book with the ominous prophecies to the ground, *furore accessus*. Thereupon his son approaches, *pacificaturus patrem*. His salutation, which is one long *captatio benevolentiæ*, is entirely geared to this purpose:

> Contra illum regulum,
> contra natum paruulum
> iube, pater, filium
> hoc inire prelium.[60]

Only after Herod has gone through a series of changing emotions does he dismiss the Three Kings in the usual manner.

But this play, which originated from an important monastery school,[61] is not representative of the genre. However much the potential of *Herodes iratus* may have been exploited for the stage business – and we may be sure that the rubrics give only a very incomplete picture – its influence on the dialogue was virtually nil. A special 'raging speech style', so typical of the mystery plays, was never developed by the liturgical drama. But above all the emotion is conceived of as a self-contained unit which exists only in the one who experiences it and hardly affects the by-standers. It does not become an element which drives the action forward; it is as static as are the interpersonal relationships in these plays.

The basically static conception of the emotions allows Herod's wrath to become visible only as a global phenomenon, not in its developing phases. This makes it independent from the point of view of the speaker. How little even Herod himself is 'in the clutches' of his wrath becomes clear from the Freising Slaughter of the Innocents (*Ordo Rachelis*), where he comments on the news of the flight of the Magi with the words:

Rex nouus ut pereat, regisque furor requiescat.[62]

Even in his first reaction to a certainly infuriating message he is capable of thinking of the end of his agitation. Basically it is irrelevant who mentions the king's wrath. In Orléans, Archelaus refers to it even before the king has had an opportunity to manifest it:

Decerne, Domine, uindicari iram tuam, et stricto mucrone querere iube pueros; forte inter occisos occidetur et puer.[63]

Wrath does not 'rise' at a particular moment, the sword is not an instrument to be used at a particular moment. Both are reinforcing signs which are attributed to Herod, the one perhaps taken from contemporary art, the other probably born of the exigencies of scenic representation. It would be a mistake to call Herod the first example of character sketch.[64] His outbursts do not yield a pattern of behaviour which could be attributed to a character in any meaningful sense of the word. His raging does not even create a type, for the essence of such a type is that one and the same character trait appears in ever new situations. All these manifestations will have something in common, but they will also be suited to the respective occasion. But Herod's raging is a stereotypically repeated course of action which is neither fitted to nor motivated by the situation in which it occurs. It does not grow out of a character trait which might be postulated as a substratum; it is simply a sign of the reaction to the religious event with which Herod is faced. The appropriate reaction would be humility, dignity, decorum. What is above all important in Herod's behaviour is that it is the opposite of all these things. He is thus characterized as an enemy of God, as an incarnation of the evil principle. In this he resembles the raging judges of the legends. He has to rage, to contrast with the liturgical dignity of the Magi. Because his behaviour is a sort of counter-liturgy rather than the expression of a psychological disposition, it does not have to be fitted to a particular occasion and to be varied according to it. Since his raging is not always directed against specific people, it often seems to occur in a dramatic vacuum. The sword which Herod brandishes before the eyes of the Magi is not so much a specific threat as a permanent attribute of the Slaughterer of the Innocents of Bethlehem. It is present even when the situation does not require it.

But just as medieval art did not persist in the technique of attribution, so the drama went beyond the stereotypical gesture.[65] The following pages will deal with the new modes of representation which the drama developed.

Laments

Grief is another emotion the occasion of which is represented on stage, but which the liturgical drama does not show as developing within the person. Only in rare instances has the religious drama of the Middle Ages – both Latin and vernacular – achieved a psychologically faithful portrayal of emotional movements. But the lament, in which grief finds expression, was capable of an achievement which was not open to the presentation of wrath: it could bring the onlooker to share the situation and the feelings of the lamenter.

It was above all through the Marian *planctus* at the Cross that the liturgical drama was able to open a new dimension of experience.[66] In the lyrical *planctus* of the twelfth century the mother of Christ expressed her grief in her own person. When these were received into the liturgy and the liturgical drama, an important step toward their humanization had been taken. Mary, who was revered as the *mediatrix*, was capable of bridging the gap between the divine and the human. The twelfth century was a period in which it became easier to identify with her grief than with the suffering of the divine Saviour.

To obtain a clearer view of the Marian laments it will be useful to see them against the background of other liturgical-dramatic laments. The laments of Rachel, which originated probably within the liturgy of Innocents' Day, go back presumably to the eleventh century and are thus likely to be older than the Marian laments. The four texts that have come down to us[67] agree in only one respect: all of them have a *consolatrix* appear along with Rachel and thus make the lament into a dialogue. The texts show a good deal of common material, though the arrangement differs. Attempts to reconstruct a common archetype have so far been unsuccessful.[68] This lament will therefore tell us little about the influence of the liturgical style on the lament.

More is to be expected from the far more richly transmitted laments within the *Visitatio Sepulcri* which were first published by Wilhelm Meyer, together with an apparatus of variants.[69] Of the stanza groups A to E which Meyer distinguished, it is above all A, B, and D which are relevant for our present purposes. The A and the B stanzas are laments sung by the Women on their way to the Sepulchre, the D stanzas are sung by Mary Magdalene alone after discovering that the grave is empty.

These stanza groups share certain stylistic features which place them within the tradition of the liturgical drama and set them off against the style of the *planctus*.[70] Their content is largely descriptive. The pain of the lamenters is frequently articulated in exclamations but just as frequently in mere assertions. With the exception of the conventional *Heu!* the exclamations consist always of complete, simple sentences which are in marked contrast to the turbulent syntax of the Marian *planctus*:

> Heu! nobis internas mentes   quanti pulsant gemitus
> Pro nostro consolatore,   quo priuamur misere,
> Quem crudelis Iudeorum   morti dedit populus.
> Iam percusso cev pastore,   oues errant misere;
> Sic magistro discedente,   turbantur discipuli,
> Atque nos absente eo,   dolor tenet nimius.
> (lines 1–6 of Meyer's 'A' stanzas, quoted Young, *DMC*, vol. 1, pp. 385f)

> Omnipotens pater altissime,
> angelorum rector mitissime,
> quid faciunt istae miserrimae?
> Heu, quantus est dolor noster!
> Amisimus enim solatium,
> Jesum Christum, Mariae filium;
> ipse erat nobis consilium.
> Heu, quantus est dolor noster!
> (lines 1–8 of Meyer's 'B' stanzas, quoted Young, *DMC*, vol. 1, p. 285)

> Dolor crescit, tremunt precordia
> de magistri pii absentia,
> qui saluauit me plenam uiciis,
> pulsis a me septem demoniis,...
> (lines 5–8 of Meyer's 'D' stanzas, quoted Young, *DMC*, vol. 1, p. 386)

The syntax of these stanzas is as clear as are their content and structure. Pain and misfortune are named as if they were objectively observable, not felt and experienced by those who are expressing them: *Dolor crescit* (D, 5), *nos... dolor tenet nimius* (A, 6). Physical symptoms are described accurately, as from outside, certified as it were for the liturgical congregation: *tremunt precordia* (D, 5), *gemitus* (A, 1). Most space is usually taken up by the explanation: in B the Women state that they have lost their *solatium*, introducing this statement with an explicit *enim*. In D Mary Magdalene says that she cannot find her Lord, while in A the Women compare themselves to a flock without a shepherd.

The causes of the grief are always reported as objectively and detachedly as the grief itself. They are always represented as facts of the past. This is another contrast to the Marian *planctus* (as well as to the later vernacular drama), where to name the grief is always to relive and thus to renew it. In the *Visitatio* laments the emotions do not break forth from the characters, nor are they refuelled by remembering the causes and their accompanying circumstances. They are testified to. This testifying is done in clear, measured language, and we may assume that it is addressed to God, since the 'B' stanzas are given the form of prayer. It is not, as in the vernacular plays, a self-description which is primarily meant to inform the audience. These laments are still embedded in the context of religious worship. In this they differ from the Marian laments to which we shall now turn.

The Marian laments rose to considerable eminence in the vernacular Passion plays, although England has little to emulate the achievements of the Continent. Apart from the *planctus* which form independent texts and which were possibly staged,[71] the Latin drama has the *planctus* only in the Benediktbeuern Greater Passion Play. This play has adopted two *planctus* which are among the oldest of the genre: *Flete fideles animae* and *Planctus ante nescia*.[72] Wilfried Werner has subjected both of them to a thorough stylistic analysis which also takes the emotional attitudes into account.[73] For our present purposes it is therefore sufficient to concentrate on those aspects which are relevant from the dramatic point of view.

Although dialogue does appear occasionally in the *planctus* – especially in *Flete fideles animae* and in *Qui per viam pergitis*, which in part derives from the former, – the connection between the Latin *planctus* and the situation surrounding it remains fairly loose. The *planctus* only verbalizes a state, not an event with its causes and consequences which can develop into a represented action. It is less precisely localized in time than the Sepulchre and Manger scenes. Mary laments at some moment between the crucifixion and the death of Jesus. Neither of these events is influenced or affected by her lament. For this reason, even the extended *planctus* printed by Young[74] are not properly dramatic, although they are richly endowed with dialogue and gesture. Mary's situation remains the same throughout the lament.[75]

Even though the *planctus* does not constitute action by itself, the question of its embedding into the action remains. How and how far does the extra-linguistic situation enter into the lament, how does it contribute to its effect?

The *planctus* are clearly distinguished from the liturgical texts, including most laments, by the stylistic ornamentation which they use to express emotions. One example may stand for the many instances of sound figures, metonymies and antitheses which W. Werner cites:

> O pia gratia   O fera dextera
> sic morientis   crucifigentis,
> o zelus, o scelus   o lenis in poenis
> invidae gentis.   mens patientis.[76]

The syntax of this quotation revels in exclamatory nominal groups. Characteristically, it is above all the facts – the sufferings of Jesus, his sinlessness, his supratemporal glory, the cruelty and abjectness of the Jews – which are represented in those exclamations. They are thrust at the listener, as it were, in the raw, without being transformed into a complete clause. Questions, requests and reproaches do not break the syntax to the same extent. There are hardly any passages which specifically refer to Mary's grief: it is revealed indirectly in the juxtaposition of those circumstances which caused it. But the devices used (sound repetition and antithesis) are calculated not so much to express emotions directly as to affect the readers or listeners. They are forced to perceive Mary's grief not merely intellectually by way of the meanings of words and sentences, but also acoustically by way of the sound.

All of this stands in marked contrast to the clearly articulated, predominantly reporting style of the liturgical drama. The difference also becomes apparent in a fundamentally different method of representing the events of the biblical story. By its ceremonial – and by binding the latter to the Church year – the liturgy creates, so to speak, an institutional opportunity to make an event like the Resurrection 'happen again'. The efficacy and validity of such repetition does not depend on the quality of the devices used, such as dialogue, gesture, impersonation, and song. It relies solely on the fact that those means are authorized by the Church and are used on an occasion that is authorized by the Church. Re-presentation is thus independent of the psychological effects which the devices used may create in the audience. By contrast, the *planctus* represents Mary's laments by devices which are part of the text itself and which can exercise their effect whenever they encounter a corresponding mood in the audience. With this change the effect becomes independent of the ceremonies and institutions of the Church and dependent on the emotional receptivity of the individual believer, and the skills of the author and the 'actor'. (The word can be used here in its modern sense.) It is a change which corresponds to the transition from cult picture (*Kultbild*) to devotional picture (*Andachtsbild*) in the history of painting.[77] This in its turn alters the position of the beholder vis-à-vis the represented events. In the liturgical drama the congregation was represented by the impersonating clerics who received the divine message. The members of the congregation did not need to place themselves in the psychological situation of those taking part in the event, e.g. the three Marys at the Sepulchre; they had to achieve both more and less: more, because their own psychological situation became fully identical with that of the represented people since what had happened to Christ's associates was happening again to the medieval congregation; less, because this identification was strictly confined to the one represented situation. No-one in the congregation had to picture her (or him!)self as virgin mother, former whore, or frostbitten shepherd. With the Marian lament this limited identification is no longer possible. The listeners must identify themselves with the entire Mary, including especially her previous biography: present grief is deepened and aggravated by past joy. The listeners' task is no longer to allow a past event to happen to them, but to feel themselves entering into another person's soul. The recipient thus assumes a psychologically active rôle, for which there was no place in the original liturgical drama.

The modern reader may well feel that here is an emotion with which he can empathize and which is more akin to his own feelings than the purely conceptual *Visitatio* laments. But even this emotion takes its shape not from what the mother of Jesus experiences at the foot of the Cross, but from a theological idea. This may be illustrated by a stanza which will probably strike the unprepared modern reader as embarrassing:

> Triste spectaculum
>   Crucis et lanceae
> Clausum signaculum
>   Matris virgineae
>   Profunde vulnerat;
>   Hoc est, quod dixerat,
>   Quod prophetaverat
> Senex praenuntius,
> Hic ille gladius,
>   Qui me transverberat.

> Dum caput cernuum,
>   Dum spinas capitis,
>   Dum plagas manuum
>   Cruentis digitis
>   Supplex suspicio,
>   Sub hoc supplicio
>   Tota deficio,
>   Dum vulnus lateris,
>   Dum locus vulneris
>   Est in profluvio.[78]

The lance with which the Roman centurion pierced Jesus' side is here said also to have pierced Mary's maidenhead. The wound which he inflicted on the crucified corpse is said to be *in profluvio*. According to most sources, *profluvium* is a medical term to describe the flow of semen or menstrual blood.[79] The acumen which intertwines death and procreation in a paradox, the insouciance which applies physiological notions to spiritual ones without regard to their 'normal' associations: all of this shows the 'medieval' character of the imagery which sees the phenomena directly in their theological sense.

While it is true that the *planctus* are more emotionalized than the *Visitatio* laments, the emotions expressed here are not simply those experienced by a human mother. The imagery and the ideas expressed are too general, too strongly shaped by theological concepts. In *Planctus ante nescia* the dying Christ is addressed merely as *dulcor unice, singulare gaudium* (st. 2a), *flos florum, dux morum* (st. 3a): however extensive the description of Christ's torments, the terms used to refer to him are associated with heavenly joys rather than human pain. For this reason the lamenting Mary does not appear as exclusively preoccupied with her present grief as she will in the later vernacular laments. The rhetorical figure of metonymy, which treats abstractions with persons and thus raises the momentary feeling to the level of general concepts, is applied not only to Christ: when Mary says that she wishes to die in her son's stead, she addresses first *Mors* (st. 7a), then the (unidentified) bystanders (sts. 8bff). The address to the bystanders does not grow out of the dramatic situation, it is merely a rhetorical apostrophe; for immediately prior to this the Jews have been referred to as *gens effera* in the third person (st. 8a). The cruelty of Christ's Passion, which forms the subject-matter of this stanza, is stated as it were objectively; it does not come in the form of a personal reproach.

Often the *planctus* present feelings in the form of self-description, which in another form will return in the vernacular plays. Here it is still of a strongly ceremonious character and is often followed by an appeal to the bystanders to join in the lament (e.g. *Pl.a.n.*, st. 13). *Flete fideles animae* even makes this appeal its main theme.[80] This is characteristic of the early *planctus*: these aim not at compassion but at co-lamenting: *ut sint multiplices/doloris indices* (*F.f.a.*, st. 1a). In her own grief, too, Mary emphasized the supra-personal, generic aspects: *materne doleo* (*F.f.a.*, st. 1b). This stressing of the symptoms at the expense of the inner causes, of the generically apt at the expense of the individually felt, is not very different from the style of the earlier liturgical drama. The linguistic alloy of emotion and decorum corresponds to the peculiar in-between position of the image of Mary at this stage. The Mary of these *planctus* is above all an object of veneration, not so much the source of the emotions which we assume to be behind her complaints. In spite of the first person singular which is used throughout, she is usually seen from the point of view of the believers. Thus the listeners become witnesses rather than participants in her grief. Although the Mary of these laments is very different from the remote *theotokos* and *mediatrix* of the early medieval hymns,[81] she has not entirely abandoned that earlier rôle. Those features which strike the modern reader as somewhat cold, the rich use of antithesis and the complex play with ideas, stem from her double nature: momentary grief is coupled with a clear knowledge of her soteriological function which transcends that moment. The compassion which is aroused by these laments is thus not their ultimate aim, it is merely an emotional support of the cult: the more grief she demonstrates, the more venerable she becomes to the believer.

EXCURSUS:
The Latin and Middle High German *planctus* in the Benediktbeuern Greater Passion Play

As is well known, the moderately emotionalized image of Mary which we have observed in the previous chapter became thoroughly psychologized and humanized in the thirteenth century.[82] The effect of this change on the form of dramatic discourse can best be seen in a brief analysis of the Middle High German *planctus* which precedes the Latin ones in the Benediktbeuern Greater Passion Play. W. Werner has convincingly shown that the soteriological view has completely disappeared from the German stanzas.[83] But there is more: the emotions do not only dominate the lament, they increase from beginning to end and thus determine its structure. In her last exclamation *Zwiv sol mir leben vnde lip* (line 264: What use are life and body to me?) her despair reaches a climax which can hardly be justified theologically: Mary no longer wishes to sacrifice her life for a higher good (as her son's life would clearly be), but she wants to die because life now appears meaningless to her. The request *Lat leben mir daz chindel min/vnde toetet mich, die muter sin* (Let my child live and kill me, his mother) (lines 261f), which is also known from the Latin *planctus*, is the direct result of seeing her tortured son. The bystanders are asked not to lament with her, but are implored for pity (line 254: *erbarmen*) which is to be the result of compassionate contemplation:

      Lat iwer ovgen sehen dar
      vnde nemet der marter rehte war.   (lines 255f)

      Let your eyes look here
      and perceive well this martyrdom.

This poses a question which is important for the interpretation of all vernacular drama: who is addressed in these stanzas? Werner believes that Mary is speaking here to the audience, and certainly their emotions are to be moved by the *marter*. But the final stanza can, strictly speaking, only be addressed to Mary's Jewish and Roman contemporaries:

> Lat leben mir daz chindel min
> vnde toetet mich, die muter sin,
> Mariam, mich uil armes wip.
> Zwiv sol mir leben vnde lip. (lines 261–4)

> Let my child live
> and kill me, his mother,
> Mary, who am a full miserable woman.
> What use are life and body to me?

The lament does not distinguish clearly between audience and Second World bystanders. The spectators are compelled to 'act' Mary's dramatic antagonists, just as in the vernacular plays they have to 'act' Herod's subjects or John the Baptist's followers.[84] In part this state of affairs was present already in the very earliest Revelation situations: there, too, the choir and the congregation had, in Young's familiar formula, to 'represent though not impersonate' the bystanders of the protagonists. But here a new aspect gains importance: those who are represented by the congregation (or the audience) are no longer defined exclusively as recipients of the religious message, but they are people who take a specific, negative attitude to the religious message, they have to be evaluated morally, as cruel and unfeeling. The spectators must apply the valuation implicit in the lament to themselves and to admit its justness before they can fully appreciate Mary's grief. The reaction to which the spectator is invited is thus a truly dialectical one: it does not stop at an identification with the sinful bystanders of the represented scene (which would leave the spectator in a state of hopeless contrition). By identifying themselves emotionally with the sinners, they overcome their moral and theological identity with them. The identification is thus of a cathartic and implicit, not of a didactic and explicit, kind. (Still less, of course, does it partake of the hieratic and ritual nature of the Revelation situations.) This cathartic element will be found frequently in the vernacular religious drama – and especially in its most impressive scenes. With the loss of the liturgical frame, it became the most important way for the drama to affect the spectators – more important even than the didactic element.[85] Often it takes the form of *argumentum ad hominem*: a theological truth is presented from the point of view of a particularly fallible or even abject person with whom the audience have to identify in the sense indicated here. Mary's virginity is promulgated by Joseph, Christ's Passion by the Torturers. The development of the drama thus becomes a mirror of changes in the history of piety. The supra-individual ritual had to be supplemented and even replaced by personal devotion, concrete-sensual contemplation, and emotional participation.

4 The dramatization of narrative sources

The transposition of mental processes into the dramatic medium

The Easter and Christmas plays, even the Herod plays, grew out of the liturgy, and their language and structure were marked by those origins. The Marian laments were originally lyrical texts and retained their character when they were incorporated into the liturgical plays. As we have seen, they acquired properly dramatic features only in the vernacular. But there is a small group of Latin plays which closely follow their narrative sources in Bible or legend. This group includes above all the miracle plays, but the transformation for the stage can be observed also in plays based on the Old Testament, in the *Hortulanus* scene which was attached to the Easter Play in the twelfth century,[1] and in the Benediktbeuern plays. Coffman has defined the dramatic technique of the miracle play as 'the application of the dramatic method to popular, legendary material of the saint's life'.[2] This definition raises the question whether this 'dramatic method' cannot be applied to other narrative material as well, and whether there is really 'the' one dramatic method which the definition presupposes. The structure of the scenes and plays mentioned above is determined not by the 'liturgical groundplan', but by the 'pragmatic nexus'.[3] The *Hortulanus* scene above all shows a liveliness of movement and interpersonal relationships that would be unthinkable in the earlier scenes of the Easter 'play'. Christ and Mary Magdalene do not face each other in the rigid, hieratic confrontation which characterized the meeting between the three Marys and the Angel(s) of the *Visitatio*.[4] Mary Magdalene's falling down before the risen Christ and his withdrawal from her[5] bear very little similarity to the measured gestures of a liturgical act which de Boor has described as 'pacing, kneeling, rising, separating and re-joining, censing, reverent kissing'.[6]

Taking 'dramatization of narrative sources' as the genus, a first specification can be reached by studying the transformation of psychological processes for the stage. For here, two groups of plays can be distinguished: those that practically forego such transformation, and those that introduce a number of new techniques, especially of a mimic kind, which hitherto were unknown to the liturgical drama.

Although the scenic movement of the *Hortulanus* shows considerable liveliness, it is one of those plays which is surprisingly unconcerned about the dramatization of psychological processes. What we learn about gesture and language reveals nothing about the emotions of the characters. For instance, laments at the Sepulchre may be prefaced with the explanation that the three Marys 'still doubt the resurrection of the Lord'.[7] The same play explains Mary Magdalene's behaviour with the words *Illa uero putans eum* [viz. Iesum] *esse ortulanum respondeat*. Clearly these words are taken over mechanically from the Bible or from biblical commentaries without regard to the problem of visualizing such mental processes. The mechanical transfer from the gospel text becomes still clearer in those *Hortulanus* scenes which have the Magdalene address Jesus with the words 'Rabbi, quod dicitur Magister.'[8]

The same phenomenon occurs in the Old Testament plays. In the *Ordo Ioseph* from Laon (thirteenth century)[9] the encounter between Potiphar's wife and Joseph is represented as a pantomime with written 'explanations' such as *uxor Phutifar diligens Ioseph* or *Illa festinat ut innocenti culpam imponat*.[10] This play shows evidence of mechanical transfer even in places which appear to render mental processes in the spoken text. Having left one of them behind in Egypt as a hostage, Joseph's brothers confess on their return journey:

> Merito grauissimam
> patimur iniuriam
> Talis retributio
> est pro fratre uendito.[11]

This stanza goes back to Gen. 42.21: *et locuti sunt ad invicem: Merito haec patimur, quia peccavimus in fratrem nostrum*. Both in the play and in the Bible the words express a somewhat complex reaction: remorse at earlier, wrongful behaviour, a remorse prompted by anxiety in view of present danger. For Joseph, the *frater venditus*, takes one of them as hostage against the promise to return together with their youngest brother Benjamin. But the transfer from narrative to play has changed the character of the words significantly: while in the biblical account they are merely the summary of a conversation, the play takes them literally as direct speech, thus making the brothers speak (or rather sing) in chorus.

Even an experienced dramatist like the wandering scholar Hilarius[12] motivates his characters' actions by extensive 'stage directions' which hardly deserve the name because they contain nothing that is representable on stage. Thus, the envious 'princes and presidents' who plan to blacken Daniel's character with King Darius are characterized as follows: *Videntes Inuidi eum* [viz. Daniel] *esse in amicitia Regis, et uolentes eum inimicare Regi, nec inuenientes causam, nisi in lege dei sui.*[13] At first sight it may seem surprising that such a skilful playwright as Hilarius should have foregone this opportunity for scenic representation, but in his reticence he has certainly shown more stage instinct than the anonymous author of the Laon *Joseph*. Apparently he felt that in drama the linguistic form of such mental processes as collective planning and decision-making must be different from the one that is required in narrative. Hilarius did not develop those forms, but he refrained from giving inadequate expression to the mental processes behind them.

These plays can be contrasted with another group which is distinguished by a very accurate feeling for the possibilities of scenic representation. Although this group is not co-extensive with any one dramatic genre, it offers a much more homogeneous picture than the previous one. The group consists predominantly of the miracle plays, but a number of biblical plays belong here too. The majority of these plays is gathered together in three manuscripts. Two of these, Fleury and Benediktbeuern, were composed in important monastic schools. The third contains the *oeuvre* of Hilarius.[14] Although, as the example of Hilarius shows, the division into two groups is not absolutely clear-cut, the manner of textual transmission does suggest that the plays originated in places where considerable stage experience was allowed to accumulate and to shape the form of the plays in question.

For these plays it is normal to transform the feelings indicated by the source into visible action. The thieves described in Hilarius' St Nicholas play as *timentes* presumably gave their fear facial and/or bodily expression. Sometimes the significance of the prescribed manner of acting or speaking is explained. St Paul, for instance, is made to preach with elevated voice, *et quasi iam credens*. The Apostle's conversion is thus expressed by a contrast to his earlier behaviour, which was described as *quasi iratus*.[15]

Why were mental processes 'dramatized' so unequally, and why was imperfect dramatization of the source acceptable in some cases? An answer is perhaps possible if we consider the occasions on which the plays were presumably produced. The Barking Easter office, for instance, was introduced because Katherine of Sutton wanted to revive the religious zeal of her convent; to this end she gave the office a festive and ceremonial frame.[16] The nuns representing the Marys had to say the *Confiteor* and receive absolution before proceeding to the Sepulchre. In keeping with its congregational nature the office was meant to influence not only the emotions of the 'audience' but also those of the 'actresses'. The instructions 'de Resurrexione Domini adhuc dubitantes', 'putans eum esse ortolanum' and 'agnoscens eum'[17] therefore do not express what the 'actresses' are to show, but what they are meant to feel and experience. Since the text of the office was probably known to the entire convent, it is legitimate to assume that the on-looking part of the community was expected to share the emotions of the actresses. This assumption finds some support in the fact that none of these instructions contains the word *quasi*.

The Barking Easter office and the miracle play[18] of the conversion of St Paul represent almost two ideal types of the relationship between gesture and emotional content. The *ira* and the elevated voice as a symptom of newly found belief as found in the 'Conversio' are of course in the tradition of the Herod scenes and the Easter office. But they have radically changed their function: the Easter jubilation asks the congregation to unite in the expression of a certitude which for Christians is always valid, Herod represents the ever-potent principle of Evil, thus demonstrating a permanent threat to the Christian's salvation; but in the life of St Paul, wrath and belief are merely episodes which, while they had lasting effects for the history of Christianity, are by themselves of no salvific efficacy and thus do not need to be perpetually re-enacted. The cleric acting the part of Paul *quasi iam credens, et predicans alta uoce*, imitates a past event: he does not give visible expression to a real emotion which he and his audience must re-create within themselves for the good of their own souls. Conversely, the nuns representing the three Marys in Barking are obliged to re-experience even those emotions which are not accessible to physical expression. What in the case of Paul was interpreted at a seemingly superficial level is presented here as a kind of abstract inwardness.

Such an interpretation, however, would not be satisfactory in the case of Potiphar's wife, although the relationship between gesture and emotion seems to be similar to that in the Barking Easter ceremony. Here, too, it may be helpful to speculate about the purpose for which the play was produced. Although there can be no certainty in these matters, some hints are to be taken from the strongly didactic tendency which is particularly apparent in the prologue of the play. This tendency is also discoverable in the *allegoriae* of the *Ordo de Ysaac et Rebecca* from Vorau,[19] a play which in many ways is comparable to the *Ordo Ioseph*. Their didacticism suggests that both plays were acted by the pupils of a monastery school, a conjecture which finds further support in the boys appearing in the *Ysaac*. If this assumption is correct, we may perhaps regard these plays as school exercises, designed to reinforce what was taught in class. If we regard the Barking Easter ceremony as a dramatic equivalent of the medieval *Andachtsbild*, then the plays under discussion here may be compared to the 'historical' image.[20] What they share with this latter is at least their slight artistic pretensions; their sole purpose is to remind the audience of a biblical story. With such an aim, it is enough if only parts of the story are represented scenically; the audience can be counted on to supply the rest from their own prior knowledge.

While these plays are addressed to a group of people who are well known to the players – and presumably to the authors as well – and who are thoroughly familiar with their intentions, the miracle play gives the impression of being performed before a 'public' in the full sense of the word.[21] It is not easy, however, to gain an accurate picture of the composition of that public. We may assume that the saints' feasts for which the Saint plays were produced at the great monasteries were not merely religious celebrations but at the same time important commercial events which attracted numerous traders and minstrels besides pilgrims.[22] But whether such an audience was able to follow the production of a Latin play must be open to debate (although lively gestures may have compensated for the deficiencies of the foreign word).[23] But there is a common element that can be discovered in the linguistic form not merely of the miracle plays but also of the other plays which can be subsumed under the heading of 'clerics' poetry'.[24] Those who are present at the production without taking part in it as actors are now completely outside it; what takes place within the play is not the re-enactment of a sacred event in which the onlookers participate along with those representing a rôle in it; it is the imitation of a past event looked at with interest and delight, but without the ontological status of an immediately effective reality. The aesthetic autonomy which the drama thus acquires has consequences not only for the relationship between the represented characters and the audience but also for the internal structure of the plays. We shall now turn to the most important aspects of that internal structure: characterization and space and time.

Rôle-type characterization

The representation of emotions in this drama was of course not an end in itself but was adopted only when the source required it. Decisive progress in characterization was made whenever a dramatic figure became the carrier of the action. There is a method of characterization which can be described as 'rôle-type', translating the German *rollenmäßig* of P. Tack, who defined 'rollenmäßige Sprachgestaltung' as a manner of expression that is fitted to character and situation.[25] To medieval drama it was first applied by Hanns Ott.[26] Although in the original the term is fraught with overtones of 'naturalness' which appear inadequate in the discussion of medieval drama, it captures well the one aspect which we want to concentrate on in this section: a person endowed with something like a character continuum which varies its expression as the situation changes. Ott illustrates this type of characterization with the Herod of the Benediktbeuern Christmas play.

Apart from the late interpolation in Freising and Bilsen, in which Herod imprisons the Magi, the Benediktbeuern Christmas Play is the first Latin play to relate Herod's behaviour to the situation. This implies that simultaneously the first beginnings of a character substratum become visible. In the true fashion of the unjust tyrant, the Benediktbeuern Herod bursts forth *cum magna indignatione* against his messengers who report the birth of the newborn king:

> Cur audetis talia
> regi presentare?[27]

Such words may be used by a certain well-defined type of person in a given situation. They contrast markedly with the neutral *Ante venire iube* of other plays. For the first time, Herod's manner of speaking is shaped throughout by his mood. These moods are now the result of situation and character, which, in turn, means that the character is capable of changing moods and reactions. At the same time the mood becomes a motive force for further action. His fear of Jesus causes the Benediktbeuern Herod to call for his advisor, the Archisynagogus:

> Nostra mordet uiscera
> duri fama nuntii.[28]

Another innovation is that Herod asks for advice *before* the Magi have arrived. This prompts his plan of seeming friendliness: Herod is to meet the Magi *sub amoris pallio* (line 421).

This arrangement is remarkable for several reasons: it introduces some sort of strategic planning and, by that token, hypocrisy, which take the dialogue far beyond the usual question and answer of the liturgical offices; it also equips Herod with a continuum of behaviour to which the categories of character interpretation are at least applicable (even if the characters may not always seem consistent). The decisive criterion is not psychological plausibility. Whether an irascible king will be prudent enough to accept such clever advice may well be debatable.[29] But what is alone important is that the Benediktbeuern play makes all his actions and reactions dependent on his one ruling passion: fear for his throne, and that this fear leads to different reactions which are suited to the occasion and call forth new actions.[30]

There are but few plays that make character the carrier of the action in a similar fashion. Some hesitant beginnings can be found in Hilarius' Play of St Nicholas, but the passage of one motive to the next is not as effortless. The *barbarus* who entrusts his treasures to the statue of the saint explains his plans and his reasons to it point by point:

> Nicholae, quidquid possideo,
> hoc in meo misi teloneo;
> te custodem rebus adhibeo;
>   serua quę sunt ibi.
> Meis, precor, adtende precibus;
> vide nullus sit locus furibus.
> Preciosis aurum cum uestibus
>   ego trado tibi.
>
> Proficisci foras disposui;
> te custodem rebus inposui;
> reuertenti redde quę posui
>   tua sub tutela.
> Iam sum magis securus solito
> te custode rebus inposito;
> reuertenti uide ne merito
>   mihi sit querela.   (lines 1–16)[31]

The speech begins with a description of the situation, which presumably is directed more at the audience than at the statue; then the speaker gives the saint his instructions, carefully explaining that he must go on a journey: and finally he explains his course of action: he feels more secure if the saint watches over his treasures. Similarly, the complaint after the discovery of the theft is more a statement of causally related facts than the outburst of sudden dismay:

> Grauis sors et dura!
> Hic reliqui plura,
> sed sub mala cura.   (lines 17–19)

It is true that the complaint begins with an exclamation, but this exclamation at the same time describes and classifies the blow which the *barbarus* has received, explaining also *why* it is such a hard blow. The psychological mechanism of the lamenter is being explained as if by an outsider. This is a speech type which is characteristic also of most of the vernacular drama. It shows that the playwright feels the need to represent reactions and impulses, which also means that he recognizes them as factors capable of releasing action. But he is content to state them; he has as yet developed no technique to make them 'shine through' the character's speech as something which is present without being directly verbalized.

In this respect, the anonymous author of the Fleury *Iconia* play is much more successful. His hero – the *barbarus* has been turned into a *Iudaeus* – at first derides the miracles with which Christians credit his saint. When he finally does put the saint in charge of his treasures, this is done with a good deal of scepticism.[32] The unbeliever's attitude is thus much more complex than in Hilarius' play; deliberation and decision are far more intricately interwoven. This thoroughgoing emotionalization becomes even more apparent in the complaint,[33] which was probably modelled on Euclio's great scene in *Aulularia* (Act IV, Sc. ix).[34] The theory of Plautinian influence is supported by the fact that the *Iudaeus* shares just those features with the Latin miser which Hilarius' *barbarus* lacks. The fact that he has been robbed is no longer stated directly but appears only in its emotional reflex. In Plautus he says:

> Perii interii occidi. quo curram? quo non curram?
> tene, tene. quem? quis?
> nescio, nil video, caecus eo atque equidem quo eam
> aut ubi sim aut qui sim
> nequeo cum animo certum investigare.   (lines 713–15)[35]

The corresponding speech in the Fleury *Iconia* play runs:

> Vah! perii! nichil est reliqui michi! cur esse cepi?
> Cur, mater, cur, seue pater, fore me tribuisti?
> Heu! quid proferri michi profuit aut generari?
>   (Young, *DMC*, vol. 2, p. 346, lines 91–9)

But the monologue also shows features which can have no direct source in Plautus. In a long outpouring (which is probably meant as a parody of characteristically 'Jewish' speech) the Jew despairs of life, even reproaching his parents for his existence. It is also worthy of note that the motifs of the present complaint are made to agree with those character traits which had become apparent in the Jew's opening speech. Unlike Hilarius' *barbarus*, he does not reproach the statue directly, he merely feels confirmed in his original scepticism: *Fides nocuit michi Christicolarum* (line 104), and even the scourging of the image is no longer a deserved and considered punishment but is an emotionally motivated act of vengeance:

> Nec solus flebo, nec inultus, credo, dolebo:
> Tu meritis subdare probris tondere flagellis.   (lines 107f)

Out of his grief over lost treasure arises the comforting thought that he will not be the only weeper if he takes revenge on the image. But his own tiredness prevents him from executing the plan, and the saint gains a night's reprieve. This sequence of reactions gives the impression that they are being uttered as they take place within the Jew. The words are symptoms of deeper sensations which are thus expressed, not merely described.

This high standard in the technique of representing emotions is rarely reached even in the vernacular drama. We may assume, therefore, that it is due to the skill of the author rather than to the conventions of the genre. But even if we neglect the factor of individual skill, we can observe a tendency in the miracle plays and the Benediktbeuern Christmas Play to regard mental impulses as factors in the dramatic action and to give them a place in the play. This distinguishes these plays from the earlier liturgical drama and places them in the neighbourhood of the mystery plays. The influence of the Roman comedies, which were studied in the monastery schools, seems still the most likely explanation.

But the miracle play is not content with transforming emotions into actions and embedding them in the psychological substratum of a person. It also represents processes in which several people interact; this leads to extensive dialogue. It is true that short 'persuasion scenes' occur also in the dramatizations of biblical scenes, such as the Benediktbeuern and Klosterneuburg Easter plays in which the Jews persuade Pilate to arrange for a watch at Christ's grave;[36] or the *Ordo de Ysaac et Rebecca* from Vorau, where Isaac is at first 'ualde stupefactus' by his mother's deceitful plan.[37] But these remain meagre dramatizations of what was found in the biblical or legendary source.[38] We have to wait for the miracle plays to find extensive stageworthy dialogues, which may even sacrifice theological doctrine to dramatic effect. The legend of the Three Daughters as told by John the Deacon,[39] for instance, presents a self-pitying lazybones who sends his daughters into prostitution to rescue the family from poverty. He himself cannot do any physical work because of his noble lineage. The saint's rescuing act – Nicholas throws gold in through the window – thus benefits a person who has no claim on the reader's or spectator's sympathies. Its motivation is exclusively theological: by a life in sin, which they would have to enter out of filial obedience but against their own will, the daughters would be risking eternal damnation. This danger is to be warded off by the saint's intervention, as is explained in a long commentary which forms the main part of the legend. The play, which must go back to the eleventh century,[40] humanizes and even sentimentalizes the story by shifting the moral emphases: the idea of prostitution is first suggested by the eldest daughter; in the Hildesheim version of the play the father even opposes it at first. Thus, the evil plan does not arise out of laziness and selfishness, but out of the will to help and extreme self-sacrifice. The unexpected gift of gold now provides an immediately satisfying solution which does not call for theological comment.

This change in theological emphasis is reflected in new forms of dramatic speech. In the way they represent interpersonal relationships, the St Nicholas plays are closer to the vernacular mystery plays of a later period than to the Latin Bible dramatizations which are roughly contemporary with them. Two words of the Latin legend, *fornicare constituit*,[41] provide the subject-matter for forty-five lines in the original version of the play which was a mere eighty lines long.[42] This is the first time that a dramatist presents contrary opinions in dialogue without finding them already in his source. It has to be admitted, however, that this dialogue is not dramatic in the sense that it changes the situation. It is not a debate whose progress we can observe step by step: it does not have to be, since a decision becomes unnecessary on account of the saint's intervention. Nor does it have a 'dramatic' climax: the most disturbing proposition comes from the eldest daughter, who speaks first. The second opposes her, while the third merely recommends that they wait for God to help them. The surprise that the miracle might produce is thus diminished rather than increased by the preceding dialogue. But when all this has been admitted, it still remains true that here for the first time a situation has been presented exclusively by means of dialogue: the participants' situation is not merely reported but presented in their reactions; the dialogue is not merely a series of statements but a chain of interlocking arguments in which the daughters' positions are clearly differentiated.

A fundamental change in the relationship between speech and speaker lies in the fact that the members of one group, the daughters, address the 'other side', their father, individually. We have seen how alien this form of dialogue is to the original liturgical drama. There, it is quite usual for a 'monologue' – e.g., the three Marys' lament or the Grave Watch's defiant song – to be divided between the members of the group. But as soon as they face an 'other side', such as the Angel or Pilate, these groups will speak, or rather sing, in unison.

The new treatment of groups, which again foreshadows the vernacular plays, is clearly a feature of the miracle play as a genre and is not due to the author's individual inclination or talent. It is to be found in the rather primitive *Tres Filiae* plays as well as in those on the *Tres Clerici* and in the anonymous play on the miraculous *Iconia*.[43] Especially the three thieves of the anonymous *Iconia* are clearly and skilfully differentiated, while their counterparts in Hilarius' play are still silent characters. Young rightly observes that the Third Thief is cleverer and more cautious than his companions:[44] he warns them of the Jew's vigilance, he discovers that the chest in which the Jew has stored his treasures is unlocked, and finally it is he also who, after the saint's intervention, recommends that the booty be returned to its rightful owner. But of course he owes these character traits to the necessities of the dialogue rather than to any psychological ambitions on the part of the author. Since a new step in the action is taken by the three only after a complete 'round' of speeches, it is inevitably the third one who speaks immediately before action is taken and who thus appears as the decisive influence. If, therefore, he seems more individually marked, this is due to the fact that he is more directly connected with the action. Character differentiation is thus not an end in itself but the by-product of skilful dialogue. It is entirely subordinate to the requirements of the action. This characterization technique, thoroughly alien to Bible and legend, finds but few imitators in the English mystery cycles. But it is typical of the author of the famous *Secunda Pastorum* of the Towneley cycle.[45]

This technique of differentiating within a group which acts only collectively is an important innovation which was introduced into the Latin religious drama only by the St Nicholas plays. The skill with which interpersonal relationships are integrated into an already existing story can best be observed in the *Tres Clerici* plays of Fleury and Einsiedeln.[46] The host, who in the Hildesheim play[47] was capable of deciding by himself, has now to ask his wife's opinion. In Fleury the *clerici* even turn first to *Vetula* to obtain their goal.[48] This detail was presumably introduced to add a little variety, not for the sake of characterization, for in the planning of the murder the wife is by no means milder than her husband.

This differentiating and psychologizing detracts from, rather than supports the miraculous element of the story. It heightens the suspense which prepares us for the crime that precedes the miracle. In general, psychological differentiation ceases as soon as the miracle has happened. The only (qualified) exception is the *Fures* in the Fleury *Iconia* play who continue their debating habits even after the intervention of the saint. But what they discuss is the merely practical question of whether to obey the saint and return the booty. In the saint play the miracle appears as the unexpected frustration of a clever plan or as the unhoped-for remedy of a desperate situation, but hardly as the revelation of the numinous.

Time and space

When relationships between dialogue partners go beyond the rigid confrontations of the liturgy, when form and content of utterances become influenced by temporal and situational context, when the continuum of a human character becomes visible behind such utterances: then the *a priori* forms of human perception, time and space, show a need for some kind of dramatic shaping. The when and the where of an utterance become dramatically significant when the liturgical office begins to represent world-containing situations. But the liturgical office will never get beyond first beginnings in the development of a continuous spatio-temporal medium. The liturgical significance of the church building and of the time of the divine service remains too powerful to give much rein to the imaginative development of the forms of perception. For these reasons, a study of the development of these forms cannot proceed from the assumption that the authors of the early offices and plays had any conscious intentions. It can only expose those objective conditions which determined their specific ways of representing time and space. This will enable us later to give a clearer picture of the peculiarities of the vernacular drama.

Already at the beginning of this part of our study we had occasion to underline the constitutive importance of time and space for the liturgical drama.[49] We saw that only the stations or *sedes* themselves belonged to the sphere of the represented world. And even the *sedes*, the Sepulchre or the Manger, were frequently identical with the altar.[50] But whether the altar itself was used as a dramatic place or some special place was erected for the purposes of representation – the place always had to receive its dramatic existence from the liturgical ceremonial. Physical similarity with the Manger or the Sepulchre remained secondary even when a special effort was made to obtain it. It remained a means to direct the senses, it was not constitutive for the ontological status of the dramatic place.

Since physical similarity was not constitutive, its further development never became a necessity for the early liturgical drama; it did not need to go beyond the merely suggestive and symbolical. The size of the Sepulchre, for instance, often did not permit the Angel to sit on it or the Marys to enter it.[51] And *a fortiori* these *loca* lacked an environment. Not until the Women stand in front of the Grave (or the Magi in front of the Manger) do they enter into any relationship with it. An – admittedly extreme and isolated – example may show how little significance the intra-dramatic distance between two *loca* was felt to possess: in the Fleury Herod play the Magi address those standing near the entrance of the choir as citizens of Jerusalem and enquire about the newborn king. This encounter is not reported to Herod as it is in Bilsen and Freising. On his own initiative, having 'sighted' the strangers (*quibus uisis*, as the rubrics state explicitly),[52] Herod sends his *Armiger* to interrogate them. The composer of the Fleury play apparently 'overlooked' the fact that the short distance between Herod's *sedes* and the entrance to the choir represents the much larger distance between Herod's palace and the

Jerusalem city gates.[53] The rubric *quibus uisis* is valuable even though it has no parallel elsewhere, because it is evidence of what was felt to be 'dramatically acceptable' even in a play as highly developed as the Fleury text: long distances between Second World places are not represented by short distances on stage (as they are in the vernacular plays); they are, theatrically, ignored and omitted.

The change which the miracle plays – or, more exactly, the plays of the clerical poetic tradition – have brought about in the treatment of dramatic space becomes apparent from a comparison between the Star procession of the Benediktbeuern Christmas Play and the earlier Magi plays.[54] In the early plays the three Magi usually approach from different ends of the church and sing in alternation the lines of *Stella fulgore* before they have actually 'met' and greeted each other.[55] To ask pedantically whether the Magi are already within earshot of each other and are now singing together a song which is known to all of them would be a gross misunderstanding of this alternation. At this point they simply have not entered the Second World governed by the rules of representation, and in that world alone such a question would be meaningful. The Second World is entered only when the Kings salute each other with *Pax tibi, frater* and are questioned by Herod's messenger. But these events remain isolated points not prepared by other Second World events, as they are in Benediktbeuern and in most vernacular plays. The unmistakably liturgical character especially of the kiss is evinced not only by its similarity with the liturgical kiss of peace, which is exchanged for instance in the High Mass between priest and deacon. More important in our context is again the absence of any situational embedding: the Magi do not introduce themselves, they are neither glad nor surprised at their meeting, they do not exchange observations concerning the Star. The salutation is a mere ceremony without any inner motivation. All of this is the more remarkable as the episode is peculiar to a few late and more elaborate Magi plays which are often described as 'realistic': even here dramatic time and space remain a discontinuous medium into which only the highlights of the story enter.

In contrast to this, the entry of the Magi in the Benediktbeuern Christmas Play marks an important advance in the concretization of space. The first of the Three discusses by himself the significance of the new star. The liturgical singer has thus changed into a Second World person who, like his counterparts in the later mystery plays, speaks a monologue. Even more significant in our present context is the Second King who discovers the First and rejoices at having found a travelling companion. This 'agreeable humanization'[56] of interpersonal relations remains, however, the exception; the Second King's becoming aware of the First is merely hinted at, it does not become part of a gradual process. When two stanzas later the Second King addresses the First, we have none of the small steps which relate this event to the previous one and which in the vernacular drama will contribute so much to establishing a spatio-temporal continuum. Perhaps most significantly, the moment when the Second King approaches the First, which always marks an important juncture in the mystery plays, is completely absent from the Benediktbeuern play (line 301). Nevertheless, an important step into new dramatic territory has been taken: the represented persons no longer move in a vacuum; the space of the church is now used to represent distances in the represented world. At the same time the Star – which of course retains its religious significance – is perceived by the dramatic characters as an object in their (represented) world. Its significance is not immediately apparent to them but must be established by a quasi-scientific – i.e. astrological – discourse. Its function is no longer exclusively that of a divine sign, it is first of all a star which has to be compared with other stars.

The same treatment of space, which already resembles that of the vernacular drama, is to be found throughout in the St Nicholas plays. A quotation from the Fleury *Tres Clerici* may illustrate this:

> Secundus Clericus:
> Iam sol equos tenet in litore,
> quos ad presens merget sub equore.
> Nec est nota nobis hec patria;
> ergo queri debent hospicia.
>
> Tercius Clericus:
> Senem quemdam maturum moribus
> hic habemus coram luminibus.
>   (Young, *DMC*, vol. 2, p. 330, lines 5–10)

Although the allusion to the horses of the sun with its pagan overtones is more learned than most of what we find in the vernacular drama,[57] the reference to the setting sun and the unknown country betrays an interest in the specific state of the environment which recalls the mystery plays. Space has become 'worldly' (*verweltlicht*) in a double sense. First, the objects claim our interest for their physical properties and perhaps the mood which they evoke, not for any transcendental meaning; secondly, reference to these objects creates a piece of the life-world of concrete human beings. Such evocative details are not to be found in the rest of the liturgical plays.

Space may be said to have been humanized in these plays. This is evidenced not only in the fact that physical objects are referred to as physical objects, but also in the way people deal with them. The thieves of the Fleury *Iconia* play study the chest in which the Jew has left his treasure: their relationship to the object is exclusively determined by practical considerations. There is (of course) no place in these plays for the solemn unveiling and processional carrying which characterize the treatment of objects in the liturgical drama proper.

This new relationship between people and their environment is also reflected in the treatment of time. Before the *Clerici* meet the host they state the fact that it is getting dark and that they have to look for shelter. On their way to the Jew's house the *fures* exchange their expectations concerning the loot; before discovering that the chest is unlocked they discuss how they can obtain the treasure. In the Einsiedeln fragment of *Tres Clerici* St Nicholas even thinks at first that the corpses of the scholars are the fresh meat which he has asked for – before he discovers the terrible truth. In contrast to the liturgical plays, but in agreement with the mysteries, it is always the moment just before the climax which is realized with particularly loving care.[58] But these moments are not merely multiplied as they were especially in some of the Herod plays; such a procedure would merely blur the story line. On the contrary, the thoughts of the characters are already directed toward what is to come, which will promptly assume an unexpected form. Thus, suspense and surprise enter the drama.

In this respect, the detailed representation of space and time creates a realism which far exceeds that of the mystery plays. But the Latin miracle play also loses something which the mystery cycles could not give up without losing their essential character: in reducing the environment to its physical and empirical aspects, the Latin miracles are confined to a reality which to a religious drama is necessarily peripheral. The sacred place, the significant moment are beyond its ken. Man's existence in the physical world is given dramatic form in these plays, but the supreme importance of that world has not yet become evident. The represented world is indeed the world in which real human beings move, but it is represented for its interest rather than its significance. And it draws its interest mainly from the fact that the saint's intervention can waive its laws at any time. The mystery plays, which could not be content with a merely anecdotal view of the empirical world, had to develop different staging conventions.

Part II

The English Creation to Doom cycle

5 The origins of the Creation to Doom cycle and its stage

Before we begin the study of the vernacular drama it is necessary to inquire into any continuity that may exist between the mystery cycles and the liturgical drama. When the German original of this book was published it was still usual for the standard histories to say that the vernacular genres had 'developed' out of the Latin. How exactly such development had taken place was not so clear. When the evolutionism of the generation of Chambers and Creizenach had fallen into disrepute, the incertitude about the nature of that evolution increased still further. Hardin Craig, who wrote the last one-man history of our genre, is probably representative of that watered-down evolutionism:

We know that liturgical plays or dramatic offices were in the hands of the clergy and that during a period of perhaps slightly more than 100 years, roughly from the beginning of the thirteenth to the beginning of the fourteenth century, the plays left the church and passed into the hands of the laity. How and why they did this we do not know with any great definiteness.[1]

Craig would probably have rejected the charge of biologism, but his wording – 'left the church and passed into the hands of the laity' – still reflects the notion that between the liturgical drama of the twelfth and the mystery plays of the fourteenth and fifteenth centuries there must have existed an uninterrupted line of progeny pretty much as it is postulated by biologists when they claim the descent of one species from another. Such thinking will always be on the lookout for transitional forms which share some of their features with the earlier, some with the later species. The impulses which gave rise to the new features will be relegated to second rank by such thinking.[2] Historians of drama, who believe that a long-term impulse towards growth is the dominant factor in the development of the genre, find these transitional forms in the very comprehensive productions of Cividale (1298 and 1304), Riga (c. 1206),[3] Regensburg and other places. They derive support for their thesis from the fact that the cast of these productions were presumably clerical, while the place of performance was certainly already outdoors.[4] Another link is often seen in the Latin plays with vernacular insets, such as the Benediktbeuern Passion Play, the Origny Easter Play, the *Iconia* play by Hilarius and the Limoges *Sponsus*.[5] The reason given for these insets is usually that the plays were to be made understandable for a lay audience.[6] But even Craig, who accepts this hypothesis as plausible, has to admit that 'at the very first the vernacular parts seem to be choral or explanatory rather than direct translation'.[7] 'Direct translation' is to be found much later, e.g. in the *Shrewsbury Fragments* and the Trier Easter Play, both transmitted in fifteenth-century manuscripts.[8] In the light of this state of affairs it is more likely that the lay audience of the French and German plays in question was in fact meant to receive a message that was different from that received by the clergy. England is too poor in bilingual texts for any valid conclusions. But for Germany Alfons Brinkmann and Wilfried Werner have demonstrated that 'father tongue' and 'mother tongue' stand for different kinds of piety in the Middle Ages.[9] The concepts offered by Brinkmann and Werner – 'theocentric' and 'anthropocentric', 'liturgical' and 'popular' existential attitudes' (*Seinshaltungen*) – can of course only be first approximations. The individual work – this has been pointed out by A. Brinkmann – will usually show a mixture of the ideal types; but they are sufficiently distinct to subject Craig's theory of gradual 'secularization' (which to him implies 'decay') to a minute form-historical probing.

The rise of the vernaculars thus means not only that existing contents were made accessible to new audiences but also that a qualitative change in those contents took place. Our present knowledge leads us to believe that bilingual plays were an attempt at synthesizing two existing kinds of drama (the liturgical and the vernacular) rather than the 'missing link' between the older and the more modern genre. This tallies well with the fact that the earlier vernacular plays are usually earlier than the earliest bilingual ones (with the exception of the *Sponsus*,[10] which has had hardly any influence on the vernacular plays). The Anglo-Norman plays *Ordo representacionis Ade* and *La Seinte Resureccion* go back to the twelfth century and 'are as different from one another as both are from any liturgical plays'.[11] From this period only *Les Trois Maries* can be regarded as a translation of the liturgical drama.[12] It is above all *La Seinte Resureccion* which anticipates the vernacular drama in its endeavour to avoid discontinuity in the representation of time.[13] Its stage, moreover, with its fourteen *sedes* representing everything from heaven to hell shows no similarity with the liturgical drama. Since the neutral area between the *sedes*, the *platea*, has lost all significance and all rapport between actors and audience after the Prologue, the *Resureccion* is even further removed from the liturgical drama than most later vernacular plays.[14] Hardison believes that these methods of representation reflect already established practice.[15] It is perhaps equally possible that they originated simply from an attempt to stage a narrative source. This question must remain open; luckily the answer is not crucial for our argument. But since the (earlier) Paris version was possibly recited by a single mime rather than acted by a troupe,[16] our text may well sit on the fence between narrative and drama, thus resembling the Latin *comoediae elegiacae*. This explanation would make it unnecessary to assume an otherwise unattested acting tradition. In any event, the dramatic technique of the *Resureccion* has nothing in common with the productions of the liturgical drama.[17]

While the structure of the *Resureccion* suggests a narrative source, the backbone of the *Adam* is taken from the Gregorian liturgy.[18] This means that even at this early period the vernacular drama shows a multitude of forms which can hardly be explained by a common origin in the liturgical drama. But these Anglo-Norman plays can no more be described simply as 'developments' of the liturgical drama than they can be called 'precursors' of the mystery cycles. Even the *Resureccion*, whose episodic structure and narrative style come fairly close to the mystery cycles, lacks important elements whose presence in the Corpus Christi cycles cannot be explained simply by gradual growth. They have their roots in the history of society and its piety, and it is now time briefly to refer to the most important of these.

Between the *Resureccion* and the first record of an English Corpus Christi play (York 1376) there is the great medieval reform movement which led, among other things, to the founding of the mendicant orders and to the introduction of the feast of Corpus Christi. In this feast, which became generally accepted in the early fourteenth century, the Church endeavoured to express a new openness to the world;[19] it marks a watershed in the history of piety which is also reflected in the development of religious drama: while in the liturgical drama man had to approach the deity reverently, it is now the deity that goes out into the world. The Eucharist leaves the precincts of the church; the history of salvation – from the Creation to the Last Judgment – takes place in the market places and the streets. The German word *Verweltlichung* captures the double nature of this process rather better than the English *secularization*: in going out into the world, the plays become *welthaft*, acquire a 'world' of their own in Lukács' sense of the word.

While the feast of Corpus Christi must have been an important factor in creating the Creation to Doom cycles, the relationship between the feast and the cycle texts as we have them is at best an indirect one.[20] Of the four cycles that have been preserved in even approximately complete form, only two are undoubtedly connected with cities. And of these only one, York, was connected with the feast of Corpus Christi. The other, Chester, was moved to Whitsun in the 1520s, when it was given more or less the form in which we know it today.[21] The *Towneley Plays* have for a long time been identified with the Corpus Christi cycle of Wakefield, but that connection now looks desperately like the fabrication of a patriotic local historian.[22] *Ludus Coventriae*, whose unrelatedness with Coventry has been known for a long time, is now usually called 'N-Town', after a reference in the 'Proclamation' of the cycle (line 527). This designation aptly expresses the fact that in all likelihood the cycle had no city connection whatever. In the case of Towneley and N-Town it is highly doubtful that they were ever performed as they appear in the manuscripts.[23]

On our present knowledge we must assume that the guilds and their desire for representation influenced not only the later development of the Corpus Christi plays but were a decisive factor already at the outset.[24] Lawrence M. Clopper has recently put a strong case for cycle plays having developed, above all, in northern cities with strong governments based on the trade guilds.[25] On this evidence the biblical cycle is a new genre which certainly adopts a few scenes and dialogues from the liturgical drama; it does not take over and translate the liturgical drama *in toto* only to liberate itself subsequently from its influence. In the case of Chester it seems even probable that the plays as we have them constitute a sixteenth-century reaction to earlier popular forms of dramatic activity.[26] The cycle has its own problems and methods of representation, which will be analysed in the following chapters. While this study is almost exclusively devoted to the four great biblical cycles, it should be remembered that the 'Corpus Christi cycle' is probably not as representative of medieval English religious drama as has been traditionally assumed.[27] The term 'Corpus Christi play' can refer to a great variety of phenomena, it hardly represents a homogeneous dramatic genre.[28]

The guilds and the feast of Corpus Christi share an important feature with the plays: the expression of religious feeling was less dominated by religious ceremony than had previously been the case. This circumstance is responsible for the decisive difference that exists between the mystery cycles and all earlier genres – the liturgical drama as well as the Latin miracle play and the vernacular *Resureccion*. Basically, this peculiarity consists in the relationship which the mystery plays establish between First and Second World. The many modifications of which this relationship is capable will become apparent in a study of the audience-address, to which we shall devote a special chapter. But the physical conditions which make these modifications possible are to be found in the form of the stage and will thus have to be examined first.

In contrast to the hierarchical situations of the liturgical drama, the Corpus Christi cycles know, and recognize, an audience; they are performed in the presence of a crowd which is not continuously drawn into the represented situation.[29] While the attitude of the congregation of the liturgical drama was prescribed by its being part of the divine worship, the public of the Creation to Doom cycles had only the suggestive power of the production to guide its responses. The play-audience relationship here is similar to that in *La Seinte Resureccion* and presumably in some of the Latin miracle plays.[30] But the function of the audience is different, as is clear from the spatial disposition of actors and audience. All reconstructions compel us to assume that the *Resureccion* was performed *in front of* an audience,[31] whereas in the English cycles the actors moved presumably *in the midst* of theirs. Play-sphere and audience-sphere, First and Second World, were thus not facing each other, but the play-sphere arose from the world in which the audience lived. The relationship between both spheres is not casual, as it will be in the case of a troupe of actors happening to come to a town or village; it is firmly grounded in the customs of the community. This gives the representation of the biblical story – of God's ways with Man – the character of festive self-representation. Although the plays are no longer religious ceremonies whose every action is invested with religious significance, they are still, taken as a whole, communal religious acts.[32]

This is of some consequence for the treatment of the spatio-temporal continuum of the Second World. The neutral space between the *sedes* is, in the mystery plays as in the liturgical plays and *Feiern*, no mere geometrical interstice but reaches out into the world of the audience. The contrast between intra-dramatic *locus* and audience-oriented *platea*, which was to be found already in the liturgical drama, returns in the Creation to Doom cycles – though with important modifications:[33] in the liturgical drama place and time – the building of the church and the hour of divine worship – were not a semiotic *tabula rasa*, their signification always shone through and affected that of the representing action. Each represented scene was embedded in the action of the service and received its significance from it. The vernacular plays, performed as they were on the pageant-waggon, the town market or the village green, were not so embedded and had to create their own spatio-temporal foundation. There, the place of the action was merely 'the Sepulchre' or 'Bethlehem', without any cultic function underlying the representational one. This brought about a fundamental change in the relationship between 'godly' and 'ungodly' *sedes*, e.g. between the *praesepe* and Herod's throne. In the church the *sepulcrum* or the *praesepe* were distinguished by their position, being placed for instance on or near the altar. Herod's throne and other *sedes* were reduced in their status by the very fact that they did not have such a marked position. By contrast, the vernacular stage did not provide such *a priori* hierarchical differences. Differences were no doubt made visible, e.g. between heaven and hell, heaven and earth, Bethlehem and Jerusalem; but they had to be the result of the acting and of the physical structure of the stage.

A peculiar double function was developed by the space between the *sedes*, a function which was to distinguish most of the English theatre down to the days of Shakespeare. The *platea* of the vernacular theatre can be open to the audience-world just as the space between the *sedes* was in the liturgical drama. But in addition to this, it is also the physically experienced space of the play-world. The people who move across the *platea* never leave the spatio-temporal continuum which relates them to the *loca*, even if occasionally they address the audience. The characters of the mystery plays never step outside their parts as for instance a cleric in a Latin *Magi* play could lapse from his 'dramatic' part back into his liturgical function. Even when the mystery actors address their audience they do so in the capacity of poor shepherds, henpecked husbands, raging tyrants, not as personal acquaintances or neighbours. Even the Shepherds walking over north country moors do not leave the world of Bethlehem. The *dramatis personae* always 'know' where they come from, and often they anticipate where they are going. The Magi for instance discuss the miracle which has been promised them, they see each other approach, they recognize the Stable on nearing the appropriate *sedes*. In a word, the represented characters experience the space in which they move as their physical environment. This important difference over against the liturgical drama compels us to qualify somewhat the view expressed by Robert Weimann and Martin Stevens that 'the shepherds of Bethlehem graze their sheep on the moors of northern England' and that the York cycle uses the 'City as Stage'.[34] It is perhaps more accurate to say that the world in which the action of the drama unfolds is not qualitatively different from that in which the audience lives; Christ, after all, had been born into the world of which northern England was a part.

Certain similarities between the late Latin plays and the mystery cycles should not be overlooked, but they need not be interpreted in the sense of a direct line of descent. They are most naturally explained by the fact that both dramatic genres adapt narrative sources and for this simple reason have to provide for some spatio-temporal continuity. Another reason is that both genres were no longer composed for self-contained communities of monks or priests but for a mixed public whose lives had to observe the exigencies of their physical environment. But whatever the similarities, we cannot emphasize enough the all-important difference:

the balance between the two stage areas was changed radically in the vernacular drama. As we have seen, the Latin miracle play works out the physical environment with loving care and yet gives it only a local, 'anecdotal' significance. The Creation to Doom cycles, too, show their characters' environment as physically experienced, and 'a new awareness of man's position in the physical world' can even be called characteristic of the genre.[35] But the Creation to Doom cycles treat the physical world much more seriously than the miracle play does. A miracle, by definition, is an occasional intervention of the deity in the physical world; in the mystery plays the deity and man interact constantly. Man's deeds in this world will be punished or rewarded in the next. And often enough the judgment seat before which he will have to appear is visible on the stage. If the *platea* often appears as the scene of a harsh, bitter and funny world far from God, that may well have sharpened medieval man's sense that this is the world which will be judged by God and which can only hope for His forgiveness to be saved. It is true that the *platea* often shows social criticism, realistic anachronism, and comic contradiction to the sacred action.[36] But a detailed study will show that all these are facets of the general condition of man, who must face the superhuman and divine on the one hand and anti-human evil on the other. The mystery stage thus makes the world-picture of medieval gradualism visible and creates, within the confines of this world-picture, the possibility of a realistic mode of representation. As far as we can tell, this 'realism' is part of the original make-up of the genre, not a late, popular and irrelevant addition.[37]

The relationship between *locus* and *platea*, moreover, is not the same in all plays. To the extent that it varies in accordance with local tendencies, it will be dealt with in chapter 7. But fundamentally it depends on the physical structure of the stage, which must concern us now. Study of the Creation to Doom cycles has been hampered by the fact that by far the most influential study of the medieval stage is based on an analysis of the plan of the morality play *The Castle of Perseverance*.[38] Southern's brilliant though widely disputed analysis has inevitably led to the Corpus Christi stage also being studied in the light of his theory. Moreover, the processional staging of the cycles is less confidently assumed now than it used to be. Even the performance of the York Cycle on pageant-waggons has been questioned.[39] While there is fairly general consensus on the 'true-processional' staging of York and Chester and while the N-Town manuscript most likely combines plays designed for both types of stage,[40] the staging of Towneley is very controversial, though the cycle seems to be designed for fixed staging.[41]

In this uncertain situation, Robert Weimann's approach has a good deal to commend it: he abstracts from the physical structure of the stage, inquiring merely into the dramatic function of its components. Taking the N-Town Joseph as an example ('Joseph's Return', LC XII), he shows how the speaker changes within one speech from a position of distance to one where he is closer to his public.[42] Joseph is capable of breaking through the play-sphere with a brief remark spoken *ad spectatores*. This will be discussed in detail in the next chapter. For the moment, suffice it to say that this rapid alternation between the two Worlds seems to be easier on the comparatively intimate pageant stage, while it appears to be alien to the elaborate stage of *The Castle of Perseverance* and parts of N-Town. Weimann illustrates his views first with the N-Town *Passion Play II*, which at one time must have been an independent unit[43] composed for a multiple stage. But the sudden sally from Second to First World which is at the centre of his attention is then exemplified by LC XII, which seems to belong to an earlier stratum of the cycle written for a pageant stage. It seems likely that the sudden change from play-sphere to audience-sphere, which Weimann rightly regards as a precursor of the Elizabethan aside, is by and large peculiar to the narrowly dimensioned pageant stage. It presupposes a degree of intimacy between actors and audience which is common in the folk-play, in large sections of the Corpus Christi cycles, in the moralities and interludes of the later travelling players, but not in *The Castle of Perseverance* or the bulk of the N-Town *Passion Plays*. One would like to think that the nature of the stage has a strong influence on the relationship between play-world and audience-world. Maddeningly, this relationship is incapable of strong proof. But the next chapter will offer a close analysis of many audience-addresses which hopefully will at least raise the level of probability for whatever relationships may exist.

6 The representation of time and space in the cycles

Sketch of a typology

Before the four cycles are discussed individually a few general remarks will be useful. The treatment of Second World time and space on the stage must face special problems whenever the events of a story are distributed over more than one (usually two) localities. We can distinguish two basic techniques, which I shall call the technique of 'continuous correspondence' and the 'cutting' technique (using a term borrowed from the movies). 'Continuous correspondence' demands that after a person's departure from place A his travel to place B be represented on stage. 'Cutting' means that the journey is 'cut out' and that the dialogue either continues at place A after the person's departure for some time or 'cuts' to place B immediately. 'Cutting' and 'continuous correspondence' can be contrasted as in Figure 1 (optional stages are enclosed in interrupted lines[1]).

Continuous correspondence is a technique which suggests itself immediately when a narrative source has to be put on stage. The sentence 'The messenger went from A to B', simple enough in narrative, becomes somewhat awkward when translated to the stage. The itinerant's uneventful journey will either have to be filled with otiose material (often with songs), or the discrepancy between Second World and First World distances will become very apparent to the audience. The 'cutting' technique shows a better understanding of the requirements of the stage and betrays a greater degree of independence from the narrative source. It seems justified, therefore, to call the technique of continuous correspondence 'primitive' and the 'cutting' technique more 'sophisticated' or 'advanced'. At the same time it ought to be understood that these adjectives do not imply any value judgment.

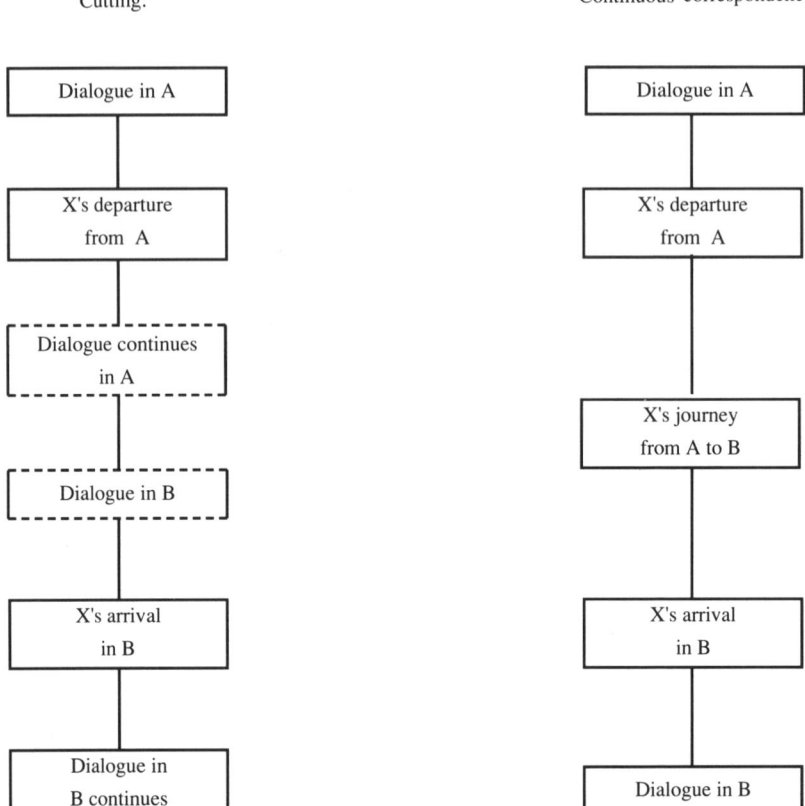

Figure 1.

Time and space in the Chester cycle

The treatment of space in the Chester Cycle is markedly similar to that in religious narrative. Quite often, however, the discrepancy between long Second World distance and short First World distance is mitigated by a reduction in the dialogue of distances mentioned in the narrative sources. In Ch IV God informs Abraham that the mountain on which he is to sacrifice his son is 'besyde' (Ch IV, 228), while Gen. 22 and the other cycles emphasize that the mountain is at a considerable distance, involving even a three-day journey. Similarly in the Lazarus play Martha tells Jesus that her brother is lying 'sicke a little herebye' (Ch XIII, 311). Here again, the play differs from the source in its treatment of spatial relations: John 11 leaves the distance somewhat in the dark, but the general situation leads us to believe that the encounter between Jesus and the messengers (not Martha!) does not take place near Lazarus' home. For when Jesus arrives there, Lazarus has already been dead for four days. These explicit deviations from the Bible are significant even if they are not numerous. (There are comparatively few episodes in the Bible which involve this kind of place-changing.) Apparently the Chester playwrights thought it necessary to inform their audiences of the identity of all the localities that were visible on stage. We may assume that the references quoted were accompanied by pointing gestures.

These explicit references to distances are remarkable above all because they would be unthinkable in the liturgical drama. The mere fact of their occurring is thus an indication of the radically new conception of space which we find in the vernacular plays. This new conception becomes even more tangible in the use of place names. Once more, the Chester Plays are the most barren of the cycles; they are content merely to mention the place without adding any description. Place names are given solely for the benefit of the audience; they are not meant to give concentrated expression to the way the *dramatis personae* experience their environment: they usually take the form of a simple announcement of the destination. Sometimes, of course, such an announcement is impossible because the beginning of the play or episode shows the characters already present at the relevant place. When this is the case we find the 'flat declaration of place' which Muriel Bradbrook finds so typical of Elizabethan drama,[2] as for instance at the beginning of the Magi play:

> Therfore these lordes and I in fere
> *in this mounte* make our prayer...   (Ch VIII, 13f, emphasis mine)

It is almost superfluous to add that the mountain mentioned here goes back to the *Legenda aurea*.[3]

But the announcement is far more common. For example, Abraham in his opening prayer says:

> Therfore of all that I have wone
> to give the teath I will begynne,   [thee tithe
> the cyttee sonne when I come in,   [soon
> and parte with thee my praye.   [prey
>   (Ch IV, 29–32)[4]

The intention to move to some other place is here subordinate to a more important plan: Abraham, who has just thanked God for having delivered him from his enemies, now wants to prove his gratitude by paying tithes to the priest-king Melchisedek. The 'cyttee' where this is to be done is of little importance; not even its name is mentioned. What matters is that Abraham intends to pay his tithe 'as soon as he comes in [i.e. to the city]'. The purpose of the speech is thus primarily to show Abraham as a loyal and eager servant of God – a quality which is to be even more severely tested in the second half of the play.[5]

In the Ministry plays (Ch XIII-XV) changes of place are announced exclusively to inform the audience about the scene of the staged events. Here again, it is merely the sense of place of the narrative source which is reflected: since the places of Christ's miracles, preachings and sufferings are important in the New Testament, they are important to the Chester playwrights as well. In an obviously late opening speech written in rhyme royal[6] Jesus says to the disciples:

> Wherfore, deare brethren, yt is my mynd and will
> to goe to Bethenye that standeth herebye,... (Ch XIII, 15f)

Ch XIV, in the regular Chester stanza, begins similarly:

> Brethren, goe we to Bethenye
> to Lazarre, Martha, and Marye;
> for I love mych that companye,
> thidder now will I wend.
>
> Symon the lepper hath prayed me
> in his house to take charitie.
> With them nowe yt liketh mee
> a while for to lend. (Ch XIV, 1–8)

References to time can be given in a similar way:

> The feaste of Easter you knowe draweth neare
> and nowe yt is at hand. (Ch XV, 3f)

The expressions of intention which we regularly find in these announcements are as devoid of emotional overtones as is the narrative formula 'Then he came to X', of which they are a slavish imitation in dramatic dialogue. They serve to inform the reader or spectator, they do not express any relationship between man and his surroundings. For a phrase like 'That seems to be X', which would express a momentary attitude to the speaker's surroundings, we shall have to wait until the York Plays.

Announcing a change of place does not mean that the journey itself is given dramatic shape in any way. The *dramatis personae* are first 'here', then 'there', they are never 'on the way'. And the 'being there' is never preceded by an 'arrival'. The many salutations only appear to contradict this claim. On closer inspection they are social conventions which do not verbalize the speaker's becoming aware of, or reacting to, a new environment. Even when elements of that environment are perceived, they are stated and characterized rather than reacted to. These are the words of the Third King after the Star has come to rest above the Stable:

> A fayre mayden yonder I see,
> an ould man sittinge at hir knee,
> a child alsoe; as thinkes mee,
> three persons therin are. (Ch IX, 128–31)

The three persons – perhaps a typological allusion to the Trinity – are exclusively characterized as specimens of their kind (maiden, old man, child). We learn nothing about their outward appearance. The speaker does not react to what he sees, he merely states.[7]

Very occasionally we find something like a process of real physical perception. This is true, for instance, of the three Marys on their way to the Sepulchre. Mary Magdalene asks the question familiar from the Bible and the liturgy:

> Suster, which of us everychon
> shall remove this great stonne
> that lyeth my sweet lord upon,
> for moove yt I ne maye? (Ch XVIII, 333–6)

But while the liturgical drama is content with this question, Ch XVIII develops a dialogue which registers progressively more details of the situation as the women approach the Sepulchre:

> MARIA JACOBI:
> Suster, maystrye ys hit nonne.
> Hit seemes to mee as he were gonne,
> for on the sepulcher sytteth one,
> and the stonne away.
>
> MARIA SALOME:
> Two children ther I see sittinge,... (Ch XVIII, 337–41)

First, Maria Jacobi dispels Mary Magdalene's worries by pointing out that the stone has already been removed. Then, Maria Salome corrects Maria Jacobi's observation that there is only one young man sitting at the open grave.[8] We shall return to this point in chapter 8.

The Chester Shepherds Play is exceptional in its cycle in that spatial relations between speakers are dramatically relevant. This is in keeping with the oft-described 'realism' which characterizes the scene in all cycles apart from N-Town.[9] As is well known, the Second and Third Chester Shepherds have to be called before they appear on stage, and the question whether they are within earshot is given considerable importance.[10]

But this is the only play in the Chester cycle in which distance and proximity become direct determinants of the characters' actions. The rest of the cycle shows its indebtedness to narrative sources precisely by ignoring this element.

For a number of plays the *Stanzaic Life of Christ*[11] is well established as the main narrative source and offers an opportunity for comparison. *St.L.*, 1777–80 and Ch VIII, 105–8, for instance, give a detailed discussion of the speed of the Magi's dromedaries.

What is remarkable about this discussion is the apparently automatic change of tone which it undergoes in its migration from narrative to drama. The ultimate source of both the *Stanzaic Life* and the Chester play, Jacobus de Voragine's *Legenda Aurea*, surveys the entire world, in which start and goal find a local habitation and a name: it explains how the Magi were able to travel in so short a time 'ab oriente' to Jerusalem 'quae in mediculo dicitur esse sita'.[12] The *Stanzaic Life*, which leaves the places unnamed, still conveys a sense of wonder at the marvellous swiftness of the Magi's travelling, even though it purports to offer an exact calculation of the dromedaries' speed:

> But wonder hit is, as clercus sayn,
> how thai come in so litel spas
> so mony myle for al hor mayn,
> In thritten days to þat plas.
>
> But, as Remyge berys recorde,
> sithen þai soȝten God almyȝt,
> No wonder thaȝe sich a lord,
> thagh way wer long, made hit but liȝt.
>
> Ierom also berys witnes
> dromedarys thay riden opon,
> that is a best of gret swiftnes
> a hundreth myle one day to gone.   (*St.L.*, 1769–80)

The Chester Vintners' Play conveys only the most superficial aspects of this astonishing ride: the fantastic speed of the animals. Talk about this necessarily becomes naïve bragging, since it comes from the mouths of the owners:

> SECUNDUS REX:
> Yea, syrs, I read us everyechone
> dromodaryes to ryde upon,
> for swyfter beasts be there none.
> One I have, ye shall see.
> TERTIUS REX:
> A dromodarye, in good faye,
> will goe lightly on his waye
> an hundreth myles upon a daye;
> such beasts nowe take wee.   (Ch VIII, 101–8)

All that is miraculous or incomprehensible has disappeared from these speeches. The possibility that the divine infant might speed up their travel is barely mentioned in an almost perfunctory, off-handed way:

that child would shorten well our waye. (Ch VIII, 110)

And the actual covering of the distance is rendered half pedantically, half naïvely: instead of merely crossing the *platea*, as usual, the Kings descend from the pageant, mount their 'beasts' and ride around on them.[13]

But this is an exception, to be explained only by the uncommon distance mentioned in the original. Where the narrative *states* that the Magi travelled from the Orient to Judaea and met Herod's messenger, the play *shows* them doing it. On the stage the phases of the action appear just as compressed as they do in the narrative. The temporal structure resembles that of a narrative poem with very extensive dialogue: in the dialogue represented time and representing time become coterminous, the long stretches between them are condensed to one sentence in the narrative and one symbolic act in the play (such as walking around the pageant waggon to suggest a journey).

The closing pages of this chapter will be devoted to instances of the 'cutting' technique which will look uncharacteristically 'modern' in light of what has been said so far about the treatment of time and space in the Chester cycle. It occurs in two scenes both of which seem to have passed through the hands of the reviser who also used the *Stanzaic Life*. This, however, does not prove that the 'cutting technique' is his work. One of the two passages is to be found in the *Nativity* (Ch VI); it is remarkable above all because it shows a messenger's errand, i.e. a scene-type which is usually represented 'continuously': we see the messenger's departure, his arrival at his destination, his departure there, and finally his return to his original place – all of this with the intervening journeys included. In contrast to this convention, the Chester *Nativity* places parts of the errand 'behind' the scene. *Preco*, Octavian's messenger, does not arrive in Palestine immediately after his departure from the Emperor's court (Ch VI, 296). Instead, the Emperor receives two senators who enjoin him to accept divine worship. Octavian seeks the advice of the Sibyl. When this advice has been given (line 372), we see *Preco* in Palestine announcing the Emperor's taxation decree. Such a 'backstage journey' will have mitigated the discrepancy between short representing time and long represented time for the audience, who in the meantime had 'stayed' with the Emperor in Rome. Exceptionally, Chester is here more 'progressive' than, e.g., Towneley IX, where the messenger goes directly from the Emperor's court to 'Sirinus' (Cyrenius) and back to the court. Comparison of Chester's skilful solution with its source suggests that the reviser was doing this consciously. For the order of the episodes in the play is exactly the reverse of that in the *Stanzaic Life*:

	St.L.			Ch VI	
ROME:	Census ordered	(309–36)	ROME:	Taxation order, *Preco* off	(177–296)
JUDAEA:	Joseph obeys; they go toward Bethlehem; Mary gives birth; story of *ara pacis*	(337–416; 445–80)			
ROME:	Octavian rejects divine honours	(539–610)	ROME:	Octavian rejects divine honours	(297–372)
			JUDAEA:	*Preco* announces census; Joseph obeys taxation order; they go toward Bethlehem; Mary gives birth; Expositor (*int. al.* story of *ara pacis*)	(373–643)
ROME:	Sibyl's vision	(611–44)	ROME:	Sibyl's vision	(644–714)

The *Stanzaic Life* begins, like Ch VI, with Octavian ordering the census. But this episode is immediately followed by the events in Judaea, while the conversation at the Roman court is reported later – precisely that conversation which in Ch VI is used to 'cover' the messenger's journey. The action of the play shifts to Palestine only after the conversation at the court and the subsequent consultation of the Sibyl. By contrast, the Sibyl's vision which prophesies the birth of the Saviour is separated from the consultation, whereas in the *Stanzaic Life* it immediately follows it. By this transposition of scenes, the Chester playwright succeeds not only in covering the changes of place; he can also make the lapse of time between events in Rome less conspicuous. In the *Stanzaic Life* there is an interval of three days between Octavian's refusal to be worshipped and the Sibyl's vision:

> Then Sibille asket a time to pray,
> then wolde ho gyf vnsuar þerto. [answer
> so Crist was born þe thridde day,
> And to þe emperour come ho. (*St.L.*, 609–12)

This manipulation of time and space is no doubt skilful and unusual in Middle English drama. Whether we regard it as an independent achievement of the Chester reviser depends on the influence which we attach to other sources. R. H. Wilson, to whom we owe the most thorough comparison between the *Stanzaic Life* and the Chester Plays, is inclined to assume a French mystery play as such a source. He can point to the *Passion de Saumur*, which also has Octavian and the Sibyl appear in two separate scenes.[14] Since the Chester reviser who used the *Stanzaic Life* was generally more interested in theological didaxis than in skilful dramaturgy,[15] a French source is a plausible explanation for the unusual display of dramatic skill in the Octavian episode. Moreover, the 'covering technique' is more at home on the simultaneous stage than on the pageant-waggon, and Chester is perhaps the one place for which the 'true-processional' style of production has been least disputed.[16] The tendency of the Chester Plays toward frequent changes of place, which leads to occasional cutting technique, is conceivably due to an older version written for a larger stage – and that version may well have been French.[17]

The other instance of cutting technique, the Slaughter of the Innocents (Ch X), shows less evidence of dramatic intention. Here, too, a change of place is 'covered' by an inserted scene; but this is nothing unusual in the English plays. Of six plays treating the subject[18] only York and Towneley make the Flight to Egypt into a separate play; all others enclose it in the Slaughter.

But the small number of preserved cycles and plays makes statistical considerations highly unreliable.[19] More important are the traditions from which the order of the scenes is derived. York and Towneley follow the Gospel according to St Matthew and the liturgical drama, which attach the Flight directly to the Magi's journey home and return to Herod's court only after this.[20] Chester and the other plays follow the *Legenda aurea* which interpolates the Angel warning Joseph between Herod's plan and its execution.[21] Salter praises the effective contrast between the raging tyrant in Jerusalem and the quiet departure of the Holy Family[22] – but this contrast had already been formed by Jacobus de Voragine. The 'cutting technique', which allows the dramatist to 'cover' a change of place, is only a by-product – but a by-product which must have been felt to be dramatically effective. Otherwise the model of the *Legenda aurea* would not have triumphed so often over that of the Bible and the liturgical drama. When the action at two places is intertwined as it is here, it is almost inevitable for characters at the first place to keep in mind those at the second. This gives the events a depth which they cannot have in the Bible and in the Yorkshire cycles. The multiple stage of the Middle Ages, on the other hand, is capable of rendering the contrasts of the narrative in ways that are closed to the 'classical' theatre of the post-medieval period.

Time and space in the Yorkshire cycles

The two Yorkshire cycles are so closely related that in most chapters they will be treated together. They are also more diverse than the Chester Plays. This will become evident in the representation of time and space. Some of the Towneley plays appear so archaic in their treatment of space that they require a detailed discussion. T VI ('Jacob') ignores changes of place in a way similar to that of the liturgical drama. Jacob appears first on his way to Laban and founds Beth-el (according to Gen. 28.10–22); immediately after this he returns with Laban's daughters, expresses his fear of Esau and finally wrestles with the angel (Gen. 32). The long time between the two scenes which he spent with Laban is neither represented scenically nor even mentioned with a single word.[23]

The journey is mentioned in a stage direction which deserves our very special attention (line 58+): 'hic egrediatur iacob de aran in terram natiuitatis sue.' Strictly speaking, this sentence is not a stage direction at all, for it is not confined to the perceptible aspects of the actors' actions. For although the subjunctive in *egrediatur* contains an *instruction* for the manner and direction of the actor's movements, it is chiefly an *explanation* of the stage events: the country he comes from and the country he goes to are named or defined. But such explanation could benefit only those who were in a position to read the script, i. e. the producer and the actors. This 'stage direction' shows the same relation to extra-linguistic reality as we found in the rubrics of the liturgical drama. In contrast to the usual procedure in the mystery plays, the move from one place to the next is verbalized in the speech following the event, not in the one preceding it.

Jacob's time in Haran with Laban is as little transferred into the dramatic medium as similar scenes were in the liturgical drama. It may be objected that the audience can easily supply the necessary information from their knowledge of the Bible and infer it from the preceding play and the following scene.[24] But such an objection touches only the periphery of the problem. Even if it is true that the audience knew about Jacob's whereabouts between the two episodes, this would only serve to underline the fact that they had to supplement the represented reality with their own knowledge of the context of the scene, just as the congregation of the liturgical drama had to do.

This state of affairs differs from that in most other mystery plays. There, the audience has to work out the details of processes and objects which the spoken word and gesture merely suggested; here and in the liturgical drama, more is required: the audience must add whole episodes which are omitted in the dramatic representation.

But it is not only the omissions which place the Jacob play in the vicinity of the liturgical drama. Similarities are hardly less when we consider the places selected for representation. The events of the first liturgical dramas took place at the altar. We have seen that the sacral function of this *locus* was responsible for the 'hierarchical' structure of the dramatized situations. In the present play Jacob's first action is to erect an altar in Beth-el, where God has appeared in his dream. The altar as the place where Man meets the deity determines the represented situation no less than in the earliest liturgical offices – even though here it is only a 'play' altar. The second chief episode of the play, the wrestling with the angel, is also an encounter with the divine, even though the violent action which it requires made it hardly a fit subject for the liturgical drama. Here, too, the encounter with the divine leads to the subsequent naming and identifying of the place: in line 110 Jacob calls it 'fanuell' (cf. Gen. 32.30f).

The localities of this play are not merely empirically given, geometrically defined places which stand in a relation of proximity or distance to other places. The space in which they are situated is physically bare but in a transcendental sense full of presence. Because it is 'not homogeneous' in the sense defined by Eliade,[25] it does not matter how the actors get from one place to the next. The localities begin to exist properly only after they have been singled out by the divine presence. This singling out, though, is not done in the same way as it is done in other mystery plays by means of the *sedes*. In contrast to Beth-el and Phanuel[26] ('Face of God') the *sedes* are usually present from the beginning of the play – not only in a merely physical, but also in a dramaturgical sense. The 'itinerant' protagonists, Noah and Abraham, the Shepherds and the Magi, have to *render* themselves to these places if an encounter with the deity is to take place; the neutral *platea* and the localized *sedes* are mutually dependent. In the Jacob play the localities are singled out only in the course of the action. Whether this found expression in the physical structure of the pageant-waggon (which may have been without a *sedes*), we do not know. Since the treatment of space here is so different from most of the Towneley Plays, one need not assume that the play was written for the type of stage which can be postulated for the bulk of the cycle.

The analogies between two scenes of the Towneley Jacob play and the liturgical drama are obvious enough. Analogy, however, need not mean influence. The hierarchical confrontations which form the nucleus of the play existed already in the source and imposed their structure on the play. It is enough to recall Auerbach's analysis of the Genesis account of the sacrifice of Isaac[27] to recognize how much the treatment of space in this play resembles that in the Old Testament. While the liturgical drama imposed a hierarchical structure on a situation which may have been structured quite differently in the source, our play has inherited that structure from its source. It is therefore not to be expected that all Towneley plays of a similar presumed age show a similar treatment of space.

Nevertheless, the first part of T XXXI ('Lazarus')[28] also shows strong traces of this liturgical 'spacelessness'. It is even more 'spaceless' than its biblical equivalent and the Latin Lazarus plays.[29] The staging of this scene is particularly difficult since much of its effect depends on the interaction between two places; whenever the *dramatis personæ* are at one place, they, and with them the audience, have to keep the other in mind. The Latin Lazarus plays exploited this bipolarity adroitly, and the highly developed spatial dramaturgy of the N-Town Lazarus play will be analysed in the appropriate chapter (LC XXV, p. 103f). All these plays use the beholder's emotional interest in the dying of Lazarus to create suspense. The sense of distance between the dying Lazarus and Jesus, who could save him, is accentuated by messengers running busily back and forth[30] and by a long mourning scene which gives ample space to the expression of human grief.[31]

T XXXI foregoes these effects by making Jesus the only centre of events. With the single exception of a brief exchange between the two sisters necessary for the completeness of the action (lines 63–7 = John 11.28f), all dialogue takes place in Jesus' presence. Thus Bethany, the 'other' place, where people long for him to arrive, never gains the dramatic independence which characterizes it in the Latin Lazarus plays. Even the distance which Jesus and his disciples have to cover is not dramatically experienced by the audience: also, the announcements of the type 'Now I am going to X', which we found in Chester, are mostly absent from this play. Where they do occur they lack the 'labelling' effect which they had in that cycle. Thomas saying 'Weynde we With oure master all' (line 38) reflects John 11.16 and is not so much naming the 'next place' as demonstrating his loyalty as a disciple. It is in keeping with the 'spacelessness' of the play that Martha should announce her brother's death immediately after this (lines 39f).[32]

In the treatment of space the two plays under discussion occupy a middle position between the liturgical drama and the majority of the vernacular plays: the localities moving along with the main figures point forward to a long tradition of the late medieval drama whose successors are still to be discovered on the Elizabethan stage.[33] That both the Jacob play and the beginning of the Lazarus play should be written in couplets may be more than a remarkable coincidence.

But however 'primitive' we may find the treatment of space in these plays, there is one respect in which they may well be called more 'modern' than many presumably later ones: in the characters' behaviour toward their surroundings. As we have seen on pp. 80–87, places are often either announced by those intending to go there or identified by those already there. Both techniques are examples of 'demonstrative speech' which normally do not occur in real-life situations and whose only justification is the need to keep the audience in the picture. It is significant that this technique should be absent from the plays under discussion here. As far as indications of place do occur, they are fully integrated into the speaker's momentary reaction. Jacob, for example, does not explicitly state at the beginning of T VI that he is on his way to Mesopotamia; the place receives merely a passing reference in his prayer. This prayer is better motivated than those which will be dealt with in the chapter on the opening prayer: Jacob prays because he is feeling helpless. But even this helplessness is not described in abstract terms, it is implied in the concrete situation which has caused it:

> Help me lord, adonay,
> And hald me in the right way
> To mesopotameam;
> ffor I cam neuer or now where I am;
> lord of heuen, thou help me! (T VI, 1–6)

In the Towneley 'Lazarus' changes of place are announced in a similarly indirect manner. One example (line 38), which is modelled on the biblical source, has already been mentioned. More interesting, because more independent, is line 66, where Mary exlaims:

> A, for godys luf let me go! (T XXXI, 66)

Let me go! announces a change of place which three lines later has already been completed.

This indirect, incidental indication of place probably strikes the modern reader as more apt than the heavy-handed announcements which characterize the medieval drama in general. But this impression must be dismissed as an optical illusion created by historical distance. The detailed study which we have devoted to these plays was meant to dispel this illusion. The appearance of greater skill is primarily due to the fact that the representation of space had not yet been discovered to be a problem. The development of the drama appears, in this respect, to parallel that of the religious narrative. The early legends, as represented for instance by the *South English Legendary*, are less interested in physical surroundings for their own sake than in the expression of pious feeling. And that expression can surely be enhanced by incidental reference to place, which may suggest the closeness or remoteness of God, as the case may be. But as soon as the representation of space is discovered as a problem in its own right, conflicts will arise between the orientational needs of the audience, which call for explicit reference, and the situational awareness of the *dramatis personae*, which makes such reference intra-dramatically superfluous. It is this conflict which has been largely responsible for the medieval drama's reputation for naïveté. But merely to state such 'naïvetés', without inquiring into the orientational needs which produced them, is clearly insufficient.

Such an inquiry may well lead to the recognition that the infelicities which strike the modern reader are not necessarily the result of 'primitive' representational techniques or the product of inept dramatists who have 'not yet' learnt how to embed scenic processes into the spatio-temporal medium. The modern philologist who has read so much about the strange theatrical conventions of the Elizabethan period and who is always admonished not to regard the medieval drama with 'modern' eyes, often has a guilty conscience when he approaches the presentational techniques of the mystery plays with the criteria of his own common sense. He is easily inclined to suspect an unknown convention behind scenes which look implausible to him. A good many of those scruples can perhaps be dispelled if those implausibilities can be shown to be not the product of a single strange convention but a cross of diverse, unreconciled presentational techniques.

To give strength to such a suspicion, let us regard a play which probably does not form part of the earliest stratum of its cycle. The Building of the Ark (Y VIII) is a separate play from the Flood (Y IX) and may be regarded as comparatively late for that reason alone.[34]

The scene is remarkable for skipping a hundred years in a single line. But the naïveté does not really consist in the equanimity with which that giant step is taken: it is not difficult to find similar examples in Shakespeare or even in modern films. What is remarkable and, for the modern beholder, strange is the manner in which Noah covers this span of time:

> Full trewe it is who will take tente,
>   Bot faste my force begynnes to fawlde,
> A hundereth wyntres away is wente
>   Sen I began þis werk, full grathely talde,
> And in slyke trauayle for to be bente,
>   Is harde to hym þat is þus olde. (Y VIII, 112–17)

These lines indicate that the dramatist is not quite sure how to interpret those hundred years: on the one hand they reflect the legendary old age which the Bible attributes to the patriarchs. According to Gen. 9.29 Noah lived to 950 years. In such a life a hundred years are certainly not too much for the building of a ship which is essential for the continuing existence of the human race. The popular religious tale, which is frequently the source of such embellishing quantification, used it merely to underline God's magnanimity.[35] But in drama this quasi-symbolic figure becomes a span of time which has actually been spent on physical work. Noah naming a hundred years' duration as a reason for his fatigue inevitably provokes the, albeit pedantic, question whether he never found time for a rest. Since he has never left the stage since he began his work, he almost forces this conclusion on his spectators. The attempt to make the symbolic legendary time a concrete experience leads to the mixing of two spheres which do not mix well and which in other cycles are not mixed. Indications of time are usually avoided here. Where Noah's gradual exhaustion does receive scenic expression, it eases the passage to a farcical quarrel with Mrs Noah. Here, however, Noah's fatigue is merely an opportunity for God to utter praise and give last orders. Comparison between this scene and corresponding ones in other cycles shows that, while the concrete details of the ship-building and the experienceable aspects of the lapse of time occur in most plays, reference to the hundred years is peculiar to Y VIII. Since the York Plays, especially in their later strata, often sacrifice dramatic logic to external effect, implausibilities like the one observed here are probably to be attributed to a late desire for embellishment and detailed description rather than to dramaturgic 'primitivism'.

The representation of the spatial environment in dramatic speech has its consequences above all in plays whose action is divided between two places. The connection between these places is usually established by messengers, as in the Chester Plays. But in contrast to the Chester Plays the journey between those places is now represented completely.[36] The suggestion of long distances by 'cuts' is unknown in these plays.

Usually the messenger scenes give an extremely undifferentiated presentation of the places they have to connect. In T IX Nuncius goes 'from Caesar' 'to Sirinus'. Sirinus' physical environment, for instance his palace or the city in which he dwells, is left completely out of consideration. Any individuality which the two places may have is as unimportant as the distance between them. What is alone important is the fact that they are at a distance from each other.

But even these 'primitive' scene-types can be used to good effect. A good example of this is the play of the Exodus of the people of Israel (Y XI) which reappears in the Towneley manuscript under the name of *Pharao* (T VIII). The soccage-service of the Israelites, the plagues which

94   *The English mystery play*

befall the Egyptians, Pharao's hard-heartedness – all these details which are required by the biblical source and are apparently quite unfit for scenic representation – have been made by the dramatist into an effective and lively play with the help of messenger's errands. The plagues are reported by Egyptians who rush in to Pharao – but not merely reported. The messengers enter not with an objective, cool statement, but with an exclamation of distress which at first contains no factual information. The king is thus forced to enquire. The way in which the fourth and fifth plagues follow each other is typical:

> *I Egiptius* Lorde, allas, for dule we dye,
>   We dar not loke oute at no dore.
> *Rex*   What deuyll ayles yow so to crye?
> *II Egiptius*   We fare nowe werre þan euere we fure.
>   Grete loppis ouere all þis lande þei flye
>   That with bytyng makis mekill blure.
> *I Egiptius* Lorde, oure beestis lyes dede and dry
>   Als wele on myddyng als on more –
>   Both oxe, horse and asse
>   Fallis dede doune sodanly.   (Y XI, 289–98)

The reporting of the fourth plague by the Second Egyptian, and of the fifth by the First, compresses what in the Bible covers a long period of time. This creates the impression of events following in rapid succession. Pharao's attempt to deceive the Israelites finds expression not only in the dialogue but also in the stage movement. For he does not admit Moses to his presence, as he does in the Bible; he merely sends a messenger with his offers. (Another skilful arrangement is to reserve the Second Egyptian for the messenger's rôle, thus leaving the First free to return to Pharao with new messages of disaster.) In this way the polarity of the pageant stage is fully exploited to underline the contrast between God's servant and His enemy. The lively to-and-fro caused by the messengers' errands, however, is responsible for Pharao's and Moses' *loca* resembling less the *sedes* of the liturgical drama than the *mansiones* of the Roman comedy. It reduces the stature of both God and Moses: the latter has been turned from an unapproachable prophet into a clever negotiator with the gift of magic immediately seeing through Pharao's hypocritical offers:

> He mon haue more mischeff
> But if his tales be trewe.   (Y XI, 311f)

Divine punishment has become 'mischeff', and from the wording one is tempted to conclude that Moses is in full authority to bring it about. God's ways with Man lose their supernatural, awe-inspiring quality. The treatment of time and space in this play is thus far removed from that of the liturgical drama; it suggests a naïve familiarity with the transcendent, which we will find again and again in the Yorkshire cycles, but judged in its own terms it does not have the inconsistency of which the modern reader will tend to accuse it.

The messenger scene is a stereotypical scene-type which does not change much in the course of the development of the cycles. This is shown above all by Y XXX and Y XXXIII (140ff, 216ff), both of which are attributed to the so-called York Realist or 'Realistic School' of York active after 1415.[37] The only elaboration which the messenger scene in Y XXX acquires is not at all in the direction of increased realism, but serves an exclusively edificational purpose by demonstrating Jesus' miraculous powers: following the Gospel of Nicodemus, the dramatist has Jesus fetched by a beadle.[38] To the indignation of all Jews present, he pays homage to Jesus. Of great significance is where this homage takes place. Logic as well as the beadle's first words suggest that he should bow as soon as he meets Christ. That would mean: in Pilate's absence. But what the Jews are indignant about is precisely the fact that all this happens in Pilate's presence (Y XXX, 318, 320; *Nic.*, line 76). Quite clearly, the dramatist is as little interested in the 'logic' of the action as his source is. What matters is its 'visibility': the fact that an uninitiated, subordinate contemporary recognized Christ's divinity demonstrates the guilt or at least obtuseness of those who did not.

This triumph of 'significance' over 'logic' in a play of the 'Realist School' must be kept in mind whenever we find closer attention paid to the ways in which space and place are experienced. It is true that the later dramas tend to render more and more details of the characters' environment, and this will often result in a remarkable psychological 'realism'. But especially the late York Plays show an even greater interest in scenic effect.

There are also plays, however, which establish an emotional relationship between the characters and their environment. This may occur by means of a casual remark as in the York Abraham play, where one of the servants expresses his dissatisfaction at having to travel through unknown country on the journey to Moriah:

> Why, sall we trusse ought forthe a towne
> In any vncouthe lande to lende? (Y X, 115f)

Here the emotional reaction to the environment finds expression in a casual remark, perhaps an aside. When the places are of religious significance such reaction can lead to elaborate descriptions. A good example is the arrival of the Shepherds in Bethlehem (Y XV), which differs interestingly from the corresponding scene in Chester. In Chester the comers were 'there' at once, in York they gradually perceive the place they are approaching and comment on it in their conversation:

> *I Pastor*   Breder, bees all blythe and glad,
>   Here is the burgh þer we shulde be.
> *II Pastor*   In þat same steede now are we stadde,
>   Tharefore I will go seke and see.
>   Slike happe of heele neuere herde-men hadde;
>   Loo, here is the house, and here is hee.
> *III Pastor*   3a forsothe, þis is the same.
>   Loo whare þat lorde is layde
>   Betwyxe two bestis tame,
>   Right als þe aungell saide.   (Y XV, 86–95)

The place is here perceived not as something abstract and unified but as a complex of constituent features. In this case the gradual process of perception serves of course to confirm the Angel's words. What is distinctive about the York Shepherds Play is that it lends this religious function precisely to the visible aspects of the locality.

The same edificational purpose is recognizable when Joseph describes the miserable stable in which the divine infant is to be born:

> And yf we here all nyght abide
> We schall be stormed in þis steede,
> þe walles are doune on ilke a side,
> þe ruffe is rayued aboven oure hede,
>   Als haue I roo;   [*as I hope to have peace*
> Say, Marie, doughtir, what is thy rede,
>   How sall we doo?   (Y XIV, 15–21)

The concrete, sensory-perceptive details are in the foreground here. The fact that this miserable shed is to be the Saviour's birthplace is of course known to the audience, but it does not figure in Joseph's speech – in marked contrast to the Chester *Nativity* (Ch VI), where the stable is merely designated as 'this stable' and the emphasis is on its moral and religious function:

> Therfore wee muste in good faye
> lye in this stable tyll yt bee daye.
> To make men meeke, leeve I maye,
>   shew him here will hee.   (Ch VI, 457–60)

In York, the birth of Christ must have been supported by a strong stage-lighting effect. Joseph, who had left Mary in darkness and cold to fetch light and fuel (Y XIV, 41–4), finds the stable immersed in shining light on his return. This moment was appreciated by Creizenach as an original idea of our dramatist.[39] Such praise overlooks, however, that the greatest event in Christian teaching is thus reduced to the private mood and gives rise to surprise and curiosity rather than to an awareness of its salvific importance:

> A, lord God, what light is þis
> þat comes shynyng þus sodenly?
> I can not saie als haue I blisse.
> When I come home vnto Marie
> þan sall I spirre. [ask (Y XIV, 78–82)

Differentiated scenery can also be used for dramatic effects which are impossible in the Chester cycle. In Y XLIII ('Pentecost') the disciples inside the house are contrasted with the Jews outside: inside and outside come to symbolize the two attitudes of fear and threat: the very moment the Holy Spirit has taken their fear from them the disciples leave the house and face the Jews (lines 175ff). The skilful treatment of space is best seen in a comparison with the source: In Acts 2, the Holy Spirit also descends on the disciples while they are still inside, but the spatial conditions of the event are left entirely in obscurity; the disciples' leaving the house is not made explicit and has to be inferred from the fact that they are suddenly speaking to a large crowd. By contrast, the York play lets the speaking in tongues take place inside (line 126); thus its function is no longer to make the disciples into preachers of the gospel, it has merely the psychological effect of encouraging the Twelve. The somewhat vague spatial relations of the scene in Acts 2 are thus accentuated in a sharp contrast which finds an effective outlet in Peter's speech.

The treatment of space in the York Plays is thus shown to be in marked contrast to that of the Chester cycle, where a place was merely named without becoming concrete and detailed for the perceptions of the audience. On the other hand, Chester does show some instances where a change of place is rendered by a 'cut'. The York Plays, in contrast, lay great emphasis on the visible, physically experienced aspects of their localities, but they are fairly careless in rendering the relationship *between* places. They seem thus more faithful to the original.

In their treatment of time and space the late plays of the Towneley cycle resemble those lively scenes guaranteeing that rapid sequence of events which we have been able to observe already in Y XI (*Exodus from Egypt*). The environment is not 'frozen into states', the spectator is not forced to 'tarry' at religiously or emotionally important places; details are selected with a clear understanding of their place in the course of events. The desire to press ahead is so strong that occasionally even God has to submit to the demands of *tempus edax*: After his decision to drown humanity in the Flood, he must go 'quickly' to Noah to warn him:

> Hym to mekill wyn, hastly will I go
> To Noe my seruand, or I blyn, to warn hym of his wo.   (T III, 109f)

Even spatial relations between the *dramatis personae* are used for comic effects, as when Caiaphas attempts to strike Jesus but misses him because He 'standys so far' (T XXI, 299).[40]

Similarly, references to time grow organically out of the speech situation, as in the Noah play T III (line 445). Changes of place as a rule are not merely stated or announced; their further effects are considered and transformed into dramatic action. For instance, when Noah must see his wife to tell her of the coming Flood, he spends an entire stanza on how best to break the news to her. In T XII, 452 the arrival of the Shepherds at the stable in Bethlehem culminates in a little friendly quarrel about who is to enter first.

The Wakefield Master succeeds even in giving new variety to such a conservative scene-type as the 'on-the-way' scene. At the beginning of the Towneley *Coliphizacio* the Torturers drag Jesus to the High Priests. This is not announced as a bare fact, but cloaked in the form of a threat:

> To Anna will we go and Syr Cayphas.
> Witt thou well: of thaym two gettys thou no grace.   (T XXI, 2f)

The journey is spread out over a dialogue of no less than forty-five lines, which is uncommon enough in itself. At its end the arrival is again embedded in the speech situation which the preceding dialogue has created. The First Torturer silences his companion with the words:

> Peas, man, we ar thore!   (ibid., 43)

Such a long journey can hardly have been enacted on the narrowly confined pageant stage. If the Towneley plays were performed on a multiple stage, as Martial Rose and Alan Nelson suggest,[41] the dialogue covering the Torturer's approach may of course have been spoken in the *platea*. But even this theory would be insufficient to explain the words with which the Third Torturer of the *Processus Talentorum* greets his fellows:

> Now are we thre commen in.   (T XXIV, 157)

One should perhaps consider the possibility that the torturers in the Towneley Passion plays began their appearance in the midst (or rather at the back) of the audience and reached the stage only in the course of their entrance speeches. This assumption gains probability if we look at the length and the movement of these speeches. The longest, that of the *Processus Talentorum*, comprises more than a hundred lines (T XXIV, 73–176). *Secundus tortor* begins with the characteristic 'war, war!' (line 113) and asks the audience to 'make rowme' (line 113), like a folk-play mummer. *Tertius tortor* even states that he 'com rynyng all at ones' (line 146).

The entire dialogue between First and Second Torturer in *Coliphizacio* (T XXI, 1–42), which verbalizes the dragging of Jesus to Pilate, would also look extremely unnatural if it were all performed on the pageant stage. But a progress through the crowd would make it rather effective. The chapter on audience-address (pp. 128–32) will endeavour to show that the relationship between First and Second World differs here from what is usual elsewhere in the cycles. There we shall also try to demonstrate that Towneley uses scene-types which are less common in York and more familiar in the folk-play.

Time and space in N-Town

While the Yorkshire cycles show great variety in their treatment of time and space, ranging from the most primitive to the highly elaborate, N-Town demonstrates a highly developed technique throughout.[42] Scholars have long recognized that the authors of the plays in this manuscript had a sure grasp of theatrical and visual effects. Their linguistic art, on the other hand, has been harshly criticized.[43] I hope to show that those 'dramatic' effects are in part at least grounded in the language and, more particularly, in the linguistic treatment of time and space.

The more primitive treatments of time and space are comparatively rare in the cycle. They occur above all in those parts which employ the thirteen-line stanza of the *Proclamation*[44] or the Chester stanza. Traditionally these parts of the cycle were regarded as early.[45]

The treatment of time and space which we find in these parts is already familiar from the other cycles. We can therefore be brief. The most notable aspect is again the abrupt change of place. Joachim and Anna, for instance, discuss their intention of going to the Temple; immediately afterwards they are already there (LC X, 27).[46] Just as quick is Joseph's return to Mary after he has been informed of the real cause of her pregnancy (LC XII, 180–3, p. 114).[47] Equally sudden is the transfer of the Shepherds from the field to the Stable in Bethlehem (LC XVI, 90). While other cycles elaborate the arrival of the Shepherds with loving care, the N-Town play does not even name the place of arrival. The only reference is wholly unspecific and occurs immediately before the Shepherds' departure from the field:

    Ffor to seke þat chylde I rede we go.   (LC XVI, 89, p. 149)

These announcements, which precede the actual change of scene as a heading precedes a chapter, are of the same type as in Chester.

The transitions in the two-stress tail-rhyme stanzas of the *Adoration of the Magi* (LC XVIII) are similarly abrupt; especially the encounters between Herod's messenger and the Magi (lines 95ff) show great similarity with the liturgical *Magi* plays. But even here our distinction between the 'spaceless' liturgical drama and the spatially embedded mystery play is borne out: the *Senescallus* declares at length his readiness to execute Herod's command (lines 103–10), thus announcing his change of place. But for all its similarity with possible liturgical models, even this scene shows an interest in the purely accidental, momentary environment which is entirely alien to the liturgical drama: the *Senescallus* greets the Kings with the words:

    Kyngys iij
    vndyr þis tre   (lines 111f, emphasis added)

But while this engaging little detail helps to underline the difference between the liturgical drama and the mystery play, it does not affect the overall picture of the cycle. The change of place is brought about just as abruptly here as it is in the plays previously discussed and as in several others which we shall not discuss.[48]

Far more concrete and detailed is the realization of the spatial environment in those parts of the cycle which are written in double quatrains and which Craig regards as 'The heart of the cycle, that which may perhaps be more characteristic of the place of its origin'.[49] But the majority of scholars hold that they were originally part of a different cycle and were taken over into the *Ludus* only after the composition of the *Proclamation*.[50] Some of the plays written in this metre have also been claimed for the pageant-waggon stage.[51] The degree to which spatial proximity can be reflected in sensual experience can be illustrated from LC XIV ('The Trial of Joseph and Mary'): the play opens with two *Detractores* who make their scandalized comments on Mary's pregnancy. Their conversation is overheard by 'Bishop' Abisacher who, unnoticed by the two, sits on his *sedes*. He interrupts them, summons them, and takes them to task:

hic sedet episcopus Abiʒachar inter duos legis doctores et audientes hanc defamocionem vocat ad se detractores dicens:
    Herke ʒe felawys why speke ʒe such schame.   (line 73, p. 126)

In the same play the Summoner, a strongly satirical character,[52] fills his walk to the Bishop with all sorts of entertaining nonsense, helping to cover the passing time. His encounter with Joseph and Mary is extended into a lengthy dialogue, which again covers the return to the Bishop's seat. The extensive to-ing and fro-ing of this play makes a performance on the pageant-waggon rather unlikely.

Even when the spatial environment is not represented scenically, it is reflected in the speakers' experience. The Bethlehem *Civis* whom Joseph addresses when looking for shelter, gives at once a detailed description of the state of the town:

> Sere ostage in þis town know I non
> þin Wyff and þou in for to slepe
> this cete · is be-sett · with pepyl every won
> And ʒett þei ly with-owte fful every strete. (LC XV, 65–8, p. 137)

The words in which Joseph describes the Stable are very similar to those in Y XIV, 15–21:[53]

> god be þin help spowse it swemyth me sore
> þus febyly loggyd and in so pore degre
> goddys sone amonge bestys to be bore
> his woundyr werkys ffulfyllyd must be.
> In An hous þat is desolat with-owty Any wall
> Ffyer nor wood non here is. (LC XV, 97–102, p. 138)

External appearances are accurately noticed, especially in an encounter between strangers. Joseph says to *Civis*:

> A cetecyn of þis cyte · ʒe seme to be. (ibid., 57, p. 137)

In a very similar way Joseph is addressed by the Midwives whom he went to look for:

> Why makyst þou man suche mornyng
> tell me sum dele of ʒour gret mone. (ibid., 137f, p. 140)

This dialogue technique which not merely duplicates, but reacts to, the environment is particularly effective in 'The Woman Taken in Adultery' (LC XXIV). The farcical elements of this play were already recognized by Gayley.[54] But he lays the emphasis on the appearance of the *iuvenis* who, caught in the Adulteress's chamber, escapes his pursuers *calligis non ligatis et braccas in manu tenens* (line 124+). He does not analyse the language, which here even reflects the way the characters move and behave in the spatial surroundings. The roguish *Accusator*, who in many ways resembles the later Vice, shows a beautiful feeling for timing:

> ȝe tary ovyr longe serys I sey ȝow
> they wyl sone parte as þat I gesse. (LC XXIV, 113f, p. 204)

The strategy to surprise the Adulteress which is developed in the following dialogue is full of implicit stage directions. *Phariseus*, for instance, says to *Accusator*:

> Goo þou be-forn [...]
> We xal þe ffolwe [...] (lines 117f)

Scriba even cries:

> Breke up þe dore and go we inne
> Sett to þe shuldyr with all þi myght. (lines 121f)

This creates stage movement which is simultaneously lively and planned, something which is usually absent from the purely religious scenes. A similar integration of speech and movement, of dialogue and group action, is familiar from the plays of the Wakefield Master. The environment in which the action takes place is of interest only in its physical aspects: how is the house constructed, how best to break into it, in what order should the different steps of the action take place? These are some of the questions to which the dialogue gives an answer. And it is an indirect answer: for the speakers do not report on the situation they are in, they react to it. A consequence of this reacting is that the situation changes continually. This is why the order of the utterances is so much more important than in the quieter scenes of purely religious content. Each phase is a direct result of the preceding one; this creates a density and speed of the action which is already to be found in the Latin miracle plays but which in the English cycles remains the exception.

The following scenes of this play, in which the Adulteress is calumniated, threatened and dragged before Jesus, of course do not offer the same opportunity for this close integration of dialogue and situation. But the author's exact sense of timing can be observed even here. Eleanor Prosser has impressively shown how the suspense is increased by the dialogue:[55] in the first phase the woman's supplications become more and more desperate and modest; when finally she merely asks for a secret and speedy execution to save her family from disgrace (lines 174ff, p. 206), the Jews take her off to Jesus. While the first phase is characterized by the increasing nastiness and cruelty of the accusers, the second contrasts their eager expectation with Jesus' persistent silence. While the accusers create ever new moral dilemmas which they hope will allow them either to kill the woman or to convict Jesus of heresy,[56] Jesus continues to write in the sand. When at last he speaks, his tone is quiet, and he does not answer their reproaches:

> Loke which of ȝow þat nevyr synne wrought
> but is of lyff clennere þan she
> Cast at here stonys and spare here nowght
> Clene out of synne if þat ȝe be.

hic ihesus iterum se inclinans scribet in terra et omnes accusatores quasi confusi separatim in tribus locis se disiungent. (LC XXIV, 229–32, p. 207)

After the dispersal of the accusers the play can end in a quiet and edifying dialogue between Jesus and the woman.

The analysis of dramatic speech confirms what E. Prosser has said from a theological point of view: it is not enough to praise with Gayley the comic aspects of the play, and it would be wrong to play off serious and comic elements of the mystery plays against each other. The farcical opening, the middle part with its high tension, and the quiet, edifying conclusion, all have a share in the play's over-all effect. They all bear witness to the author's skill in embedding speech in the extra-linguistic situation. Emotions are part of that situation.

A very 'modern' method of handling Second World space, which we have termed the 'cutting technique' and which we have been able to observe in the Chester Plays, is also to be found in the double quatrains of N-Town. A simple specimen is LC XXI ('Christ and the Doctors'). During the entire play the core of the action is the dispute between Jesus and the Doctors in the Temple. Joseph and Mary appear only in a short interlude, when they discover that Jesus is not with them (lines 201–32, pp. 184f). Here, however, the 'cutting' goes no further than it does in the other cycles or, for that matter, in the biblical source (Luke 2.44–6).

A masterpiece in this respect is 'Lazarus' (LC XXV, pp. 210ff).[57] The story, as told in John 11, begins in Bethany with Lazarus lying sick. Messengers are sent to Jesus, who tarries for two days before he arrives in Bethany four days after Lazarus' death. We also learn that Martha goes and meets Jesus before he enters the village. Finally Jesus visits the grave together with the sisters and their neighbours. This involves at least four changes of place, which in the other cycles are rendered exactly in accordance with the source: the scene there often changes literally between the lines, and is probably marked only by a few steps across the acting-area. York and Towneley simplify the problem even further by beginning the play with the messengers' appearance before Jesus. Rather than imitate such simplification (which is unknown to the Latin Lazarus plays),[58] the N-Town play even further differentiates the scenes and moves between them in a way that would be quite acceptable to a modern audience. At the beginning of the play we do not find Mary and Martha lamenting, but we see Lazarus who complains about his poor health and even asks his sisters to move him to an adjacent room (lines 10, 14). The place where Lazarus dies is thus not simply a geometrical point at some distance from another geometrical point, but it is differentiated in itself. It is a house the details of which are fully represented on stage as far as they are relevant for the action. This house becomes the scene of extensive laments and consolations, from which a messenger is sent to inform Jesus (line 100). For about another fifty lines after the messenger's departure the dialogue continues in Lazarus' house (until line 152), to be then continued at the place of his burial (to line 192). Not until then do we see Jesus and the messenger in conversation (lines 193–212). After a dialogue between Jesus and his disciples (which we find in all plays on the subject, following John 11.7–16), the scene returns to Bethany. But the encounter between Martha and Jesus is delayed by another lament. The same pattern is repeated when Martha, following Jesus' orders, calls Mary: only after we have watched her for some time in the midst of a group of *consolatores* does Martha inform her about Jesus' request. Thus the action at one place always begins with a sort of prelude which does not further the action and is not mentioned in the gospel but which adds to the atmosphere of the play. The company which the newcomer joins is thus not 'virgin territory' merely waiting to be put into action, but is engaged in activities which are independent of him and which his arrival will interrupt. Each place is thus furnished with its own life.

In 'Lazarus' and the 'Doctors' Play' the cutting is obviously the author's own work. In other plays, especially in 'Noah' (LC IV, pp. 35ff) and in *Passion Play I* (pp. 225ff) it is clearly added by a later reviser. Changes of scene often coincide with a change of metre or with a gap in the manuscript. This suggests that earlier plays, which may have been meant for the pageant-waggon stage, were adapted for a larger theatre in the round.[59] Usually the points of transition are characterized by tumbling measure or long octaves which are regarded as the mark of later compilers.[60] Since the textual history of *Passion Play I* is inordinately complex, we shall begin with the Noah Play. This play, originally written entirely in 'Proclamation thirteeners' (Spector's term), later had a scene in long octaves added to it. The interpolated scene is above all concerned with the murder of Cain by his great-great-great-grandson Lamech,[61] but the interpolation begins a little before this incident: an angel instructs Noah to begin the building of the Ark (line 118). It ends with the end of the Flood and is thus identical with the end of the play. The fact that it extends beyond the Lamech episode argues against its being introduced merely for its entertainment value, as Gayley would have it.[62] The true motive for the interpolation is probably to be found in the indirect stage direction which we find in Noah's speech shortly before Lamech appears:

A shyppe for to make now lete us hens pas. (LC IV, 140, p. 39)

Immediately afterwards Noah and his family clear the stage for Lamech. When they reappear in line 198, a hundred years of shipbuilding (line 206) and the forty days of the Flood (line 242) have passed. The building of the Ark and the Flood have thus taken place 'during' the Lamech episode and 'behind' or rather outside the stage. The composition of this scene does not correspond entirely to the schema presented on p. 80, since the interpolated scene is causally unconnected with the rest. But the result is similar: the audience is saved from watching the unrealistically fast passage of long stretches of time.

In one respect, however, the effect of this interpolation is different from that served by the 'cutting technique' in 'Lazarus': There, the goal was to create a feeling of continuity in spite of the action being spread over several places. The cuts replaced the principle of 'continuous correspondence' by a continuity of audience interest. Here, the only recognizable goal is to cover long, uneventful stretches of time with an entertaining, visually effective episode.

An interest in visible effects becomes even more apparent in the detailed stage directions of *Passion Play I*. The order of the scenes in this play provides effective contrasts which must have influenced the responses of the audience more strongly than those of the Noah play. A stage direction after Jesus' entry into the house of Simon the Leper reads:

here Crist enteryth in-to þe hous with his disciplis and ete þe paschal lomb and in þe mene tyme þe cownsel hous beforn-seyd xal sodeynly onclose schewyng þe buschopys prestys and jewgys syttyng in here Astat lyche as it were A convocacyone. (LC, p. 245, line 397+)

After the conspiracy of the priests a new quire begins in the manuscript (the famous 'quire O'). It is opened by Mary Magdalene with a long speech in the thirteen-line stanzas used in the *Proclamation*:

As a cursyd creature closyd all in care
and as a wyckyd wrecche all wrappyd in wo
Of blysse was nevyr no berde so bare
as I my-sylf þat here now go. (LC, p. 247, lines 462–5)

The same stanza is used in the anointing scene which follows Mary's speech. Judas' criticism and Jesus' reply are given in a combination of tail-rhyme and alternate rhyme (aaab cccb dede) which is unlike either of the surrounding scenes. The Last Supper which follows and from which

Judas rises to conspire with the priests is in long octaves (abab bcbc). The first part of this ends with the stage direction

here judas rysyth prevely and goth in þe place *and* seyt now cownter[*fetyd*. (LC, p. 251, line 589+)

After this stage direction more than a page in the manuscript is left empty, and quire P begins with Judas' speech. The first words of this speech are the same as the last of the 'stage direction': *Now cowntyrfetyd*. Judas' speech and the ensuing dialogue with the Jews use the same rhyme scheme as the dialogue at the Supper though on average the lines seem somewhat shorter. Quire O shows the editing of someone who knew the following scene. In his speech (lines 590ff) Judas reveals a delight in his own villainy which resembles that of the Vice in the later interludes and which we also find in some of the other double-quatrain scenes in N-Town:[63]

> Now cowntyrfetyd I haue a prevy treson
> My Maysterys power for to felle
> I judas xal A-say be some encheson
> On-to þe jewys hym for to selle.   (LC, p. 251, lines 590–3)

This arrangement is an interesting mixture of 'cutting' and 'continuous correspondence': the interpolation of the conspiracy allows a many-layered response which allows the betrayed and the betrayers to be seen simultaneously, but the interpolated scene itself shows the 'itinerant' on his way, allowing him to draw the audience into his confidence while crossing the *platea* ('place').

It has to be remembered, though, that this treatment of space in the two *Passion Plays* is probably a remnant of older strata. These must have been independent plays at one time,[64] and in most cases the on-the-way scene has lost that closeness to the public which in other plays is provided by the *platea*.[65] The messengers' errands which are more typical of these plays bridge the distance between the *loca*, but instead of making the contact between play-sphere and audience-sphere more intimate they increase the pomp and circumstance of the production. These plays show even more clearly than the late York plays the loss in dramatic vitality and in actor–audience contact which is the price of theatrical effects. Much has been written about the 'secularization' of the religious drama of the late Middle Ages. Usually this means such comic scenes as we find in the *Secunda Pastorum*. But also cycles with a strong ecclesiastic element show a tendency toward more and more decoration which 'externalizes' the religious content and leaves little room for the simple pious emotions of the early Towneley Plays.

That the increasing distance between play-sphere and audience-sphere has little to do with modern theatrical illusionism becomes apparent from the treatment of space in those plays which Craig regards as the remnants of an originally self-contained St Anne's Day play.[66] In LC XIII ('The Visit to Elizabeth') a journey is bridged over by a narrative insert: while Mary and Joseph set out to visit Elizabeth, Contemplacio paraphrases the account of *Legenda aurea*:[67]

> Sovereynes vndyrstondyth þat kynge davyd here
> Ordeyned ffoure and twenty prestys of grett devocion
> In þe temple of god · Aftere here let apere
> Þei weryd clepyd summi sacerdotes · ffor here mynistracion
> And on was prynce of prestys.   (LC XIII, 23–7, p. 116)[68]

From afar this recalls the narrative antiphon *Currebant duo* which accompanies Peter and John on their race to the Sepulchre which the Marys have just reported open. But here it is not a choir of singers celebrating an event unfolding before their eyes, but an extra-dramatic figure uses a 'break' in the presentation to give the audience the fullest possible information on the previous lives of Zachary and Elizabeth. The goal of the journey is not a sacred place reverently to be approached by a congregation, but one to be presented to an audience and embellished by biblical and legendary ornament.

Even when a ceremony of divine worship is presented it becomes a 'show'. We shall illustrate this with two scenes which also originated presumably under the influence of *Legenda aurea*. In the *Legend's* account, the fifteen steps to the temple which the three-year-old Mary mounts are an image of the fifteen psalms of degrees (Ps. 120–34). The play (LC IX, 84ff, pp. 74ff) changes this image into a ceremony which accompanies each step with an allegorical explanation given by Mary and ending with the incipit of one of the psalms.

When Joachim is rejected from the Altar for his childlessness, this incident receives just one sentence in the *Legend*.[69] In the N-Town play, the words of the priest change it into a solemn, slow ceremony where each movement is controlled and deliberate. The immolants are told exactly by the Archpriest where to go and where to stand:

> Comyth up, serys,...
> A-byde a qwyle, sere!...
> Therefore comyth up and offeryth here alle! –
> Þu, Joachym, I charge þe fast out þe temple þu go!
>   (LC VIII, 73–83; Meredith, 98–108)

Comparison of this scene with a play like 'The Woman Taken in Adultery' makes clear that the range of relationships between the spoken word and scenic movement can be very wide indeed. In that play, the spoken word was simultaneously a spontaneous reaction and a trigger for new action. It was thus integrated into a complex of vivid, quick linguistic and non-linguistic action. Here, the authority of the speaker automatically gives his speech acts the character of commands. This finds physical expression in the speaker's sedentary position which places him physically and hierarchically 'above' the movements which he causes.

The contrast between the two plays marks the stylistic range which is to be found in the cycle as a whole: on the one hand a scenic realism which resembles that of the late Towneley plays, on the other a tendency toward a ceremonious formality which we do not find in other cycles.

7 Address to the audience

General aspects

Liturgical 'forerunners'

The audience-address has no true equivalent in the liturgical drama. It is, therefore, particularly suited to become a distinctive feature of the type of drama that has developed in the vernacular. The extent to which this type of dramatic speech is peculiar to the mystery play (and later to the morality play) can best be seen by passing briefly in review those sections of liturgical drama which have on occasion been regarded as early forms of the vernacular audience-address.

Berthold Venzmer and, in his wake, Karl Young, believed that the expository characters who appear in some mystery plays are foreshadowed in the narrative antiphons sung by the choir, the best-known of which is the *Currebant duo* of some extended versions of the *Visitatio Sepulcri*.[1] Yet these antiphons – although they narrate and thus also inform – do not, strictly speaking, address anyone.[2] Basically they perform the same function as the dramatic presentations themselves and the *lectiones* from the Bible (which they originally were): they praise God's deeds, and it does not matter who hears them – apart from the extollers and God himself. A further difference is that these utterances are purely narrative, while the function of the audience-address is above all to explain and instruct. It is significant that they always recount the action they accompany in the preterite. The vernacular expositor can use this tense only at the end of plays in summaries which generally deal just with those episodes not presented on stage.[3] In a text running absolutely parallel to the action on stage, the mystery play knows only the present or the immediate future, as for example in phrases like 'Now I will...'. Such speeches accompanying the action are moreover never entrusted to extradramatic characters, but always to characters acting in the play itself. These characters often address their explanatory remarks to the audience; but the very explanatory and accordingly detailed nature of such speeches (such as that of Noah building the Ark) clearly shows how the mystery play differs from the liturgical drama, which would have no use for such elucidation since no one is ever so far 'outside' the performed action as to have need of it. The action, which even in gestures is only vaguely intimated, is not explained but merely reported in the utterances of the liturgical drama. Thus it is clear that narrative antiphons like the *Currebant duo* have no real analogue in the mystery play. In such antiphons the relationship between word and action is still that of religious ceremony. The use of the past tense is symptomatic of this. Priority is quite clearly given to the text which is sanctioned by the church authorities. By virtue of its origins in the historical books of the New Testament, this text is perforce of a narrative character and thus committed to the past tense. In the light of this the action can only perform illustrative functions. In the mystery play, on the other hand, priority lies in visual action and the task of the text is to comment on it.

If, therefore, only slight and moreover peripheral relations exist between the narrative antiphon and the expositor, then the question remains whether one could not detect a forerunner to the audience-address in the 'Revelations' which are directed to the choir, for instance, by the three Marys, Mary Magdalene or the Shepherds. But these 'Revelations' are always directed at persons who are in the same situational context as the Revealers. This may be seen most clearly by the fact that the choir is able to enter into a kind of dialogue with the characters and that in the course of the evolution of the liturgical drama new characters – e.g. the Disciples or the Magi[4] – break away from the body of the choir and take over original choral antiphons as part of their rôles. While in the mystery play the character addressing the audience steps out of the Second World, the liturgical performer draws, as it were, the choir into it.

This is where we find the crucial difference between liturgical drama and the mystery play: the former does not really have a viewing public, but simply a congregation that participates.[5] This difference, which is reflected in the situational embedding and the directionality of the utterances, means that the liturgical office or drama knows no audience-address. One may indeed ask whether the laity in the liturgical drama had not already been pushed into the passive rôle of an 'audience'; their participation, as we know, was restricted to the traditional hymn 'Christ ist erstanden'. Yet the laity were not spectators in the sense that the plays were performed *for them*. The ceremonies would not have become meaningless if there had been no onlooking laity.[6]

The mystery play, on the other hand, is a play for spectators who are addressed, receive explanations, and who are, above all, to be instructed, edified, and entertained as well. The plays as a whole show the awareness that there are people beyond the sphere of action for whom, after all, the play is performed. So strong is this awareness that the plays not only do justice to it by their didactic and comic elements but they even address the public over and over again. The audience-address must above all be understood as an expression of this new awareness; for this very reason the search for 'forerunners' is bound to stick fast in superficial similarities.

There is, however, one aspect which, although it has no bearing on the essentials, has to be mentioned in order to complete the picture. Even if there was no need for the functions of the audience-address in the genuine liturgical drama, yet there are two Latin plays – *Ysaac* from Vorau in Styria (Austria) and *Ioseph* from Laon[7] – in which the choir is used for the purposes of the audience-address. The choir-singing of these plays provides theological commentaries, as in *Ysaac*, or moral exhortations, as in *Ioseph*. Whereas the *allegoriae* sung by boys, which interrupt the action of *Ysaac* at regular intervals, give no indication whatsoever as to whether they are directed at an audience – although their didactic nature makes this seem likely – this is clearly the case with the moralising prologue of *Ordo Ioseph*, which asks its addressees to be silent (*silentium*, line 4) and to listen (*Audite*, line 21).

In both these plays, standing as they do quite alone in the tradition of Latin drama, we are confronted with the genuine forerunners of the later audience-address. Nevertheless, we must stress the unusually restrained character of the audience-address which is still bound to the liturgical style. I have already intimated that the audience in *Ysaac* is never directly addressed; and the one explicit address of the *Ioseph* Prologue, too, contains only the *Audite* mentioned above. All other exhortations are disguised in the third person:

Letetur hodie	Sequantur homines	
chorus fidelium;	Ioseph consilium	
quiescant fabule,	vitent mulieres	
crescat silentium.	nature uitium.	(lines 1–8)[8]

These are not admonitions to certain persons but general rules of behaviour. The tone here is still impersonal and detached. Here we feel nothing of the friendly humility used by the Expositor of the Chester Plays to court attention for his explanations and not even the merest hint of that humorous acquiescence which so often seems to exist in the Yorkshire cycles between actors and spectators. The thoroughly impersonal style does nothing to close the gap between play and audience or to bridge it. This gap has not yet been discovered as something to be mastered by formal or artistic methods. In this respect *Ysaac* and *Ioseph* are still closer to the liturgical drama.

The significance of the audience-address for the vernacular drama

The audience-address deserves our interest not only because it happens to be an innovation of the mystery play over the liturgical drama. It also represents an essential structural difference between the two genres which one might define approximately by the categories 'lyric' and 'epic'. The liturgical drama, which arose out of the ritualistic re-creation of moments of the Christian history of salvation, went on to heighten the effect of such moments by lyrical commentaries that reflected the mood of the persons represented but also committed the feelings of the performers and the participating congregation. The stage directions of the *Regularis Concordia* show that the performers of the liturgical drama were not only bound to give physical expression to the emotions of the Second World persons they represented, but that they were expected to feel them inwardly as well. In the *Regularis Concordia* the priests are expected not only to approach the *sepulcrum* 'pedetemptim ad similitudinem quaerentium', but also to sing the seven penitential psalms 'cum magno cordis suspirio', to kiss the Cross 'humiliter' and to perform certain actions 'mente deuota'. Finally, at the end of the Easter dialogue the priest begins to sing the *Te Deum* 'congaudens pro triumpho regis nostri'.[9] The liturgical stage directions do not need to differentiate between the gesture and its content, the *signifiant* and the *signifié*, because the one is contained in the other and because the identity of visible representation and the idea to be represented is guaranteed by the liturgical setting.

In the vernacular drama on the other hand, one was always aware of the difference between the representation and the things represented. In the mystery play the history of salvation is not 're-presented', not 'made present' again, but performed, told scenically. This changes the relationship between actor and rôle. 'Re-production' is replaced by 'showing'. Whereas the performer in liturgical drama took his rôle upon him as a ritual task, the actor in the mystery play seems, so to speak, to step 'alongside' his rôle. In contrast to the genuine liturgical performer, he is therefore able to talk about the actions and motives of the character he represents as he would talk about a third person, he can describe what is difficult to see and explain what is difficult to understand. In the later plays we will even find him responding to probable reactions of his audience. His theatrical style – as far as we can gather from the texts – thus resembles that of the epic theatre, where the actor is supposed to 'narrate' his part.[10] In the medieval theatre, however, where the audience is always present as a silent partner, the audience-address never brings about the destruction of a dramatic illusion (as do its modern counterparts). Such an illusion is not the intention of this drama (although there are conventions in which a potentially illusionary effect is inherent). The audience-address is a particularly striking aspect of the general principle of telling and showing which dominates the medieval theatre as a whole.[11]

As the medieval audience-address does not mean a short leave-taking from the strict rules of a naturalistic drama, it is much more capable of interpretation than its modern residuum, the 'aside'. It is far more than a temporary opening of the 'fourth wall', very often it is even the authentic summarizing of the 'message' of the play.[12] At the same time it is an important indicator for the assessment of all the other characteristics of form and style. This aspect will be analysed later on when the individual cycles are discussed. Let it suffice here to point out that we can distinguish two types of audience-address which at the same time are distinctive of different cycles: an 'edificational' type characterizes the Chester Plays and largely the N-Town cycle, while the York and Towneley cycles are predominantly marked by a type which we can call 'histrionic'. The 'edificational' audience-address usually stands out very clearly from the rest of the text and stylistically is also different from the dialogue; the result is that the 'World' of the play generally remains closed. Utterances are always to be taken at face value, they are in no way coloured by the subjective attitude of the speaker, but give particularly clear expression to the objective content of the play. The 'histrionic' audience-address, on the other hand, sallies forth from the 'World' of the play, keeping it thus open to the First World of the audience. It is similar to the later aside in that it manifests an understanding between the spectators and individual characters in the play. It has recourse to experiences which are shared by Second-World characters and audience.[13] In contrast to the 'aside', however, it hardly arouses the feeling that the other characters are not meant to hear it; thus it does not normally give the impression that the audience is better informed than some of the *dramatis personae*. Neither does it imply that this understanding is in some sense against the rules of the game which audience and actors are playing together. On the contrary, it reinforces those rules of telling and showing which are basic to the medieval, pre-illusionist theatre.

Recognizing the audience-addresses

Before making a thorough analysis of the audience-address in the four cycles, we must deal briefly with the question of how audience-addresses are to be identified. Only in a very few cases may we hope for some sort of information from the stage directions.[14] More rewarding is the examination of the texts themselves; vocatives and second-person pronouns which cannot refer to characters in the play or information which is familiar to these can be regarded as sure signs that the audience is being addressed. In the Chester Plays and in the N-Town cycle we even find characters whose sole task is to inform the audience about what is going on.[15] Yet it is in the Chester Plays that we find many speeches, especially self-portrayals in the form of monologues, which are not addressed openly to the audience but which have a similar explanatory function as the overt audience-address. It will not always be possible to classify these speeches unambiguously. Since it is futile to speculate on the supposed intentions of the dramatists, we shall merely ask whether or not these speeches differ stylistically from unambiguous audience-addresses. It will be methodically sound always to distinguish such speeches from clear audience-addresses. Often we shall find that the presence or absence of the second-person pronoun (to mention only the most important indicator) is not merely accidental but has important stylistic reasons.

The audience-address in Chester[16]

Edificational audience-addresses

In keeping with the serious general tone of this cycle, we find the edificational audience-address almost universally predominant, together with a strong tendency to a closed play-sphere. This tendency limits the possibilities to use audience-address considerably. With very few exceptions, we do not find it in the mouths of the *dramatis personae*. In order to inform and edify the audience while at the same time keeping the play-sphere closed, the Chester cycle has developed two types of extra-dramatic character.

Purely factual information, i.e. exposition, the introduction of characters and occasionally the explanation of the emotions and motives of the characters, is usually dealt with in the dialogue and thus kept within the play-sphere. This is particularly true of the exposition, in which the interlocutors are often informed about facts which, from a 'realistic' point of view, ought to be already familiar to them.[17] Even the bragging monologues of Herod, Pilate, and Antichrist, which are rich in expository material, are probably to be read as dialogue openings addressed to the other characters present on the stage.[18] In other instances, prayers and similar invocations of the Deity are used to avoid an unveiled address to the audience.[19] Sometimes the speaker of the exposition even appears as actually talking to himself. This is the case, for instance, in the reflections with which Satan begins the Temptation (Ch XII). Similarly, the play of Emmaus (Ch XIX) begins with a complaint by Luke, which is uttered in the presence of Cleophas and is responded to by the latter, but in which Luke still appears to be speaking to himself.

Paradoxically, a more important device for preserving a closed play-sphere is to be found in those audience-addresses which are uttered by characters standing outside the play-sphere proper, such as Nuntius (Ch IV, 1ff; VI, 177ff) and Expositor (Ch IV, V, VI, XII, XXII).[20] Characteristically, these figures are confined to certain definite positions relative to the action: Nuntius always begins, Expositor always ends, a scene.[21]

The brief appearances of Nuntius need not detain us for very long.[22] Their function is primarily to ask the public for quiet and attention – a task which in other cycles is shouldered by the main characters themselves. What is deserving of note is the measured tone of his speeches and the fact that the part should have been introduced at all. Taken together, these two facts are some indication that a dignified tone and a closed play-sphere are expressions of the same stylistic tendency.

Expositor's speeches are far more interesting. A brief stylistic analysis will be the best way for us to discover the kind of relationship between audience and play which these speeches are designed to establish. They are somewhat verbose and full of periphrases. Although Expositor has to make theological points, he does not assume the stance of the prophet promulgating some supra-personal truth.[23] Expositor appears quite openly as an interpreter whose thoughts on the matter at hand do not claim any ultimate authority. Since his own understanding is represented as possibly faulty, he is nearer to the audience than the biblical figures on whose deeds he comments. He thus becomes a true mediator between play-sphere and public. To be sure, this unassuming attitude is above all a rhetorical pose; it does not indicate an honest belief in the possibility of error on the part of Expositor and it is quite compatible with an occasional condescending remark on the 'unlearned' (Ch IV, 115). Nevertheless, this pose pervades his speeches and is to be observed in a number of stylistic traits: he addresses the audience as 'Lordings', he qualifies his own exegesis with conditional clauses and with formulae like 'vnderstand may I'[24] or 'as I reade',[25] or affirms it with 'in good faye'.[26] However much these formulae may be occasioned by the rhyme, they do give the impression that Expositor wants to make himself and his message agreeable to the audience. This is also shown by the fact that he describes his own speech as 'in meke mannere' (Ch XXII, 76) and that he includes himself among the addressees of the Christian message.[27] The emotional attitude which he tries to establish is, however, rather plain and arid. He does little more than call biblical persons and events 'good',[28] or ask his listeners to accept the message 'with good intente'.[29] The prime objective is not the creation of a pious mood, but the teaching of clearly ordered theological knowledge,[30] which also seems endowed with a sort of practical usefulness:

> Nowe that you shall expresselye knowe
> these Prophettes wordes upon a rowe,
> what the doe signifie I will shewe [they
> that mych may doe you good. (Ch XXII, 25–8; see also Ch IV, 464 (DM))

Know, signify, show, expound are frequently recurring key-words which underline the sober, didactic tenor of the Chester cycle.[31] It is only at the end of his last appearance that Expositor allows himself some slight emotional appeal. There he admonishes his audience to lead a life which may pave the way toward eternal bliss. But even here, where the emphasis is clearly on the Hereafter, utilitarian considerations are unmistakeable:

> Nowe have I tould you, in good faye,
> the tokens to come before doomesdaye.
> God give you grace to do so aye
> that you them worthye bee
> to come to the blysse that lasteth aye.
> As mych as here wee and our playe,
> of Antechristes signes you shall assaye.
> Hee comes! Soone you shall see! (Ch XXII, 333–40)

This tone, which is didactic rather than edificational, is very similar to that of the *Stanzaic Life of Christ*; even the wording is sometimes almost identical.[32] Since, with the exception of Ch XII, Expositor appears only in plays which are recognizably influenced by the *Stanzaic Life*,[33] it seems likely that this didactic tenor, which is usually attributed to the high age of the Chester cycle, owes its existence to a late revision.[34]

Open play-sphere and 'histrionic' audience-address

It is in keeping with the serious tone of the Chester cycle, which addresses itself to reason rather than the emotions and which expounds a somewhat homespun theology, that the histrionic audience-address should appear only in isolated instances. In the Yorkshire cycles it is, for instance, common for the *dramatis personae* to greet the audience when entering and to bid farewell when departing.[35] These speech acts, which create a certain intimacy between play-sphere and audience-sphere, are almost completely absent from the Chester Plays. It is true that many of the Chester plays end with blessings, but these are worded in such a way that they are primarily addressed to the characters on the stage.[36] We may assume, however, that the audience is included in these blessings. This idea is at least suggested by the close of Ch XIX, where Jesus says:

> *Christe* give you grace to take the waye. (line 273, emphasis added)

The fact that Jesus speaks of himself here in the third person and thus leaves the play-sphere suggests that these parting words were taken as conventional formulae which were but loosely connected with the main body of the play. But the very fact that in spite of their conventional character the play-sphere was kept closed in most cases testifies to the importance which the Chester Plays attach to this stylistic feature.

A similar case of breaking the play-sphere is to be found in Ch XI, 327ff, where the Angel ends the play with the words:

> Now have you hard, all in this place,
> that Christ is commen through his grace –
> as holye Esau prophecied hase –   [*recte* Esaie
> and Symeon hase him seene.
> Leeve you well this, lordes of might,
> and keepe you all his lawes of right,
> that you may in his blisse so bright
> evermore with him to leene.

These farewell words, however, have clearly lost their connection with the contents of the preceding play: They refer only to its first half: to the Purification and the Presentation in the Temple, on which originally they must have provided the closing comment.[37] When the second part, *Christ and the Doctors in the Temple*, was taken over from York, the Angel's speech was simply transferred to the end of this second episode. It is hard to think of a less ambiguous proof of the independence of this speech from the preceding play.

There is but one further parting salute which is explicitly and unambiguously directed at the audience. It comes from the Gartius of the Chester Shepherds Play (Ch VII, 693–6). This is the only one of the Chester Plays which shows throughout that easy-going fluctuation between play-sphere and audience-sphere which is a necessary prerequisite for the histrionic audience-address. Even this play has only comparatively few passages which can be shown to be directly addressed to the audience. But these passages are of much greater significance for the general tone of the play than those discussed so far. The Third Shepherd, for instance, addresses the 'husbandes that benne here abowt'

(Ch VII, 86) pretty much as do his counterparts in the plays by the Wakefield Master, and the First Shepherd says at the beginning:

> Here be more herbes, *I tell yt you*;
> I shall recken them on a rowe:
> fynter, fanter, and fetterfowe,
> and alsoe pennyewrytte. (Ch VII, 25–8, emphasis added)

The introduction of the second person pronoun in a confirming formula is fully integrated into the rest of the speech; it gives us the right to regard the whole speech as directed at the audience even if other incontrovertible evidence is lacking. The local adverb here which is often used at the beginning of a stanza, indicates that the Shepherd is showing something to the audience and not merely discovering it for himself. The very regularity with which the word is used demonstrates its ostensive function. Similarly, the announcement 'I shall recken' (line 26), which is immediately followed by the deed (lines 27f), shows that something is being demonstrated. The sequence of the statements with their parallel syntax, especially the repetition of 'here be', 'here is', is symptomatic of a descriptive manner of speaking which we shall encounter again in other types of discourse in this cycle:

> Loe, here bee more herbes saffe and sownde,
> wysely wrought for everye wounde – (lines 17f)
>
> Here be more herbes,... (line 25)
>
> Here is tarre in a pott,
> to heale them from the rott;... (lines 33f)

The speaker here is clearly showing and naming from his fund of knowledge, not expressing a momentary experience. This manner of speaking is so natural for the audience-address that one may well wonder why other plays in the cycle avoid that address and why the Shepherds Play is allowed an exception. The answer must be speculative to some extent, but presumably the lofty effect of the biblical events would have been felt to be at risk if the characters had been allowed to put themselves on a level with the audience. The desire to keep a certain distance between play-sphere and audience-sphere found expression, as we have seen, in the introduction of a mediating figure such as Expositor, a fact which, by constituting a third plane, underlined the necessity to mediate between play and audience. The Shepherds, who were quite incapable of such elevated effects, symbolized the fact that the Christian message was first received by simple folk. The spectators can regard them as their equals, with whom it was possible to be on a familiar footing.[38]

In the Adoration of the Shepherds the audience-address corresponds to a play–audience relationship that is characteristic of the entire play, notwithstanding the heterogeneous origins of the play.[39] In all other plays of the cycle it constitutes an inorganic interpolation. An example of this is Ch III ('The Deluge'), in which lines 97–112 clearly interrupt the smooth flow of events and are usually regarded as a comic addition, possibly on the model of Y IX.[40] In the course of this interpolation Noah calls on the audience to witness his matrimonial sufferings (line 108). This type of audience-address, which exploits experiences shared between audience and character for comic effects (as opposed to the edificational ones in the Shepherds Play), is represented by only a few scattered examples in Chester. In other cycles, as we shall see, it is firmly established.[41]

Finally, Chester also has an audience-address of the 'bombastic' type, which will be treated in more detail below: Ch V 124–63 are an interpolation in MSS B A R (called B W h by Deimling) which re-enforces the bragging element and which characteristically contains a direct turn to the audience (lines 126f).[42]

The interpolations in Ch III and V resemble the mass of the cycle very closely both in terms of metre and style. This is not true of the speech of Demon carrying Herod off to hell (Ch X, 434–57). Here, the strong alliteration and the largely anapaestic rhythm suggest a later origin. This devil shows a certain resemblance to the demons of the folk-play. He threatens above all the tapsters (only in B H) who pour out too little beer with his promise to 'come agayne and fetch moe' (line 455). He carries a 'Croked Cambrock'[43] with which he threatens to 'cloe' the backs of the audience (DM, line 437), and he introduces his speech with 'Warre, warre' (line 434).[44] Also his manner of presenting himself differs from what is usual in the mystery plays. It does not characterize the speaker so much as it describes his movements and his external attributes. This is a feature shared with many of the self-introductions of the folk-play.[45]

Being few and presumably late, these examples can only underline what has already been said: the breaking of the play-sphere remains an alien element in the Chester cycle which stands in marked contrast to its older surroundings.

Speech-types resembling the audience-address

Our analysis so far has demonstrated a strong tendency towards a closed play-sphere in the Chester Plays and a corresponding tendency to avoid a direct address of the audience, especially its histrionic variant. At the same time the predominance of a descriptive manner of speaking became apparent, placing a certain distance between the actor and his part and by that token tending to stretch the boundaries of the play-sphere. When this manner of speaking occurs in dialogue we will experience a certain tension between the form of the speech and its function, but the context of the action will usually be strong enough to prevent an actual stepping out of the play-sphere. In such cases there will be no question of an audience-address.

The situation is quite different where there is no context of action. This is true above all of the Prophet plays, of which there are two in the Chester cycle. One, which resembles the Prophets Play familiar from the Continent, exists only in MS H, where it forms lines 297–432 of ChV.[46] The other, Ch XXII ('The Prophets and Antichrist'),[47] is peculiar to Chester. Apart from these, mention should be made of the speeches of God (Ch I-III, XXIV). The utterances of the dead souls delivered by Christ from hell (Ch XVII) can also be regarded as belonging to this type, although it must be admitted that here the context of situation gradually becomes more important.

Hanns Ott has coined the happy term 'statuarische Person' (statue-like person) for this kind of dramatic character. More in keeping with today's terminology, we might perhaps call them 'de-contextualized'. Ott has demonstrated that these figures still show features which testify to their origin in the sermon; their main function is to serve as theological mouthpieces, and they appear above all in 'action-less' plays. Apart from that, they usually introduce themselves and directly address the audience.[48] These observations made apropos the German drama are largely true of the English as well. As far as Chester is concerned, however, a direct address of the audience is usually avoided. The prophets in Ch V prefer to introduce themselves by name, but none of them uses even the most casual form of address. The utterances emphasize their relevance for the whole of humanity, which, however, is mentioned only in the third person.[49] This is consistent with a solemn, apodictic style which is free from subordinate and especially conditional clauses and is confined to lapidary statements. Moreover, the prophets do not merely propound their prophecies but also show themselves in the gesture of prophets, e.g.:

    I, Joell, saie this sickerlye,...   (Ch V (App. IB), 377)[50]

The effect of this manner of speaking relies in part precisely on the absence of an explicit addressee. This absence gives the prophecies their general validity and supermundane authority.

The prophets of Ch XXII speak somewhat differently. They also avoid any direct address of the audience, but still they are not so totally removed from it as their counterparts in Ch V. They address humanity throughout (which in Ch V appeared in the third person only).[51] This is accompanied by a slight but distinct change of tone. The speakers no longer establish their own speech situation,[52] they find it established before they begin to speak. The speech situation is no longer conceived of as general and outside time and space, it is clearly specific. St John the Evangelist for instance begins his speech with the words:

> There sawe I manye a wondrous thinge.
> One which I tell you anon. (lines 179f)

In a similar vein Daniel emphasizes the *hic et nunc* of his prophesying (lines 131f). Many of the utterances contain elements of subjectivism and even of perplexity.[53] Since the speeches are about visions, the manner of experiencing these can be introduced into the telling. Such opportunities exist also in Ch V, although there they are never exploited.

All this shows that the manner of speaking is more subjective here than it is in Ch V. Craig's belief that these prophets are not 'merely taken over from the *Prophetae*'[54] is supported not only by the theological arguments which Craig adduces, but also by the speech style of these figures.

The stylistic differences which we have observed point to strict, removed objectivity in Ch V and to a distinct subjectivism, however slight, in Ch XXII. Craig, who believes that the eschatological plays differ in origin from the rest of the cycle, might find support for his views in our stylistic findings. But the findings of Clopper and Travis make it virtually certain that the two plays, at least in the form preserved in the manuscripts, are the product of one process of 'major transformation' in the early sixteenth century.[55] Differences are thus better explained by the different homiletic functions of the plays. The message of the eschatological prophets is more immediately relevant to the audience; hence it will influence their behaviour more directly than that of the messianic prophets.

Whichever way we decide the question of authorship, we shall have to admit that the audience-address, which is normally regarded as a feature of a 'naïve' dramaturgy, is capable of subtle differentiation and can be minutely adapted to a number of dramatic-homiletic functions. Above all, our perhaps rather humdrum principle of always observing the occurrence or non-occurrence of the pronoun of address has proved most useful. This seemingly surface phenomenon reveals important distinctions concerning the nature of the intended audience: while Expositor can address himself only to those actually and physically present, the prophets can address mankind in its totality.

The audience-address in the York and Towneley cycles

Absence of separation between the two spheres, especially in the earlier strata

The two Yorkshire cycles, which are closely related, correspond much more nearly to the received opinion, according to which the medieval drama did not separate between play-sphere and audience-sphere.[56] But even here developments and differentiations are in evidence which make this crude formula at best problematic. Unfortunately, it is rather difficult to prove those developments, since the compositional history of the two cycles is inordinately complex. This complexity reveals itself even in a casual glance at the enormous variety of their metres. To this day it has proved impossible to arrive at a generally accepted chronology of the individual plays.[57] Alterations are not confined, as they are in Chester, to a few additions which can be fairly confidently identified. Anyone setting forth to sketch the development of dramatic form in these cycles has to tread with extreme care. Nevertheless, a few differences between early and late plays will become apparent.

Plays conventionally regarded as early are clearly marked by a strong and unforced fluctuation between play-sphere and audience-sphere. Pharao in Y XI, 1ff (= T VIII) addresses not only the Yorkshire spectators, but also the people of Egypt (Y XI, 14, 18). He thus 'transforms' the audience into his Old Testament subjects. This transformation of the audience is characteristic of most tyrants' monologues, but more typical of the early strata seem to be those plays which seriously dramatize a 'Revelation' situation.

One of the most instructive examples of this is the Towneley *Iohannes baptista* (T XIX), in which John informs the audience directly about his own family history. He does not merely narrate the story, though. At the very beginning he praises God and prays Him to bless the audience. Such blessings can be quite formulaic and may have nothing to do with the part played by the speaker.[58] But John's hope that the audience may be kept from sin is clearly grounded in his rôle as preacher. The real self-introduction begins only in line 9. The almost intimate tone which John adopts is clearly calculated to impress the circumstances of his birth on the spectators:

> My name, for sothe, is baptyst Iohn,
>   My fader zacary ye knaw,
> That was dombe and mayde great mone,
>   Before my byrth, and stode in awe.   (T XIX, 13–16)

The closer he draws to his spectators, the more marked becomes the distance from his Jewish contemporaries listening to his preaching. Not only does he speak of them in the third person, but he underlines their ignorance and blindness by giving first an account of the miraculous birth of Christ and then adding:

> Yit the Iues inqueryd me has
> If I be cryst; thay ar begyld.   (T XIX, 21f)

The following stanzas are devoted to a glorification of Christ and his passion. In true Franciscan fashion he endeavours to arouse sympathy for Christ's sufferings (lines 35f). He identifies himself with the audience by emphasizing that he and they are equally in need of salvation by Christ (lines 37, 47). This identification is carried to such lengths that John looks at the scene of action as it were from the outside:

> In water clere then baptyse I
> The pepyll that ar *in this coste*;...   (T XIX, 41f, emphasis added)

Such local references – usually in the form of 'this place' – are highly characteristic of the prologues in medieval drama. In this John is similar to the Chester Expositor and other extra-dramatic figures: the position thus acquired enables him better to guide the reactions of the audience than would be possible from within the closed play-sphere. And it is quite in keeping with the prologue-like function of this speech that in the concluding prayer (lines 51–64) he should make himself the spokesman of his audience, just as the expository character Contemplacio does in LC XI.[59]

The characters of the *Processus Prophetarum* (T VII) have a similarly informal manner of addressing their public. Moses, it is true, begins by addressing the 'folk of israell' (line 1), but his closing remarks are clearly directed at the audience. He briefly sums up the previous history, he informs them about the locality ('monte synay', line 87), he admonishes them in a somewhat colloquial tone, and above all he gives them the parting salute 'And haue now all good day!' (line 90). The audience here can take on the rôle of the *dramatis persona's* contemporaries much as the choir of the liturgical plays fluctuated between the rôles of celebrating congregation and (e.g.) the disciples of Christ. But there is also an obvious difference: the rôle of the audience of the mystery plays is bound to remain a passive one; it can only listen, it cannot speak. Nor is there any evidence that it sings. Unlike the liturgical choir, it is outside the play-sphere to begin with, it can only be drawn into it by the characters of the play. Thus, the separation of play-sphere and audience-sphere is at the root of the mystery play as it was not at the root of the liturgical play. It makes sense, therefore, to study the further development of the mystery play in the light of this separation.

Moses' colloquial, good-neighbourly tone, which never allows us to forget the presence of the audience, returns in the other speeches of the play (which, however, has come down to us only in a fragmentary state). It shows in the freely used pronouns of address which are entirely missing in Chester, in expletive phrases like 'I warne you then' (line 26), in the division of the audience into groups like old and young, rich and poor, etc., and in the use of conditional and other subordinate clauses (e.g. lines 58, 100, 167). Such minstrel-like features, which are supported by the tail-rhyme stanza, are concentrated above all in the speech of David, who, with 'my harp and fyngers ten' (line 110) promises to 'myrth make' (line 118).[60] Employing the first person plural in his leave-taking, David associates himself more closely with the audience than Moses and the Sibyl do:

> he that maide vs all with his wytt,
> sheld vs all from hell pytt,
> And graunt vs heuen lyght! (T VII, 160–2)[61]

This style suggests an intimacy which is possible between a minstrel and his listeners – that is, between people who are spatially fairly close together. This intimacy in prophecies which are addressed to the people of Israel and thus to the whole of humanity in expectation of the Saviour, may strike us as odd. But the relationship between First and Second World which it creates still bears some resemblance to that created by the ceremonious, formal style of the liturgical drama: like the religious congregation, the physically present audience has to represent humanity as a whole. It is the manifest recipient of a message addressed to a far larger audience. But in spite of these similarities, the differences between the linguistic media are not merely external. The change from liturgical Latin to the minstrel's English has also altered the nature of the identification between the physically present and the larger audience. In the liturgy, this identification was, as it were, institutionally guaranteed. The ceremonial rigidity avoids an appeal to the natural emotions of those present. While being physically near to their audience, the liturgical *dramatis personae* are emotionally and rhetorically remote from it. The mystery play, by contrast, uses a tone in which physical and emotional nearness are matched. The appearance of secular, minstrel-like features in a play as little amenable to 'secularization' as the *Processus Prophetarum* suggests that in the Yorkshire drama at least the so-called 'secular element' is not necessarily the late addition as which it appears in Chester and in parts of N-Town.[62]

But the relationship between *dramatis personae* and audience does not always correspond to that of the 'Revelation' situation. In the scenes discussed so far the audience had to take an imaginative leap into the presence of the Second World characters. In other plays, this change of time and place has to be achieved by the characters. It is they who move back and forth between play-sphere and audience-sphere. This is manifest in the audience-address, but it is implied in other types of discourse as well. A particularly significant example of such a technique is provided by the prayers in some early plays of the York cycle, where the speaker begins by addressing God in the second person but soon lapses into the third, thus talking *about* God *to* the audience.[63] Among other things these prayers serve the purpose of self-presentation and self-introduction. Noah and Abraham, while praying and thanking God, inform the public as to why they pray and thank God. But information of the audience is not the only function of these prayers; they are a synthesis of religious and dramatic acts which is familiar from the liturgical drama. In 'donning' his part, the actor makes himself the spokesman of his fellow citizens. A detailed analysis of the prayers, especially of the relationship between the speaker and God, must be reserved for the chapter on the opening prayer. But we can already say something about the relationship between the speaker and the audience: although the prayers are uttered by persons existing within the play-sphere, these persons are placed in a situational context which is by no means required by their intra-dramatic rôles. Noah and Abraham are not merely the biblical patriarchs alone with their God, they also inform and remind their fellow citizens of the deeds which God has done for those patriarchs.

In most of these prayers the audience is not addressed directly, but Noah's prayer in Y IX[64] does contain such addresses. In tone it differs so little from the others that one is inclined to regard the absence of direct audience-addresses there as a statistical coincidence.[65] The identity of style between apparent monologue and overt audience-address is of course a much more important indicator than the mere frequency of unambiguous audience-address. The very identity of tone permits us to assume in the early plays what we have called 'fluctuation' between the two spheres (which does not know sharp 'breaks' or 'transitions' from one sphere to the other). This fluctuation seems to be found above all in the earlier York plays. Those plays for which there is evidence of composition after 1415 define the position of the speaker relative to the play-sphere much more clearly.

The fact that the prayers move so smoothly and easily between play-sphere and audience-sphere is certainly a fair indication of the closeness between these two 'worlds'. But to determine this relationship more accurately, we have to analyse the various audience-addresses individually, which we shall now do. The possibly older plays are distinguished by a type which we may call 'confidential'. It consists largely of the blessings and greetings by which the actors take leave of the audience.⁶⁶ These greetings are little more than social phrases. This is borne out by the fact that they make no reference to the contents of their respective plays.⁶⁷ They contain no didactic message as did Expositor's speeches in Chester, nor do they exhibit his ingratiating politeness. Occasionally one is inclined to believe that the mood of the leave-taker is influenced by the events of the play, as when Mary Magdalene exclaims after her encounter with the risen Christ:

> I am as light as leyfe on tre,
> ffor ioyfull sight that I can se,
> ...
> To galyle now will I fare,
> And his dyscyples cach from care;
> I wote that thay will mowrne no mare,
>   Commyn is thare blys;
> That worthi childe that mary bare
>   he amende youre mys. (T XXVI, 623–34)

But this is probably little more than a casual by-product of the convention. For our study these parting words are of interest precisely because they are formulaic and almost void of content. This shows that they are not meant to establish a relationship but that they are the expression of an already existing one. And such a relationship exists only between the actors and their fellow-citizens the spectators. With the parting words we are thus back into the First World, and the process which we observed at the beginning of many plays has now been reversed: just as the actor then 'donned' his part by introducing himself as a *dramatis persona* and by telling that persona's life-story, he is now 'doffing' it. The easy passage from actor to part and back shows both similarities with and differences from the relationship obtaining in the liturgical drama. It is similar in that here as well as there the actor never completely disappeared behind the part; the ecclesiastical rank of the subdeacon for instance was not allowed to be forgotten even when a thurible (taken to represent the spices of Mark 16.1 and Luke 24.1) identified him as one of the three Marys at the Sepulchre.⁶⁸ But the subdeacon differs from the mystery play actor in that he is reduced to a single rôle even outside the play-sphere (namely to that of his ecclesiastical rank) and that his relationship to his 'audience' (the chorus of his fellow clerics) is determined by and limited to his liturgical function, while the carpenter or fisherman acting the part of Noah always remains the neighbour whose relations with his fellow citizens comprehend the fullness of everyday life. In the liturgical drama the sphere surrounding the play-sphere is regulated by an elaborate, highly formalized ceremonial which reduces human relations to rôles as much as the liturgical drama does, whereas the sphere surrounding the play-sphere of the vernacular play is the much fuller, richer world of everyday life which is far less regulated and reduces human relations to a far lesser extent. Thus the tone to which he returns on leaving the play-sphere is that of everyday life.

The blurred borderline between play-sphere and audience-sphere and the narrow, always bridgeable gap between the two make it possible even for Jesus to address the audience *in propria persona* (and in this he differs most decisively from his opposite number in Chester):

> ȝe þat haue sene þis sight
> My blissyng with ȝo be. (Y XXIV, 208f)

The Saviour of the play-sphere here speaks directly to the audience. Since there is no qualitative difference felt to exist between the world of the play and that of the audience, such blessings are acceptable even in plays whose vivid dialogue and realistic characterization have been justly praised.[69] In the Towneley *Salutacio Elezabeth* Elizabeth says:

> That lord, that the with grace infude,
> he saue all in this place. (T XI, 89f)[70]

These parting salutations as between neighbours turn the performance into a communal enterprise. The enterprise differs from the religious service in that it is not *regulated* by rigorous ceremonial but only *guided* by the quality of the play-acting. Nevertheless, it is not completely 'secularized'.[71] If by this term we mean only the simple (though consequential) fact that Second World events are now placed in the framework of civic society and its code of behaviour (and no longer in that of the Church and its ritual) – then the term may pass. But even then one has to remember that the guilds which supported the production of the plays were not exclusively secular organizations in the modern sense of the word.[72] But under no circumstances must 'secular' be understood as an antonym to 'religious' or even 'pertaining to the Church'. For the incomplete identification between actor and part, which makes entering and leaving the play-sphere into special processes that are even relevant for the effect of the plays, never turns into that discrepancy between illusions and unmasked reality popular in the Mummers' Play, which presupposes that the process of ritual impersonation has already been superseded by dramatic mimesis and theatrical self-consciousness (*ästhetische Publikumsbewußtheit*).[73] Such discrepancy cannot evolve in the mystery play for the very reason that the 'donning' of the part in which we have recognized an inheritance, however altered, from the liturgical drama has never claimed the status of ritual impersonation, which has been held to have been present in the pagan origins of the folk play. However one may differ in one's estimate of the amount of pagan strata in the mystery plays, there can be no doubt that the basic structure of these plays was determined by the official religion.

Later tendencies towards a closed play-sphere

The findings of the previous section must not obscure the fact that the presumably later parts of the York and Towneley cycles do tend to close the play-sphere. This can be demonstrated in those plays which Towneley took over from York and which, after the adoption, were changed in one of the cycles.

Two relevant examples are to be found in Y XXXIX, 148f and IX, 191ff. Both are late plays the predecessors of which appear to have been preserved in Towneley.[74] In each case the earlier version shows a direct turn to the audience, while the later one refers to it only in the third person. This becomes particularly clear in Y XL ('Emmaus') which was presumably written after 1415 and which shows the marks of the ornate 'Northern alliterative school'.[75] The simple, conventional lines

>   That blyssid childe that marie bare
>   Grauntt you his blys. (T XXVII, 379f)

are changed into the much more elaborate

>   Here may we notte melle more at þis tyde,
>   For prossesse of plaies þat precis in plight.
>   He bringe to his blisse on euery ilke side,
>   þat sofferayne lorde þat moste is of myght. (Y XL, 191ff)

'Popular' audience-addresses

The audience-addresses we have considered so far still follow the basic liturgical pattern. Although the principle of hierarchical gradation has been abandoned, contact with, and overt awareness of, the audience is confined to certain well-restricted phases of the play (chiefly beginning and ending). But it is characteristic of the mystery play (as well as of the other genres of the medieval vernacular drama) that audience-contact is conditioned not only by phase, but also (and chiefly) by character. There are certain characters in the plays who establish momentary contact not between the play as a whole and the audience, but between themselves and the audience. They do not 'fluctuate' between the two spheres but they occasionally 'break' the play-sphere. The best-known of these characters is Joseph, whose very impact on the audience depends on this 'breaking'. He is physically frail, he thinks he is a cuckold, he at first does not believe in the marvellous events in which he plays a part – this has often been interpreted as comic relief in an otherwise too solemn story. But what is more important in terms of play–audience relations is that it is exactly Joseph's all-too-human qualities which give him his function in the history of Man's salvation. This weak, sometimes egocentric and unlovable person, who at first does not even believe in the divine message, is a particularly apt representative of average Man. The public, as it were, was in a position to hear the news of the conception of Christ with his ears[76] and to achieve that moral-psychological identification which distinguishes the mystery play from the liturgical drama. Joseph addresses the audience in long, extensive narrative (T X, 227ff) as well as in short proverbs and warnings which grow out of the dialogue (T XV, 149f). These laments of the hen-pecked husband, which recur in the plays of the Wakefield Master (Noah, T III, and the Second Shepherd, T XIII), clearly resemble the later 'aside'. Like the aside, they cause the public to differentiate between the *dramatis personae*. In this they differ from the audience-addresses we have studied so far. As long as the relationship between the two spheres is articulated in entrances and exits, the audience is addressed, as it were, on behalf of the whole troupe. The spectators are not invited to identify with the speaker. All this changes as soon as the audience is addressed out of the midst of the dramatic situation. The speaker of the aside is somehow 'closer' to the audience than his fellow characters. He causes the public to take sides, to react emotionally, above all: to sympathize. This is a reaction for which the liturgical drama has little use.

The above remarks about similarities with the later aside have to be qualified, however, especially as such qualification may help us to define the ontological status of the play-sphere vis-à-vis the audience-sphere. The fact that the play-sphere is being momentarily 'broken' indicates, it is true, an artistic consciousness of the separateness of the two spheres. But what the audience hears is not, as it were, 'information smuggled through the fourth wall', as might be purveyed by a talkative servant in a Roman or Restoration comedy. Joseph's relationship to the public resembles rather that of Hamlet, Apemantus, or a Shakespearean fool, who can share his own reflections with his public because his experience of life is representative of the audience's. Robert Weimann is surely right in assuming that Shakespeare, in the figures mentioned, is exploiting a convention that he has inherited from the popular theatre which preceded him.[77] But the popular roots of the Shakespearean drama must not let us forget the fundamental difference between Joseph's aside and that of a Shakespearean character.[78] An extreme but still characteristic example of the Shakespearean type is provided by Apemantus, the 'churlish philosopher' whose 'aside' position at Timon's feast is signalled by his sitting at a separate table:

O you gods, what a number of men eats Timon, and he sees 'em not! It grieves me to see so many dip their meet in one man's blood; and all the madness is, he cheers them up too. (*Timon of Athens*, I, ii, 38–41)[79]

Here, too, the stage character and the audience share a common experience of life. But here this sharing enables the audience to assume a critical stance against the vain, foolish, and hypocritical activities of the other stage figures. The audience thus is allowed to feel superior to those characterized by the speaker. The mystery stage does not arouse this feeling in its audience. Quite the contrary: in realizing that a biblical figure articulates an experience which is familiar to them, the spectators are drawn closer to the sacred events reproduced before them.[80] The secular experience which Joseph shares with the audience and which at the same time leads the spectators to a profounder understanding of their own situation is underlined and made subservient to the religious message by the aside.

Agreement between stage figure and audience makes it possible to differentiate within the audience: often it is only a section of the audience which is addressed. For instance, warnings against marriage are usually directed only at the *young* men in the audience.[81]

This type of audience-address which 'breaks' the play-sphere appears not only in the mouths of normal, 'decent' human beings like Joseph, Noah, or the Shepherds. It is also used by Demons (T XXX; cf. also Ch X), wicked tyrants (T XXII) or impudent servants. In such cases it can make parts of the public even into satirical butts. Tutivillus in the Towneley Judgment play for instance threatens the

> Ianettys of the stewys
> and lychoures on lofte...
> All harlottys and horrys. (T XXX, 349ff)[82]

Pilate explicitly addresses the wicked ones in his audience (T XXII, 23ff, 36ff), and Cain's servant Pikeharness, announcing the arrival of his master, teases the audience with the words 'Som of you ar his men' (T II, 20). In these late plays the general, good-neighbourly relationship between play-figures and public is transformed into an accompliceship between certain figures and certain parts of the audience. The originally homogeneous community of the mystery plays has thus been polarized. The biblical reality of the play and the social reality of the audience have already drifted so far apart that the occasional contact between the two creates a special, usually satirical effect; there is no longer the fluctuation of the earlier plays. Within the mystery play this development has never progressed beyond the first steps. It is a late development which follows the earlier stages with a certain logic. The relationship between play-sphere and audience-sphere has here become more diversified than for instance in the Chester Plays, the play–audience relationship of which we have already described and which leaves very little room for the 'histrionic' audience-address.

It is perhaps significant that this 'selective' audience-address should be found above all in plays which were either written or revised by the Wakefield Master. This dramatist, to whom we owe the *Secunda Pastorum* with the famous Mak episode, is well known for his extensive use of popular motifs and customs,[83] and the figures who use the 'histrionic' audience-address show distinct traces of popular origins. As Weimann indicates, they all have 'an original speech pattern quite unlike the descriptive narrative of medieval prose and the sermon'.[84] Though Weimann may be underestimating the dramatic and even histrionic potential of the medieval preacher in this statement, his explanation serves well to bring out the profound difference between these speeches and those of the patriarchs.[85] For these 'popular' figures show their closeness to the public already by responding to its reactions (which presumably presupposes that they have provoked them by mime and gesture):

Wote ye not I com before?   (Cain's servant *Garcio* in T II, 5)[86]

ye wote not wel, I weyn / what wat is commen to the towne.
(Pilate in T XX, 10)

Garcio and Pilate do not confine themselves to describing their external appearance and their other characteristics, but they accompany their entries with words like 'Here come I' or a similar exclamation underlining their arrival. In this they resemble the Jack Finney and the Beelzebub of the Mummers' Play, as well as the Torturers of the Towneley Passion plays. If, as was suggested on p. 99, the Torturers enter from the back of the audience, this will create a rather unusual relationship between the two spheres.[87] Unlike the more respectable figures of the mystery play, who 'create' the play-sphere in their opening monologues, the Torturers resemble the characters of the folk-play in that they presuppose this sphere and enter it from outside. As soon as they have entered it, however, they break it in their address to the audience. This creates a highly paradoxical effect: by breaking the play-sphere they make the audience conscious of its existence and thus help to strengthen its dramatic autonomy. The comic effect of these speeches relies to a large extent on their 'impropriety'. If this is so, the play as a sphere obeying its own laws must already have been sufficiently set off from the world of the audience to make the bridging of the gap between the two worlds aesthetically significant. This significance was lacking in the 'fluctuating' relationship which characterized those pageants described in the previous section. But the relationship here differs also from the greetings and partings of the older plays: the actors no longer 'doff' their parts, but they address the audience in their character as *dramatis personae*.

The development of the bragging speech

The entry speeches of the servants and torturers are not the only possible form of establishing a comic relationship with the audience. The bragging speech, which, thanks to Chaucer's 'Pilates voys',[88] is probably the best known speech-form of the English mystery plays, was established in the mystery plays long before the folk-figures entered it. It is attested in some of the early fragments and may even have its origins in the *Herodes iratus* of the liturgical plays.

The 'popular' and the potentates' audience-address are well distinguished as to their form. It will be our task to find out these differences and to discuss the problems arising from their occasionally meeting in the text. This, by the way, is the reason for our treating the later type first. We hope to show that the problems hinted at occur only when the tyrant's bragging speech is prefixed to other scenes, prominent among which is the popular entry speech.

Paradoxically, the significance of the tyrants' speech is proven by the fact that few of them have been transmitted from the oldest strata of the cycles. Apparently those plays which offered an opportunity for a tyrant's ranting speech were frequently revised. Because of the popularity of the tyrant's speech which is here in evidence, we have only two specimens that can be regarded as comparatively early. They are spoken by Pharao in Y XI[89] (= T VIII) and Caesar Augustus in T IX. Martin Stevens' thorough linguistic analysis of the latter play has demonstrated that its dialect is predominantly Northern English and that it may well have been written at about the same time as those plays which Towneley took over from York, i.e. 1415 at the latest.[90] Possibly we are dealing with a play which was discarded in York and thus did not find its way into Burton's 1415 list.[91]

Neither Pharao's speech nor that of Augustus exhibit any features which *unambiguously* serve a comic effect. It is true that the potentates swear by 'Mahowne', but there is none of that peculiar comedian-like enjoyment of blasphemy which is so palpable in the later plays. They show pride in their power just as *Rex vivus* does in the roughly contemporary morality *The Pride of Life*.[92] Our speeches resemble the one in the morality also in giving a hint of the limitations and transitoriness of earthly power. They are still too firmly grounded in the homiletic tradition to allow free aesthetic exchange between play-sphere and audience-sphere. Although the spectators are insulted and threatened and are thus, as it were, made the subjects of the biblical potentates and drawn into the play-sphere, the transition from one sphere to the other occurs without any dramatic effect, without any actual 'break'. This becomes particularly obvious with Augustus, who begins by praising himself as an omnipotent ruler,[93] and who then, apparently to underline his claim, gives his name and glories in his own beauty – something nearly all tyrants do. But unlike other tyrants, Augustus passes from boast to complaint:

> Bot one thyng doys me full mych care, (T IX, 37)

and this 'care' causes Augustus to turn to his *counsellars* (line 40) for consolation. The self-presentation, which here includes boast and complaint and which is clearly spoken *ad spectatores*, yields the psychological motif for turning to the other *dramatis personae*. This fluctuation is quite similar to that which we found in the prayers of Noah and Abraham, there is none of that conscious transgression which we observed in Joseph's proverbs and which we shall re-discover in the later boasting speeches.

The same fluctuation between play-sphere and audience-sphere is also in evidence when Augustus describes his realm. In claiming 'all ... that vp standys, / Castels, towers, townys, and landys' for his property (line 13f), he evokes the image of a medieval town rather than of the Rome of antiquity. In this respect the speech is an instance of the well-known medieval anachronism. But with its stereotyped enumeration this anachronism differs in style as well as in content from the powerful images that are used as a vehicle for social criticism in the later bragging speeches. In the case of Augustus it seems to be unintentional, the equality of social conditions in ancient Rome and medieval Yorkshire is presupposed without question, there is thus no need to point it out and no possibility to exploit it for satiric purposes. This 'naïve' anachronism, however, is a necessary precondition for the later satiric one: it shares with its successor the belief that there is no essential difference between the world into which Christ was born and that in which the medieval actors and audience live together.

Before discussing the development hinted at here we must first recall to mind a feature which distinguishes the tyrants' bragging speech from the plebeian entry speech both in its dramaturgy and in its composition. While the entry speech can only introduce a scene, the bragging speech can stand by itself and form a scene of its own. A dramatist wishing to heighten the effect of a play can do this very easily by prefixing a bragging speech to it. In most cases he will fill up the scene with counsellors and messengers, but even they are not strictly *de rigueur*. Entry speech scenes, on the other hand, are possible only if the torturers or soldiers appearing in them can be employed in the following scene as well. We may assume, therefore, that the rise of the tyrants' speech in the later strata is largely due to the facility with which it can be attached to already existing plays. The fact that the Wakefield Master in his maturer plays prefers the plebeian entry speech may thus be taken as an indicator of his skill as a dramatist. Special problems arose when the bragging speech was prefixed to an already existing plebeian entry scene. We shall see that the York Realist and the Wakefield Master solved these problems in rather different and in each case highly characteristic ways.

But before such problems of dramatic composition can be discussed, we must find some plays which demonstrably had a bragging speech scene either added to them or revised. Such plays, which can tell us something about the development of dramatic style and of scenic composition, do in fact exist, and some of them can even be dated with some accuracy. First we shall discuss a group of scenes in which the genetic relationships are so clear that we can trace the evolution of dramatic form almost step by step. Insights gained in the analysis of these scenes will help us in the placing of those speeches where we have to rely solely on internal criteria. The group referred to is constituted by Y XVI (Beadle's numbering) and T XIV, i.e. by plays dramatizing the encounter between Herod and the Magi. The relations between these plays have been thoroughly studied by Mendal G. Frampton.[94] In the manuscript of the York register the Magi Play appears as two plays and is so printed by L. T. Smith (as Nos. XVI and XVII).[95] Beadle has re-united them as No. XVI. According to him the play became the joint responsibilty of the Goldsmiths and the Masons in 1432–3. 'At or soon after this time an additional Herod "scene" was composed for the Masons and placed at the beginning of the play.'[96]

T XIV, which the majority of experts regard not as the original York play but as a revision of it, is seen by many as having originated in the second decade of the fifteenth century.[97] Herod's bragging speech in T XIV shows a metrical peculiarity which may allow a few inferences – however cautious – concerning the composition of the play: the first few stanzas exhibit *concatenatio*, a metrical device which was popular in York[98] but is not to be found in the non-York parts of Towneley. This metrical ornament repeats the last few words of a stanza at the beginning of the following one. In T XIV *concatenatio* stops the moment Herod turns to *Nuntius*, the very character who seems to have been absent from the original York version of the play. This may suggest that the scenic embedding of the bragging speech, as we find it in the manuscript, took place after the play had been borrowed by Towneley.

We may conclude, therefore, that T XIV and Y XVI represent revisions of an earlier bragging speech, traces of which are still visible. But such revised speeches are also to be found in a number of Towneley plays where they are not required by the plot. These plays cannot be attributed to a common origin: Two of them – T XX (*Conspiracio (et Capcio)*) and T XXII (*Flagellacio*) – go in part back to York originals, while the origin of T XXIV (*Processus Talentorum*) is as contested as its high dramatic art is universally admired.[99] Another play showing an 'unmotivated' bragging speech is T XXIII (*Processus Crucis*). In all of these four plays we can recognize the hand of the Wakefield Master. In T XX and T XXIV the introductory bragging speeches are written in his stanza and may thus be attributed to him even though they do not show the elasticity of his complete plays.[100] In the case of T XXII and XXIII his authorship of the introductory speeches is less unambiguous.[101] The metrical similarities are not conclusive, although both plays do exhibit his stanza in other parts.

The second and the third decades of the fifteenth century saw a rapid development of the York cycle. From local documents we know that the most important reason for the appearance of new plays and the disappearance of old ones was the economic fortune of the gilds concerned. When a play was divided between two guilds the two parts could be brought to the appropriate length with the help of a tyrant's speech. Or, several less prosperous guilds joined forces:[102] a bragging speech was then a suitable and effective beginning. Since the insertion of the bragging was often due to such obviously practical motives it would be foolhardy to assume a conscious artistic principle behind every one of these speeches. But practical necessity gave birth to a treasure of dramatically effective conventions on which the great dramatists of the period, the York Realist and the Wakefield Master, were able to build and without which they would have been unable to reach the heights of their art. In order to assess and understand their achievement it is thus necessary to discuss these conventions beforehand. This discussion will show that both cycles developed different conventions which were then perfected by those two great dramatists.

Peculiarities of Towneley

On the whole, the Towneley cycle preserves more archaic speech forms. It treats the integration of the prefixed scenes into the following action with characteristic carelessness. The bragging speech remains a closed episode which, being closed, does not lay any claim to dramatic illusion. Throughout the cycle we find the tyrants hinting that they will be present only for a short while.[103] Often the tyrant suggests that people 'here' do not yet know him. This, too, is a reflex of the real extra-dramatic situation, in which the English spectators relegate the tyrant's Jewish or Roman subjects to the background.[104] Whether the ruler appears as the biblical enemy of Christ or as a medieval feudal magnate,[105] his presence is an occasion for histrionic enjoyment. In one of the later plays, however, the relationship between time-represented and time-of-acting is considered worthy of comment, which presumably suggests that it is becoming problematical:

> ffor I am he that may / make or mar a man;
> My self if I it say / as men of cowrte *now* can.
> (T XX, 19f, emphasis added)[106]

What these entering speeches gain in contemporary relevance is of course accompanied by a corresponding loss: their connection with the ensuing play is scanty at best. Nothing happens in these speeches or even scenes that could be regarded as antecedent to the following action. The elaboration of the tyrant's opening speech thus creates a gap which might well be dangerous within the conventions of the illusionist theatre. The gap tends even to be emphasized optically and scenically: when the tyrant has stopped ranting, the action at his *sedes* is interrupted for the time being. The attention of the audience turns to another part of the stage, and the occupants of that part will gradually have to take the action back to the tyrant's *sedes*. But the Towneley playwright(s) do not seem to have regarded these gaps as aesthetically dangerous. Ironically, it is probably the earliest of the plays under discussion that shows at least an attempt to bridge the gap: in T XIV Herod sends his *Nuncius* to look for potential adversaries.[107] In this way the encounter between the messenger and the Three Magi is being prepared for. The Passion plays aim at quite another sort of nexus. The mighty potentate, who, by vaunting his own strength and beauty, demonstrates his vain confidence in earthly goods and thus shows himself to be an enemy of God, has been turned into a petty provincial tyrant whose speeches reveal the injustices of contemporary society, thus making Jesus a victim of those social forces under which the spectators had to suffer in their everyday lives:[108]

> ffor I am he that may / make or mar a man;
> My self if I it say / as men of cowrte now can;
> Supporte a man to day / to-morn agans hym than,
> On both parties thus I play / And fenys me to ordan
>   The right. (T XX, 19–23)

What is new about this passage is not that biblical and contemporary reality become one, but that the unintentional anachronism of the earlier speeches has been turned into a highly intentional and conscious one. Christ has been turned into the 'common man', and his sufferings can be experienced with maximum intensity if they are situated in the world of his worshippers. And this 'world' does not consist merely of the horrid details of physical suffering, as they are depicted in Pseudo-Bonaventura's mystical meditations,[109] it includes the whole system of social dependence, of unfeeling torturers and fraudulent office-holders.[110] This creates an intricate double-bottomed interplay between the contemporary and the biblical world which, while relying on the 'naïve' anachronism of earlier plays, goes far beyond it aesthetically.

In the monologue which precedes the Torturers' scene of T XXII written in Wakefield stanzas and which may thus be assumed to be later than the work of the Wakefield Master,[111] Pilate introduces himself as a virtuoso deceiver:

> I am full of sotelty,
> ffalshed, gyll, and trechery;
> Therfor am I namyd by clergy
>   As mali actoris.
>
> I shall fownde to be his freynd vtward, in certayn,
>   And shew hym fare cowntenance and wordys of vanyte;
> Bot of this day at nyght on crosse shall he be slayn,
>   Thus agans hym in my hart I bere great enmyte
>   ffull sore.   (T XXII, 10–13, 31–5)[112]

It is probably no coincidence that Pilate should here call himself the friend of those 'backbiters' (line 36) who anticipate the later Vice in many of the early plays.[113] At the same time, Pilate functions as a sort of 'Presenter', a diabolical producer who directs this particular act of the cosmic drama and is as much above it as God is above the drama as a whole. The *Tortores* who appear after his speech – a typical trio in the popular Towneley tradition – are not merely Pilate's accomplices in his struggle against Jesus. In their capacity as actors they are also his underlings who have to amuse the audience at his command:

> Therfor shall he suffre mekill myschefe,
>   And all the dyscypyls that vnto him drawes;
> ffor ouer all solace to me it is most lefe,
>   The shedyng of cristen bloode, and all that Iury knawes
>   I say you.
> My knyghtys full swythe
> Thare strengthes will thay kyth,
> And bryng hym be-lyfe;
>   lo, where thay com now!   (T XXII, 44–52)

Contributing thus to the amusement of the crowd, Pilate creates a peculiar solidarity between himself and the public which gives a new colouring to his earlier words which at first seemed to serve above all the purpose of satire and social criticism. It was probably not for nothing that Pilate said:

> *ye men* that vse back-bytyngys,
> and rasars of slanderyngys,
> ye ar my dere darlyngys,
>   and mahowns for euermore.   (T XXII, 36–9, emphasis added)

This speech seems to say: basically you are all 'backbiters' and 'slanderers', 'fals endytars, / Questgangars and Iurars' (lines 23f). The audience are now confronted with a new experience: earlier tyrants had berated them as Christian dogs or as opponents of 'Mahowne'; now, instead of being attacked for their virtues, they are being praised for their vices. This is a double-bottomed game which they may enjoy with the *actor*, with whom they are presumably united in their rejection of social evils, but this enjoyment is diminished by the feeling that they are also united with the *dramatis persona* in practising those evils.

The new relationship to the audience is characterized above all by the fact that these opening speeches no longer merely describe the tyrant's character, but at the same time play on the audience's expected reactions. A simple example is T XXIII, the opening speech of which, spoken by Pilate (lines 1–28), is a metrically heterogeneous, probably late addition. Here, the self-presentation of the hero is no longer the main element, description and demand are no longer as neatly separated as in York, in quantitative terms they fall back behind the threats:

> Peasse I byd euereich Wight!
>   Stand as styll as stone in Wall,
> Whyls ye ar present in my sight,
>   That none of you clatter ne call;
> ffor if ye do, youre dede is dight,
>   I warne it you both greatt and small,
> With this brand burnyshyd so bright,
>   Therfor in peasse loke ye be all.
>
> What! peasse in the dwillys name!
>   harlottys and dustardys all bedene!
> On galus ye be maide full tame,
>   Thefys and mychers keyn!   [pilferers
> will ye not peasse when I bid you?
>   by mahownys blode, if ye me teyn,
> I shall ordan sone for you,
>   paynes that neuer ere was seyn,
>   And that anone!   (T XXIII, 1–17)

The new quality of these lines is not in their content but in the handling of dramatic speech: not the mere fact that Pilate is threatening, but the manner in which he does it. Most interesting of all is the first word of the second stanza. Pilate, who just before has pointed to his sword, interrupts himself with an exclamation which at the same time is a rhetorical question. The audience, we must assume, has not sufficiently heeded Pilate's first demand for 'peasse', and the question is a reaction to this sign of disobedience. The following curses give an impression of the violence of the tyrant's reaction and add force to his demand. Since the first demand for 'peasse' (line 1) is not followed by such curses, lines 9ff create an effect of variation and climax. In a similar way, the threats of lines 14–17 are connected with the question of line 13. The repetition of the demand for 'peasse' does thus not become monotonous, but contributes even to the aesthetic organization of the speech, while at the same time creating, on the psychological level, the impression of spontaneous ranting. As we shall see,[114] this represents a marked contrast to the corresponding speeches in York. There, we shall find a rhetorical pattern which is independent of such factors as person and situation: demand, reasons given for the demand by means of self-presentation, renewal of demand. Here, in Towneley, the organizing principle of the speech is given by the intentions which the speaker wants to realize in a given situation. Self-presentation (a fundamentally static activity) takes second rank in comparison with the interaction with the audience. Pilate no longer states what kind of person he is, he makes the audience infer his character from his behaviour. Character is no longer conceived of as something static and independent of the situation, it exists exclusively in its symptoms and manifestations.

It is these formal features which make Pilate's speech in T XXIII a representative example of the audience-address in the late Towneley plays: its apparent lack of rhetorically preconceived *dispositio*, its integration with situation and character. Again it is the Wakefield Master who demonstrates this technique of characterization-through-style-of-speech at its best. This becomes particularly clear when he has several characters address the audience in sequence. The finest example is probably the *Prima Pastorum*, in which the strongly conceptual, antithetical style of the First Shepherd is set off against the lively, associative manner of the Second.[115]

This lively speech-style, which is rooted in the mood of the speaker and interacts with the partner, is by no means confined to the audience-address. It does however create a special effect there, because the histrionic interplay between dramatic characters becomes one between character/actor and audience; it is thus combined with the interplay between the two spheres. In these audience-addresses the public are not simply informed: they have to interpret the speaker's utterances pretty much like those of a real interlocutor and even react to them.

In some plays the public are required to cooperate even more. In T II (*Mactacio Abel*) and T XVI (*Magnus Herodes*) there is not only no self-presentation of the main characters, but what is more, the servants announcing them give a partly misleading picture of them. Cain is described by his boy as *A good yoman* (T II, 15), whereas the rest of the play will reveal him as a type of the tight-fisted farmer. The picture of Herod which is presented by his *Nuntius* is even further removed from the truth. The latter describes his master as 'the heynd kyng,... Gracyus you gretyng' (T XVI, 10–13) who is offering *grith* to his people (line 4) – provided only they keep quiet. As in the Cain play, this introduction is soon given the lie by Herod's own appearance (lines 80ff). The servants' introductory speeches in these plays may thus be said to function similarly to the self-introductions in the plays treated previously: they are not to be taken as valid information but as conscious misrepresentation, they are thus to be understood as 'in character' by the audience.

In these plays the introductory speech has attained a stage which can be compared to that reached by the aside: even those pieces of information which are directed *expressis verbis* to the audience must not be taken at their face value. In such a situation the 'play' character of the performance will largely supersede the objective validity of the presentation. The function of the audience-address in these plays differs radically from that in the Joseph plays: there, an everyday character served to reduce the distance between the miraculousness of the story and the everyday world of the audience; here, the audience is invited to criticize, i.e. to gain distance from, the stage characters out of its own experience. Once more, the Wakefield Master uses traditional characters and speech-forms for his social criticism. But he remains much closer to the dramaturgical conventions of the bragging introductory speech than does the York Realist, to whom we now turn.

Peculiarities of York

Originally, the dramaturgic conventions in York must have been similar to those observed in Towneley; a play like the *Tres reges* mentioned by Burton cannot have been too different from the Towneley *Oblacio Magorum* (T XIV). As was demonstrated above (p. 134, and note 97), a *Nuntius* must initially have been missing from both plays. Thus we may assume that the original York play, like the preserved Towneley one, began with a bragging speech which presumably was relatively unconnected with the rest of the play. Consequently, the messenger who appears in the preserved versions of the York play of Herod and the Magi (Y XVI in Beadle's edition) fulfils different functions from his Towneley counterpart. We do not watch Herod sending him out. Instead, he enters near the end of a dialogued court scene and announces the coming of the Three Kings. The 'scenic gap' so characteristic of Towneley is thus avoided in York. Y XVI shows the Magi only at the moment of arrival, not during the entire phase of their approaching. Herod's bragging speech itself passes over into dialogue and thus avoids isolation from the following scene. After extensive self-glorification Herod addresses his soldiers:

> How thynke ʒe þer [= these] tales þat I talde?   (Y XVI, 21).

The bragging speech, which thus becomes a court scene, anticipates in its 'Trauerspielelemente'[116] those formal features which were to distinguish the tragedies and histories of the sixteenth century. Although the speeches of the Renaissance plays are unmistakably patterned on the classical model, it is nevertheless conceivable that indigenous models were also influential. This is the more likely since the opening scenes of the Renaissance plays share one important feature with those of the York Realist: they are 'monologues', not 'soliloquies':[117] the speakers do not give the impression of talking to themselves, they are clearly giving forth information which is meant for listeners (i.e. the public), factual exposition remains independent of 'mood exposition', to which it is usually subordinate in Seneca.[118] The endeavour to remove the opening speech 'from the apron' (von der Rampe zu lösen) is thus earlier than the influence of Seneca. It appears already in the mystery play – and what is more, it appears in a form which is closer to the Renaissance drama than the morality which at first may appear as its direct predecessor.

The two features which anticipate in York the 'classical' unity of space – the immediate appearance of those characters who are needed for the scene following the tyrant's speech and the tyrant's turning to his courtiers – return so routinely in the late alliterating plays and reveal such dramatic skill that we may assume them to be inventions of the York Realist[119] or perhaps the 'realistic school' of York. But more important than the question of authorship is the stylistic tendency which becomes apparent in such conventions. Clearly, York aimed at an effect which is much nearer to the illusionist theatre than Towneley's play on the two spheres. But what is gained in terms of a closed play-sphere, is bought by a loss of scenic effect. The spectators cannot interact with the characters to the same extent as in Towneley. The change in the relationship with the audience also appears in the language. In the York Herod's speech there is not a single word that could be described as conditioned by the speaker's situation, and there is no explicit address to the audience. Correspondingly, there is no allusion to contemporary conditions. The entire speech is nothing but an amplification of the descriptive element. *Descriptio* is of course bound to occur in all opening speeches, but only in York is it allowed to throng out all other rhetorical strategies. The author's intentions become apparent in the astronomical bombast of the speech, which may even be influenced by the *miles gloriosus*[120] and which is meant to produce the appearance of learning, while in reality it reveals deplorable gaps of knowledge:[121] the dramatist wants to impress his audience with a multitude of meaningless words. But with this tactic he foregoes the possibility of *dramatic* effectiveness. Abandoning the popular acting conventions of the pageant stage, the medieval drama was bound to be petrified in bombast. But what needs to be emphasized is that this petrification, which at the same time was an impoverishment of the religious *and* the social meaning of the plays, was an end- and by-product of learned and clerical influences.[122]

This development towards the bombastic is, however, not an isolated case. About a decade before Herod's speech in Y XVI was probably written (1422–32) there was a remarkable dramatist writing in York who gave to the cycle a number of impressive plays.[123] But his dramaturgical principles led away from the popular playing conventions which had arisen with the pageant stage and the theatre in the round. He, too, opened most of his plays with a bragging speech, but the unforced fluctuation between the two spheres was replaced by a somewhat pedantic sequentiality, in which the tyrant first absolved his raging rather like an operatic 'number', before he began the action proper of the play by turning to the other *dramatis personae*. In each of these speeches one can point exactly to the moment at which the tyrant begins to speak to those who are with him in the dramatic world. In consequence of this neat separation of the two worlds, the bragging speech itself changes its character and becomes different from the traditional audience-address. The speech of Pilate in Y XXX ('Christ before Pilate') may serve as an example. Like those in other plays, this tyrant threatens his audience to be quiet. But the way in which he lends force to his threats is entirely different. He does not describe himself as a corrupt contemporary official, but as the legendary Pontius Pilate, the son of Caesar and Pila, the grandson of Atus. His life and his career are not placed in a neutral time which the audience may identify with their own present, but he describes himself explicitly as the former governor of the province of Pontus (line 20) and as the present Judge of the Jews (lines 21–4).

There is hardly room here for anachronism and social criticism, and they are rare in the other plays of the Realist as well. To do him justice, however, one should not pass without mention a passage of considerable histrionic interest in Y XXIX ('Christ before Annas and Caiaphas') in which Caiaphas reveals his own corruption by imitating an unfair trial in tone of voice, choice of words and presumably gesture:

> What wyte so will oght with me
>   Full frendly in feyth am I foune;
> Come of, do tyte late me see
>   Howe graciously I shall graunte hym his bone. (Y XXIX, 10–13)

Here, an effect is achieved which is familiar from other bragging speeches: The audience is allowed to feel superior to the villain who has revealed his true character. But the means by which this effect is achieved are thoroughly unconventional: the objective value judgment does not come from the villain's own mouth, it has to be inferred by the audience from his behaviour. The invitation to see through the braggart is thus made indirectly, by purely stylistic means.

But this scene is an exception. Everywhere else in the Realist's plays social criticism takes second place to putting the audience in the historical context of the staged events. The apparently cynical frankness of other villains is also missing: powerful and threatening as the Realist's potentates are, they all resemble Caiaphas in not making the criteria for their moral evaluation explicit. The stylistic consequence of this is that one feature of the older bragging speech becomes now dominant to the exclusion of others: self-glorification. The descriptive element which we found so exuberant in the play of Herod and the Magi (Y XVI) dominates the speeches of the tyrants in the cycle's Passion plays as well and submerges other language functions such as the appellative. The effect of this can be studied in the structure of the speeches and in the relationship to the audience which they establish. This can best be exemplified from the demand for *Peasse!* Although it is still fulfilling its theatrical task, it has at the same time become a peg on which to hang any number of descriptive details. In spite of local exaggerations and the wildness which they suggest, the structure of these speeches is surprisingly clear. When the tyrant praises himself, this appears as a reason for demanding 'Peasse!'; on occasions self-glorification is followed by a renewed demand for 'Peasse' which is then introduced by a causative 'therefore'.[124] The speeches are thus patterned according to an argumentative schema similar to those which we shall find in many later monologues. They go beyond the monologue in that they openly address the audience, but their structure reveals that it has only a very passive rôle to play. It is not, as it was in Towneley, a potentially reacting partner whose behaviour the actor has to reckon with but which he can also manipulate by his acting.

Much of what is lost here in interaction between players and spectators is compensated for by a rich dialogic to-and-fro within the dramatic world. The bragging speeches in York are never isolated from the rest of the play (as they so often are in Towneley), but are always embedded in lively little scenes. A rich imagination and a sure eye for typical detail enable the York Realist to transform processes into scenic events which in the narrative sources (especially the *Northern Passion* and the *Gospel of Nicodemus*) were represented only by a single verb.[125]

But if you embed a bragging speech into a scene, you also have to create an ending for that scene. Three of these scenes are ended by the protagonist's going to bed. The York Realist was certainly not the first to end a tyrant's scene in this way,[126] but no other medieval English dramatist has used this device with greater skill. The N-Town Herod for instance abruptly ends the discussion about Jesus which he had with his *milites* by saying that he needs rest;[127] in contrast to this, the characters of the York Realist first take a few drinks, which offers an opportunity for creating a convivial atmosphere and differentiated relationships between characters[128] and causes the ensuing sleepiness in a most natural way. The ending of the scene, which is necessitated by the story, is thus given intra-dramatic plausibility.

The structure of the following scenes, in which the action proper begins, also shows a new type of composition. The 'gaps' in the nexus of events, which we observed in many Towneley plays, are removed by the York Realist – again by foregoing the use of popular elements. Instead of the descriptive speeches with which the *milites* of the Towneley cycle accompany their entry, we now find short dialogues at the palace gate and short reports which give rise to renewed conversation between the potentates. The stage business can thus remain where it began with the bragging speech. Even the potentates' desire for rest which had ended the previous scenes is causally connected with the following dialogue which the arriving *milites* occasion by their request for permission to enter; for the palace guard are of course less than willing to disturb their master's sleep (Y XXX, 236ff; XXXI, 59ff). With his 'predilection for discussion and argument among his characters'[129] the York Realist creates a density of causal nexus which is probably unsurpassed in the drama of medieval England. At the same time, however, he turns into intra-dramatic comedy scenes what in Towneley are anti-processions studded with folk-play elements.

The price which has to be paid for the virtuoso quality of this type of scenic composition is considerable: the Torturers, who entered presumably from behind the audience asking for 'room!' and who forced the audience into a highly complex identification, which in its mixture of humour and horror was highly effective cathartically,[130] are replaced by comedy types who have withdrawn into an aesthetically closed world and have lost all direct contact with the audience.

The York Realist is continuing a tradition which can be observed in other speech-types and in plays which have not been ascribed to him: the original bipolarism of *locus* and *platea* and the interplay between audience and *dramatis personae* is reduced in favour of a more 'verbal' dramaturgy.

The audience-address in the N-Town cycle

Changing speaker perspective in the 'Proclamation thirteeners' and short octaves

The heterogeneity which this cycle betrayed in its treatment of space can also be observed with respect to the audience-address. The differences here are perhaps not quite as apparent, though; in particular there are similarities between the Old Testament plays in short octaves and those in thirteen-line stanzas. Nevertheless, the basic situation is the same here as it was before: instead of the continuous development of forms which were popular in one place and which therefore allow us to recognize a unifying principle behind the differences, we encounter radically disparate formal conventions which presumably were joined together only in the third quarter of the fifteenth century.[131] Therefore, we cannot, in this cycle, speak of the predominance, e.g., of the closed or open play-world, of the 'edificational' or 'histrionic' audience-address. We shall have to accept the fact that both types of play exist side by side.

The Old Testament plays which are written in the two basic metres,[132] are still characterized by a changing speaker's perspective. This may give credit to the opinion that these are the oldest parts of the cycle.[133] Noah, Abraham, and Moses begin their plays with self-introductory prayers, just as they do in York and Towneley. The self-introduction of the Prophets and Kings in LC VII clearly resembles that of the Towneley *Processus Prophetarum*. Moses' point of view fluctuates in the by now familiar way: at first Moses speaks about God in the third person (LC VI, 1–4, p. 51), then he addresses Him. Self-introduction proper follows only in this direct prayer. The illusion that the speaker is alone with God in his prayer is given even less room in this play than in other cycles. For Moses, who apparently is the only character on stage, speaks continuously in the plural: he includes the audience in his prayer:

> I am Moyses þat make þis bone
> I pray þe lord god with all my mende
> to us incline þi mercy sone
> þi gracyous lordchep let us fynde. (LC VI, 5–8, p. 51)

He explains, as it were, to the audience that he is praying for them. His prayer is of so general a character that it does not with a single word relate to the dramatic situation. This, however, is exceptional and is to be explained by the special nature of this *Moses* play, which merely serves as an induction to the following *Prophets* play.[134] Moses is – as are the Prophets and Kings – conceived of as a 'statue-like' person.[135] A dramatic situation out of which he might appear to be speaking is barely hinted at in the beginning, in the further course of the speech it vanishes altogether.

Noah and Abraham clearly set off their prayers against their self-introduction. In this they are in marked contrast to Moses and the characters of the *Radix Jesse* play, as well as to their counterparts in other cycles.[136] The fluctuation between addressing God and speaking about God, which is the norm elsewhere, does not exist here. This betrays a formal, distanced attitude toward the audience which is also characteristic of the later strata of the cycle. When the characters turn toward the audience they do not merely actualize what is always latently present, but they assume a position which contrasts with the previous one. The patriarchs no longer naïvely tell the audience their previous history, as for instance the York Noah did (Y IX, 15ff), they solemnly inform them about their theological significance. Noah says that with him the second age begins (LC IV, 14ff, p. 35), Abraham describes himself as a 'patriarch' (LC V, 10, p. 43). On top of that they introduce their families who are present with them on the stage:

> my wyff and my chyldere here on rowe   (LC IV, 11, p. 35)
>
> Ysaac lo here his name is tolde
> My swete sone þat stondyth me by.   (LC V, 13f, p. 43)

The pointing gesture which they employ in these speeches and the ceremoniously descriptive manner of speaking with which they refer to their own praying (IV, 12; V, 5f, 17) give to these plays a measured solemnity which is lacking in York and Towneley. In the N-Town cycle the characters do not draw the audience into their confidence; they function rather, as we may say with some slight exaggeration, as their own *Expositores*. This can be seen above all in the strongly theologizing posture which they assume toward their own rôles, but also in the neat separation of prayer and self-presentation. Addressing the audience from 'within the play' does, therefore, not result in an approximation between audience-world and play-world, but rather in an increased distance.

Apparently this distancing was not a product of mere chance, but was an effect which the dramatists worked for. Perhaps it was even meant to underline the dignity of the patriarchs. This conclusion is forced upon us when we observe that they do not take leave of the audience with the brief friendly blessings which are customary in York. The *Noah* and the

Abraham plays are concluded – as are most of the other plays – by thanksgiving prayers or songs which do not refer to the audience at all. The religious ceremonial which in the liturgical drama waived the separation of audience and *dramatis personae* has practically inverted its function. Though its nature requires not spectators but participants, it is produced by actors on the stage. Consequently it transfers the events of the play into a closed sphere which ignores the spectator, who can now only view it from without. It has become a show.

The plays in short octaves[137] often end with the *dramatis personae* calling God's blessing upon the audience. Frequently this is accompanied by a marked change of tone and perspective. Moses for instance, when expounding the Ten Commandments, uses 'man' and 'þou' to address his audience. In the closing stanza he changes to 'frendys' and 'ȝe' (LC VI, 187ff):

> Fare well gode frendys for hens wyll I wende
> my tale I haue taught ȝow my wey now I goo. (LC VI, 193f)

On two occasions at least the play that is about to close is explicitly referred to. The *Prophets* or *Radix Jesse* play ends with a stanza spoken by King Amon:

> Thus we all of *þis genealogye*
> Accordynge in on here in þis place
> Pray þat heyȝ lorde whan þat we xal dye
> Of his gret goodnesse to grawnt us his grace.
> (LC VII, 131ff, p. 62, emphasis added)

And the disputation between Christ and the Doctors is called 'þis pagent' by Primus Doctor:

> all þat hath herd þis consummacion
> of þis pagent ȝour grace þem saue. (LC XXI, 287f, p. 187)

More ambiguous is the opening of the play-sphere in the 'Nativity' (LC XV) and 'The Raising of Lazarus' (LC XXV). In the 'Nativity' the midwife Zelomye bids farewell with a phrase which in the context must refer to Mary and Joseph but which is usually applied to the audience:

> And I Also do take my leve here
> Of all *þis blyssyd god company*. (LC XV, 313f, p. 145, emphasis added)

Similarly ambivalent is the end of the 'Lazarus'. Here, too, the context is clearly that of Christ's coming Passion, but the expression used by Jesus obliterates the distinction between First-World and Second-World beholders:

> Now I haue shewyd *in opyn syght*
> of my godhed þe gret glorye
> to-ward my passyon I wyl me dyght.
> (LC XXV, 449ff, pp. 224f, emphasis added)

In 'The Woman Taken in Adultery' Jesus himself addresses the audience directly. But in doing so he assumes the point of view of the actor representing him:

> Now god þat dyed ffor all mankende
> saue all þese pepyl both nyght and day
> and of *oure* synnys *he us* vnbynde
> hyʒe lorde of hevyn þat best may.
> (LC XXIV, 293–6, p. 209, emphases added)

In the plays written in 'Proclamation thirteeners'[138] this opening of the play-sphere towards the audience at the end is extremely rare. It occurs only in the play of John the Baptist (LC, pp. 188ff). But with John audience-address is a conventional feature which is also traceable in all other plays that have come down to us (Y XXI, T XIX).[139]

The open play-sphere, which in York and Towneley was a pervasive feature, is in N-Town almost limited to a metrically well-defined part of the cycle. This fact should support those who, like Greg and Spector, believe that metrical differences also point to different origins.

The farewells and blessings are of interest to the historian of dramatic form because they enable us to characterize strata within the cycle. But their significance as 'index fossils' must not allow us to forget the fact that the majority of the plays are governed by a principle which is diametrically opposed to direct audience-address. Most of them conclude not with a good-neighbourly opening toward the audience but with extensive, liturgical-solemn prayers, which, being prayers, point beyond the immediate events of the play but whose aesthetic function is to remain within the play-sphere. They thus contribute to that distance between audience and play which distinguishes the N-Town cycle from all others.

The 'histrionic' audience-address in LC XIV, with a digression on the early history of the Vice

It is in accordance with this serious tone, which keeps the spectators at a distance, that the 'histrionic' type of the audience-address occurs only very occasionally in the N-Town cycle. The few speeches that are at all subsumable under this heading deviate in important particulars from the corresponding speeches in other cycles.

If we neglect the almost obligatory audience-addresses like the 'Old Man's Lament' by Joseph believing himself to be cuckolded by Mary (LC XII, 49ff, p. 110), the purest representative of the type is to be found in LC XIV ('The Trial of Joseph and Mary', pp. 124ff), a play in short octaves whose coarse humour gives it a position apart.[140] Nevertheless, the integration of the play into the cycle can be determined at least relatively: since the description of the play in the *Proclamation* (p. 6, lines 183–6) is in a stanza different from the rest, we may assume that this play is later than most others. On the other hand it must have entered the cycle before the 'Mary Play', many parts of which (LC VIII, IX and XIII) are not mentioned in the *Proclamation* at all. Our own observations concerning the treatment of space suggest that the play belongs with LC XXI ('Christ and the Doctors'), XXIV ('The Woman taken in Adultery'), XXV ('Lazarus'). With these and other plays (mainly in short octaves) it shares the property of being headed by a Latin title. The wording of the title, however, is peculiar to this one play: 'Hic intrabit pagetum de purgacione Marie et Joseph ·' (p. 124). A further distinction of the play is a comic prologue spoken by a summoner who is called Den in the speech headings but is addressed as 'Sym somnore' by the Bishop (line 105, p. 127). Of this prologue more anon.

Having approximately determined the pageant's position in the cycle, it remains for us to define its formal qualities. The audience-address will lead to rather surprising results in this respect. A lengthy quotation may first give a general idea of the style of these speeches:

> PRIMUS DETRACTOR
> A A · serys god saue ȝow all
> here is a fayr pepyl in good ffray
> Good serys telle me what men me calle
> I trowe ȝe kan not be þis day
> ȝitt I walke wyde and many way
> but ȝet þer I come I do no good
> to reyse slawdyr is al my lay
> bakbytere is my brother of blood....
> Now be my trewth I haue a syght
> Evyn of my brother lo where he is
> Welcom dere brother my trowth I plyght
> ȝowre jentyl mowth let me now kys.
> SECUNDUS DETRACTOR
> Gramercy brother so haue I blys
> I am ful glad we met þis day.
> 1ᵘˢ DETRACTOR
> Ryght so am I brothyr i-wys
> mech gladdere than I kan say.
> but ȝitt good brother I ȝow pray
> telle all þese pepyl what is ȝour name. (LC XIV, 1–8, 17–26, p. 124)

The entrance speeches of the two *detractores* resemble to an astonishing extent those of the Vices of the later moralities: they begin by greeting the audience in a very familiar, suggestive style, they describe their own activities and goals, welcome each other as accomplices and are obviously pleased in mentioning their own telling names (Raiseslander, lines 7 and 33; Backbiter, lines 29f). Typical of this manner of speaking is above all the cat-and-mouse game with the audience, who are entertained by being teased (lines 3f). The two villains do not lose their awareness of acting in front of an audience even when they are together. Clearly, the audience-address in this case does not merely exist to inform the audience – that could be achieved more easily by a single speaker. Its main purpose is entertainment. The similarity with the speeches of the Vice, which was first observed by Spivack,[141] is the more astonishing as it is not confined to aspects of style. All the features which are characteristic of the Vice can be found here as well: the two detractors act without any motive, the intention to slander exists before a suitable victim is in sight. Their main desire is not to impress or frighten the public, their greatest delight seems to be to caricature themselves. From the devils they differ chiefly in being detractors rather than seducers. But their most important characteristic, which undoubtedly anticipates the Vice, is their amoral, non-serious speech-style, which reveals only one feeling: the virtuoso pride in their own doing, the destructive character of which is not felt.[142] It is often said of the medieval villains that they know that they are villains. That is not true of our present pair: their artistic function has become more important than their moral or homiletic one.

The entry speech of the Vice is to be encountered here in its pure form almost a hundred years before the word became a recognized term.[143] This discovery, however, does not mean that such a stageworthy figure went out of existence for almost 100 years before surfacing again. For the morality play *Mankind* (1465 × 70)[144] also shows the characteristic features of the Vice's speech fully developed.[145] There, however, this speech style is used by figures whose very names – Myscheff, Nought, New-guyse, Now-a-days – suggest their kinship with the personified abstractions of the traditional moralities; by themselves they thus do not disprove the thesis pronounced by Spivack (and before him by Eckhardt) that the Vice originated in the personified vices of the morality play. In LC XIV, on the other hand, we are clearly dealing with types rather than allegories. Contrary to received opinion,[146] the type thus appears to be older than the allegory, the virtuoso villain earlier than the vice conceived of in terms of moral theology.

But in matters of priority one should tread perhaps even more warily. The 'prototype' of the allegorizing morality play, *The Castle of Perseverance* (c. 1425),[147] which probably is even earlier than LC XIV, already shows a character who calls himself 'Backbiter', but whose name in the Latin stage directions is *Detractio* rather than *Detractor*. Type and abstraction are thus not distinguished in this earliest dramatic occurrence. *Detractio* is often classified as a subtype of envy and thus belongs in the context of the Seven Deadly Sins.[148] But the Backbiter of *The Castle*, like the *Detractores* of LC XIV, behaves rather differently from the major Sins. Admittedly, there is more pathos and less self-indulgent playfulness in his speech,[149] but here too we encounter that virtuoso element in which free comic play is sometimes more important than the theological message. Backbiter can even feel satisfaction at the misfortunes of his own companions. Having denigrated Gluttony, Sloth and Lechery with their leader, Flesh, he rejoices when they receive a hiding from the latter:

> Now, be God, þis is good game!
> I, Bakbyter, now bere me wel.
> If I had lost my name,
> I vow to God it were gret del.
> I schape þese schrewys to mekyl schame;
> Iche rappyth on oþyr wyth rowtynge rele.
> I, Bakbyter, with fals fame
> Do brekyn and brestyn hodys of stele. (*Castle*, lines 1,823–30)

This is not the place for a definitive statement concerning the origins of the Vice. But the early association of his speech style with the name of 'Backbiter' may at least be a pointer. The detractor is a figure which the sermon liked to use for satirical sallies and vivid, detailed character portraits.[150] The stage, however, invests these figures with an aesthetic autonomy which they cannot have in the sermon. They are too obviously pleased with themselves, they fail too miserably and too soon to cause that horror which they provoke in narrative and homiletic presentation.[151]

The aesthetic autonomy which the detractors have gained inside LC XIV is still surpassed by Den the Summoner's prologue, which was apparently prefaced to the play when it was included in the cycle.[152] Den flirts with the public already in the original play, treating it with obscene threats and apparently asking for money:

> Do me sum wurchep be-for my face
> or be my trowth I xal ȝow make
> If þat I rolle ȝow up in my race
> Ffor fere I xal do ȝour ars qwake.
> But ȝit sum mede *and* ȝe me take
> I wyl with-drawe my gret rough toth
> gold or sylvyr I wol not for-sake
> but evyn as all somnorys doth. (LC XIV, 121–8, pp. 127f)

The redactor who incorporated the play into the cycle resumed these motifs and expanded them into a prologue of thirty-two lines which addresses no fewer than thirty-four imaginary spectators in person:

> both Johan Jurdon and Geffrey Gyle
> Malkyn mylkedoke and fayr mabyle
> Stevyn sturdy and Jak at þe style
> and sawdyr sadelere.   (lines 9–12, p. 123)[153]

Here again we find the stylistic devices which are familiar from the 'histrionic' audience-address, but its cumulative and de-functionalized use suggests that the convention has become automatized: the singling out of addressees, which in Towneley was used for satirical purposes, has here been turned into one of those alliterative jingles which are so popular in later plays.[154] But more important than such quality judgment is the historical discovery: in the N-Town cycle the histrionic audience-address apparently is earlier than the edificational one, which appears only in those parts which were not included in the *Proclamation*.[155]

Other parts of N-Town

Speeches of tyrants and devils

In the other cycles the most usual form of histrionic audience-address is the tyrant's bragging speech. That speech-type is only minimally represented in the N-Town cycle. It is used only by the two Herods, who speak in those long alliterating lines which are generally considered to belong to the latest strata of the cycles (LC XVIII, 1ff, 69ff (pp. 151f, 153f) and LC XXIX, 1ff (pp. 271ff)). In LC XVIII ('Adoration of the Magi') we are, moreover, faced with implausible insertions which disturb the course of the play. This makes it probable that, in contrast to York, the bragging speeches in LC are not late representatives of a well-developed type, but that the type itself is extraneous to the original cycle.

The existing speeches differ from those of York and Towneley in important respects. The entry speech in LC XVIII preserves important topoi such as praise of the speaker's own power and beauty, but it does without the usual threats to the audience. The notions used in the self-glorification are more aristocratic than in other cycles. This Herod is apparently the only tyrant of medieval English drama whose horse (lines 2, 10, 17)[156] and palace (lines 14, 16) are specifically mentioned. Also his rich robes receive more emphasis than usual (lines 9, 12, esp. 70), whereas physical strength and violence play hardly any part at all. Only

Address to the audience

line 71 offers some of the picturesque detail that other cycles abound in. But even here N-Town is unique in evoking the world of chivalry, albeit in comparatively crude style:

> Dukys with dentys I dryve in to þe dych.

Chivalrous values are also evoked when Herod vaunts his *dowty dedys* (1. 72, similarly lines 7 and 15). Strangely enough, Herod does not introduce himself as an ally, but as an opponent of the Devil (line 9).

This will not be the last time that we encounter aristocratic features in the cycle. They show in the tone in which the characters communicate with each other, but also in the measured ceremonial of the audience-addresses of the 'Mary' and Passion plays.

This measured tone also characterizes the speech of Herod in 'Passion Play II'. Recalcitrant Christians, it is true, are threatened with death by hanging, but even this is done in the form of a matter-of-fact statement (line 11, p. 272). The conventional demand for silence is put into words which never allow the speaker's royal dignity to be forgotten:

> Now sees of ȝour talkyng · And gevyth lordly Audyence
> Not o word I charge ȝou þat ben here present
> noon so hardy to presume · in my hey presence
> to on-lose hese lyppys Ageyn myn intent. (lines 1–4)

These speeches have recourse neither to the social criticism of the Towneley cycle nor to the popular legend-telling of York. The Herod of the N-Town cycle is the only tyrant who is characterized not by general bragging but by specific crimes taken from the Bible (lines 17f). That he should emphasize his own cruelty is also unusual, though not unique:

> to se hem hangyn or brent · to me is very plesauns. (line 14)[157]

This objective attitude toward his own actions and feelings, which is quite different from the unthinking boastfulness of other tyrants, places the N-Town Herod in the neighbourhood of the personified vices of the moralities, which have been credited with an influence on LC.[158] But the similarity is too unspecific to allow us to assume such influence here. It can be explained equally well out of a tendency of the period which transferred homiletic modes of presenting evil into the drama.[159]

At the beginning of this section it was claimed that the N-Town cycle has not developed a specific speech-style for its tyrants. This claim can be corroborated by the similarities between the speeches of Herod and those of the devils in LC XXVI (pp. 225ff) and XXXI (p. 287).

Like the speeches of the Herods, those of the two devil figures lack any comic element. Like Herod they give their own actions that objective evaluation which is characteristic above all of the morality vices. The didactic element is most pronounced in the devil called 'Lucifer' in LC XXVI (p. 225), who says that he has come 'A matere to spelle' (line 4) and who introduces himself as 'Norshere of synne' (line 5).[160] Similarly objective warnings are to be found in the speech of 'Sathan' in LC XXXI (p. 287). Both give ample space to the telling of the preceding story. Nothing in their speeches resembles the comic self-complacency of the two *detractores* of LC XIV.

Contemplacio

From the point of view of audience-address, the most rewarding figure in the cycle is Contemplacio. It would be more correct to speak of two figures, since the parts of the cycle in which Contemplacio appears – the 'Mary Play' and Passion Play II' – are probably not of identical origin. As an extra-dramatic figure he remotely resembles the Chester Expositor, though his influence on the style of the cycle as a whole is less strong than that of his Chester counterpart. While Chester shows a tendency toward a closing of the play-sphere even in those plays in which the Expositor does not appear, the N-Town cycle does not show such a tendency even in the plays framed by Contemplacio's speeches.[161] One reason for this is presumably that within the *Contemplacio* group earlier plays have remained which were originally designed for the pageant stage. Understandably, those plays would retain the fluctuating speaker's perspective and the histrionic audience-address which are natural for such a stage and which we do find in LC X (p.83: Abysakar) and LC XII (p. 110: Joseph).

The overall character of the *Contemplacio* group (the 'Mary Play') is determined not so much by the use of different audience-addresses as by the ambiguities of Contemplacio himself. While the Chester Expositor was limited to narration and theological didaxis, Contemplacio must fulfil at least three functions: he introduces the plays, narrates events which are not represented on stage, and says a prayer before the beginning of the 'Parliament of Heaven' (LC XI, pp. 97ff). Of these three functions, the last is certainly the strangest, since here Contemplacio is addressing not the audience, but God. He is thus not bridging the gap between play-world and audience-world, but he merges these two worlds into one unit, acting as its speaker before God. The lack of separation between the two worlds is evidenced also by the fact that the prayer is a link in the progress of the action. Contemplacio prays that God assume human form to redeem humanity, which is precisely the outcome of the 'Parliament of Heaven'.[162] He thus creates a relationship between audience and action which resembles that of the liturgical plays rather than that of the vernacular drama. It is not the *dramatis personae* who step forth from the play-sphere to address the audience, but the audience which, represented by Contemplacio as the liturgical congregation was by the choir, takes part in the represented action. This makes Contemplacio's prayer in LC XI unique in the English religious drama, so that an eminent expert like W.W. Greg was led to call it 'a mere blunder on the part of the scribe or else a very clumsy piece of botching on that of the reviser'. But such a verdict hardly does justice to the playwright,[163] who was probably well aware that he placed this unusual prayer at a point which, from the Christian point of view, is decisive in the history of humanity. The proximity to the liturgical drama becomes even more marked if we assume, as many scholars do, that the *Contemplacio* group was meant for performance on St Anne's Day. The play would then refer to the represented events not only by way of dramatic mimesis, but also by virtue of being connected to a particular day of the Church year, which may after all be regarded as a reduced copy of the history of man's salvation. The play would then be literally a *re-praesentatio*, as the Mass is a repetition of the sacrifice of Christ.[164] By celebrating St Anne's Day, the congregation becomes, in a heortological sense, a contemporary of the saint, and it is perhaps appropriate that it should partake in the soteriological events of the saint's life.

There is yet another occasion on which Contemplacio resembles the liturgical choir more than the expositor or doctor of other vernacular dramas: after Joseph and Mary have set off to visit Elizabeth, their journey is bridged by a speech by Contemplacio,[165] just as the liturgical Apostles' Race was accompanied by the antiphon *Currebant duo*. What is remarkable about this episode is not that it is handed over to a narrator; that also happens in other cycles, notably Chester. What makes this scene different is that it is narrated *and* staged with Mary and Joseph remaining silent, just as Peter and John remained silent during their race to the Sepulchre. Contemplacio's speech, not unlike the antiphon, serves as a kind of 'background music' to the action.

The parallel, however, should not be pressed too far. An important characteristic of the liturgical choir was always that it addressed no-one except God. In contrast to this, Contemplacio makes explicit reference to the audience by addressing it as 'sovereynes' (line 23). The resemblances to the liturgical play-type should thus not be overestimated; taking the cycle as a whole, they are not too important. But that they should appear at all constitutes a remarkable exception in the English cycles that have come down to us.

Contemplacio's third function is the expository one which is familiar to us from Chester.[166] His tone, however, is quite different from that of his Chester counterpart. Where the latter was kind and perhaps a little condescending, Contemplacio is reverent and keeps his distance;[167] the use of the word 'sovereynes' (line 23) is an example of this. At the beginning he refers to the audience in the third person as 'this congregacion' (p. 62, line 1), and nothing in the rest of the play suggests any familiarity between speaker and audience. For all his reverence, he uses no formulae suggesting modesty which might make the audience more accessible to his words. When he speaks about the contents of the plays his attitude is that of a sober, detached reporter who has no wish to inculcate his audience with religious feelings. In so far as he does attempt to move his audience, he is not concerned with the religious content of the plays but exclusively with the actors' manner of presenting them.[168] This becomes particularly clear at the end of the group:

> Now most mekely we thank ȝou of ȝour pacyens
> and beseke ȝou of ȝour good supportacion
> If here hath be seyd ore done Any inconuenyens
> we Asygne it to ȝour good deliberacion
> Be-sekynge to crystys precious passyon
> conserve and rewarde ȝour hedyr comynge... (lines 29–34, p. 122)[169]

This is perhaps the first time in medieval English drama that the manner of presentation receives more attention than the subject-matter. The emphasis on externals corresponds with the style, whose Latinisms and whose obtrusive alliteration, which often results in diplology, suggest an unskilful variant of the aureate style. The alliteration often binds together unstressed Latin prefixes and colourless synonyms like 'sad and sure' (line 4, p. 62); often it is created merely by the adding of expletives, such as 'sentens to be seyd' (line 4, p. 62).[170] It is not for nothing that these speeches have been attributed to John Lydgate.[171]

A rather different tone is to be observed in Contemplacio's prologue to 'Passion Play II', which shows none of the frosty ornament and neutral attitude toward the events of the play which we have found in the 'Mary Play'. Instead, the speaker wants the audience to be moved by Christ's Passion:

> ...we be-seche ȝow þat ȝour wyllys be good
> to kepe þe passyon in ȝour mende þat xal be shewyd here.
> (lines 7f, p. 271)

When he renders the contents of the play he does not limit himself to the mere facts, but addresses himself to the emotions of the audience and emphasizes the soteriological importance of the Passion:

...mekely his deth to take
And how he made his mawnde · his body ʒevyng þan
to his Apostelys avyr with us · to A-bydyn for mannys sake.
(lines 10–12, p. 271)

These considerable differences add weight to Swenson's conjecture that this Contemplacio has nothing to do with that of the Marian plays.[172] 'Passion Play II' belongs to a different, much more unified type of play. With its actor–audience relationship it represents the same basic pattern as Chester, but it pursues different ends and therefore uses a different tone: here as there, the world of the play is closed, which is both framed and interpreted by the Expositor. But while the Chester Expositor imparts above all theological knowledge, the audience in 'Passion Play II' is humbly 'besought' (line 7, p. 271; see above) to assume a certain emotional attitude, namely that of meditative empathy.

'The Assumption of the Virgin'

In contrast to the Contemplacio of 'Passion Play II', the prologue of the 'Assumption' (LC XLI) shows considerable resemblance to the prologues and epilogues of LC VIII-XI, even if he is called Doctor and not Contemplacio. These similarities have led Greg to believe that the 'Assumption' is by the same author as the Contemplacio speeches.[173] Against this it might be said that Contemplacio is always anxious for a short, compressed presentation, which finds its expression in many almost stereotyped *brevitas* formulae.[174] The Doctor of the 'Assumption' on the other hand amplifies his statements by pedantically adding sources and calculations. But perhaps these differences should not be given too much weight, since they are brought about by means that were taught in almost any handbook of rhetoric or poetics and since the Doctor's speech follows the *Golden Legend* almost point by point.[175] It is perhaps more important to observe that the attitude to the subject-matter is throughout that of the Contemplacio of the Mary plays. In both cases the facts are reported in a dry *résumé*. The aim of the presentation is completeness of the sequence of events rather than the effect of single events on the pious mind. The prologue therefore uses 'serializing' devices such as parataxis, which is often supported by parallelism. All events are of equal importance since they are connected with the life of the saint; none has to be emphasized in particular; evaluative expressions are rare.[176] All this results in an evenly objective, didactic style which is ornamented merely by strongly Latinized diction and by occasional diplology such as *wrot and tauht* (line 3) – in this, too, resembling the Marian Contemplacio speeches.

The attitude to the audience also shows important resemblances. The spectators are addressed as 'Ryht worchepful souereynes' (line 1), whom it 'may please' (line 1) to hear about Mary's assumption; the Doctor concludes his prologue 'preyng you of audience' (line 26). The Doctor thus resembles Contemplacio in that he does not address the audience as simple believers who regard watching the play as a religious duty and as beneficial for the good of their souls, but as social superiors whose attention has to be begged rather than demanded.

This attitude does not appear elsewhere in the mystery cycles, although it is not unique in the religious drama of the English Middle Ages. In this respect, two of the Digby Plays, *Herod's Killing of the Children* and *The Conversion of Saint Paul*, are similar to this part of the N-Town cycle.[177] The speaker of the prologue of the *Conversion*, who is called 'Poeta', addresses his 'wyrshypfull audyens' with the words:

> Honorable frendys, besechyng yow of lycens
> To procede owur process, we may [shew] vnder your correccyon,
> the conuersyon of Seynt Paule, (lines 7–9)[178]

And he concludes with an expression of modesty which still surpasses that of Contemplacio:[179]

> Thys lytyll pagent thus conclud we
>   As we can, lackyng lytturall scyens,
> Besechyng yow all of hye and low degre,
>   Owur sympylnes to hold excusyd and lycens,
> That of retoryk haue non intellygens,
> Commyttyng yow all to owr Lord Jhesus,
> To whoys lawd ye syng: '*Exultet celum laudibus!*' (lines 656–62)

These protestations of inability return in the prologue of the *Killing of the Children*:

> We be comen hedere as seruauntes diligent,
>   Oure processe to shewe you, as we can.
> Wherfor, of benevolens we pray euery man
> To haue vs execused that we no better doo –
> An-other tyme to emende it if we can,
> Be the grace of God if our cunnyng be thertoo. (lines 19–24)

And similarly in the epilogue:

> Honorable souereignes, thus we conclude
>   Oure matere that we haue shewid here in your presens,
> And though our eloquens be but rude,
>   We beseche you alle, of youre paciens,
>   To pardon vs of oure offens,

Address to the audience

> For after þe sympylle cunnyng that we can,
> This matere we haue shewid to your audiens,
> In the worshippe of Oure Lady and hir moder Seynt Anne.
>
> (lines 551–8)

The intrusion of such modesty topoi into the religious drama is not merely an indication of the growing influence of rhetoric but also of the increasingly 'artistic' character of the plays – a feature that is shared by N-Town, some of the Digby Plays, and York.

8 Intra-dramatic speeches

The great importance which the relationship between play and audience has in the English mystery cycles must of necessity reduce the intra-dramatic relationships. The spectator views the situations which arise in the course of a play not with the eyes of those within the situation, since the bragging speeches, self-introductions and theological comments convey a perspective which is constant throughout the play. But even this rigid perspective, which is one of the most important causes of the 'two-dimensional' effect of medieval drama, cannot annihilate every relationship between people and situations within the drama. Rather, we shall see that – unlike the liturgical drama – the mystery plays do try to cope with these relationships and that the impression of *'naïveté'* which the medieval drama so often creates in its modern readers is largely due to the great care which the dramatists took to convey them.

Their verbalization is the subject of this chapter. We shall see that the form of the dramatic speeches is primarily determined by the extra-linguistic situation in which they are embedded. For this reason, these situations will be the *causa partitionis* of the following sections. If we order the speech-types which we can thus identify in an ascending order of complexity, we shall obtain first the 'revelation speech' in which God himself speaks without addressing anyone, second the 'opening prayer' in which the speaker addresses God at least rhetorically. These two speech-types have this in common with the audience-address: they can impose a certain point of view on the spectator. Other speech-types cannot do this; they offer more opportunities for expressing the subjective feelings of individual speakers. For that reason they will be represented by such speeches whose purpose it is to express emotions and interpersonal relationships, i.e. affect speeches and dialogues. The class of 'affect speeches' will be further limited to representations of sorrow and grief, i.e. to laments, since anger and rage have already been extensively discussed in the chapter on audience-addresses. (It is a significant feature of the cycles that anger and rage, to the extent that they are expressed in monologues, hardly appear outside the audience-address. It seems that these emotions systematically avoided forms that invited the audience to identify with the speaker.)

In the section on laments it will not be apposite to discriminate too carefully between monologue and dialogue. Since, on the other hand, a characteristic type of dialogue, which I shall call the 'serial' dialogue, is often used for laments, a certain amount of overlap cannot be avoided.

Revelation speeches

This term will be used for those speeches in which God or Christ 'reveal' their nature and deeds. Since this type is well represented in York and Towneley and shows a considerable variety of forms, the usual order of treatment of the cycles will be modified in this part of the chapter. Instead of beginning with Chester we shall open the chapter with York and Towneley, hoping that this will also enable us to put the phenomena occurring in Chester in better perspective. Chester has only two representatives of this speech-type, which formally are far apart from each other, and their place in the history of dramatic forms is probably best assessed against the background of York and Towneley.

Revelation speeches occur primarily in the plays dealing with the Creation, the Last Judgment and Christ's Harrowing of Hell. Their function is similar to that of the self-introductions and the planning monologues of human speakers. Yet they cannot be dismissed as simply a more solemn variant of these latter.

On a purely formal level they differ from self-introductions by the absence of any form of audience-address. Their speakers do not address anyone, and their words are not embedded in a situation out of which they might be said to grow. The speeches seem to be addressed to an audience which is too vast to be physically present. They differ also from the didactic speeches in that they make no attempt to adjust themselves to the understanding and feeling of the listeners: there are neither explanations nor homely comparisons, only assertions and causal arguments. The subject of these assertions remains identical over many sentences and even stanzas, so that every sentence must return to the point of departure of the previous one.[1] The result is that 'closed sound shape of a movement circling in itself with firm, closing cadence, an as it were "ritual" tone of voice' (geschlossene Klangform einer in sich selbst kreisenden Bewegung mit fester, abschließender Kadenz, ein sozusagen 'ritueller' Tonfall), which according to Wolfgang Mohr forms part of a revelatory speech (*Verkündigung*)[2] and which clearly distinguishes these speeches from the self-introductions of human speakers.[3] Two short quotations may serve to illustrate the difference:

> Ego sum alpha et o,
> I am the first, the last also,
>   Oone god in mageste;
> Meruelus, of myght most,
> ffader, & son, & holy goost,
>   On god in trinyte. (God in T I, 1–6)

> That Lord þat leves ay-lastand lyff,
>   I loue þe euer with hart and hande,
> That me wolde rewle be reasoune ryffe,
>   Sex hundereth yere to lyffe in lande.
> Thre semely sonnes and a worthy wiffe
>   I haue euer at my steven to stande;
> Bot nowe my cares aren keene as knyffe,
>   Bycause I kenne what is commannde. (Noah in Y IX, 1–8)

God in Towneley makes ever new statements about himself, the subject of his sentences is *ego* or *I*, the second half of the stanza consists exclusively of predicative nouns depending on the *I am* of line 2. The York Noah, on the other hand, speaks first of his love for God, then about his family, and finally about his worries concerning things to come. The theme of the stanza, Noah's state of mind, is divided into a number of sub-themes. These sub-themes are not always the subjects of his sentences. The non-identity between sentence structure and communication structure gives the speech a movement which God's speech in T I lacks. Cohesion between these statements is supplied not by surface syntax but by the emotional state of the speaker. The contrast between past family happiness and present cares which is expressed by 'Bot' again exists primarily in the emotional state of the speaker. The unvaried syntax of God's speech does not allow such emotions to become apparent. Even when God passes judgment (as he does in the great introductory speech of 'The Last Judgment', Y XLVII), his judgment appears as logically and objectively substantiated.[4] It is not, as is frequent with human speakers, the product of moods. The hieratic, rigid posture which we have sketched here finds its purest expression in the entry speeches of Y I, II, III and XLVII. But more archaic representatives of the type are presumably T I and Y XXXVII (=T XXV). They shall therefore be dealt with first.

At the beginning of the 'Harrowing of Hell' (Y XXXVII) Jesus announces his intention to free the souls of the departed from Satan's bondage:

> The forward of my fadir free
>   Haue I fulfillid, as folke may fynde,
> þerfore aboute nowe woll I bee,
>   þat I haue bought for to vnbynde.
>   þe feende þame wanne with trayne

>   Thurgh frewte of erthely foode,
>   I haue þame getyn agayne
>   Thurgh bying with my bloode.   (Y XXXVII, 5–12)

The work of redemption announced here is treated in unemotional, almost juridical language. There is hardly a word of hostility against Satan since the stress is upon the idea of buying back (= redeeming) the souls by the death of Christ.[5] Christ particularly underlines the fact that by his death he has already gained the right to the souls of the dead. Christ is not speaking about a plan which conceivably might fail; the hearer is to feel that an already established fact is being announced. Accordingly, Jesus does not mention the technical details of his plan to conquer Hell, he merely describes the state of eternal bliss which his victory will bring about:

>   And so I schall þat steede restore
>   For whilke þe feende fell for synne,
>   þare schalle mankynde wonne euermore
>   In blisse þat schall neuere blynne.   (Y XXXVII, 13–16)

Admittedly, this gives his speech a tone of combative resolution and proud certainty which is not quite in keeping with the pure revelation speech.

God's entry speech in the Towneley 'Creation' merits a special comment because it allows comparisons with corresponding speeches in York. The descriptive mode of speaking, which is characteristic of all revelation speeches, becomes particularly apparent here because the author was unable to adapt the tail-rhyme stanza to his theme. The different acts of creation are dealt with point by point. In some phrases, which presumably were primarily added for the sake of the rhyme, we hear a tone of naïve, reverent awe which is carefully avoided in York. In T I, God appears to himself as 'meruelus' (line 4), the light is 'fayre to se' (21), the oceans of the earth are 'so wyde' (37). God is here speaking with the voice of his human worshippers who are unable to grasp the wonders of the Creation. The rigid ornamentation of the York Creation group was unattainable for the Towneley dramatist. References to God's grandeur and power are less frequent than in York.

Two thematically related passages will permit detailed comparison:[6]

>   Sen I am maker vnmade, and most es of mighte,
>   And ay sall be endeles and noghte es but I,
>   Vnto my dygnyté dere sall diewly be dyghte
>   A place full of plenté to my plesyng at ply,
>   And therewith als wyll I haue wroght
>   Many dyuers doynges bedene,
>   Whilke warke sall mekely contene,
>   And all sall be made euen of noghte.   (Y I, 9–16)

> I am without begynnyng,
> My godhede hath none endyng,
>   I am god in trone;
> Oone god in persons thre,
> Which may neuer twynnyd be,
>   ffor I am god alone. (T I, 7–12)

Both revelation speeches are basically descriptive in character. But if we regard those parts of the sentence which are not purely descriptive, we will note important differences. The rich linguistic ornament emphasizes the individual line as a unit and gives the York speeches a rigour and weight which the tail-rhyme stanzas in T I lack. For all their massiveness the York stanzas are well-structured. The predominance of causal conjunctions corresponds with the dogmatic thrust of the plays, whose aim is to teach theology and to impress the listeners by amplification and repetition (Y I, 2/9, 5/7, 8/10).[7] References to God's dignity, power, and glory (Y I, 9, 11, 20ff; Y II, 47) support this effect. In keeping with this notion of God, Y III regards man primarily as the worshipper of God, whereas in T I (lines 162ff) he appears first of all as the master of God's creation. In the Creation play proper of the York cycle (Y II) it is not the grandeur of the created world which is emphasized, but its obedience toward God and the pleasure which it gives Him. The waters below and above the Heavens (Gen.1.7) are 'þere cursis lely for to lere' (Y II, 34), and at the end of the day God says:

> þis warke is to my pay
> Righit well, withoutyn wyne. (Y II [Smith], 25f)[8]

The somewhat rigid effect of the York speeches which carefully refrain from conveying any particular mood, is usually emphasized by parallel verses without enjambment. Alliteration does not serve to underline emotionally loaded words, it rather produces nearly synonymous pairs such as *gracyus and grete* (Y I, 1), *formaste and fyrste* (ibid., 4), *teche and tell* (Y XLVII, 39), whose effect is above all ornamental.

Expressions which could appeal to the emotions occur in frozen collocations, a fact which strongly reduces their suggestive power (*blithe moode*, Y XLVII, 27; *harte-bloode*, 31).

But what is more important is the stylistic tendency which is here revealed: the words are not meant to appeal to the senses; such appeal is rather to be avoided. The description of specific detail, which is so important in some of the Passion plays,[9] for instance, is hardly to be found here. The rich rhetorical ornament leads as it were an independent existence quite separate from the meaning of the text. It befits the contents as a whole – and of course especially God as the speaker – its task is not to emphasize the effect of specific details or of ideas that may be evoked by the text. On the contrary: those emotional reactions which we encountered in God's speech in T I – and which, admittedly, were human, not divine emotions – are carefully eliminated in York. The aesthetic function of the rhetorical *ornatus* could be compared to Lydgate's aureate diction and to the golden background of medieval painting:[10] instead of highlighting individual details, it produces an aura of general solemnity. In the liturgical drama that solemnity was guaranteed by the frame of the cult, while the vernacular cycles had either to forego it altogether or to create it by linguistic means.

Having emphasized the stylistic differences between the revelation speeches in York and in Towneley[11] we should not, however, neglect the features which these speeches have in common in both cycles: the 'static' features of speech and of 'non-situational' speaking. In T I they were intermingled with humanly naïve awe and a certain delight in colourful presentation, in York they dominate to the exclusion of all others, in the interest of a decorum which is oriented at the rank of the speaker.

Decorum is the stylistic principle which governs these speeches in the cathedral city of York. Other developments were also possible, as is shown in the work of the Wakefield Master, who has, however, left us only one revelation speech. And we may assume that his main interest was not in this speech-type. It occurs in *Processus Noe cum filiis* (T III, 73–117), which owes its great aesthetic success above all to the comic scenes dealing with Noah's wife.[12] In humanizing God, the Wakefield Master resembles the author of T I, but he executes his picture of God with superior dramatic skill.

That skill becomes evident immediately at the beginning of the speech. In the Noah plays of the other cycles God begins with a detailed retrospective on the days of the Creation and especially on the intentions which guided him in creating Man. This is usually followed by a statement to the effect that he is sorry to have created Man and, finally, by the resolution to exterminate all humankind with the exception of Noah and his family. As a result, these three thoughts are clearly separated from each other. In contrast to the normal approach the Wakefield Master's *Deus* barely mentions the Creation in a by-clause, proceeding straight on to what preoccupies him most: his very worldly annoyance at the behaviour of the humans, which he describes in vivid detail:

> And now in grete reprufe full low ligys he,
> In erth hymself to stuf with syn that displeasse me
> Most of all. (T III, 84–6)

This annoyance is not the subject of a separate section of the speech to be followed by a further section in which the decision for the Flood would be taken. No, it becomes the basic mood which pervades the entire speech and is palpable even where it is not explicitly mentioned. Above all it finds expression in the implicit contrast between what God might reasonably have expected and how mankind really developed. The contrast feeds and re-feeds the basic mood of profane annoyance and finally produces the decision to submerge everything in the Flood. But this decision does not come like the well-formulated and premeditated sentence of a judge; it takes shape gradually, as would thoughts of revenge in the heart of one offended. At first the plan appears only in vague outline, with an undertone of grim satisfaction already audible:

> That bargayn may thay ban
> That ill has done. (T III, 94f)

The plan takes on a more definite shape only a few lines later:

> Therfor shall I fordo all this medill-erd
> With floodys that shall flo and ryn with hidous rerd.
> I haue good cause therto; for me no man is ferd. (lines 100–2)

The last sentence betrays once more God's rather human desire to justify himself, which he does not show in other cycles. The Flood, too, is described from the human point of view: it will 'ryn with hidous rerd'. Such graphic details certainly make the speech livelier than in other cycles, but the price for this is high: divine judgment has been changed into a human catastrophe.

The humanization of God becomes most evident at the end of the monologue, which introduces already the dialogue with Noah:

> Hym [Noah] to mekill wyn, hastly will I go
> To Noe my seruand, or I blyn, to warn hym of his woe. (lines 109f)

God does what he never does in the other cycles: He himself goes to a human being to transmit his message.[13] While other dramatists have God sit immovably at a presumably raised *locus*, the Wakefield Master forces Him to go from one place to another, as any other person would have to do. He thus robs God of his usual omnipresence. The humanization of God has influenced not only the speech but also the staging. He even has to go 'hastly', as if it were not in his power to begin the Flood at a time of his own choosing. But the Wakefield Master's God, moved by anger and haste as he is, has to follow other considerations: to depict details vividly and powerfully, to develop speech continuously so that each idea grows out of the previous one – these things are now more important than the dignity of the part which we found in York and which required that the speech place the listeners at a befitting distance.

Intra-dramatic speeches

The wealth of formal devices which we found in the York Creation speech has no equivalent in the *Chester Plays*. Although the author of the Chester 'Creation' is stylistically more skilful than his Towneley counterpart, the two are more alike in their basic conception of God and His dramatic situation than their superficial differences would lead us to suspect. In both cycles God's words follow Genesis 1 in considerable detail:

>Now will I in waters fishe forth bringe,
>fowles in the firmament flying,
>great whalles in the sea swymminge,
>all make I with a thought. (Ch II, 57–60; cf. Gen. 1.20f)

The passage from one day to the next is brought about by the almost stereotypical formula 'Now will I make'. This formula, variants of which appear in the 'action speeches' of human characters,[14] destroys that continuity of the process of creation which was still to be felt in T I and which Y II had developed into a firm concatenation between the various acts of creation.

Unlike York, Chester does not organically develop this speech-type. The introductory speech Ch I, 1–51, which Craig incomprehensibly describes as 'obviously old',[15] represents the only attempt to swell the simple verses of the original by added splendour.

Instead of the exquisite and disciplined *ornatus* which we found in York, Chester seeks to impress by the use of polysyllables which are sometimes used without much regard for their meaning:

>The wholl foode of parente is sett
>in my essention.
>I ame the tryall of the Trenitye
>which never shalbe twyninge,
>pearles patron ymperiall,
>and Patris sapiencia.
>
>...
>
>For all the meirth of majestye
>is magnifyed in me.
>Prince principall, proved
>in my perpetuall provydence,
>
>...
>
>set in substanciall southnes
>within selestiall sapience.
>
>...
>
>Nowe sithe I am soe soeleme
>and set in my solatacion   [*prob.*: isolation
>a biglie blesse here will I builde,
>a heaven without endinge,
>and caste a comely compasse
>by comely creation.   (Ch I, 7–12, 20–23, 36–41)

When 'Deus' describes himself as 'Patris sapiencia', this weak echo of a long theological tradition is all but incomprehensible.[16] Through the stanzas there is no recognizable progression of ideas: 'Sapience' is referred to again in line 27, once more without any reference to the other two persons of the Trinity. God is seen not so much as the Creator but as the greatest monarch ('patron ymperiall', line 11). His wish to create the world is plausibly motivated by his isolation (line 37), but this is implausibly joined with his 'solemnity' (*soeleme*, line 36). Latin words like *essentia* (misspelt as *ession*, line 8), *sapiencia* (line 12), *potencia* (line 16), and *licentia* (misspelt as *licentill*, line 19) confirm the impression that the function of this speech is to impress rather than to instruct. God's power is rendered by rhetoric rather than logic.

The revelation speeches in N-Town do not attain to the splendid remoteness of their counterparts in York. This may surprise at first sight, since the N-Town cycle is above all known for its ecclesiastic, non-popular character. But the plays which offer an opportunity for revelation speeches belong to the 'old-fashioned' part of the cycle which is written in 'Proclamation thirteeners' (LC I, II, XLII) and which has no share in the quasi-courtly 'aureatizing' style of the Passion plays and the *Contemplacio* group. The small importance of God's dignity becomes apparent in the fact that in this cycle God walks up and down while creating the world – in decided contrast to other cycles which place him at an awesome height:[17]

> My werk for to make · now wyll I wende   (LC I, 2, p. 16)
>
> I am þe trewe trenyte
> here walkyng in þis wone.   (ibid., 14f)

While York is governed by a style of general solemnity which often submerges the meaning of individual words, the N-Town speeches make precise statements using well-defined theological concepts:

> in my self restyth my reynenge
> it hath no gynnyng ne non ende
> And all þat evyr xal haue beynge
> it is closyd in my mende   (LC I, 3–6)
>
> I am oo god · in personys thre
> knyt in oo substawns.   (ibid. 12f)

The attitude which is here suggested to the spectator is not the hieratical veneration of York or even more of the Marian parts of N-Town; neither is it the naïve awe of Towneley. Heaven, it is true, is once described in a phrase that would not be out of place in Towneley – as 'ful fayr and bryth'. But this expression, which is also motivated by the rhyme, stands completely isolated in a purely descriptive enumeration which deals with the entire Creation week in merely two stanzas:

> Now hevyn is made ffor Aungell sake
> þe fyrst day and þe fyrst nyth
> The secunde day watyr I make
> The Walkyn also ful fayr and b[r]yth...   (LC II, 83–6, p. 19)

In the other cycles the world is usually created by a command or at least by an announcement. Here it is sufficient for God to *state* that he is creating the world. The world is thus not *created by* the word; the word merely accompanies the creation of the world. God's speech is thus not stylistically distinct from the 'action speeches' which run parallel to, but do not interact with, the events that take place on stage.

The principle of decorum is missing here as it is in Towneley. But unlike Towneley, where this decorum never takes hold,[18] the N-Town cycle lacks it only in the 'Proclamation thirteener' plays.

The opening prayer

God, one of whose attributes is infiniteness, can reveal himself in a speech-type which dispenses with situational embedding and even with an explicit addressee. Human beings cannot do that. Since the mystery play does not normally allow them to talk to themselves, they must either address the audience – or God. For expository purposes the 'opening prayer' thus fulfils approximately the same functions as the direct audience-address.

Like the revelation speech the prayer offers the possibility of instructing the audience without actually addressing it. This possibility is not exploited throughout, presumably owing to the less exalted position which praying humans hold in comparison to God. It is sufficient here to recall the many speeches, especially in the earliest parts of York, which fluctuated between prayer and audience-address.

The opening prayer in the Chester Plays

It is somewhat rarer here than in other cycles. As a result of the fairly rigid conception of the cycle, which is more concerned with dogmatic clarity than with vivid stage business, the characters mostly appear or speak in a strictly hierarchical order. In the plays in which God appears he is the first to speak; at times he is also given the exposition (as for instance in the Chester Noah play Ch III). His human partners can do little more than answer and obey; a genuine prayer is hardly possible under such circumstances. This disposes of two opening prayers which

170   *The English mystery play*

are very prominent in other cycles: those of Noah and of Abraham before the sacrifice of Isaac. Since Chester does not contain a play on the Baptism of Jesus, this leaves us with only five opening prayers: Ch II, 425ff (Adam before the Cain and Abel episode), Ch IV, 17ff (Abraham before the encounter with Melchisedech), Ch VIII, 1ff (The three Magi), Ch XI, 1ff (Simeon in The Purification of Mary), Ch XVII, 1ff (Adam in The Harrowing of Hell).

As this series shows, opening prayers occur chiefly in those plays in which God acts in the person of the Father. Only after the Baptism can Jesus assume the rôle of the divine agent. Insofar as his interlocutors are aware of his divine nature, they treat him with reverence and obedience, but they communicate with him in forms which they would also use with other humans: he is asked, informed, entreated, but not prayed to.[19]

The opening prayers in the Chester cycle follow a fairly uniform pattern which is all the more remarkable as three of the five opening prayers belong to plays which according to some scholars were written later than the majority of the cycle.[20] All prayers begin by praising God's greatness and might. The praying person has experienced God's power and also His goodness. In offering thanks for what he has received he can tell his own life story. The prayer thus becomes a pretext for the exposition. Although the prayers are formally thanksgivings, they do not give the impression that they arise out of a feeling of gratitude. Such emotional colouring will be found in the Yorkshire cycles; in Chester the fate of the speaker is above all an *exemplum*, an illustration of God's long familiar goodness and magnificence. The words of Adam offer a characteristic example for this relationship between praying man and God:

> Hight God and highest kynge,
> that of nought made all thinge –
> beast, fowle, and grasse growinge –
> and me of yearth made.   (Ch II, 425–8)

God is addressed with titles which arise not from the personal or momentary attitude of the praying person, but which belong to Him objectively as the king of the world. The titles are often followed by by-clauses and appositions which emphasize God's deeds or characteristics.[21]

After this general introduction the speaker mentions the special dispensation of mercy which he has received:

> thou gave me grace to doe thy wyllinge.
> For after great sorrowe and sikinge
> thou hast mee lent great likinge,
> too sonnes my hearte to glade.   (Ch II, 429–32)[22]

Here the opening prayer serves as a substitute for narrative, which is otherwise hardly possible in drama. This becomes particularly evident in those plays which were influenced by the *Stanzaic Life*, where the prayer easily glides into autobiography. But autobiography is strictly confined to what is relevant to the story at hand, herein also following the model of the *Stanzaic Life*. York's excursions into the history of the world with their theological colouring do not occur in the Chester prayers. For these excursions, Chester has the Expositor.

The retrospective is often coupled with a request to God, but after that the attitude of prayer is regularly given up, and the speaker's attention turns to his own present. What follows is often linked to the preceding prayer by 'therefore'.[23] This word shows in an almost exemplary fashion the manner of connecting things in Chester: there is an unambiguous and objective reason for everything, nothing arises from the agents' mood or emotions.

The schema of the prayers turns out to be very strict even in minutiae. Whether they are to be found in early or in late plays, whether they are spoken by patriarchs or kings – their structure is the same. Since all prayers are constructed according to the same pattern, they never give the impression that they are a product of the specific situation. The thoughts, which follow each other in strict order, are ready made before they are uttered, they do not gain shape in the speaking. Clearly, logically structured, uncoloured by any subjectivity, these prayers resemble largely the revelation speeches uttered by God.

The opening prayer in York and Towneley

The play of Jacob in the Towneley cycle (T VI), which has been described as one of the dramatically most 'primitive',[24] is surprisingly lively in its treatment of the prayer situation. The expository material is integrated into the prayer without giving the audience the feeling that these things are mentioned only for their information. For instance, the fact that Jacob is on his way to Mesopotamia is not given as a flat statement, but is part of a request directed at God:

>Help me lord, adonay,
>And hald me in the right way
>To mesopotameam. (lines 1–3)

At the same time the audience learns about accompanying circumstances which are irrelevant for understanding the situation but convey something of the mood in which Jacob experiences it and which accordingly makes his prayer the more urgent:

>ffor I cam neuer or now where I am. (line 4)

This prayer tells us nothing about the speaker's ancestry or present standing which take up so much room in most other opening prayers. Even the momentary situation – the strange country, the long journey – is not given as a series of objective facts, but is reflected in Jacob's tiredness and fear. This psychological effect finds expression in the repetition of 'help me' (lines 1, 6) and thus aids in structuring the prayer. Unlike other entry speeches, Jacob's prayer does not give us a description of the situation, but the speaker's reaction to that situation. The firm grounding of the speech in the psychological situation and the smooth transitions between psychological states should qualify this prayer as dramatic even to the sternest naturalist. If the play as a whole affects us none the less as 'undramatic', this is due largely to the treatment of time and space and the absence of a link between speech and action.

But the Jacob play is atypical with respect to the opening prayer, as it is in its treatment of time and space. The structure of the typical opening prayers of these cycles is superficially similar to that of the Chester prayers: an invocation of God is followed by a recalling of His deeds and afterwards by the speaker's autobiography. In this last part the speech-addressee changes from God to the audience: God retreats into the third person singular.[25] But the internal nexus between these elements is quite different from that in Chester. These differences show already in the titles with which God is addressed. While in Chester he was above all remote and throned in majesty, he is now, more simply and more actively, the helper (T IV, 4) and the ruler (Y IX, 3). The relationship between God and the speakers is direct, personal, and exclusive. The speakers do not appear as representatives of the human race which in its entirety is the object of God's attentions, but they appear as standing in exclusive relationship to Him.

The facts touched upon in these prayers always appear in the light of this relationship, not as something to be reported objectively. Abraham even says explicitly that what he is saying is just now passing his mind:

> This musys mekill in my thoght. (T IV, 12)

'This musys' remains the keynote of the entire prayer. In the six stanzas of his monologue Abraham does not report anything the significance of which is generally recognized, but he shows his own, personal reaction to the fates of his forefathers:

> when I thynk of oure elders all,
>   And of the mervels that has been,
> No gladnes in my hart may fall,
>   M[y] comfort goys away full cleyn. (T IV, 33–6)

Abraham's speech is not merely superficially emotionalized. His sympathy for his dead forebears occasions God's command to sacrifice Isaac. For God decides to answer Abraham's prayer for the dead if he finds Abraham obedient, and to test his obedience with that command. Isaac, a prefiguration of Christ, has thus assumed part of the Saviour's function.[26] In spite of all changes in detail, the opening prayer of the Yorkshire cycles will continue to be thus embedded in an emotional substratum.

Since the two cycles are so closely related, we can illustrate the development of the opening prayer in a detailed comparison of the two Magi plays. The comparison between the two bragging speeches of T XIV and Y XVI[27] can thus be followed up by one between the 'opening prayers' in T XIV and Y XVI.[28]

In the stylistically simple T XIV the Magi are completely overawed by the 'selcouth light' (line 104), the significance of which they do not know but hope to discover with God's help. Their prayers are thus dominated by requests and therefore oriented towards the future. The audience is informed only about what the kings hope and look for, not about where they come from. The more ambitious Y XVI strives for a more complete presentation of its figures and accordingly must bring in the past and the ancestry of the kings as well. In particular, the prophecy concerning the Star must be mentioned at the very beginning (Y XVI, 59–65). This disturbs the equality between the three Magi which in the other cycles is strictly observed: in T XIV all three are equally astonished, in Ch VIII all are equally knowledgeable, but in Y XVI the first knows, while the others do not.

Apart from these asymmetries, which are basically alien to the mystery play, the endeavour to present a full picture of the main dramatic figures harbours the danger that the emphasis of the speeches shifts from the future to the past. The more the speeches indulge in narrative, the more difficult it becomes to maintain that distance from the audience which properly belongs to the dignity of these figures. The Three Kings would thus be in about the same relationship to the audience as Noah and Abraham are. This development was avoided by making the narrative passages both in respect to syntax and content dependent on the invocation of God. Thus the unity of the prayer-situation is at least formally preserved.

The York play thus shows no change in the basic attitude or in the relationship between *dramatis persona* and audience. But a closer study of stylistic detail indicates an increasing tendency toward linguistic ornament and a solemn, measured speech style. By frequently referring to themselves and their own pietal attitudes[29] the kings in York create an appearance of simultaneity between speech and inward attitude which is part of cultic praying. While in T XIV the kings praise God above all as the bringer of the Star, thereby stressing the playwright's interest in the concrete detail which arises from the personal situation of the praying person, the prayers in York show their supra-personal, situation-independent character in the use of stereotyped formulae[30] and also in praisings of general validity for which the Third King may serve as an example:

> Lorde God þat all goode has bygonne
>   And all may ende, both goode and euyll,
> That made for man both mone and sonne,
>   And stedde yone sterne to stande stone stille,] (Y XVI, 81–4)

EXCURSUS: The prayers of the Three Kings in Coventry
As they offer particularly good opportunities for comparison, the prayers of the Three Kings in the Coventry *Shearmen and Taylors' Pageant* will be analysed here in addition to those of the complete cycles.[31] The extraordinary heterogeneousness of the Coventry Plays should caution us against any attempt at placing them in any line of development, but a comparison with the Yorkshire cycles, which clearly represent a similar tradition, may be of some interest. Coventry shows the simplicity of Towneley in some places, the decorum and dignity of York in others. This sense of decorum, of dramatic appropriateness, is evinced, for instance, in the fact that the meaning of the gifts is not explained at the beginning of the scene, as it is in Towneley, but at the offering (Y XVI, 317–20, 330–2, 341–4). The didactic element is thus integrated into the dramatic situation, while in Towneley it is unashamedly given in the opening speeches. Both solutions are consistent in themselves. In Coventry we find instead a mixture of both: the Second King, on meeting the First, explains his gift of incense (STCo, 580f), while gold and myrrh are not mentioned.

A similar change, equally not quite consistent, is to be found in the prayers. The First King expresses his gratitude in the simple, awe-struck tone which is familiar from Towneley:

> Now blessid be God of his swet sonde,
>   For yondur a feyre bryght star I do see!
> Now ys he comon, vs a-monge,
>   Asse the profet seyd thatt yt shuld be. (STCo, 540–3)

By contrast, the Second and the Third speak first about their having lost the way, and they pray to God that he may indicate to them the direction in which they have to go (lines 560f, 584f). Only after that does the Star appear (lines 562ff, 586ff), whose significance, however, they can explain at once. To create a momentary emotion and perhaps an external stage effect, an illogicality in the motivation is accepted: if the Star appears only now, the reason for the kings leaving their respective home countries remains unexplained. It is probably no mere coincidence that the stanzas which indulge in this externalism are distinguished by a particularly rough and tumbling metre:

> III. REX. I ryde wanderyng in veyis wyde,
>   Ouer montens and dalis; I wot not where I am.
> Now, Kyng off all kyngis, send me soche gyde
>   Thatt I myght haue knoleyge of thys cuntreys name.
> A! yondur I se a syght, be-semyng all afar,
>   The wyche be-tocuns sum nevis, ase I troo;
> Asse me thynke, a chyld peryng in a stare.
>   I trust he be cum that schall defend vs from woo.   (STCo, 582–9)

The child appearing in the star, a borrowing from John of Hildesheim's *Three Kings of Cologne* which does not occur in the cycles, is characteristic of Coventry's tendency to overburden the story with ornamental detail.[32]

Craig, whose introduction gives a fairly precise analysis according to rhyme-schemes, ignores the rhythmical differences and thus regards all parts of these prayers as belonging to the oldest strata, since all of them are quatrains.[33] Since rhythmical and stylistic criteria discriminate in the same way, it seems probable that we have to distinguish at least two strata in these prayers. If this assumption is correct, the plays cannot, as Craig believes, represent the earliest stage in English.[34] It is true, as Craig says, that the decisive parts of these cycles are 'free from comicality and bombast',[35] but this very general characterization is not sufficient to guarantee the age or simplicity of a mystery scene. 'Comicality and bombast' is not the only direction in which a play can 'degenerate'. Another way is the development toward the 'Schaubild' which conceives only of the externals of the surrounding reality.[36]

In the Magi play Y XVI the prayer had lost its original task of expressing a pious mood and had assumed that of giving an intra-dramatic report instead. Y XXI ('The Baptism') also avoids direct audience-address. A comparison between this play and the corresponding T XIX, which structurally is very similar,[37] should help us find out what happens to the contents of an introductory speech when it is cloaked in the form of a prayer, instead of being directly addressed to the audience.[38] In T XIX John the Baptist informs the audience directly about his pre-history. His closeness to the public helps him emphasize that he needs redemption through Christ just as much as his spectators. Having thus identified

176   *The English mystery play*

with the audience, he is able to make himself the mouthpiece of his English audience in the prayer which follows the self-introduction.

All of this is different in Y XXI, where the function of the introductory audience-address is assumed by a prayer. The central topic of the speech is now the error of the people who mistake him for the Messiah. In Towneley this was mentioned merely to lead on to Christ's Passion. The York playwright apparently considered this very specific reference to future events inappropriate in the intra-dramatic situation of the prayer and so omitted it. One result of the facts being clothed in the dress of prayer is that they do not stand out as clearly. The prayer is not a report, but an expression of feeling for which the facts are merely the occasion. It is probably characteristic that John does not speak of 'Jews' but of Man in general (Y XXI, 2). The facts themselves are not important but their evaluation:

> Full woundyrfull is mannys lesyng,   [*lesyng* = falsehood, error
> ...
> Men are so dull þat my preching
> Serues of noght.   (lines 2, 6f)

Even if facts are reported in the following stanzas, they are primarily an illustration of the complaint which John brings before God. The procedure is comparable to that narration-within-prayer which we found in Y XVI.[39] In the further course of the prayer in Y XXI the narrative gains considerable independence, even to the extent that John quotes from his own sermons (lines 29–49). The quotation is duly introduced by 'saide I' (line 29),[40] but in the performance it must have struck the audience as a movement from the narrative past to the present of exposition. The audience will thus be placed in the rôle of John's contemporaries, at whom this sermon was originally addressed. The York John here achieves something which is impossible to his Towneley counterpart: he can address his audience without descending to its level. For now it is not John who steps out of the play-sphere but the public which is drawn into it. The relationship between the two spheres thus resembles that in the liturgical drama: just as the chorus of the clerics was placed in the rôle of the disciples vis-à-vis the Easter message, the citizens of York now 'become' the Jewish listeners of John's sermon.

The comparison between T XIX and Y XXI confirms what we observed in connection with the audience-address: that the presence or absence of an explicit audience-address is closely connected with the stylistic level of a speech and that a growing feeling for such hierarchical distinctions leads to a diminishing of the naïve-confidential type. We can now add: the change in the rhetorical situation – from audience-address to prayer – also conditions a change in the facts mentioned and in the attitudes taken toward them. In the prayer, mere reporting takes second place to evaluation and reflexion.

Joseph's prayers in Y XIV, 1ff (Nativity) and Y XVIII, 1ff (Flight into Egypt) hold an intermediate position between the Magi in T XIV and those in Y XVI. They are dominated by a unified mood into which the description of the situation and the invocation of God are embedded. The external circumstances under which the couple will have to spend the night are described with a sure understanding for the emotional effects of specific details:

> And yf we here all nyght abide,
> we schall be stormed in þis steede. (Y XIV, 15f)

This description is not merely a presentation of things but clearly grows out of the fear of what is coming. The prayers do not merely fulfil the function of an exposition but also have to arouse the spectators' sympathy. In this prayer the conventional Joseph, who is always halfway into the emotional world of his spectators, is enriched by a new method of creating and presenting dramatic figures.

The miserable stable, the cold, his own weakness and old age – all of Joseph's physical experiences are as close to the everyday world of his audience as they are in other cycles. But their everyday character is now differently expressed linguistically. There are no proverbs and no general reflexions on the plight of the old man married to a young woman (as, e.g., in T XV, 44f, 92ff). When he complains about the decrepitude of old age, it is his momentary weakness which he bemoans. His complaints are no longer addressed at the public and thereby lifted out of the sphere in which they are experienced. They are offered in the form of exclamations and are thus integrated into the personal emotions that are articulated in the prayer:

> And we are weyke and all werie
> And fayne wolde rest.
> Now, gracious God, for thy mercie,
>   Wisse vs þe best. (Y XIV, 25–8)

> Thow myghtfull maker, haue mynde on me
> And se vnto my sympplenes.
>   I waxe as wayke as any wande,
>   For febill me faylles both foote and hande. (Y XVIII, 15–18)

These prayers arise out of the needs of the moment. God thus becomes the confidant of the human heart and its anxieties. The prayers are the expressions of momentary needs, not proclamations of official religious tenets.

But these features should not be regarded exclusively under their formal aspect. The change in the manner of speaking entails one in the character. In these plays Joseph no longer presents himself as a type. That is why he does not claim general validity for his experience; he does not use proverbs which, after all, express general truths in concrete terms. He does not see himself as an exemplar of a general state of affairs, and thus he cannot appeal directly to the public, who know this general state of affairs from their own experience. He therefore loses his proximity to the public and his plebeian comicality. He experiences his fate as unique, and this sense of uniqueness fills his prayers. Solidarity with the public has to be established indirectly: it is not Joseph who generalizes his experience, but the public has to empathize with him, distilling as it were the general from the individual. Joseph is still the representative of the public: of the common people into whose community Christ was born. But it is now for the public to establish the connection between themselves and their representative.

This is a far cry from what is generally known as popular acting conventions. But the change in acting conventions also has consequences for the theological significance of the part. To the extent that he ceases to be a representative of contemporary (or rather: timeless) Man, Joseph ceases to be conscious of his soteriological function. In his prayers he is not the husband of the mother of God, but only a man in his creaturely needs and hoping for individual help.

The prayers in the middle of the plays are similarly psychologized. Inasmuch as the presentation of momentary feelings replaces generalized description, the entry prayers lose their expository character and become an expression of momentary feeling. This psychologizing of originally dramaturgical speech conventions will be observed more frequently in the later strata of the York cycle.

While the opening prayers in Chester were largely of the same type, the Yorkshire cycles offer a multitude of different forms which, however, does not represent a simple continuum from naïve self-presentation to more penetrating psychology. Prayers in Towneley are strongly determined by the speaker's mood but reveal very little about his nature. York ranges from a Joseph who is represented with a great deal of psychological empathy to the Magi of Y XVI whose prayers are petrified in ceremonial. In the later plays of the York cycle there is a strong tendency for the rank of the speakers to determine the style of their prayers.

The opening prayer in the N-Town cycle

After the variety of forms which the opening prayer has to offer in York and Towneley, we are now again approaching a cycle which treats this speech-form as uniformly as does Chester. In view of the extreme heterogeneousness of the cycle this is surprising and contrary to what we should expect from our previous observations. The reason is chiefly that the Old Testament plays, to which the opening prayer is largely confined, are of a fairly unified type, even if they are not all of the same origin.

There are four prayers belonging to this type: Noah (IV, p. 35), Abraham (V, p. 43), Moses (VI, p. 51), and Lazarus (XXV, p. 210). Lazarus' prayer differs in many respects from those of the Old Testament, as the entire play is totally different from the other three. But these are so similar to each other that they can be treated together. Like almost all prayers, they begin with an invocation of God which emphasizes, as in Chester, God's grandeur and majesty. God is not the good, powerful friend of the Yorkshire cycles, with whom the speaker is on almost intimate terms and by whom he feels personally protected. Above all, the relationship to God does not have the naïve exclusiveness which it had in York and Towneley and which allowed the characters to address Him out of a momentary mood and to reveal their emotional attitude to Him. The N-Town cycle, on the other hand, resembles Chester in that God is addressed by titles which belong to Him by a sort of religious protocol and which therefore allow no inferences concerning the personal attitude of the speakers. In distinction to Chester, however, these titles are now adapted to the expansive aureate style of N-Town, which also makes them occur much more frequently. Instead of a simple 'highest kynge' (Ch II, 425) we now read, e.g.:

> God of his goodnesse · and of grace grounde
> By whoys gloryous power all thyng is wrought
> in whom all vertu plentevously is ffounde
> with-owtyn whos wyl may be ryght nought. (Noah, LC IV, 1–4, p. 35)

or

> Most myghty makere of Sunne and of mone
> Kyng of kyngys and lord ouer all
> All myghty god in hevyn trone. (Abraham, LC V, 1–3, p. 43)[41]

God, it appears, is again the distant great ruler whom Man can approach only in the most ornate language.

A further difference from Chester is that the prayers do not go beyond these titles and definitions. We learn nothing about what God did either to humanity as a whole or to the speaker himself. Instead, the prayer always leads into a request for protection from sin and for a life that is pleasing unto God:

> My lord my god to þe I kall
> with herty wyll lord I þe pray
> In synfull lyff lete me nevyr fall
> but lete me leve evyr to þi pay. (LC V, 5–8)[42]

The prayers are limited to generalities and have no connection to the specific topic of the play. The result is a pronounced gap between prayer and exposition proper which is not even bridged by a conjunction – as it was for instance by *therefore* in Chester. The prayers may be said to serve as pious introits without any dramatic function.

The Lazarus play, which stood out for its unusual treatment of space, is equally unusual for its opening prayer. There are no titles here; the few things that are said about God are immediately related to the specific situation of the dying man: God has created all things, and puts an end to every creature's life (line 1f). Out of this statement emerges a prayer which is motivated by a sort of *argumentum ad Deum*:

> Saue thyn handwerke þat þou hast wrought
> ...
> of my dysese now comforte me. (LC XXV, 3, 6, p. 210)

Dysese is the cue for the following description:

> Which þurowe syknes hath such penawnce
> On-ethys ffor heed Ache may I now se. (ibid., 7f)

Description enters into this prayer, too; here, too, do we find a piece of exposition. But these lines, the subject of which is the present state of Lazarus' health and which contain nothing of his previous life, as they would in other plays, help give added weight to the prayer. By virtue of this the prayer shows a degree of homogeneousness and dramatic vivacity which is rare in the cycle.

The verbal presentation of mourning and grief

As we have seen, the opening prayers were not entirely limited to their expository function, although it is certainly to this that they owe their existence as a relatively well defined speech-type. The Yorkshire cycles especially showed a tendency to embed the expository matter of the prayer in the speaker's mood – for instance, in concern or gratitude. This by itself is an indication of how important it would be to study the emotions and their presentation in medieval drama. But such a study – which above all would need to view the drama against the background of medieval emotionality in general[43] – would far exceed the scope of the present book. Instead, we shall attempt an analysis of the verbal presentation of that emotion which shows the strongest tendency to form a speech-type of its own.

The field of human emotions is one of those aspects of medieval drama which is particularly difficult to assess adequately. Since the interest of the Middle Ages in the individual was comparatively small,[44] it is hardly surprising that moderns should regard medieval presentations of emotions to be largely insufficient, particularly with regard to the medieval drama. It was quite common for the older surveys and introductions to standard editions to point out, even apologetically, that one could not expect a subtle play of emotions from the religious drama and to dwell the more lovingly on the few cases which did seem to show a more differentiated psychology.[45] But even these remarks remain general and do not proceed to a detailed analysis of the techniques of emotion presentation. Consequently, the specific character of emotion as represented in medieval drama remains ill-defined.

There is a considerable literature on the Marian lyric, some of which has extensively studied the relationship between the lyrical and the dramatic *planctus*.[46] But since the dramatic *planctus* so clearly derive from the lyrical ones, to the point even of verbatim quotation, they are rather atypical of the dramatic lament in general. Often they could be lifted from the plays without loss to the progress of the action. They represent an important special problem, but they must not be taken to represent the dramatic lament as a whole.

In the early 1960s Eleanor Prosser produced a study of one very important emotion.[47] She regards the late medieval emphasis on penitence as a decisive impulse for the development (possibly even the origins) of the mystery plays. Accordingly, she investigates the presentation of this emotional state in a number of dramatic figures. In spite of this programmatically *geistesgeschichtliche* position, however, she explicitly acknowledges the timelessness of value criteria[48] and subscribes to the modernist prejudice that subtle psychology and skilful characterization form the height of dramatic art.[49] Although this approach yields many valuable insights and observations, it must be said that she views the representation of feelings mainly under the aspects of characterization, composition, and (to a lesser extent) language. With this approach, the dramatic figures are not viewed against the background of linguistic and acting conventions which the religious drama of the Middle Ages had developed for the representation of human emotions.

Moreover, repentance, being theologically less suspect than other kinds of emotional pain, avoids the complications of other types of lament. Suffering and mourning always involved the danger of rebelling against the wisdom of God's decision.[50] One of the important differences between the liturgical drama and the vernacular mystery cycles is that the latter made it possible to articulate such clashes between divine command and human feeling. The fact that the Sacrifice of Isaac is the one episode to have come down to us in as many as six plays is an indication of the importance of this very conflict to the medieval playwrights.[51] This fact alone should warn us against regarding the presentation of natural human emotions (as opposed to liturgically stylized ones) as a mere by-product of the vernacular plays. It is necessary to determine the specific relationship between human emotion and divine will for each situation separately.

For this it is necessary to differentiate and supplement Prosser's results. This will now be done, at first by a systematic stock-taking, which on the one hand will consider human character only in its relevance for the emotion under investigation and on the other will extend the area of laments beyond that of repentance. In this way, it is hoped, repentance will be placed somewhat more precisely in the context of the presentation of emotion.

The peculiarity of the subject makes it necessary to deviate somewhat from the pattern followed in other chapters. Because of their special status, the Marian laments will be dealt with before the others. And since York and Towneley show so many differences with regard to the emotions, the two cycles will be dealt with separately in this chapter.

The Marian laments

If the presentation of grief in general posed delicate problems for the medieval dramatist, this was even more true of that very special grief felt by the Blessed Virgin Mary. Significantly, the early Middle Ages debated extensively whether Mary at the foot of the Cross felt grief, wept, or complained. As the Mother of God, she had to be without sin, which meant that she could not doubt her son's divinity. At the same time, she had to be a model mother and servant of God, and as such she had to love her son and participate in his torments. This dilemma, which was clearly felt by the exegetes of the early and high Middle Ages, found greatly varying solutions in the development of medieval piety.[52] The Latin *planctus* preferred, as was shown, a ceremoniously distanced style which invited the listening congregation to *lament* rather than to *suffer* with Mary. The vernacular *planctus* on the other hand, arising as they do from popular piety, are distinguished by a desire not only to venerate but to feel with the Virgin, to present a human mother who is entirely submerged in her momentary grief. The limits of this humanization will become apparent when the laments of the other figures have been investigated. For the moment, this much may suffice: Mary's laments never exploit the tension between *locus* and *platea*, which so often symbolizes the theological contrast between the divine and the human. The situational embedding of these laments is highly tenuous, for they can be expanded *ad libitum* and use laments which were originally independent, lyrical texts.[53] Their full integration into the dramatic situation takes place comparatively late in the development of the genre, notably in the work of the York Realist.

An exception to this rule, i.e. a dramatic integration of the Marian lament before the period of the York Realist, occurs in Y XXXIV (*The Road to Calvary*) and the partially identical T XXII (*Fflagellacio*).[54] Both plays share a version of the *planctus* which originates probably from the Gospel of Nicodemus.

A comparison between the two plays is made difficult by two facts: the York play lacks a leaf between lines 141 and 142, and the Towneley play has been swollen by much foreign, metrically distinct material. Nor can we be certain that the metrically uniform Y XXXIV does not contain later stanzas.[55]

According to the Gospel of Nicodemus John flees from the entourage of Christ to inform Mary and her companions that Christ has been condemned by Pilate. The *planctus* is thus embedded in a dialogue situation. The fact that it is addressed to a dramatically present listener influences its linguistic form. The laments in Towneley – those in the 'original' metre rhyming aabaabcbcb as well as the probably later ones in other metres – are more situationally embedded than those complaints which are the exclusive property of Y XXXIV. The laments of the Second and Third Marys above all are constructed according to a constant pattern which exploits contrasts for their rhetorical effect:

> II MARIA: Allas þis is a sithfull sight,
> He þat was euere luffely and light
>   And lorde of high and lawe,
> Oo! doulfully nowe is he dight. (Y XXXIV, 150–3)

> III MARIA: Allas, þis is a cursed cas.
> He þat alle hele in his hande has
>   Shall here be sakles slayne. (Y XXXIV, 180–2)

A quotation from T XXII may indicate how much more simply and directly similar ideas are worded there:

MARIA IACOBI: This lord that is of myght / dyd neuer yll truly,
Thise Iues thay do not right / if thay deme hym to dy. (T XXII, 332f)

Here it is *stated* that Jesus is without sin and 'dyd neuer yll', while in York the Marys *complain* that he shall be 'sakles slayne'. In York we are not informed that Jesus is without sin, but we experience the affects which are aroused by the condemnation of a guiltless person.

The style of the Towneley laments is somewhat prosaic. But this prosaic style is balanced by a clear grasp of scenic possibilities. Grief and tender sympathy appear as a psychological interplay which is immediately translated into stage action. John trying to break the news to Mary is at once interrupted by the anxious question: 'whi, Iohn, is my son slayn?' (T XXII, 283).[56] John, who now must tell more precisely what has happened, is at once asked by Mary Magdalene to step aside, lest Mary be overwhelmed by the terrible news (T XXII, 292–4). Concern for Mary is thus expressed scenically as well as verbally, while in York it is merely mentioned in John's monologue:

But in myn herte grete drede haue I
þat his modir for dole schall dye. (Y XXXIV, 136f)

In T XXII John reacts immediately to Jesus' entry:

Lo, where he commes vs euen agayn
with all yond mekyll prese!
All youre[57] mowrnyng in feyr/ may not his sorow sese. (lines 312–14)

Similarly, Mary begins her lament immediately on sighting her son (line 315); out of her sympathy for her son's suffering she wants at once to carry the cross. Every utterance is thus made to arise out of, and to fit, a specific moment in the action: from the words of the bystanders we can infer the moment when Jesus must appear on stage. (None of the lines quoted, by the way, belongs to the parts shared by both plays and thus presumably earliest.) In York, the wording of the laments reveals nothing of this kind.

The two plays thus reveal a contrast between York and Towneley which will be confirmed by laments in other plays. York always shows more rhetorical ornament, while Towneley prefers a simple, concrete style and often shows emotions as arising out of the situation. Often this contrast can be explained by the hypothesis that Towneley preserves an older version of York. But the Towneley play we are dealing with here demonstrates that evidently later insertions, too, follow the stylistic principle of the Towneley Plays. Since the Wakefield Master has revised this play (sts. 5–27 (= lines 53–259) are in his metre, and the last, st. 49, is only one *frons* short),[58] it is at least possible that he selected these laments with an eye to their scenic potential, even though he may not have written them. They certainly distinguish the Towneley play from its York counterpart.

The *planctus* proper of the Towneley cycle which occur in T XXIII (*Processus Crucis*), do not show the same integration as in Y XXXIV and T XXII. Mary's only function in this play is to lament the death of her son. She abruptly begins her complaint the very moment that the Torturers have dropped the cross into the mortice, with Christ already nailed to it. The force of the fall is intended to break Jesus' bones. Mary's lament is again metrically heterogeneous, and again the Wakefield Master's hand has been suspected in this part of the play – probably with less justification.[59] It is true that the play contains a Wakefield stanza (st. 57 = lines 372–81),[60] and there are also a number of lines which could be regarded as either Wakefield *frontes* ($a_3b_3ababab(ab)$) or Wakefield *caudae*, but especially the '*caudae*' – they are really tail-rhyme stanzas ($a_3aab_3c_3ccb$) – occur too often in batches to suggest much similarity with the Wakefield stanza (esp. sts. 50–4 = lines 313–60). Moreover, the rhythm is mostly smoother than in the work of the Wakefield Master. It seems more likely, therefore, that the two stanza-types in question represent different metres and different origins. Both metres also show distinct differences in style. The '*frontes*' are often shrill in their tone, use *cherché* images, apostrophize Death, and frequently emphasize the destruction of Christ's beauty:

> Alas! thyn een as cristall clere/ that shoyn as son in sight,
> That lufly were in lyere/ lost thay haue thare light,...   [lyere = face
> (T XXIII, 361f)

But above all it is Mary's own feelings which are in the foreground, and the emphasis is on the boundlessness of her grief: it causes her to 'drowpe' and 'dare in drede' (line 309), it makes her 'mad', 'redless and rad' and causes her to 'rafe' (lines 383f). This makes her grief intense but altogether human.

The effect of the '*caudae*' is quite different. The tone is plain, the attitude is one of pious adoration; the various sufferings are enumerated in simple but feeling language and are made the object of quiet contemplation. All sensationalism is avoided. Epithets, so far as they do occur, appeal to a pious, sympathizing soul. The same is true of the few details which are described somewhat more extensively:

> Alas! thi holy hede
> hase not wheron to helde;   (lines 321f)

> ffestynd both handys and feete
> With nalys full vnmete.   (lines 329f)

Another characteristic is the description of Christ's blood drops as tears (line 335). Mary's own motherly sorrow is mentioned only by way of apology:

> how shuld I stand in sted
> To se my barne thus blede? (lines 325f)

John, who reminds Mary that Christ has accepted his death voluntarily (lines 350ff), replies in the same tender tone. The religious purpose is thus always kept in mind beside the human grief.

Although the tenderness of this scene will no doubt appeal to the spectator, it remains, dramaturgically speaking, an insertion without connection to the rest of the play and without dramatic movement of its own. This changes in the *planctus* which the York Realist wrote for Y XXXVI ('Death of Christ'). The rich stylistic arsenal of the rhetorical York school is used here again: the strict structuring of, for instance, the eleventh stanza (lines 131–43) in which every other line begins with 'Allas', the *cherché* imagery which likens Jesus, among other things, to a 'blossom so bright' which 'untruly is tugged to this tree' (lines 137f). In addition to this, emotionally important words are underlined by alliteration, thus heightening their impact. Occasionally it may even be possible to read the hesitant speech rhythm of deep sorrow into these alliterations:

> My lorde, my leyffe,
> With full grete greffe. (Y XXXVI, 140f)

But the most prominent feature of this lament is its translation into a genuine dialogue. Jesus begins with an apostrophe to mankind patterned on the *Improperia* (lines 118–30).[61] Thus far, the York Realist follows the tradition. But whereas in other cycles Jesus listens to his mother's lament in silence, here he exhorts her to cease her 'weeping', since he dies at his father's command to save mankind (lines 144–7). Mary replies that she can only weep since her separation from her son is imminent (lines 148–52). This gives an added motivation to the well-known passage from John 19.26f: Jesus' words

> Womanne, instede of me,
> Loo, John þi sone schall be. (lines 153f)

are a direct answer to Mary's complaint, and they also motivate the tender tone of caring reproach in which John tries to calm her. With this exact feeling for the right moment the York Realist creates what is perhaps the most moving moment of the play: Mary, who has not yet realized that Jesus has died after receiving the drink of vinegar and gall, asks him to address her for a last time:

> Now dere sone, Jesus so jente,
> Sen my harte is heuy as leede,
> O worde wolde I witte or þou wente.
> Allas, nowe my dere sone is dede. (lines 261–4)

It was observed earlier that the York Realist writes in a tradition which has already lost a good deal of the original pageant-waggon dramaturgy.[62] We have often seen what losses of histrionic as well as edificational potential this entails. But here the later type with its tendency toward the closed play-sphere is in a better position to render the complexity of interpersonal relationships. The *dramatis personae* are indeed able to 'forget' the presence of the audience and to work out the details of the emotional interplay so that the audience can empathize with it.

This high art of representing emotions is hardly present in the Chester cycle (Ch XVIA, 241–64 and 333–6 in Lumiansky/Mills (MS Hm), Ch XVI, 625–64 and 733–6 in Deimling/Matthews (MS H)). Here we find once more the type of the 'inserted' lament which remains unconnected with the surrounding drama. The beginning is characteristic: Pilate has completed the inscription 'INRI' and is reprimanded for it by the Third Jew. In answer to this the cross is erected, and at the same time Mary advances. MS H carries an unequivocal stage direction: *tunc omnes Crucem exaltabunt et veniet Maria*. Since all iconographic conventions suggest that Mary's lament takes place at the foot of the cross, no other solution seems possible, even though the other MSS are not so committal. The scene in which Mary is to lament is thus created for the purpose. Mary begins with vehement complaints; she does not *describe* her emotions (only in line 242(LM) = 626(DM)) but transforms her grief at once into wishes, asking Jesus to come to her aid, to have mercy on her suffering since he has the power to do so:

> Alas! my Boote looke thou be,
> thy mother that thee bare!
> Think on my freut! I fosterd thee,
> and gaue the sucke vpon my knee;
> vpon my payne haue thou pitty!
> thee faylës no power. (Ch XVI, 627–32, Deimling/Matthews)

The lament is not uniform as far as style and piety are concerned. On the strength of the manuscripts we can distinguish two parts: one, Ch XVI, 625–40(DM)/Ch XVIA, 241–56(LM)[63] and Ch XVI, 657–64(DM)/Ch XVIA, 257–64(LM), is common to all MSS; the other, Ch XVI, 641–56(DM)/apparatus p. 315(LM), occurs only in MS Harley

2124 (H) which Deimling and Matthews chose as the base text for their edition and whose superiority was recognized by such an authority as W.W. Greg.[64] More likely than not, the lines unique to H are a later insertion, but other variants in H, which concern the stage movement of the *dramatis personae*, suggest that H was closer to Chester stage practice than the other MSS.[65] We may conclude, therefore, that the interpolation was actually staged and was meant as a kind of counterpoise to the original part.

The differences between both parts are considerable. In the text common to all MSS, a very worldly mother is speaking who above all asks her son for help in her own grief. She even implores him to have pity upon *her* grief (XVI, 631(DM)/XVIA, 247(LM)). Her own life seems to her meaningless in view of her son's death pangs, which she describes in brief, powerful, rhythmically effective words:

> Alas! why ne were my lyfe forlorne?
> to fynd my foodë my beforne
> Tugged, Lugged, all to-torne
> with Traytors, now this tyde?   (XVI, 633–6(DM)/XVIA, 249–52(LM))

Even her wish to die in her son's stead, which is traditional in the *planctus*, takes the form of a (gentle) maternal rebuke:

> alas! my sorrow why wilt thou not slake,
> and to thes Traytours me betake,
> to suffer death, Sonne, for thy sake,
> and doe as I thee say?   (XVI, 657–60(DM)/XVIA, 257–60(LM))

In all of this there is little pious contemplation or *compassio*. The dominant feeling is that of her own creaturely grief. The precarious balance between maternal love and acceptance of God's will which we found in York and even in parts of Towneley is abandoned here.

But this one-sided emphasis on the human aspects of the Mother of Sorrows must have given offence at a later period. This at least is the most plausible explanation for the entirely different tone which we encounter in the interpolation (XVI, 641–56(DM)). Here, Christ is no longer the child which she has held on her knees and suckled (XVI, 630(DM)/ XVIA, 246(LM)), but the God who chose her for his mother (XVI, 645(DM)). Her speech-style changes accordingly. She is no longer the mother who may expect assistance and obedience from her son – even from *this* son – but the praying woman who certainly has been distinguished by becoming the mother of God and who may mention this contribution to the salvation of mankind in support of her prayers, but who always remains conscious that she directs her prayers to one infinitely greater than herself. The very fact that she gives reasons for her prayers, thus giving them the character of a plea, is characteristic of these sixteen lines.

The author of the insertion must have been conscious that too excessive human grief would be detrimental to the impression of a *compassio* which is believed to have a share in the salvation of mankind. His Mary almost prays forgiveness for her grief:

> how should I apayd be or in peace,
> to se thee in such Penaunce? (XVI, 643–4(DM))

Neither does he forget that Mary, for all her grief, is always aware of the joy which is awarded by Christ's presence:

> Alas! the sorrow of this sight
> marrs my mynd, mayne and might,
> but aye my hart me think is light,
> to looke on that I love. (XVI, 649–52(DM))

This joy, she continues, could be even heightened if she were allowed to die together with her son (XVI, 653–6(DM)). The death wish of the older part (XVI, 657–64(DM)/XVIA, 257–64(LM)) appears thus in an entirely new light.

Our hypothesis that the interpolation was written with the intention of mitigating the unabashedly human passion of the original lines gains in strength when we consider the interpolation with regard to its position in the lament as a whole. The 'apologies' which Mary offers for her complaints immediately follow those stanzas in which she gives her grief a free rein, and her wish to die together with Christ (XVI, 653–6(DM)) immediately precedes her request to die in his stead (XVI, 657–60(DM)/XVIA, 257–60(LM)). The interpolation introduces no new themes, but only sheds a new light on those which were already introduced in the original. For these reasons Deimling seems to be right in regarding XVI, 641–56 as a later insertion in H (p. xxiv). Unlike Deimling, however, we believe that there are good reasons for such a hypothesis. If our assumption is correct, our view of the didacticism of the Chester cycle has been differentiated in one not altogether unimportant respect. The endeavour to achieve theological correctness would have continued after the great revision which led to the incorporation of much material from the *Stanzaic Life of Christ* and probably to the introduction of the Expositor as well.

The N-Town Cycle is the one which devotes most space to the Virgin Mary. Marian laments appear here in places where they are unknown in other cycles.[66] Two shorter laments are produced at the *Depositio* and immediately after the Resurrection (LC XXXIV, p. 311, and XXXV, p. 321). Both laments are unknown to the other English mystery cycles.[67]

Even more important is another lament, equally unique to LC, which occurs at the end of *Passion Play I* (Block, pp. 267–9). In this scene Mary Magdalene hurries to the Virgin to inform her of her son's capture.[68] She does not, however, address her as one would a good acquaintance, but rather like a figure who already enjoys cult-like veneration:

> O in-maculate modyr of all women most meke
> O devowtest in holy medytacion evyr A-bydyng.
>
> (LC, p. 267, lines 1,041f)

Mary, however, does not react like the distant Queen of Heaven that one might expect after such an address. She shows much more of her human nature than is the case in the other Marian laments. She asks herself why the sinless one must die: this is a motif which in York and Towneley was voiced only by the other Marys. She believes herself guilty of her son's death (line 1,063), she even argues with God the Father and asks finally if there is no other way to save mankind (lines 1,077f). But immediately after this last rebellion she accepts her fate (line 1,079) and finally begs Christ's pity for humanity, explicitly including herself:

> On All man-kend now haue þou pety
> And Also thynk on þi modyr þat hevy woman.   (lines 1,083f)

This is clearly a very different Mary from the one we have met in the other cycles. The pains of a mother become less important than Mary's rôle as a model of piety, who is above all conscious of the fact that her own sins have contributed to her son's Passion.

In marked contrast to the didacticism of this lament is the scene at the foot of the cross, which psychologically is probably one of the best and most sensitive of all cycles. The scene (LC XXXII, pp. 298ff) begins, as in Chester, as a great entry: after the cross has been erected and the Jews have sat down for their dicing game,

xal oure lady come with iij maryes with here and sen Johan with heme settyng hem down A-syde A-fore þe cros · oure lady swuonyng and mornyng (p. 298, line 769 +)

After two highly rhetorical stanzas which are adorned with apostrophes to her son, to her own heart, and to death (three times), another new stage direction commands: *here oure lady xal swonge A-ȝen and ore lord xal seyn þus* (p. 299, line 777 +). But instead of answering his mother, Christ implores God's forgiveness for his murderers, promising even one of the malefactors a place in Paradise (lines 808f). Mary's complaint that she is the only one to whom he has not spoken is common to all cycles, but here it gains in force from the high pathos of her preceding lament – especially since the lament now following is altogether different in style. Instead of pathetic exclamations we hear questions which, for all the grief they express, are uttered in an intimate, almost colloquial tone:

> what haue I defendyd þe
> þou hast spoke to alle þo · þat ben here
> and not o word þou spekyst to me. (lines 811–13, p. 300)⁶⁹

This lament dispenses entirely with the depiction of gruesome detail: Mary's sorrow is grounded solely on the fact that she believes her relationship with her son disturbed. The same tender consideration which takes the mood of the hearer into account is to be heard in Jesus' answer:

> Now syn it is þe wyl of my fadyr it xuld þus be
> Why xuld it dysplese þe modyr · (lines 830f, p. 300)

Complaint and consolation create a genuine dialogue which even furthers the action. Mary is asked by John and Mary Magdalene not to increase her son's pain (lines 836f, 842ff). At the same time, the complaint does not allow the dying of Christ to be forgotten: John leads Mary away from the Cross to a 'temple' saying:

> ffor he is Al-most redy to go his way (line 845, p. 301)

The author of this play has created a dialogue which is unique for its situational embedding and empathy. This kind of emotional representation remains largely alien to the mystery cycles. In this respect, the N-Town cycle stands together with the Brome and Dublin Abraham plays, whose staging methods and probable audience will be discussed in a later section.

Apart from the great cycles there is one Good Friday and Easter Sunday Play which bears hardly any similarities to the mystery cycles but which for its wealth of Marian laments must be considered here. *The Burial and Resurrection of Christ* was edited by Furnivall together with the *Digby Plays*,⁷⁰ although it has certainly never formed part of that collection.⁷¹ Although the modern editors admit that the *Burial* and the *Resurrection* 'are two parts of one religious drama, or acted meditation', they treat them as two plays and number the lines separately (in contrast to Furnivall).⁷² They have demonstrated the Carthusian origins of MS *e Museo* 160 which account for its strong emphasis on affective piety.⁷³ The *Burial and Resurrection* has been called an 'elaborate planctus' by Chambers.⁷⁴ G. C. Taylor succinctly sums up the special character of the play: 'If the planctus are cut out of the cyclic plays, fairly complete plays are left; Digby would not be a play without the planctus.'⁷⁵

Among these *planctus* there are masterpieces like 'Who can not wepe, com lern at me'⁷⁶ which by its vivid description of the wounds asks the listeners to relive the cruelty of the torturers and the greatness of the

Passion. But the linguistic and emotional intensity of this *planctus* only makes it clear how little the author of our dialogues was able to create anything equivalent. Although he does master the art, rare in the mystery cycles, of meshing speech and stage events, he does not have the finer nuances of feeling at his command which are necessary for a dialogue made up of complaint and consolation. The story of the Passion is trivialized when John asks Mary simply to forget the events of Good Friday:

> From your remembraunce, rayse owt at þe last
> Of his passione the crueltee. (CB, 473f)

Later on, Mary's complaint will be motivated just as superficially: it is to provide her 'ease' and 'content' (CB, 608). The lament which is to recall the Passion of the Lord is thus placed on the same level as the oblivion which was recommended earlier: both are considered, anthropocentrically, for their therapeutic value. Mary's grief thus is equated with the grief of any human mother. But even sympathy with this secularized grief is limited to externals. Fundamentally, the consideration of the bystanders is not directed at Mary's feelings, but at her behaviour. After her very first words she faints and elicits a comment from Mary Magdalene which in its soberness sounds like an involuntary parody:

> Lo! I was sure sho walld falle in a swown! (CB, 459)

John is now faced with the very practical task of bringing Mary back to consciousness. He accompanies his efforts with such friendly reproaches as the following:

> Ye promesit me ye wold not do thus. (CB, 467)

In the further course of the action the group are more concerned to moderate Mary's behaviour than to alleviate her grief. John's words allowing her, subject to good conduct, to be present at the burial, have a ring of almost juridical pedantry:

> Lady, if ye wille haue moderation
> Of youre most sorowfull lamentacion,
> Do as ye list, *in this case*. (CB, 600–2)[77]

Joseph of Arimathia especially seems to fear that Mary's moaning may disturb the work at the burial. Several times he tries in curt, even rude words to make her go:

> Haue hir hence, John, now I desire. (CB, 550)

As she appears in these dialogues, Mary justifies such fears. She is not even above scoring minor debating points. When Joseph says:

> We wald not haue you here (CB, 564),

Mary retorts:

> Wold ye renewe mor sorow in me? (CB, 565)

No sooner has Joseph denied this than Mary draws her conclusion, almost as in a comedy dialogue:

> Than late me abide hym nere! (CB, 567)

For all the violence of her lamentations, Mary appears as a resolute middle-class woman.[78] The accusations and imprecations which she hurls against Judas may serve to illustrate this aspect of her character:

> O, Judas, why didist thou betraye
> My son, þi master? What can þou saye,
>   Thyself for tille excuse?
> ...
> Callyt not he þe to his supere and last refection?
> Cowth þou not put owt þi pesyn and infection
>   Saue thus only,
> Vnto thy master to be so vnkind?
> Was his tender gudness owt of thy mynd
>   So vnnaturallye?
>
> Gaue he not to the his body in memorialle,
> And also in remembraunce perpetualle
>   At his suppere there?
> He that was so comly and fayre to behold,
> How durst thou, cruelle hert, to be so bold
>   To cawse hym dy thus here? (CB, 526–8, 532–43)

The former beauty of Christ is a popular motif in many *planctus*, but usually it contrasts with the disfiguring wounds which he has received from his torturers. The memory thus conjures up a contrast which rekindles the mother's grief. But here the motif has been transferred mechanically and now seems to add an aggravating circumstance to Judas' betrayal. Judas is scolded like any villain who ought to have chosen a fitter object for his destructive inclinations. The automatically attached theological commonplaces (like 'his body in memorialle', line 538) and the synonyms of Latin origin which merely duplicate the native word help but to underline the platitudinous rationality of the reproaches.

This lament shows the characteristic limitations of the medieval religious drama which will reappear, on a much higher level, in the lament of the York Judas: whenever this drama attempts to 'understand' its villains and their motives it risks becoming melodramatic or even involuntarily comical. Although these limitations become apparent primarily in the representation of evil characters, they are also effective in that of the good ones, becoming manifest as externalization and sentimentalization. The reduction of Judas to the level of a normal villain finds its counterpart in the fact that Mary's grief has become hardly more than a series of swoons which disturbs the business of the deposition and a 'good cry' which softens her pain but has lost its dimension as salvific *compassio*.

Other laments

Laments in the Towneley Plays

The Towneley cycle, which owes its fame primarily to the comic genius of the Wakefield Master, is comparatively poor in laments. Those which do occur are usually assigned to the earlier strata of the cycle and impress the reader as somewhat archaic. Only the *Annunciacio* (T X) has been severally praised for its tenderness, which is enhanced by linguistic simplicity.[79] As far as the representation of emotions is concerned, the *Annunciacio* resembles the Towneley *Abraham* (T IV), which has received far less praise.[80] Perhaps we are here in the presence of a convention which the York cycle has lost in the course of its development.[81]

In both plays the emotion has first of all to be triggered by a specific external cause. Such external causes can be concrete objects or extra-linguistic situations. In any case the expression of feelings thus becomes a reaction, it is not an utterance of the soul entirely detached from external circumstances. This unison of speech and object, of the inward and outward, creates that simultaneous impact on the mind and the eye of the spectator which is characteristic of probably all stage genres from the liturgical to the Shakespearean drama. These early plays resemble the liturgical drama in that they make the extra-linguistic phenomenon the immediate trigger of the psychological reaction. Unlike Hamlet with his skull, Joseph and Abraham are not in a position to choose an object as a reason for their reactions.

The beginning of Joseph's lament (T X, 155) is a typical example of this way of reacting: Joseph enters and, in evident agitation, reports Mary's pregnancy:

A, hyr body is grete and she with childe! (T X, 158)

The situation is thus realized in its physical, visible aspects, and it is this sensual impression which provokes Joseph's further reactions:

I irke full sore with my lyfe (T X, 161)

In the further course of the play the close connection between his emotional outbursts and immediate external factors becomes even more apparent: he goes to Mary to discover the identity of the child's father. Mary's repeated answer that it is his and God's (lines 187, 195, 204) can only irritate him further as an evidently blasphemous lie. This impression becomes the dominant motif of his utterances in comparison to which even the feeling of having been cuckolded takes second place.

The emotional potential of concrete details becomes apparent in the dialogue with Sara which Abraham imagines to himself and which brings home to him the horror of God's command -- immediately before Isaac is spared:

> What shal I to his moder say?
> ffor 'where is he,'
> If I tell hir, 'ron away,'
> hir answere bese belife – 'nay, sir!'
> And I am ferd hir for to slay. (T IV, 225–9)

Abraham's complaint resembles that of Joseph since the emotional 'trigger' does not need to be immediately present. But it has to be a vivid impression on the speaker's senses.

Among the most effective impressions in the sense indicated here are the spatial relations between the speaker and other characters, especially their presence or absence. The words just quoted are spoken 'aside' by Abraham: two stanzas previously he had turned away from Isaac to hide his tears under the pretext 'I mys a lytyll thyng' (line 214). Already before the journey to the place of sacrifice Isaac's entries and exits served to make Abraham's grief verbal (lines 9ff, 105ff). But even this grief disappears before the necessary preparations for the journey:

> And it is good that I be war,
> To be avised full good it were.
> The land of vision is ful far,
> The thrid day end must I be there. (T IV, 113–16)

Moods here do not have continuity in time. As far as their emotions are concerned, the characters seem to have no 'memory': what they experience now is not coloured by what they remember. In keeping with this, Joseph's telling of his marriage to Mary (T X, 227ff) is entirely separate from what has preoccupied him until then. This report, addressed to the audience as it is, is hardly 'logically motivated by his growing frustration'.[82] On the contrary: by its lack of emotional grounding it acquires that tone of objective validity which makes the tale of the miracle independent of the credibility of its teller.

As we have seen, the tale of Joseph's marriage is emotionally discontinuous with the irritated Joseph of the previous scene. Presumably this tale, which has all the signs of an audience-address, was also spoken at a different part of the stage from the preceding dialogue with

Mary. We may assume that *Deus* and Mary each had their respective *sedes* at either end of the stage. Between these two *sedes* there was a neutral space which was above all dominated by Joseph but which had also to be crossed by the Angel when announcing Christ's birth to Mary or informing Joseph of the true cause of Mary's pregnancy. This is not the place to discuss the physical nature of the two *sedes*,[83] but we may assume that after his taking leave of Mary Joseph went to the centre front of this neutral space and addressed the audience from there. If the neutral space here serves as the place of religious proclamation, this is only one of its functions. Earlier in the play the same spot had served Joseph for his lament on the infidelity of young women – that is for a speech on an extremely worldly and commonplace subject.[84] The betrayal of old husbands by their young wives was considered a well-known, proverbial fact in that speech:

> I myght well wyt that yowthede
> wold haue lykyng of man.
> ...
> It is ill cowpled of youth and elde; (T X, 165–70)

Platea and *locus*, the biblical characters' closeness to God and the everyday person's remoteness from Him: this contrast is most acute in the Towneley Abraham play. When God has told Abraham to sacrifice his son, Abraham is at first incredibly willing:

> *ffayn* wold I this thyng ordand. (T IV, 79, emphasis added)

But immediately after he says:

> This commaundement must I nedis fulfill,
> If that my hert wax hevy as leyde;
> Shuld I offend my lordis will?
> Nay, yit were I leyffer my child were dede.
> What so he biddis me, good or ill,
> That shall be done in euery stede;
> Both wife and child, if he bid spill;
> I wille not do agans his rede. (T IV, 81–8)

Between the two quotations, the editor has added an 'Exit Deus'. We may assume almost certainly that God found some way of withdrawing from the spectators' sight after Abraham had declared his willingness to obey. Abraham's further words may thus be considered a *platea* speech, even if we do not assume that Abraham left the foot of God's *sedes* immediately. The *platea* thus changes the inhumanly faithful servant of God into a father who cannot detach himself from his creaturely, fatherly emotions even though he still considers God's command as binding. There is thus no question that 'the fundamental inhumanity of that story was, of course [!], not apparent to our medieval ancestors'.[85] The medieval stage was quite capable of juxtaposing the human horror of the story and its salvific relevance.

Laments in the York Plays

According to some scholars (especially in the earlier half of this century) the Towneley plays which formed the centre of the previous chapter may well have been earlier versions of the corresponding extant York plays. In the case of the Joseph play (T XIII) this assumption amounts to something like certainty,[86] for the Abraham play it is at least a strong possibility:[87] the style of these plays may thus be representative of an older way of representing emotions which was later discarded in York. This opens a field of fascinating speculation, but for our purposes it is sufficient to state that York exhibits a type of lament which is as uniform as the one in Towneley and which in at least one case can be assumed to be a revision of the Towneley type.

An important difference between the two types of lament is revealed by the language. In Towneley the emotions become manifest only in verbs and adjectives: they are attributes of their carriers without an existence of their own. Since these carriers are normally human beings or a human organ like the heart, these laments demonstrate a naïve and vivid realism:

If that my hert wax hevy as lede;	(Abraham, T IV, 82)
Might I speke to myn hart brast,	(Abraham, T IV, 110)
I irke full sore with my lyfe.	(Joseph, T X, 161)

In York, by contrast, these emotions are hypostasized. They become the subject of the sentence and can even be qualified by a metaphorical adjective:

Oure cares ar comen bothe kyne and colde, With fele fandyngis manyfolde;	(Eve, Y VI, 46f)
Mournynge makis me mased and madde,	(Adam, Y VI, 82)
This is to me a perles pyne,	(Abraham, Y X, 239)
Of grete mornyng may I me mene	(Joseph, Y XIII, 1)

Such phrasings go back to a process of abstraction which raises original predicates to subjects on which new predications can be made and which now appear, at least metaphorically, as efficacious forces. Such predications may be alien to everyday thinking and to the concrete laments of the Towneley plays, but they are as familiar to the philosophy of the medieval schools as they are to modern psychology.

This removal from popular language entails also a structural change of the laments. In contrast to Towneley, where they are normally kindled by some concrete, specific object or situation, the York laments find their internal coherence in the mood of the speaker. External situations and events do not provoke reactions, but are on the contrary evoked, called forth by the speakers. They are the material which feeds the mood. In consequence of this the stark immediacy of the individual impression becomes less important than the general characterization of the situation. Whereas Joseph in Towneley said already near the beginning of his lament: 'hyr body is grete and she with childe!' (T X, 15), he needs more than four stanzas before he can express the same state of affairs rather more mildly: 'My ʒonge wiffe is with childe full grete' (Y XIII, 43). Not the body is *grete*, but only Mary herself. In T X observation and inference were offered separately, each by itself conveying the psychological impact which they must have had on Joseph. The audience was thus invited to follow the cuckold's discovery in the same succession as he had made it. In York Mary's physical appearance and her state are summarized in one expression; *grete*, especially as it does not stand at the beginning of the lament, loses some of its direct, optical impact: it means hardly more than 'pregnant'. In combination with *ʒonge* in the first half of the line it concentrates the hearer's attention much more on the supposedly moral aspect of the matter. The loveliness which surrounds the conventional picture of Mary is far less disturbed than in T X.

The aspects which are evoked to illustrate the mood are always related to one another in such a manner as to make the speaker appear to be the one who arranges and orders them. Joseph's present grief is fed by the memory of his miraculous and apparently auspicious marriage with Mary.[88] In the same way Adam and Eve underline their present misfortune by contrasting it to their lost happiness:

>   ADAM: To byggly blys we bothe wer brought;
>   Whillis we wer þare
>   We hadde inowe, nowe haue we noghte -
>   Allas, for care.   (Y VI, 42–5)

The contrast between once and now can also be viewed as a nexus between cause and effect, which at the same time implies acceptance of God's punishment as just:

>   EUA: Allas, þat euyr we neghed it nere,
>   þat tree vntill.
>   With dole now mon we bye full dere
>   Oure dedis ille.   (Y VI, 65–8)

Such antitheses can verbalize contrasts which the Towneley plays represent spatially and scenically. The contradiction between divine command and human inclination which in the Towneley Abraham play was conveyed by the *Figurenposition* (Weimann) is expressed in a syntactic parallelism in York:

It is Goddis will, it sall be myne. (Y X, 243)

The distance between the two which persists in spite of Abraham's willingness to obey, is expressed in the repetition of *sall* (lines 244, 245). While in Towneley the divine and the human sphere are spatially separate, they collide within the human psyche in York. This conflict is not as subtly expressed as for instance in the Northampton Abraham play: it is reflected, rather, in a somewhat frosty striving for theological correctness. Isaac says, for instance: '*My flessche* for dede will be dredande' (Y X, 210, emphasis added). In spite of the theological interest of the play it is hardly correct to call it less emotional than other Isaac plays.[89] To be sure, Isaac appears more clearly than elsewhere as a type of Christ,[90] but Towneley also emphasizes that the sacrifice of Isaac is to serve the salvation of mankind (T IV, 49–56, 65–73).[91] And the personal fates of Abraham and his family are stressed more strongly in the opening prayer of York than in that of Towneley. York is distinguished from Towneley not so much by emotional restraint as by an attempt to harmonize the conflict between divine and human concerns. Inevitably, the human predicament becomes idealized in the process, especially since the York Abraham does not show that intense inner struggle which characterizes his counterpart in the Northampton play. That play, whose unity of dramaturgy and emotional expression is unique in medieval English drama, will be discussed later.

Intensity of the inner struggle, however, concerns differences of artistic rank, whose importance for the history of dramatic form is certainly not negligible but which is nevertheless secondary compared to the genre-specific divide which runs between York and Towneley – between the two Abraham plays as well as between the two Joseph plays. The York plays differ from their Towneley counterparts in that dramatic space and dramatic action have become psychologized, even if the former strike the modern observer as less skilful and somewhat frostier.[92]

The 'psychologizing' of the York plays under discussion is largely a matter of rhetorical technique, and this is probably the reason why modern critics have never been happy with these plays. The story relies for its effect on verbal means rather than on the immediate force of the senses. The skilfully but somewhat bookishly employed rhetorical figures pay little heed to the extra-linguistic situation, they are available *ad libitum* and thus tend toward prolixity. Lengthy descriptions of the speaker's state of mind and descriptions of gesture (e.g. Y VI, 77–122; X, 223–94; XIII, 1–20; XXXIX, 1–22) with numerous exclamations and rhetorical questions make the action slow down and cause the dramatic tension to slacken. It is hard to imagine a greater contrast than that between the quick exchanges shortly before Isaac's sacrifice in T IV, 177–212 and the aria-like complaints extending over many stanzas in Y X (especially lines 201–94). Dramatic speech has been transformed into a lyrical-rhetorical effusion.

When dramatic speech becomes detached from the situation in which it is uttered, the function of traditional speech forms and stage positions also undergoes some radical changes. The Joseph of the Towneley *Annunciacio*, by reflecting on the fate of elderly husbands in general sentences, stepped out of the dramatic sphere and into the situation of his spectators and fellow citizens. A longer quotation may serve to illustrate how differently this matter is handled in York:

> ADAM: Do way, woman, and neme it noght,
>
> > For at my biddyng wolde þou not be
> > And therfore my woo wyte Y thee;
> > Thurgh ille counsaille þus casten ar we
> > > In bittir bale.
> > Nowe God late never man aftir me
> > > Triste woman tale.
> >
> > For certis me rewes full sare
> > That euere I shulde lerne at þi lare,
> > Thy counsaille has casten me in care,
> > > þat þou me kende. (Y VI, 144–54)

A sentence like 'Nowe God late never man aftir me triste woman tale' would be quite conceivable in a speech of the Towneley Joseph; but the justification which would follow it would ignore the dialogue situation. The York Adam, by contrast, returns immediately to his dialogue partner with the words 'þi lare'.

Occasionally the complaints become genuine dialogues. In our case Eve asks Adam to be quiet and not to mention the matter again (line 155). A similar interplay of attitudes occurred at the beginning of the same play, when the Angel asked Adam to stop his moaning, pointing out that it was all his own fault (lines 30ff) and not even accepting his excuse that he had been seduced by his wife (lines 34ff). But this interplay works here in only one direction: each complaint is rejected by the Angel; Adam and Eve do not answer the Angel's refutations but turn to the next topos of complaint.

A strange and perhaps symptomatic contradiction between outer and inner form becomes visible when we consider the verse ornament of the play. The majority of the stanzas are connected by *concatenatio*. One would think that this device is particularly well suited for the exchange between complaint and refutation which is being verbalized here. The part of speech in which a complaint reaches its climax could easily become the starting point for the refutation in the following stanza, a refutation could be turned into self-reproach, and so forth. But very little of this actually happens. The exchange between the Angel and the expelled is accompanied only twice by a verbal repetition (lines 23/4 and 51/2). But *concatenatio* is dispensed with exactly when the Angel replies to Adam or Eve directly (lines 30, 36, 69) or when a real exchange between Adam and Eve arises (lines 144, 155). The result is that *concatenatio* dominates primarily the Angel's introductory speech (lines 1–23) and Adam's long complaint (lines 77–122). Apart from these instances it appears when Adam and Eve take turns with their complaints (lines 41–51, 61–8, 123–34). It is a device which dominates above all the un-dialogical parts of the play and is more characteristic of the play as a whole than the dramatic exchanges between dialogue partners. These exchanges remain largely a decorative-formal element. Again, it is tempting to compare the composition of the play with an opera: instead of a living, permanently changing relationship between two partners we hear a duet of complaints. This duet is dialogical in the sense that it contains the element of mutual reproach – but only as a rigid, unchanging element which is added to the other element of the lament over lost happiness. The two elements do not intermingle. If we interpret the differences between Towneley and York correctly, then turning away from the audience and increased stylistic *ornatus* are two aspects of the same tendency: both are meant to lift the action out of the everyday existence of the spectators. We can only speculate as to the causes of this tendency, but it seems reasonable to assume that the style was to the liking of the affluent men who controlled the Corporation of the City of York in the first half of the fifteenth century.

On the whole it needs to be admitted that this development has led to a loss of dramatic vitality. But it must be admitted, too, that the conventions established in the York cycle produced some remarkable achievements. It is above all the York Realist who has to be seen against this local tradition. It is our belief that Robinson's thesis, which was taken up approvingly by Weimann, requires to be somewhat modified: Robinson thinks that the York Realist adopted and perfected the conventions of the mystery play.[93] In our opinion he has perfected the conventions which he found *in York*. But these had already undergone learned influence and were removed from the popular forms which we can observe in Towneley. These, with their strong reference to the present which often takes the form of anachronism, their *tua res agitur*, can be regarded as a transposition of the medieval sermon into the dramatic medium.[94]

In York, on the other hand, the play-world is comparatively closed to the audience-world and by that token to the present. The use of rhetorical devices gives it a certain aesthetic autonomy. The extent to which the York Realist is indebted to this rhetorical tradition is best shown in one of his recognized masterpieces, the repentance monologue of Judas (Y XXXII, 129–152). It begins with a passionate self-desecration in which Judas also includes his parents.[95] This emotional root position is followed, in clear rhetorical disposition, by the explanation. But again the explanation is not given as a dry report; we do not learn why and under what circumstances Judas has betrayed Jesus, but only those aspects of the story are mentioned which trouble Judas' conscience. There is first of all the moral wrongness of his action:

> For I so falsely did to hym
> þat vnto me grete kyndnesse kidde.   (lines 134f)

The contrast between Jesus' trust and Judas' breaking it is the basis for the entire monologue. The mood which takes possession of Judas in the face of his own guilt and damnation leads his thoughts to the situation in which he supposes Jesus to be now:

> Shamously myselfe þus schente I
> So sone for to sente to his slayng.
> Nowe wiste I howe he myght passe þat payne.   (lines 145–7)

Thinking of the suffering which he has brought upon Jesus, he decides that he now wants to save him:

> Vnto þe Jues I will agayne
> To saue hym - he myght passe free,
> þis ware my will.   (lines 149–51)

We thus become witness to a psychological development leading from mood to resolution. About this resolution we learn little more than that it is made. This reinforces the impression that Judas' plan is not yet developed in all its details but is gradually taking shape in his troubled mind. Word order and alliteration contribute their share to making the speaker's emotions credible.[96] Several times the beginning of the line is marked by words in which the expression of the emotion is concentrated (lines 141, 143, 145). The alliteration, which occasionally even underlines the contrast between Jesus' innocence and Judas' treachery, works in the same direction:

> Sakles I solde his blessid body.   (line 141)

No doubt there is an author at work here who has a rich arsenal of stylistic devices at his disposal and who knows how to use them effectively. But there can be no doubt either that this arsenal is a product of the schools.[97] The poetic ambition and the stylistic virtuosity which are in evidence here are certainly greater than in the work of the Wakefield Master, and the pathos of Judas' speech would probably have been unattainable for the creator of Mak. If in the last resort we find this speech less excellent than the *Secunda Pastorum*, the reason is that here something is attempted which must remain outside the scope of the mystery play: the monologue is devised to create for Judas that sympathy which we can bestow only on the sovereign antagonist of secularized tragedy who sets his own goals and purposes. Judas, who after all is only an instrument in God's plan of salvation, cannot claim such sympathy – even compassion with the damned is originally alien to Christian thinking. The influence of classical rhetoric demonstrates thus in its most successful products how little suited it is to the genre of the mystery play.

Laments in the Chester Plays
Nowhere is the didactic tendency of the Chester cycle more in evidence than in the complaints. Since this speech-type lends itself to the expression of emotion rather more easily than most others, it is particularly well suited to demonstrate the exclusiveness with which the speakers' every utterance is subordinated to the didactic purpose of the cycle. Although of course all cycles want to instruct their audiences on the basic tenets of Christian belief, Chester is distinguished in that it gives this instruction directly even in situations in which York and Towneley show above all a state of strong emotional agitation. In the preceding sections we tried to show that the theological, exemplary effect of the characters and events need not be destroyed and can even be heightened by such emotionalization. In that sense York and Towneley are didactic too. But they achieve their didactic effect as it were by a detour: via pious empathy, via cathartic emotion, and via recognition of realistically depicted everyday reality. It is the absence of this broad spectrum of empathetic effects which gives the Chester cycle its characteristic stamp.[98]

This is probably the reason why the cycle has received such different evaluations. There can be no doubt that the Chester plays impress the modern reader as particularly strange and dry. This may have encouraged scholars to give credence to those traditions which attribute a particularly early date to the cycle[99] and to consider it particularly 'medieval'.[100] Belief in an early date has clearly influenced the aesthetic evaluation of the cycle, which often corresponds to the ideological position of the critic. While E. K. Chambers deplores the lack of a 'human element' in the cycle, Craig praises the conservatism of the citizens of Chester: 'they performed a miracle in keeping their plays, as a whole, unspoiled by modernity.'[101] However contrary these judgments, both reveal a comparatively undifferentiated notion of the essence of 'the' Middle Ages and of the medieval drama in particular. But the *laudator temporis acti* does not *a priori* have a better key to the past than the optimistic believer in progress, and such re-evaluation remains fundamentally sterile.

It seems more useful to study the expressive and affective devices of the mystery play and its stage in its own development (which may well be retrogressive). This is probably the best way to discover the specific achievement of which the genre is capable, which plays develop the potential creatively and which leave it unexploited. In the latter case we believe ourselves justified to diagnose 'undramatic' tendencies, using this term not in an anachronistic sense which would be uncritically taken from the horizon of expectations raised by modern drama but in an historically meaningful one which is relevant to the development of the genre itself. We hope to show that this 'undramatic' tendency is represented by the Chester plays. Our litmus test will be an exemplary analysis of the Chester *Abraham and Isaac*, which for our purposes has the advantage of being influenced by two sources: first, the narrative *Stanzaic Life of Christ* and second, the famous Abraham play which has come down to us in the well-known commonplace book of Brome.

But before considering this rather complex case of double influence, the other laments in the cycle are to be analyzed. There are far fewer of them than in York or Towneley, and the analysis will demonstrate how the objective viewpoint of the dramatist predominates over the subjectivity of the *dramatis personae*. The characters in this cycle view themselves far more as exponents of moral and theological principles than as people who are placed in a given situation and the mood that goes with it. The fact that they hardly exploit the scenic potential of the pageant stage is an additional proof that we are not using the expression 'undramatic' ahistorically. An example may illustrate this:

> Alas, now in longer [languor] I am ilente!
> Alas, nowe shamely am I shente!
> For I was unobedyente,
> of weale now am I wayved.
>
> Now all my kynde by mee ys kente
> to flee womens intycemente.
> Whoe trusteth them in any intente,
> truely hee is disceaved. (Ch II, 345-52)

The abstract diction of this lament of Adam resembles that of its counterpart in York and is rather unlike that of Towneley. This is almost sufficient to justify the assumption that we are here faced with a conscious abandonment of the popular tradition, not with an original, 'naïve' use of dramatic language. It is true that compared to York there is far less rhetorical or stylistic *ornatus*. The psychological states are not being evoked or circumscribed but are stated drily and directly (line 345). The schematism of the lament makes it appear as constructed from the 'outside' rather than from the 'inside'. It is conceived intellectually rather than emotionally. At first Adam describes his own situation on a most abstract, general level, without any emotionally effective detail. Continuing in this argumentational development, Adam proceeds to the cause of his present state, which he evaluates morally as disobedience, rather than describe it as a specific deed. The identification of the cause is followed by a moral application which, for all its platitude, is frequent in this context: that the enticements of women should not be followed (line 350). This moralizing tendency is kept up in the following double stanza in which Adam enumerates four deadly sins into which he has fallen: his 'licourouse wyfe', 'the devylls envye', '[h]is wrathe' and 'hir glotonye' (lines 353–8). This is once more followed by the conclusion that man should follow neither woman nor devil (line 360).

These 'applications' show obvious similarities to the *platea* speeches and proverbs to which we are used, for instance, from the Towneley and N-Town Joseph. Nevertheless the differences are also important. Fortunately, the Chester plays contain a 'Joseph's Lament' (Ch VI, 123ff) which will enable us first to develop the similarities to the Chester Adam, then their common differences from the Joseph of the other cycles. The Chester Joseph's lament is, like that of the Chester Adam, basically unemotional. Emotional agitation is manifest only in a few exclamations and rhetorical questions. Apart from this Joseph's 'lament', too, is pure report. If we disregard these islets of emotional expression, we recognize at once that the structure of the speech is highly logical and purely argumentational. The ideas follow each other not as they would surface in the mind of a bewildered and surprised individual, but in a strictly logical order. Mary's visible pregnancy is not, as it is especially in Towneley, the point of departure but the conclusion of the lament: first the abstract state of affairs is dealt with, then its concrete proof. In keeping with this, the lament remains completely separate from the planning speech which follows it. It is true that the idea of Mary's infidelity returns in the planning speech (Ch VI, 153–60), but it does not appear as reverberating in Joseph's psyche, as it does in Y XIII and LC XII, where it is still capable of confusing Joseph by virtue of the agitation which it has aroused in him. In Ch VI, lament and planning stand in the

206   The English mystery play

same purely successive relationship to each other as in the probable narrative source:

> When he segh ho with child was,
> then hade Ioseph in hert any,   [annoyance
> supposyng in hir gret tresspas,
> And thoȝt to leue hir pryuely.   (*St.L* 297–300)

The key-words of this stanza could easily be used as headings for the sections of Joseph's speech in Ch VI: *any* (124–8), *supposyng gret tresspas* (129–36), *thoȝt to leue* (137–44). Only the proverb-like reflections on old husbands of young wives (145–52) are characteristic of the mystery play. But if we compare the Chester Joseph's words with those, e.g., in LC XII, 49–51, 81–3, we see immediately how little contact the Chester Joseph has with the audience. In LC he calls directly and emphatically upon the men in the audience, especially of course on the old ones, asking them to learn from his sad experience:

> ȝa ȝa all Olde men to me take tent.   (LC XII, 49, p. 110)

In contrast to this, Ch VI shows only a pale prayer whose tone is by no means distinct from the rest of the speech:

> God, lett never [an] old man
> take to wife a yonge woman.   (Ch VI, 145f)

These words may, of course, be equally directed at the public by the actor. But unlike the corresponding words in the other cycles they do not *force* the actor to turn to the audience. The dramatist did not write the play with that view to scenic possibilities which we discern in other cycles. That solidarity between character and audience which the mystery stage makes possible does not find expression in the text of Chester.

Laments at the sacrifice of Isaac in the Brome and Northampton plays (with a view to Ch IV)

The subject-matter of Abraham and Isaac is clearly fruitful for the study of the dramatic presentation of feeling. In York and Towneley this story was rendered in ways that were typical of their respective cycles. In Chester the matter is somewhat more complicated, since the play in question (Ch IV: 'Abraham, Lot, and Melchysedeck; Abraham and Isaac') is, in the part concerning Isaac, largely identical with a play which to our knowledge has never belonged to a cycle and which has come down to us in the manuscript commonplace book of the Cornwallis family in Brome (Suffolk).[102] The relationship between the two plays was recognized already in the first edition of the Brome play, which also gave the most obvious parallels.[103] What has been much more controversial is the direction of the influence. In our context it is worth noting that the dispute over this question has always involved a discussion of the rôle of didacticism in the history of the mystery play. Carrie A. Harper, who has convincingly demonstrated the artistic superiority of the Brome play and the strong didacticism of that of Chester, concluded from these findings that Chester contained the older and more primitive version.[104] J. Burke Severs has studied the corruptions of the Chester text and demonstrated that as a rule they are due to misunderstanding and errors of transmission. Chester contains a number of repetitions and contradictions which are due to degeneracy rather than primitivism.[105] Severs concludes that the Isaac part of Ch IV is 'a corrupt, deteriorated version of the original Brome play'.[106] Severs' study is of particular value to us because he confines himself to a well-defined problem and is not guided by any preconceived notions concerning the history of the genre.[107] This makes his witness all the more important.

Alongside Brome and Ch IV we shall include the Northampton Abraham play in our analysis, because it resembles the Brome play especially under the aspect of the presentation of emotion.[108]

The technique of presenting emotions in Ch IV can be regarded as representative of the cycle only in so far as the play diverges from the intentions of its model, which we may believe to possess in the Brome play. This is true, above all, of the beginning of the scene. While the Abraham of Ch IV, 217ff appears entirely willing to obey God's command, the behaviour of his counterparts in Brome and Northampton is much more complex. Interestingly, the basic features which we recognized in T IV are still to be observed in these highly psychologizing plays. The Northampton and Brome Abrahams are like their counterparts in the cycles in that they begin by declaring their obedience (Br 68f, Nh 68ff) and afterwards deplore the impossibility of reconciling the conflict between the love of God and the love of the son. That these movingly human laments belong to the *platea* (as they do in T IV), can, for Northampton, be inferred from a stage direction: '*Et vadit angelus et dicit Habraham.*' What had to be conjectured in Towneley is here made explicit: after receiving God's orders Abraham is left alone in his bewilderment. The situation in Br is slightly different: Here, the Angel asks Abraham to follow him 'vpon thys gren' (line 67). We can assume that Abraham hereupon rises from the altar at which he must have been kneeling (a *locus*), to cross the *platea* together with the Angel. During his inward struggle he finds himself thus in a position in which the playsphere is traditionally opened to the audience. But this Abraham is not as helpless in his pain as his counterpart in T IV. He has more nuances at his disposal to express it. The nature of the conflict is different, too: it is no longer one between love of the son and obedience to God, but between love of God and love of the son. Abraham tries to accept God's command with his heart:

> And ȝyt my dere Lord, I am sore aferd
> To groche ony thyng aȝens ȝore wyll. (Br 79f)

The importance of this inner struggle is underlined by the Angel's answer, who commends Abraham for his obedience but adds the further demand:

> But in thy hart be nothyng dysmayd. (Br 93)

Unlike Chester and York, Br and Nh still adhere to the conventions developed by the mystery stage for presenting emotions, although they refine them psychologically. Like the much more primitive T IV they show a fine feeling for the exact placing of emotions. With this dramatic sense it is possible to show Isaac's increasing fear as a process developing in time rather than as momentary highlights. With a subject like this the emotion develops not only in time but also between the partners. In Br Isaac's fear awakens gradually, then is kindled more and more by his father's answers which are meant to be soothing. This creates a *crescendo* which is probably without parallel in the English mystery play (Br 135–67).[109] Nh goes even one step further; not only do we observe the gradual rising of Isaac's fear of death, but the impending horror dominates the mood of the play. This creates a very modern effect: the mood is reflected not only in direct hints by Abraham but also in utterances by persons who do not know of the coming sacrifice. Sara's very first words betray fear. When her husband returns from his prayer she greets him:

> Without fayle, I haue had gret doute
> Last any thinge did you grevaunce. (Nh 90f)

She is also against Isaac accompanying his father (Nh 109ff, 134f). This opposition, too, springs from a fear for which there is no rational explanation and which cannot be justified by what Sara knows. In this way interpersonal relations are influenced by the coming event even though it is not so much as mentioned.

Nh achieves a level of psychologizing and above all emotionalizing which is unique in the English mystery plays. We are confronted here with the altogether unusual phenomenon of an 'emotional atmosphere' (disregarding for the moment the rather different Shepherds Plays of the Towneley cycle), in which emotions are present without being explicitly uttered. The French influence which has been assumed for this play[110] is perhaps to be found in these structural similarities rather than in the verbal parallels adduced by Brotanek and rightly contested by Waterhouse.[111] There is, however, one similarity between Nh and the *Viel Testament*[112] which is important as well as tangible: both give Sara and two servants speaking parts. The everyday world which surrounds the main characters is here specified to an extent which is quite alien to the Bible as well as to the other mystery plays.[113] It creates the physical basis for what we have called the 'atmosphere'.

The question why this refined psychology appears of all things in two single plays which no one so far has convincingly brought into connection with any craft productions,[114] can find only a speculative answer which can be based, however, on the transmission of these plays. Both plays have come down to us in manuscript books which noble families kept for their daily needs, both spiritual and secular. In the case of Br we may even assume that we know the original owners of the book.[115] We cannot know whether the plays were included in the books merely to be read. But since performances in noble households were no rarity in the second half of the fifteenth century, it is quite possible that they were in fact performed.[116] A comparison also shows that Br is much more stageworthy than Ch IV. Even if it was not 'copied out for someone intending to stage the play' (cf. note 116), it may well have been copied from a staging text. Plays as means of devotion are not at all rare. Let it suffice to recall the so-called Digby *Burial* and *Resurrection*.[117] Furthermore, one of the finest medieval theatre pictures has been transmitted in a devotional book, in the *Book of Hours* of Etienne Chevalier.[118]

Laments in the N-Town cycle

A study of the laments in N-Town will confirm the position apart which is characteristic of this cycle, but will also show it in a new light. The laments of the cycle show features which are obviously employed with a view to their possible scenic effect and which also succeed in achieving it, as we hope to demonstrate.

If, progressing from the general to the particular, we attempt to define the special nature of the N-Town laments, it will become apparent that here the same rhetorical conventions for the presentation of emotions are at work as in York. In N-Town, however, they are not used mechanically and are therefore not in danger of being dysfunctionally expanded. It is probably symptomatic that Eleanor Prosser's original but controversial approach, which repeatedly investigates the emotional effects of the cycles, yields interesting and rewarding insights especially in the case of the N-Town plays.[119] But the fact that we agree more with Prosser in this chapter than we do in most others does not mean that we will follow her slavishly. We are not concerned with speculations about the emotional effect which the plays aimed at or achieved (and we are sceptical about the attempt to reduce the cycles or parts of them to *one* intended effect – even if it is as important as the idea of repentance). We shall confine ourselves – at least for the time being – to a global characterization of the effects and shall then try to determine the means by which this effect has been achieved.

As in other cycles, the most important laments are those of Adam and Eve, of Abraham and of Joseph. It is our task now to establish and to specify the characteristics of N-Town in these laments. A look at the expulsion from Paradise (LC II, 365ff, pp. 26ff) shows that the effect is produced, similarly to York, by emotional contrasts:

> in blake busshys my boure xal be
> In paradys is plente of pleye
> Ffayr frutys ryth gret plente
> þe ʒatys be schet with godys keye. (lines 381–4)

But at the same time important differences become apparent; for here we are not offered an abstract antithesis between 'blisse' and 'peyne' (as in Y VI, 88, 93), but powerfully evocative details are named which contrast the present and the former state of the speakers. One of the themes of the speech is certainly the subjective feeling of happiness and grief (as in York): Eve walks 'in welsome way' (line 380), i.e. in the 'wild', unrestrained manner of one lamenting, which contrasts vividly with the 'plente of pleye' (line 382) of Paradise. But this lament is not primarily about personal feelings; what is more important is the objective state which depends on divine mercy and which in its turn creates the conditions for bliss and grief. Thus the colours 'blake' and 'Ffayr' are not merely – and not primarily – a reflection of Eve's mood, but they symbolize the state of present lostness and the former life in divine mercy. It is symptomatic of this objective point of view that the lost Paradise should be described as something which still has an objective existence. This objectivity gains significance by the fact that in the preceding stanza the Angel has prophesied the regaining of that lost state (lines 374–7). Whereas Eve is restrained and 'objective' while she describes her own state, her language becomes vehement when she turns to Adam's situation. Conscious that she has caused his destruction, she even asks him to kill her. Such a request surely is excessive, but it does create a truly dialogical relationship within the lament: Adam gains an opportunity to quiet and comfort her (lines 391–403). This is a feature which returns in many of the N-Town laments and which is almost unknown in other cycles: individuals are not left alone with their feelings, and they even try to influence those of their partners.

The 'Sacrifice of Isaac' (LC V, pp. 43ff) shows a similar combination. There, too, the speakers treat their own feelings objectively and are full of consideration for their interlocutors. Abraham's very first reaction to God's command (which is here delivered by an angel) is characteristically different from those in Towneley and York. Abraham does not reveal his own attitude – for instance he does not declare, as he did in Towneley, that he will 'ffayn' (T IV, 79) obey God. Instead of the conflict of feelings which appears in other dramas we are confronted with an almost businesslike weighing of contrary principles:

> Now goddys comaundement must nedys be done
> All his wyl is wourthy to be wrought
> but ȝitt þe fadyr to scle þe sone
> grett care it causyth in my thought.   (LC V, 89–92, p.46)

Although Abraham is full of grief about what he has to do, he also knows that he must not yield to that grief:

> but ȝit my sorwe avaylith ryght nowth
> for nedys I must werke goddys wylle.   (lines 95f)

The following lines make it clear that this knowledge does not alleviate the grief, but they make it equally clear that there can be no genuine struggle between grief and obedience. Abraham cannot even find a few short *platea*-bound words of rebellion. The language in which his feelings are clothed is purely descriptive and realized in a series of declarative sentences:

> In byttyr bale now am I brought   (line 93)
>
> With evy hert I walke and wende.   (line 97)[120]

Abraham talks about his feelings as about something outside himself; he is always capable of characterizing and assessing them accurately: he knows, above all, that they will not prevail with God. They are not so much his own personal feelings as those of any mortal father, their purpose is apparently not to arouse sympathy with Abraham. The conflict is rather too complex to be exhaustively described by the pair of terms 'typical/individual'; a comparison with York can perhaps make clearer what is meant. While even York does of course not represent an individual, unique father–son relationship, it does mention aspects which are not shared by all such relationships and which bring a humanly touching element to the scene: Isaac is 'semely to sight', his father loves him 'full wele', and finally even the age of the son is given (Y X, 79–82).[121]

The horror of Abraham's situation is brought home to the audience by making them relate Abraham and Isaac to the fathers and the sons of their own sphere of experience. The specific is enlisted as an emotional support of the generic. N-Town, on the other hand, needs to create this emotional impact directly.[122] Abraham is not saddened by having to kill his *own* son, his sadness is not fed by Isaac's personal and by that token accidental virtues, but solely by the fact that an order which is both natural and divine appears to have been stood on its head: 'þe fadyr to scle þe sone' (LC V, 91, p. 46). The wording here is so general that the statement applies not only to the human father but also to God the Father, who sacrifices his son not in obedience to a command, but out of his unforced love for mankind. The analogy suggested by the typological juxtaposition is clear: if the human father feels such pain, how much greater must be the pain felt by God.

The analogy between God and Abraham corresponds to that between Jesus and Isaac. Like Jesus, Isaac allows himself to be led to the slaughter. The N-Town Isaac shows no signs of fear; in this he differs from his counterparts in all other cycles, even in York, although York makes more of the typological element. Isaac's fearlessness in N-Town is such that he can console his father, even tell him not to mourn, since such mourning would already imply rebellion against God:

> I pray ʒow fadyr be glad and fayne
> trewly to werke goddys wyll
> take good comforte to ʒow agayne
> and haue no dowte ʒour childe to kyll.
>
> ffor godys byddyng for sothe it is
> þat I of ʒow my deth schulde take
> Aʒens god ʒe don amys.   (lines 149–55, p. 48)

A conventional motif in this scene thus acquires a new function: when Abraham blindfolds Isaac, he does so not to spare his son the sight of his raised sword but to save himself from looking into his dear son's eyes:

> with þis kerchere I kure þi face
> In þe tyme þat I sle the
> Thy lovely vesage wold I not se
> not for all þis werdlys [sic] good   (lines 179–81, p. 49)

The details of this play are thus carefully designed to emphasize the father's grief and to minimize the son's fear.

The plays discussed so far show a fairly uniform technique of representing emotions. In contrast to these, LC XII, 'Joseph's Return', deserves our attention because it represents emotions in two clearly distinct ways. In one of them we can recognize the popular dramatic tradition, in the other, the conventions of emotionalized theological didacticism. To substantiate this thesis, a brief look into the compositional history of the play is required. In the manuscript as we have it, LC XII stands in the midst of what once may have been an independent St Anne's Day play and what its latest editor, Peter Meredith, calls *The Mary Play from the N.town Manuscript*. Yet it is mostly written in 'Proclamation thirteeners', which may suggest that it was part of the original cycle.[123] It is mentioned in the general prologue, the 'Proclamation' spoken by the three *vexillatores*,[124] but not in the introduction to the 'Mary Play' spoken by Contemplacio.[125] Moreover, the preceding play, LC XI, ended originally with a stage direction which fits not LC XII but LC XIII: 'The words *And þan mary seyth* follow on as part of this direction, but have been crossed through in red ink.'[126] And finally, the blanks preceding and following LC XII in the manuscript (ff. 66v and 70v) indicate that the scribe did not have the play at hand when copying the *Contemplacio* group, though he must have known its approximate size.[127] This also suggests that the play formed part of that corpus from which the scribe drew most of his cycle. If we assume with Greg that the compiler-redactor who brought the cycle into its present shape handed his material piecemeal to the scribe,[128] it seems likely that part of our play is in fact the work of that redactor. This assumption is supported by a study of the metre. The play shows two stanzaic forms whose juxtaposition is surely to be explained by the compositional history of the play.[129] The predominant form is the well-known 'Proclamation thirteener' in which the better part of the cycle is written. Besides this rhyme-scheme we find the ten-line stanza $aa_4b_3aa_4b_3bcbc_4$, which is rare in this cycle.[130] It might conceivably be argued that the change of stanza is conditioned by the content. But such an opinion is hardly tenable in view of the fact, hitherto overlooked, that lines 84–7 together with lines 118–26 form a complete Proclamation thirteener. The second stanza-type may thus be regarded as proof of an interpolation which presumably is not earlier than the compilation of the cycle in its present form. A further argument in favour of this theory is that the thirteen-line stanzas by themselves yield a complete, coherent play, while the ten-liners are merely adornments which can be removed without leaving a gap. The extensive critical studies which the play received, above all in the 1960s, neglect its textual history.[131] The following analysis, it is hoped, will demonstrate that this neglect has misled Eleanor Prosser into overestimating the play.

Taken by themselves, the thirteen-line stanzas yield a play which is quite similar to the other Joseph plays: Joseph returns home and asks to be let into the house in a scene which has been described as 'noisy comedy' (*lautstarke Komik*) (lines 1–8, the *cauda* of the first stanza has been lost).[132] He asks Mary how she is faring, discovers that she is pregnant and upbraids her vehemently (lines 21–37). Her reply (lines 38–42 and 48) he calls a lie (lines 43–47). There follows an Old Man's Lament, a warning addressed at the old men in the audience (lines 49–61). Mary's claim that the unborn child is God's son and the story of the Angel's visit (lines 62–70, a 'thirteen-liner' with only one *frons*), are equally rejected by Joseph (lines 71–83). Thereupon Mary prays to God that He may 'comforte' Joseph (lines 84–7). Joseph, who does not know where to turn in his humiliation, asks all men (in the audience) to pity him and leaves Mary (lines 118–26). When the Angel informs him that Mary has in fact told the truth (lines 147–59) he returns to Mary and becomes reconciled with her (lines 180–92).

By contrast, the ten-liners yield only a repetition of the Old Man's Lament and a plan for leaving Mary which is full of contradictions (lines 88–117); this is followed by a prayer by Mary which repeats the content of lines 84–7 but adds as an additional motive that Mary wants to keep the real circumstances of the conception secret from Joseph (lines 127–46). In view of the fact that her maid, Sephor, had already given an account of the conception (lines 67–70, in thirteeners), this is a rather futile endeavour. After the Angel's revelation a thanksgiving prayer by Joseph is inserted (lines 160–79). The last of the interpolations (lines 193–212) closes with Joseph's request that Mary tell him the story of the conception of Jesus. This request is met by Mary in twelve lines showing the otherwise unusual rhyme-scheme abababbbaba (lines 213–24).

If we compare the two parts with regard to their respective ways of representing emotion, it will again be seen that the thirteeners are very similar to other Joseph plays. Joseph reacts vehemently, even somewhat vulgarly, to Mary's account. He scornfully rejects her explanation that the child is God's:

> God dede nevyr jape so with may. (line 44)

In a similar manner he sneers at her account of the visit of the Angel:

> It was sum boy be-gan þis game
> þat clothyd was clene and gay
> and ȝe ȝeve hym now an Aungel name. (lines 75–7)

In keeping with the popular style which he employs in these stanzas, Joseph generalizes his apparent cuckoldom into an everyday experience which characteristically takes the form of an audience-address (lines 49ff). This audience-address shows a number of familiar features: in warning his audience Joseph draws practical conclusions from his

Intra-dramatic speeches 215

experience and in visualizing the consequences he has recourse to (apparently current) *tournures*:

> all men may me now dyspyse
> and seyn olde cokwold þi bow is bent
> newly now after þe frensche gyse (lines 54–6)

The 'Olde men' (line 49) are admonished to learn from Joseph's unhappy experience, and for himself he also draws practical conclusions: he will leave Mary (line 60) and considers where he might go – 'whedyr xal I' (line 118).

There are further elements of the conventional Joseph that we know from other cycles: the first answer which he gives the Angel appearing in his dream[133] and the abrupt change in his mood, which in its turn manifests itself in physical symptoms and in his immediate return to Mary:

> Good sere lete me wepe my ffylle
> Go forthe þi wey and lett me nowght. (lines 149f)

> Alas ffor joy I qwedyr and qwake
> Alas what hap now was this
> A mercy mercy my jentyl make
> mercy I haue seyd al Amys
> All þat I haue seyd I for-sake
> ȝour swete fete now lete me kys. (lines 180–5)

Some of these features are also to be found in the ten-liners, e.g. the Old Man's Lament in lines 88ff. But soon there are important differences to be discovered. While Joseph normally decides without hesitation to leave Mary, he is now thinking and rethinking his course of action; his planning seems to be affected by his inner agitation and by the consideration that Mary's apparent trespass is hardly compatible with the meekness he has come to know in her (lines 101–5). Mary's prayer (lines 127ff) also differs from her previous one (lines 84–7): she now excuses his behaviour before God; it is only 'vnknowlage' (line 130) which makes him act as he does. Nor do the repentance and the gratitude which Joseph feels after his encounter with the Angel have any equivalent in the other cycles:

> I myght wel A wyst parde
> So good a creature as she
>   wold nevyr A done trespace. (lines 163–5)

In other cycles Joseph is also full of repentance for his behaviour,[134] but that refers only to the fact that Mary did not really deserve his harsh words. It does not mean that Joseph should have been able to recognize the unjustness of his suspicions from the very beginning.

This insight into his own faultiness is closely connected with the edificational and revelatory functions which Joseph assumes in N-Town. As soon as he has been enlightened about the true story of Mary he remembers the prophecy of the child who is to redeem mankind (lines 171f). Joseph sees himself as the bearer of a soteriological function and as the mediator of objective soteriological truths. This striving for edification may help to explain that the end of the play shows Joseph having the account of the conception of Jesus retold to him. Not what Joseph *wants* to hear is important in this part of the play, but what the audience *is meant* to hear.

Thus the nuanced emotionalism and moral-theological teaching which Prosser discerns are to be found exclusively in the ten-line stanzas. From this it follows that some of her notions concerning the composition of the play as a whole are untenable. As far as the sharp contrast in Joseph's behaviour which Prosser claims to have discovered exists at all, it must be regarded as an accident resulting from the play's textual history.[135] Joseph's doubts concerning Mary's trespass appear already in the first half of the play (again of course in ten-liners, cf. lines 101-3). And the double account of the story of the Angel hardly has the subtle psychological motivation with which Prosser credits it.[136] Prosser is right to emphasize, with Greg and Block, that the compiler of 'Joseph's Return' borrowed from Nicholas Love's *Mirrour*, but she is wrong in assuming that he deliberately modified his borrowings. On the contrary, he took them over unaltered into a play whose conception of Joseph was diametrically opposed. The theological-didactic element with the theme of repentance as one of its most important concretizations is not the core of the play but merely a late and poorly integrated addition.

Dialogues

'Serial' dialogues

Dialogue has already been touched upon in the chapter on mourning and grief because these particular emotions occasionally involved the consideration of interpersonal relationships. But in that chapter we also saw that truly dialogical emotions, in which the feelings of one partner appear to influence and modify those of the other, are comparatively rare in the mystery play.

It may appear paradoxical to treat precisely those scenes with non-dialogical emotion in the chapter on dialogue. The reason is that these very scenes offer good illustrations for the specific difference between the liturgical drama and the mystery play. In the liturgical drama we

Intra-dramatic speeches

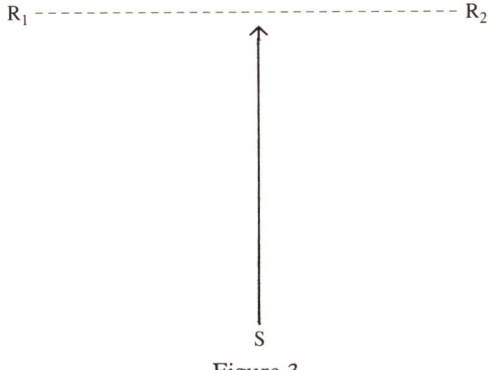

Figure 2.

Figure 3.

distinguished between 'Revelation situations' and 'world-containing' ones, both being distinguished by their respective type of dialogue. Schematically the parties in a revelation dialogue can be seen as standing in a straight line in the extension of which the spectator is to be found (Figure 2).[137] In 'world-containing' dialogue the spectator's view-line is perpendicular to that of the *dramatis personae* (Figure 3).

The peculiarity of the mystery play is that it transforms even those situations which in the liturgical drama were purely 'revelational' into 'world-containing' ones. This applies particularly to the Women at the Sepulchre and to the Shepherds and the Magi at the Manger. But since the ceremonial character of the revelation must be preserved, a new kind of partner-relation arises which is worthy of closer study because it provides an element of the liturgical drama with a new form and a new function. The type of dialogue which this new partnership creates shall be called 'serial' because its participants do not form a group whose members can enter into varying relationships with each other but can merely multiply an attitude or an emotion which could quite sufficiently be represented by a single speaker, were it not for the requirements of the liturgical ceremony from which the scenes derive. This multiplication results of necessity in a serial order in which the first, the second, and the third speaker (normally we are dealing with triads) utter the same content in this order.

To make this clearer, we had to turn to an aspect of the *Visitatio* laments which was not considered when dealing with the liturgical drama.[138] There, we investigated only the form in which emotions were expressed. Now we must ask what the subject expressing these emotions is like.

Originating as it does in choral antiphonary singing, the dialogue of this liturgical drama is essentially a group dialogue. The group acts almost without exception in *unison*: the Angels (if there is more than one) ask together, the Women answer together. Even when the group is alone on the scene it sings *unisono*, it conducts a collective monologue. The *Visitatio* laments are one such collective monologue. When the collective monologue gives way to single-voice singing, it is merely divided between the singers. One example is enough to illustrate this: The Easter Play of Rheinau monastery uses the hymn *Heu! nobis internas mentes* in the following manner:[139]

Qua[140] *finita, tres Mulieres figurantes prime ad Sepulcrum procedentes singule singulos versus humili uoce decantant.*
    PRIMA, VERSUM:
        Heu! nobis internas mentes   quanti pulsant gemitus
        Pro nostro consolatore,   quo priuamur misere,
        Quem crudelis Iudeorum   morti dedit populus.
    SECUNDA, VERSUM:
        Iam percusso cev pastore,   oues errant misere;
        Sic magistro discedente,   turbantur discipuli,
        Atque nos absente eo,   dolor tenet nimius.
    TERCIA, MARIE MAGDALENE PERSONAM EXPRIMENS, VERSUM:
        Sed eamus et ad eius   properemus tumulum;
        Si dileximus viuentem,   diligamus mortuum.

The three parts develop one complex thought: first, the fact and the object of the three women's mourning, secondly, the state of the mourners, finally, the decision which 'nevertheless' ('sed') has to be taken. There is no argument between the three speakers. Normally, a speaker would either disagree or agree with his or her predecessor. Not so in this dialogue. The thought that is expressed here is a unit from the start, it does not acquire unity in the to-and-fro of discussion. Unity without prior debate characterizes not only the lament, but also its utterer, who always appears in the plural as *nos*. There is no *I* arising from this *We*. That the individualizing of grief does not even appear as a remote possibility becomes apparent in the treatment of Mary Magdalene. As the most prominent of the three women she is always raised above the rest. But this does not mean that she is given a particularly moving lament. It merely means that she takes either the first[141] or – more frequently – the last part.[142] She is thus distinguished not by her words or her deeds, but merely by her position.

In all these respects the Middle English *Visitatio* laments are the exact opposite of their liturgical Latin counterparts.[143] Instead of one common 'We' there are now several 'I's' speaking, each of them uttering a relatively self-contained thought.[144] The speakers now appear singly, although they are by no means individualized. Differences between the various parts do not imply characterization of the speakers. That a differentiated relationship between them is not among the goals of these dialogues is indicated by the fact that the speakers always speak in the same order. The dialogue consists of 'rounds' each of them made up of three 'turns'.[145] Even here, Mary Magdalene is not psychologically distinguished from the other two,[146] but her part has undergone a characteristic change. She is no longer merely the most distinguished of the three who receives an elevated position in the ceremonial, but she is also the leader and initiator. The reason for this change is to be seen in the ceremonial character of the liturgical drama on the one hand and the mimetic character of the mystery play on the other. Frequently in ceremonies the most distinguished person appears last. Since the order of the ceremony has been arranged in advance, he or she need not demonstrate their rank by taking the initiative. Real actions, as they are imitated in drama, are not prearranged in this way, and so the triggering of the various steps must be shown to make it convincing. The taking of initiatives needs to be represented in drama, thus creating a new means of rendering a person prominent. If Mary Magdalene is to suggest the embalming of the dead Christ's body (as she does in all plays except Chester), she must take the first turn in each round of the dialogue.

Although the dialogues of the three Marys and the three Magi are among the simplest in all cycles, their simplicity cannot in every case be attributed to the model of the liturgical drama: the Chester *Magi* plays (Ch VIII and IX) go back directly to the *Stanzaic Life of Christ*.[147] For the N-Town plays no source has so far been discovered; but their strong didacticism and the total absence of any reference to the extra-linguistic situation also suggest an influence from religious narrative.

The simplest form of the *Visitatio* lament (disregarding LC XXXVI, where it is missing completely) occurs in Ch XVIII, 309–32. This play illustrates well the minimal difference between Latin and Middle English *Visitatio* laments. Each of the Chester Women utters a thought that is complete in itself, but there is no interaction between the utterances. None of the women responds to the words of the others, all of them merely modify slightly the same thoughts: grief over Jesus' death, anger at his murderers. The motifs of the lament are still (or again!) as severely simple as in the liturgical drama.[148] The sparseness of the liturgical drama reappears also in the fact that the idea of embalming Christ is, by way of exception, uttered already at the end of the first dialogue round. But even this exception demonstrates the 'separateness' of the dialogue turns which is characteristic of the mystery plays. While in the liturgical drama the embalming is a plan shared by all, in the mystery play it is the personal intention of one of the women, motivated by her own relationship to Jesus:

> Alas, nowe marred ys my might.
> My lord through whom that *I* was light
> shamefullye slayne here in *my* syght!
> *My* sorrowe ys aye unsought.
> Syth *I* may have no other ryght
> of these dyvelles that have my lord so dight,
> to balme his bodye that ys so bryght
> boyst here have *I* brought. (Ch XVIII, 325–32, emphases added)

While *Heu! nobis internas* showed unity without discussion, this dialogue shows neither discussion nor unity.

The absence of any discussion in these 'dialogues' becomes apparent above all when the utterances of the speakers contradict each other. On seeing the sepulchre, Maria Jacobi says:

> for on the sepulcher sytteth one,
> and the stonne away. (Ch XVIII, 339f)

Without remarking on the contradiction Maria Salome continues:

> Two children I see ther syttinge –
> all of whyte ys there clothinge –
> and the stonne besydes lyeinge.
> Goe we nere and see. (Ch XVIII, 341–4)

We would be seriously misunderstanding the passage if we were to assume that Maria Jacobi had not looked closely enough and that she was

Intra-dramatic speeches

being corrected by Maria Salome. We are merely dealing with two versions of the Scriptures being juxtaposed after the manner of the gospel harmonies.[149]

A similarly unrelated juxtaposition is to be found in 'The Offerings of the Three Kings' (Ch IX). Each of the three Magi describes his own gift as the best (lines 71, 73, 86, 162), but they are, of course, not competing with one another. The gifts are not being compared one with the other, they are merely being considered in relation to Christ, one of whose qualities (king, priest, dying man) each of them is meant to allegorize. The kings refer to each other only in phatic formulas, such as: 'You saye full well, syrs, both two.' (Ch IX, 80) But the contents of their speeches are exclusively addressed to the spectators.

In the York 'Resurrection' (Y XXXVIII, 187ff = T XXVI, 334ff) the lamenters also fail to relate to each other. Only the rather external ornament of *concatenatio* is used occasionally to link the turns of two speakers (Y XXXVIII, 204–5, 210–1). But as soon as the laments, which form the first round of the dialogue, are finished, the utterances do relate to each other. When Mary Magdalene suggests going to the grave and embalming the body of Christ, Mary Salome's reply contains both agreement and reservation:

> Goo we same my sisteres free,
> Full faire vs longis his corse to see.
> But I wotte noght howe beste may be,
> Helpe haue we none.
> And who schall nowe here of vs thre
> Remove þe stone? (Y XXXVIII, 217–22)

From this moment every utterance is a reaction to the previous one.

The Magi plays of the two Yorkshire cycles, which have already proved useful in the analysis of the opening prayer, also offer a good illustration of the difference between 'serial' and 'real' dialogue. The conversation of the Three Kings after their encounter is treated in T XIV ('Oblacio Magorum') very much as in Ch VIII and IX. Each of the three points to the Star and phrases his statement as if he were the first to discover it.[150] All three open their dialogue parts by referring to the Star with phrases that are typically used on a first mention: 'this starne' (T XIV, 149), 'yond starne' (152), 'yond light' (153). This is against the rules of ordinary dialogue which requires the non-first speakers (in this case, the First and the Second King) to use some substitute such as either a pronoun or a more informative, more elaborate phrase. Moreover, the First King specifically asks his companions to look at the Star (169f) and follows his request with a detailed discussion which is continued by the Second. This round closes with the Third King explaining the significance of the Star. But his explanation does not appear as the fruit of extensive reflexion, it is merely the climax of shared contemplation. It is clearly introduced as an effective highlight, not as the product of an intellectual process:

> Certys, syrs, the sothe to say,
> I shall dyscry now, if I may,
> what it may meyn, yond starne veray,
> Shynand tyll vs. (T XIV, 193–6)

After the meeting with Herod again each phase occupies a full round of the dialogue: discovering that the Star has disappeared (493–504), praying for its reappearance (505–22), rejoicing over the answered prayer (523–40),[151] prayer to the Christ child (541–58). The dramatist is clearly not interested in showing how the Magi reacted to the miraculous event whose witnesses they became. We do not see them surprised by the Star's sudden appearance or pondering lengthily over its significance. They merely show pious astonishment and believing acceptance of the prophecy. The Star is not just an unusual natural phenomenon which after some observation becomes familiar and understandable. It is accessible not to reason but only to revelation.

In Y XVI, whose dialogues sound much more 'natural', and in the Christmas play of Coventry, which has been revised less skilfully but with a similar tendency, the Star cannot have this effect. In York the Kings know the meaning of the Star before they meet. As a consequence, they are less concerned with impressing its wonderful presence on the audience (and on each other) than with the practical business of finding their destination. The Star is discussed almost like a curiosity; the Third King mentions perfunctorily, in reply to the Second, what he has heard about it (Y XVI, 103ff). The First does not waste time confirming the prophecy, but directly draws the conclusion: That makes us travelling companions (Y XVI, 109)! In Coventry the dialogue is even completely confined to questions concerning provenance and destination (STCo 594–602, 671–81), though these are simpler and more vivid than in the ceremoniously measured York play. The Star in these plays is part of the physical environment among others, and the dialogue proceeds briskly in registering that environment:

> Sir, here is Jerusalem,
> To wisse vs als we goo,
> And be-yonde is Bedleem,
> þer schall we seke alsoo. (Y XVI, 113–16)

The events on the journey from Jerusalem to Bethlehem appear similarly condensed. No sooner has the Third King suggested praying for the reappearance of the Star than the First discovers the house above which the Star has come to a standstill (Y XVI, 277–284, STCo 689–98). Instead of prayers and thanksgivings (T XIV, 505–40) we have an exchange with *Ancilla* (Y XVI, 185–96) and a short conversation between the Three Kings (Y XVI, 297–308) which again emphasizes empirically palpable aspects of the events. That the Star has shown them the way is called 'courtesy' (Y XVI, 298), the inhabitants of the stable are a 'clene companye' (Y XVI, 300), and the Third King is concerned about giving precedence to the First: 'Brother, ȝe shall begynne' (Y XVI, 308). The author of this play clearly knows how to create the impression of rapid movement in dialogue and how to suit the diction to the high rank of his characters. But in the process he loses much of the intense emotional effect which the Towneley playwright achieves by the even sequence of the closed *imago-pietatis*-like dialogue-rounds, each of which is entirely devoted to the triple expression of *one* emotion or *one* attitude: awesome astonishment, consternation, prayer, or gratitude.[152]

In the Magi plays it is customary to have the members of the group enter one after another; this gives rise to a dialogue of salutation which enlivens the scene. Of the Resurrection plays there is only one which uses this opportunity. The *Visitatio* laments of the 'Digby' *Burial* and *Resurrection* repeat what we have already observed in the Crucifixion laments. It was apparently the same redactor, endowed with a somewhat prosaic mind but with a sound instinct for the requirements of scenic speech, who also provided these laments with connecting text. Mary Magdalene enters first; the most 'interesting' character can thus utter the longest lament. Her great entry monologue ends characteristically: she deplores the fact that Christ is nowhere to be found although it is already the morning of the third day, and that she cannot see her 'sister' Mary Cleophas either, with whom she had arranged to meet for a visit to the sepulchre (lines 918–24). After this she swoons theatrically. The spheres of human private life and of religious significance are rubbing shoulders here. This undiscriminating vicinity is to be kept clearly distinct from the well-known 'naïve anachronism' which represents Pilate as a contemporary feudal magnate and has the Shepherds plod through the cold English winter. The good shepherds and the evil tyrants, also Joseph and Noah, the apparent cuckold and the really henpecked husband – all of these represent exactly that world which celebrates its community with the Son of God in the Feast of Corpus Christi. The 'double-bottomed dramaturgy'[153] of the mystery stage guarantees that the polarity between the divine and the human is always preserved. In the 'Digby' *Resurrection* the distinctions are blurred. Christ as well as Mary Cleophas appear as relatives missing an appointment.

This particular type of humanization must of necessity make the religious feeling seem shallow, even sentimentalize it. But it also gives us an opportunity to study dialogue techniques which are interesting in themselves even if they have no future in the religious drama. Dialogue here abandons the principle of serialization and contributes to the distinction between different human attitudes. During the entire scene Mary Magdalene represents the behaviour of natural man, being unable to cast off her creaturely grief and doubts. She too knows the promise that Christ will rise the third day, but this cannot remove her uncertainty (CR 55ff, 107ff). Even the Angel's message cannot alleviate her sadness (CR 141ff, 168ff). This Mary Magdalene is the only character in all English Resurrection plays that is ambivalent in her feelings. Several times she is criticized for this by her sisters, whose unwavering faith is made to contrast with her doubt.

The Magdalene's love of Christ is made to repose entirely in her personal relationship to Him. This helps the dramatist overcome a dilemma the seeds of which were already planted in the liturgical Easter office and which came into the open with the increased psychologizing of the vernacular drama: in the syncretism of the Middle Ages the *Hortulanus* from the Gospel according to St John followed directly the *Visitatio* which was taken from the synoptic gospels. This created a conflict between the jubilation of the *Resurrexit* which concluded the liturgical *Quem quaeritis* dialogue and the weeping of the Magdalene which was required by the *Hortulanus*. Our play represents her grief as so profound that only the sight of the risen Redeemer can console her, thus removing the psychological implausibility. But it is important to notice the exact point in the history of the genre at which it is removed: only when the events of the Salvation have been toned down to the plane of private and even homespun emotions, do the dramatists strive for psychological plausibility of the kind described.

Dialogues of strife and insult

At the opposite pole of possible dialogue techniques we find some of the best-known and most popular scenes of the mystery cycles. Their evaluation in modern criticism, however, is highly controversial, largely owing to the comic element which is particularly strong here. The first modern students of the mystery plays[154] praised these scenes as precursors of modern realism and as the beginning of English comedy in general.[155] More recently, their rough comic action has been regarded as a weakening of the religious message, as an 'escape from piety'; 'comic relief' has acquired the status of an extenuating circumstance.[156] The most eloquent exponent of this point of view is Hardin Craig, who gives the 'devils, tyrants, and clowns' short shrift as 'excrescences and aberrations' which can only detract from the religious purpose of the cycles.[157] Developing this criticism further, Eleanor Prosser has postulated that comedy is acceptable only when it supports the theological tenets of the play.[158] Ironically, these postulates were sharply rejected by Craig himself.[159] But such narrow didacticism contradicts the vitality of the mystery plays, and especially of their comic scenes, too obviously to find general acceptance. A. P. Rossiter, who drew on similar scoffing rituals among primitive peoples for comparison, diagnosed a 'zest-for-unholiness', an urge to denigrate what is held in general reverence.[160] Rossiter has found followers in Germany,[161] but the general drift of Anglo-Saxon scholarship has been against him. A number of articles, chiefly on the plays of the Wakefield Master, are concerned to demonstrate that the comic scenes, too, help support the religious message.[162] The merits and disadvantages of this harmonizing tendency can be made clear only after a detailed study of individual scenes; it has found its culmination point in Kolve's *The Play Called Corpus Christi*. Leaning strongly on E.R. Curtius, B. White and others, Kolve discusses at length the evaluation of laughter in the medieval Church.[163] His quotations confirm the well-known thesis that laughter was acceptable to the teachers of the Church only if it arose from *Schadenfreude* at the failures of God's enemies. This kind of laughter is indeed common in medieval drama, from the popular *risu*[*s*] *propter Synagogam expulsam* of Philippe de Mézières' *Praesentatio Mariae*[164] to the devil scenes in the mystery plays.[165] But Kolve's conclusion that the mystery plays knew *only* this ecclesiastically acceptable kind of laughter fails to recognize the important – and, as we hope to show, unambiguous – differences that are to be found in the linguistic shape of various scene-types. It also represents the psychological mechanism which creates the laughter as cruder than it really is. Kolve is misled by his approach into inferring the reality of the dramatic experience directly from the theoretical pronouncements of the authorities of the time. This forces him to assume that the obvious pleasure which the Torturers find in their activities is not shared by the audience.[166] Unfortunately, Kolve does not discuss Irena Janicka's study, which gives a much more differentiated survey of the possible place of the comic:

although the writer may use the comic as a means only, making it serve a serious purpose (for instance to show the vices of man) and not as the aim in itself (for amusement's sake), the comedy will nevertheless be independent of the serious idea while it is having its immediate effect on the audience (or reader). It then performs an independent aesthetic function, which has a value of its own.[167]

Rainer Warning goes even one step further. To him laughter is an 'answer' to that which has been excluded because it stands in opposition to the commanding forms of life and existence; more precisely: a positive answer, i.e. one which accepts what has been excluded as being a positive part of the whole of existence, confirms it, and plays it off against the excluding principle.[168]

What has been said here about the comic is, *mutatis mutandis*, equally true of cruelty: here, too, something that has been excluded by the official doctrine is reintegrated into the complex whole of existence.

If we concede this possibility, then those theories receive a certain plausibility which regard the Crucifixion scenes as a remote echo of pagan-Dionysiac sacrificial rites and as a safety valve for blasphemous tendencies.[169] Historical proof, however, will hardly be forthcoming. Only a careful analysis of individual scenes can hope to find the basis for a decision between conflicting theories. Since each scene type presents its own peculiar problems, this chapter will adopt a different principle of division from the previous ones. We shall follow one scene-type through all the cycles. Naturally, the greatest amount of space will be needed to take up those scene-types in which the comedy is irrelevant for, or even contradictory to, the theological message. This is true first of all of the Torturing and Crucifixion scenes of the Passion plays, but also of some of the Shepherds plays and the plays of Cain and Abel in the Yorkshire cycles. But to obtain an exact picture of the comic elements and their linguistic form, it is useful to begin with those scenes in which the comic element is clearly put to religious use. For this we choose Lucifer's Fall and the Devil scenes of Christ's *descensus ad inferos*.

Devils' dialogues

What the devils' dialogues share with other strife-and-insult dialogues is their rudeness and occasional obscenity. Whenever devils appear on the stage they call each other 'lurdan' (Y I, 108, 115, 117), 'rebal' (Y XXXVII, 99), 'false fayture' (Ch I, 238 (DM 217)), etc. Even N-Town, which knows of no quarrel between the Shepherds and which treats the scenes of Cain and Abel and the Torturing of Christ very briefly, has its Lucifer exclaim:

> Ffor fere of fyre a fart I crake (LC I, 81, p. 19)[170]

But the very fact that such a line does occur in a generally restrained cycle like N-Town suggests that rudeness and comicality in general assume in the devil scenes a different value from that which they have elsewhere. The quoted line tells us where the difference is to be sought: the obscenity helps to bring out the speaker's wretchedness, it does not express an aggressive feeling of superiority. The devils differ from other comical or evil figures in that they are fully aware of their own state. They refer to themselves as 'two feeyndes blacke' (Ch I, 251) and repeatedly deplore their own ugliness (e.g. T I, 137; Y I, 100), they describe the state denied them as 'blys' (Ch XVII, 162) or 'joy' (T I, 150) and are quite unambiguous in the evaluation of their own deeds. Thus, Satan declares in the Chester Harrowing of Hell: 'I tempted the folke in fowle manere' (Ch XVII, 130). The criteria for the devils' self-concept are thus purely negative: they conceive of themselves exclusively as separate from God, not as creatures with their own substantive goals.[171] The Satan of the mystery plays is not a proud rebel, he could never say with Milton's Satan: 'Better to reign in Hell, then serve in Heav'n.'[172] He is not confined in his own subjectivity like, for instance, the quarrelling Shepherds, the cruel Torturers, or even the avaricious Cain. While the latter are capable of believing in the rightness of their cause, Satan knows that he is and that he represents evil. Thus, his speech and that of his companions can only be a complaint in dialogue form, often peppered with vulgarity. The complaints are neither accompanied by action, nor do they constitute a true debate between dialogue partners; this makes them rather static, for all their violence. Calumny can only produce new calumny, it does not alter the relationship between the interlocutors. Since none of the speakers recognizably aims at changing the situation, the dialogue can create neither tension nor suspense; since, moreover, the dialogue merely underlines the wretched condition of the speakers, it cannot carry along the audience as ecstatically as some of the dialogues surrounding Christ's Passion can. The form of the comic which prevails here could be described as 'objective' (Eduard Eckhardt's *objektive Komik*[173]): the devils are not even superior in a limited field, as the Torturers are in that of brute force, and the Vices and Backbiters in that of seducing and verbal joking. There, the spectator is forced into an ambivalent attitude: he enjoys the virtuosity of these figures and their absorption in their own activities; at the same time he must call himself to order for this enjoyment and recognize that the virtuosity is wasted on despicable skills. No such ambivalence is possible toward the devils. Here the spectator can do unreservedly what according to Kolve he should do whenever he is faced with a comic or grotesquely cruel scene:[174] he can feel separate from and superior to them, he can laugh at them and thus apply that laughter which met with the approval of the Church and which was meant for the enemies of God.[175] The devils of Lucifer's Fall and of large parts of the Harrowing of Hell call for *Schadenfreude* as the most adequate attitude. Those figures to whom we now turn invite different reactions.

Cain and Abel
The aspect which we have deliberately isolated yields but few results for

the Cain and Abel plays of Chester and N-Town. These cycles – and the plays in question in particular – are too homiletic and too 'conceptual' to produce an actual quarrel between the two brothers. It is only shortly before the murder that Cain begins a lengthy diatribe (Ch II, 601–16; LC III, 144–56, p. 33). But their very placement prevents these speeches from becoming truly dramatic: Abel has no chance of a reply, the speeches can only reflect Cain's mood, underline his wrath; they cannot modify the relationship between the two brothers. These speeches follow the rules of rhetoric as they were also observed in medieval narrative: in the manner of *sermocinatio* a prominent event is underlined by a speech which fits the occasion and the character of the speaker.[176]

The Cain and Abel plays of the two Yorkshire cycles differ from their counterparts in Chester and N-Town in that they use the first murder in human history for a representation of *discordia*. This, however, involves massive alterations of the biblical model. The world in which the murder occurs is not void of human inhabitants but is peopled by a society which the spectators must have recognized as their own: in both plays Cain has a servant, in Towneley the two wrongdoers fear the bailiffs more than God; and in a farcical concluding scene they proclaim for themselves the King's Pardon (T II, 405, 419–38).

The social world in which the biblical event has been embedded contains the potential for conflict and thus for the mood which ultimately leads to the murder. Admittedly, neither in Chester nor in N-Town do Cain's jealousy and the ensuing murder come altogether unexpectedly. But that Cain is disposed toward such a course of action is made clear only in a highly abstract manner. In his objective self-characterization he tells us what kind of person he is. But we are not allowed to observe the concrete and specific circumstances under which his avarice and self-righteousness become manifest.[177] By contrast, the Cain of the Yorkshire cycles appears in circumstances which are perfectly familiar to his audience; his reactions and attitudes are also of a sort that the medieval burgesses have no difficulty recognizing themselves in them. Though Cain, as unwilling to sacrifice, is clearly marked as evil, he does offer arguments which at least sound plausible.[178] He doubts, for instance, that God could be in need of those things which he himself has given (Y VII, 60ff). His complaints about the burden of his labour (T II, 96, 239–42) must also have rung familiar with a large part of the audience – all the more so since the offering of tithes is clearly brought into connection with the demands of the contemporary Church (T II, 104).

The mean farmer is represented by very different methods in the two plays. Y VII, from which two leaves have been lost (which also contained the killing of Abel), still allows us to see that the dialogue between Abel and Cain (Y VII, 34–72) was conceived of as a didactic dispute – notwithstanding the many curses employed by Cain. Cain opposes his own indolence to Abel's pious zest. Apart from the rude insults by which his replies are always introduced, they are confined to offering counter-reasons to Abel's proposals. When Abel wants to hurry to the sacrifice 'with hert ful hende' (Y VII, 44), Cain simply 'list noʒt nowe to rouk [bow] nor rowne [mutter]' (line 48). The tithe is rejected by Cain with the argument that God, being 'moste in myghte and mayne', can hardly be in need of such gifts (lines 65f). Here, too, Abel has a theological counterargument at hand:

> He has non nede vnto þi goode,
>   But it will please hym principall,
> If þou, myldly in mayne and moode,
>   Grouche noʒt geue hym tente parte of all.   (Y VII, 67–70)

This speech is typical. It answers the propositional content of Cain's speech, it does not betray a reaction to the latter's tone, although Abel's preachiness is in the strongest possible contrast to Cain's cursing. If Cain is admonished to act 'myldly' and not to grudge, this remains subordinate to the theological argument. The fact that people react not merely to what is said but also to how it is said does not find expression in the dialogue technique of this play.

In this respect the Cain and Abel play of the York cycle differs markedly from its Towneley counterpart. When, for instance, the Towneley Cain exclaims impatiently 'How long wilt thou me appech' (T II, 85), Abel has in fact spoken at great length – and very sanctimoniously. The language is rich in proverbs, Cain's speech is strongly emotional, even violent, rhetorical questions find an answer immediately, for instance:

> Shuld I leife my plogh and all thyng,
> And go with the to make offeryng?
> Nay, thou fyndys me not so mad!
> Go to the dwill, and say I bad!
> What gifys God the to rose [= praise] hym so?
> Me gifys he noght bot soro and wo.   (T II, 91–6)

Word and gesture mesh precisely, as in T II, 99–100:

> Yit boroed I neuer a farthyng
> Of hym – here my hand.

or T II, 62:

> Com nar, and other drife or hald.

These are features of a highly developed dialogue technique which far excels that of Y VII. Less conspicuous, though not less remarkable, is the fact that Abel's speech texture shows similar signs of emotional reaction. He is not content to argue, as he is in Y VII; he attempts above all to soothe his brother, especially in his openings:

Caym, leife this vayn carpyng	(T II, 97)
Leif brother, say not so	(ibid., 130)
Leif brother, whi sais thou so?	(ibid., 167).

Clearly, there is more at work here than merely a delight in rude language: the playwright brings his insight into the impulses driving human conversation to bear on both characters, regardless of their 'stageworthiness'.

This realism is closely related to the tendency toward blasphemy and obscenity which is to be observed in the speeches of Cain and his servant although the two tendencies may well go back to different sources. Our play uses speech-types which form part of the repertoire of the moralities and interludes. Weimann has pointed out the parodistic 'Sprachspiel' with which Pikeharness glosses the 'King's Pardon' near the end of the play in his asides.[179] Similarities between Pikeharness and the Jack Finney of the Mummers' Play had already been observed by Tiddy.[180] Cain interrupting his brother's edifying speech with blasphemies resembles the Vices in the moral play *Mankind* (*c.* 1465 × 70), Cain's ploughing-team may also derive from non-religious acting traditions. The fact that he ploughs with no fewer than four horses and four oxen[181] has led to speculations on the size of the stage which are almost certainly misguided;[182] it seems much more likely that eight boys were disguised with animals' skins as oxen and horses. This would also make Cain's frequent scolding of *individual* animals more understandable: boys disguised as animals can be told when to buck or to balk; real animals, hardly. If this assumption is correct, we are observing a transfer from the Plough Monday Play into a mystery play.[183] There are more similarities than this: the Plough Monday Play has a killing (which, however, is purely comical), and unlike all other Abel plays the Towneley *Mactacio* resembles the Plough Play in allowing Abel a last outcry after he has received the deadly blow.

If we want to evaluate the *Mactacio*, we must not stop here. We must try to integrate our findings into the medieval conception of Cain on the one hand and into the structure of the play on the other. The moral evaluation of Cain – as opposed to the dramatic conception of the character – is entirely traditional. Unless we keep that firmly in mind, we are running the risk of suspecting secret heresy or even residuary paganism in the play. The Towneley Cain has precisely those features which have been part and parcel of the medieval tradition since the

Venerable Bede and Peter Comestor. Cain complaining about the hardness of his work, blaspheming against God, and even lacking respect in prayer is simply being faithful to the tradition established by Bede: *minus perfecta pietate in agenda carnis cura laboraverit, minus perfecta devotione ad offerenda Deo munera accesserit.*[184] Cain – miscounting the sheaves in his own favour, reviling his brother for being preferred by God, attempting even impudently to deny the murder – is merely a scenic representation of Peter Comestor's brief résumé: *Non recte divisit, fratri invidit,...procaciter negavit...*[185]

The Wakefield Master's great achievement is not merely to mention these qualities, but also to present them dramatically. To this end, he has placed them in the real, medieval environment of his spectators. One question, however, remains: is not Cain, by thus being brought closer to his audience, also rendered harmless? Does not the first murderer receive unwarranted sympathies when he complains about the meagre wages of farming and the pressing burden of the tithe? The modern reader may feel that Christian teaching is becoming relativized if the opposition is allowed to speak in its own, subjectively convinced voice. But this voice, which always talks of debts and payments, never of love and obedience, is too clearly the voice of *avaritia* to be able to count on the sympathies of a contemporary audience.[186] A thorough analysis of the play shows that the Wakefield Master knew very well how to determine the dramatic effect of Cain's blasphemy and vulgarity. He is careful to show Cain as a *rich* peasant.[187] He is introduced by his servant as 'A good yoman' (T II, 15), the size of his ploughing-team has already been mentioned. His complaints about hard work, about thistles and thorns in the harvest (T II, 202) must therefore not be taken at their face value, but as a realistic portrayal of his hypocrisy. This rich farmer who beats his servant and his beasts in his anger (T II, 25ff, 48ff, 387ff) will certainly not find it difficult to obtain the King's Pardon. Certainly, he is 'close to the public', but only in that sense in which murderers and exploiters are close to their victims. And it is the truly popular boy Pikeharness, patterned on the model of the folk-play ruffler,[188] who unmasks the proclamation of the Pardon in his parody. The audience laugh *with* the servant whose wit and impudence deny his master's claim, but they laugh *at* the rude and irascible farmer, who was only too familiar to them from their everyday lives.[189] The apparent externals which surround the first murder make him into an ever-present, threatening reality. This presence is guaranteed no longer – at least not primarily – by the typological significance of Abel's death as a prefiguration of the Crucifixion, but by its being rooted in the psychological and social causes which can become manifest only in specific social surroundings and which every spectator also had to suspect within his own heart.

The Torturing and the Crucifixion of Christ[190]

The problem of the representation of evil becomes even more acute in the Passion plays. Conflicting conceptions of the nature of the mystery plays come to a head in the evaluation of these scenes. Any attempt at coming to grips with the cycles must here find its touchstone. The scenes are so central to the cycles as a whole that no interpretation can be called satisfactory that regards them as mere decadent concessions to the secularized tastes of a rude populace or an adulteration of the original character of the religious drama.[191] The very number of opinions that have been voiced on this matter makes one thing clear at least: the plays in question are profoundly disturbing to modern sensibilities.

From contemporary witnesses we know that the plays sometimes aroused mirth rather than compassion.[192] This has given rise to the theory that in the Passion plays there is to be found an undercurrent of irreverence and even blasphemy which runs against the plays' official, religious purpose. The most seminal representative of this view is probably A.P. Rossiter, who discovers in the Towneley *Buffeting*

> the presence of two rituals at once, of which the one is the negation of the faith to which the piece is ostensibly devoted. The very values of martyrdom – of *any* suffering as significant – are implicitly denied by thus making game of it.[193]

Rossiter sees the two rituals, the two sets of values, as on an equal footing. He denies the possibility that the universal authority of the Christian faith in the Middle Ages was sufficient to keep the 'negation of the faith' in an unambiguously subordinate position. In another context, he discovers an 'ambivalence' whose 'evaluated effect...reaches out towards a searching irony' (p. 72).

Rossiter has found a follower in Robert Weimann, who emphasizes above all the 'pagan heritage' in his discussion of comedy and horror in the English mystery plays and who joins Rossiter in regarding the union of 'the legacy of Joculator and Jougleur' with 'the spirit of the comic rejoicings of the folk' as 'the most important part of the medieval heritage'.[194] The difference between Rossiter and Weimann is chiefly one of evaluation: while Rossiter shows himself 'disturbed' by the 'doubleness-of-tone' which he senses (p. 69), Weimann welcomes it as a sign of emancipation from clerical domination. With an uncharacteristic lack of dialectical subtlety he yokes together the 'pagan' and the 'heretical', neglecting the fact that it was precisely the 'heretics' who accused the 'miracle plays' of paganism.[195]

A close study of the relationship between speech and action may help us to evaluate these interpretations. Although we shall never know exactly how action and speech were fitted to each other, a systematic study of the language will allow reasonable hypotheses. On the whole, it can be said that the English mystery plays correlated speech and action in a way that is peculiar to them and which I propose to call 'parallelism': a speaker announces what he is going to do or describes what he is doing. He will not, like a real-life speaker, reflect and deliberate on his actions.

To illustrate the implications of these considerations for the Buffeting and Scourging scenes, it is perhaps best to start with our idea of a prototypical beating: clearly, words and blows can be offered simultaneously. But we will not announce or describe our blows. Speech and action will normally not 'parallel' but reinforce each other. When we beat someone we will not waste our breath to state this obvious fact, we will use it to add insult to injury. Normally, there will not be any obvious coordination between these two activities. Any order would be in conflict with the violence of the emotions and actions involved.

If we can trust the evidence of the texts of the mystery plays that have survived, the performances of most Passion scenes did not conform to this protypical idea of a beating. The relationship between word and action *was* ordered, and it was largely 'parallel' in the sense described.

Neither is the effect of this combination of word and deed difficult to imagine: it will slow down the pace of the stage business. To use a metaphor from electronic data processing: we will not get the events 'in real time'. In the Passion scenes, this must have reduced the violence considerably. If this is accepted as a general acting principle, detailed study of the precise relationship between word and action will yield interestingly different results for the four English cycles.

As in many other respects, the N-Town cycle differs most from the other three. Its Scourging and Buffeting scenes are by far the shortest, and the mesh between word and action seems to be less thoroughgoing.

These short dialogues are accompanied by stage directions which are extremely long even by the standards of the N-Town Passion plays. What is more, the dialogues in the Herod and in the Pilate scenes reveal nothing on the relationship between action and word. In the Herod episode, the Third Jew distributes whips, apparently to his fellows, and exhorts them to 'spare not whyl þei last' (LC, p. 286, line 446). After this exhortation a stage direction says: 'and qwan þei han betyn hym tyl he is alle blody þan þe herownde seyth'. One has to assume, thus, that the whipping itself takes place in silence, which would no doubt underline its non-realistic, ritualistic character. Two methods of making Christ's body 'alle blody' are conceivable: either the whips were treated with a substance which left red traces on the skin, or the actor representing Christ wore a flesh-coloured, tight-fitting suit hiding guts filled with red liquid. The guts would burst under the impact of the strokes, and the liquid would colour the actor's suit.[196] In either case, the actor would have been able to sit or stand still, visibly expressing that patience which figures so prominently in the meditative Passion literature of the period. The effect must have been very different from what was to be seen in Oberammergau in 1990, where Christ winced under every stroke. During the entire Scourging scene he had to face the audience, to hide red streaks previously painted on his back. These became visible only when he was led off.

The N-Town Scourging before Pilate shows a similar divorce between action and dialogue, though the action does not take place in silence. According to the stage direction, Pilate's sentence is greeted by the Jews with loud cries of joy, but there is little articulate speech. A long stage direction of eleven lines in all is interrupted by two lines of speech from *Primus Judeus* which may be interpreted as a threat but shows no direct connection with the Scourging (LC, p. 294, SD 675+, 677+). This distribution of speech and action theoretically allows for tortures of indefinite length, but the measured speech by Pilate which precedes them and at the end of which Pilate rises and goes to his scaffold seems to be more in keeping with a brief, stylized execution of this part of the sentence. The Scourging is immediately followed by the laments of two women bewailing the 'rewful syth' which Jesus offers (p. 295, line 682). This, too, argues in favour of briefness and stylization.

In the Buffeting the separation between speech and action is not as thoroughgoing as in the scenes previously discussed. For here the action is reflected partly in the stage direction, partly in the speeches:

here þei xal bete jhesus A-bout þe hed and þe body and spyttyn in his face and pullyn hym down and settyn hym on A stol and castyn A cloth ouyr his face · and þe fyrst xal seyn (LC, p. 276, SD 160+)

After this stage direction, which suggests some silent action, the First Jew warns his comrades to be careful about what they do to Jesus, because he is a prophet. The Second and the Third will at once test the prophetic abilities of their blindfolded victim by striking him. In the words of the Third Jew:

Whar whar now wole I
Wetyn how he can prophecy
ho was þat.   (lines 165–7)

Between the second and the third line of this quotation, he clearly strikes Jesus. If this integration of speech and action seems more like what we shall find in the other cycles, it has to be remembered that the blasphemous requests for prophecy have their origin in the gospel reports and can hardly be rendered in any other way. The Buffeting is almost as short as the Scourging; like it, it is followed by a scene which stresses the compassion with Jesus which the Christian is to feel: after

Intra-dramatic speeches 235

Peter's threefold denial and the crowing of the cock Jesus silently looks on Peter, causing him to weep and to lament his own faithlessness. Thus, everything shows that the N-Town 'Passion Play II' keeps the torture scenes short, thereby preventing them from becoming overly dominant.

In Chester the Buffeting (Ch XVI, 70–109) and the Scourging (Ch XVI, 307–54) scenes are longer. Especially in the Buffeting we have a more 'normal' alternation between 'announcement' and 'execution'. The announcements are usually one stanza long. Stage directions like 'dans alap*am*' (in the singular) suggest that there was only one stroke per stanza. This would again have given the action a rather stylized character. Stage directions in the Chester manuscripts are of course not impeccable evidence, but our conclusions agree well with those of Peter W. Travis: that the brutality was 'probably highly stylized' and showed formality 'to the point of ritual'.[197]

The York Buffeting (Y XXIX, 353–79) has no stage directions and shows a somewhat different, closer relationship between word and action which however is still 'parallel' in our definition of the term:

> III MILES
> I schall fande to feste it[198] with a faire flappe –
> And ther is – iij; and there is iiij.
> Say nowe, with an nevill happe,
> Who negheth þe nowe? Not o worde, no!
> IV MILES
> Dose noddill on hym with neffes that he noght nappe.
> (Y XXIX, 363–7)

The Third Soldier addresses Jesus directly and is disappointed at his failure to obtain an answer. The Fourth Soldier interprets Jesus' silence ironically as a 'nap' and encourages his comrade to 'noddle' him in order to keep him from falling asleep. Speech is here not limited to the announcement of actions but includes the reaction to the results – in this case disappointing results – of those actions. At the same time, the soldiers not only vie with each other, they also give each other advice, thus weaving a tighter net of interaction between them than was found in Chester.

Attention to effects is carried to much greater length in the Scourging (Y XXXIII, 349–426). The Crowning with Thorns is described in these words:

> I MILES
> Now thryng to hym thrally with þis þikk
> II MILES
> Lo, it heldes to his hede þat þe harnes out
> III MILES
> Thus we teche hym to tempre his tales –
> His brayne begynnes for to blede.   (Y XXXIII, 398–401)

Most of the Buffeting and of the Scourging is written in stichomythia. Since most lines announce an action, we may have to reckon with almost one action per line. This, together with the increased length of the passages, is likely to make the scenes faster and more brutal than in Chester. On the other hand, enough time is left for a detailed description of Christ's brains and blood running down on him. The soldiers would hardly have described these effects if they had not had the means to create them. The closing line of the scene is in the same vein:

> II MILES
> Lo, his flessh al beflapped þat fat is.   (Y XXXIII, 431)
> (*fat* may be a macabre pun on the possible meaning 'anointed'.)

While the Chester Torturers are content to announce (and realize) their intentions, their counterparts in York also glory in pointing to effects. This must have interrupted the barrage and monotony of violence from time to time. Above all it must have prevented Christ's suffering from being submerged in the excitement of the Torturers. Christ visibly becomes the Man of Sorrows. The isolation of Christ is thus more marked in York for including more aspects of his suffering. The York Realist is not open to the charge, frequently heard in modern media criticism, that to ignore the victim is one of the worst stimulants of brutality.

In the Towneley cycle the Buffeting and the Flagellation form two distinct plays (T XXI and XXII). The 'Flagellation' is a heterogeneous piece, metrically and probably genetically as well. The Scourging episode, almost entirely in the well-known 'Wakefield stanza', is followed by laments of Christ's followers in a variety of stanza forms. It seems likely that the so-called Wakefield Master revised the Scourging episode of a formerly more homogeneous play. But even considered by itself, the Scourging episode appears ill-focused. The Torturers, who lead Jesus from Herod back to Pilate, beat him even before Pilate has given them leave to scourge him. Unlike other Torturers, they positively relish the prospect of causing him pain:

> *Secundus tortor.*
> Bot more sorow thou hase / oure myrth is incresyng,
> No lak.   (T XXII, 74f)
> *Tercius tortor.*
> My hart wold all to-bryst / bot I myght tyll hym glyde.
> *Primus tortor.*
> A swap fayn, if I durst / wold I lene the this tyde.   (T XXII, 135f)

These strangely 'conditioned' threats are followed by the fastest series of blows that we have witnessed so far: each of the short lines of the stanza's wheel appears to be accompanied by one:

> *Tercius tortor.* haue att!
> *Primus tortor.* Take thou thatt!
> *Secundus tortor.* I shall lene the a flap,
>   My strengthe for to kythe. (T XXII, 139–42)

The same procedure is repeated in the following stanza (T XXII, 148f). At the same time, the Torturers strangely bear witness to Christ's divinity. The First Torturer comments:

> The great warkys he has wroght
> Shall serue hym of noght. (T XXII, 58f)

And the Second Torturer promises:

> I shall spytt in his face / though it be fare shynyng. (T XXII, 72)

The 'if I durst' in an earlier quotation (line 136) is in the same vein. This manner of speaking may recall the 'objective' speeches which we often hear from the evil characters in the morality plays, but here the 'objectivity' is confined to brief remarks that do not even make up full sentences.

More than any other play, the Towneley 'Flagellation' shows, at least intermittently, that 'gusto' which Rossiter found in Grünwald's 'Christ Mocked'. The 'Buffeting' is of course a much more unified play,[199] though it shares with the 'Flagellation' an interest in the psychology of the Torturers which the other cycles do not betray. But while the Torturers in the 'Flagellation' show sadistic enjoyment in their work, their colleagues in the 'Buffeting' are surly, loutish *Spießbürger* before the beating and cool, callous professionals during it. On their way to the High Priests they vent their resentment against Jesus the troublemaker who proposes to change the law of the land. Instead of relishing the prospect of beating Jesus themselves, they merely tell him that he will 'get no grace' from Annas and Caiaphas, strongly conveying, however, that this will serve him right. When they have been ordered to 'wake Jesus up with their knocks' (line 322), they go about their business without the least enthusiasm. Caiaphas promises his blessing to him 'That knokys hym the best' (line 341), thus making the buffeting into a competition. The Torturers of this play seem to be the only ones in English drama to be extrinsically, rather than intrinsically, motivated. At their work, they soberly assess, rather than triumphantly exhibit, their achievements. Christ's body is a physical object on which they exercise their craft:

> 1 *Tortor.* Now sen he is blynfeld, I fall to begyn;
>   And thus was I counseld the mastry to wyn.
> 2 *Tortor.* Nay, wrang has thou teld; thus shuld thou com in.
> *Froward.* I stode and beheld – thou towchid not the skyn
>   But fowll.

> 1 *Tortor.* How will thou I do?
> 2 *Tortor.* On this manere, lo!
> *Froward.* Yei, that was well gone to;
>   Ther start vp a cowll.   [*a swelling*   (T XXI, 397–405)

The number of blows per line – if this perverse statistic is permitted – seems lower than in other plays, and yet the cruelty is perhaps more depressing, because the men are so uncomfortably 'normal' in many ways. Froward, the youngest of the three who seems to be some kind of apprentice (and the only one with a name), is unwilling to obey the orders of the other two and complains about his miserable wages. In this he behaves exactly like the youngest of the three Shepherds in the two *Pastorum* plays. The Torturers seem to practise a trade which is organized like any other trade in the society of which they are part. Rather than delight in the pain they will inflict on Jesus, they argue about their work.[200]

One would lose all sense of Christ's divinity were it not for two remarkable references which can even qualify as dramatic irony:

> 2 *Tortor.* Ther is none in this towne, I trow, be ill payde
>   Of hys sorow,
>   Bot the fadyr that hym gate.   (T XXI, 364–6)

> *Froward.* Cryst curs myght he haue
>   That last bond his heade!   (T XXI, 394f)

But even though the divinity of Christ is relegated to the background, his opponents are not allowed to triumph. While Christ, almost unable to lift his feet (line 430), is led away by the Torturers like an animal to the slaughter-house, the High Priests are left to quarrel among themselves, thus falling into the familiar pattern of defeated devils. Even in this most brutal and callous of all Passion scenes, Jesus triumphs by refusing to play the game of his opponents.[201]

However different the nexus between speech and action in the cycles that have come down to us, it is always calculated to restrain the ecstatic potential of the Passion scenes, to keep the spectators in the relatively distant position of beholders, not to let them become 'participants' in the Bakhtinian sense of the word.

Comparing the Torture scenes of various cycles, we will notice a similarity between York and Chester which is surprising in view of the differences observed in other respects. Probably Chester has here preserved the remnants of an earlier stratum which elsewhere was abolished by the didactic reviser to whom we owe, among other things, the *Expositor* and the echoes of the *Stanzaic Life*. This conjecture finds support in the fact that a Passion play is known to have existed by 1422[202]

Intra-dramatic speeches 239

and that the verse lines of the Torturing and Crucifixion scenes (Ch XVI, 45–101 (DM 49–120), 307–78 (DM 313–84), XVIA, 73–216 (DM XVI, 457–600)) are shorter than in the rest of the play (or plays) and than in most of the cycle. A similar metrical deviation occurs in the Chester Shepherds Play (Ch VII), which also exhibits a style which is atypical in Chester and, as will be shown, may well be archaic.[203] But it is equally possible that we are dealing with a stylistically motivated variation designed to underline the special character of the Torture episodes. Such an assumption might derive some support from the fact that it is entire scenes, not just interpolations, which use the deviant metre. This would make the assumption of later revision in the surrounding text superfluous, but would leave the Torture scenes as original parts of the play. This hypothesis, too, would make it probable that a style for the Torture scenes existed which was known beyond York.

Just as striking as these similarities are those which appear in the Crucifixion scenes (Ch XVIA, 153–216, Y XXXV, 1ff). The ecstasy of the previous scene is here replaced by the cold brutality of professional hangmen. The cruelties depicted in these scenes – Christ's arms are stretched to fit them to the holes to which they are to be fixed – go back chiefly to such narrative sources as the *Northern Passion*.[204] The transfer into the dramatic medium made the individual moments of Christ's agony much more piercing and terrible than they had been in the narrative. The difference becomes apparent when we consider the form of the dialogue. After the Third *Miles* (Y XXXV, 100) has fixed Jesus' left hand, it is discovered that the distance from the right hole is too great. This discovery gives rise to the following exchange:

> *I Miles* Saie sir, howe do we þore?
> þis bargayne may not blynne.
> *II Miles* It failis a foote and more,
> þe senous are so gone ynne. ...
> *I Miles* Why carpe ȝe so? Faste on a corde
> And tugge hym to, by toppe and taile.
> *III Miles* ȝa, þou comaundis lightly as a lorde,
> Come helpe to haale, with ille haile.   (Y XXXV, 105–16)

Similarly in Chester:

> *Primus Judeus*:
>   Yea, but, as mote I thee,
>   shorte-armed is hee.
>   To the booringe of this tree
>   hit will not well last.
> *Secundus Judeus*:
>   A, therfore care thou nought.

> A sleight I have sought.
> Roopes must be bought
> to strayne him with strength.   (Ch XVIA, 181–8)

The dialogue here does not merely accompany the action, it reacts to events and discoveries. Inferences are drawn and call forth new actions. Curses and challenges go back and forth, as they do in the Towneley *Coliphizacio* (T XXI). Dramatic speech thus becomes a dialogue the parts of which interlock by thought-processes and emotional reactions. The emotions themselves are transformed in the process. The Torturers are no less cruel than in previous scenes, but the sadistic enjoyment is gone. Like the Buffeting in Towneley, the Crucifixion in York, Towneley and Chester is a technical problem which they know how to solve, not without bragging about their strength and their skill.

In a co-operative exercise like the Crucifixion such interlocking dialogue seems to have been the rule rather than the exception. In less labour-dividing activities like the Buffeting and Scourging, 'serial' dialogue appears to have been more wide-spread. The Wakefield Master went beyond his contemporaries in providing even these scenes with truly interlocking dialogue.

The Shepherds
Of the six Shepherds Plays which have been preserved for us are three which have repeatedly commanded the interest of modern critics:[205] that of the Chester cycle (Ch VII) and the two plays known as *Prima Pastorum* and *Secunda Pastorum*, which the so-called Wakefield Master has contributed to the Towneley cycle (T XII, T XIII). The fact that these three plays have so often been grouped together owes a good deal to the aspect concerning us now: all three plays supplement the account given in the gospel according to St Luke with episodes which are unmistakably taken from the everyday life of English medieval shepherds. In our context it is worth noticing that the nucleus of these supplementary scenes is always a quarrel, either between the Shepherds themselves, or with a fourth person who enters later. It hardly needs to be mentioned that these episodes have played a considerable rôle in the critical debate on the 'realism' of the medieval drama and have received highly diverging evaluations, depending on the point of view of the critic. The present writer has elsewhere expressed the opinion that the term 'realism' has been used too uncritically, both by its early advocates and by its later critics, and that it has been used almost exclusively to refer to the subject-matter of the plays. It seems more useful to consider the *manner* of representation under the aspect of realism and to inquire into the nexus between speaker, speech, situation, and action.[206] Robert Weimann's

Intra-dramatic speeches

subtle analyses are based on a similar concept of realism.[207] Weimann, however, studies above all the connection between mythical-ritual tradition and realistic representation which the Shepherds Plays manifest and is thus primarily interested in those features which the plays have in common. He confines himself to the statement that realistic means of representation are indeed present in these plays and demonstrates convincingly the highly complex and aesthetically most effective, by no means 'naïve' combinations into which they enter with both mythical and commonplace contents.

Weimann's contention that 'new realism and pristine heritage [viz. of popular/pagan traditions]' are not mutually exclusive in these plays[208] is certainly correct as far as the Towneley Shepherds Plays are concerned, but an analysis of the quarrel in Chester, which still shows clear traces of ritual *flyting*,[209] will allow us to determine more clearly the achievement of the Wakefield Realist, the traditions which he was faced with and which he transformed. The description of the Chester quarrel as a *flyting* implies already that there can be no question of a truly realistic intent. The heavily revised state of the scene scarcely allows us to identify anything like the 'intent of representation' – whether in the original or in the final version.[210] But this much is certain: none of the revisers was anxious to achieve a dramatically realistic nexus between action, speech and character. The authors of the later strata were at pains (among other things) to soften the rude aggressive tone which the entry of Trowle brings into the play (line 165). This was done chiefly by the insertion of scenes which emphasize the notion of peace and express friendly feelings also toward Trowle. The contradiction to Trowle's bitterness and loneliness which is thus created was apparently accepted as a lesser evil.

The strong similarities between the three plays exist not only in detail but also in over-all structure. They are due probably not to borrowing but to *Urverwandtschaft*. Modern research has shown that the quarrel scenes are not to be interpreted as superficial 'comic relief'[211] but are related to the biblical events by a multitude of correspondences.[212] This is an important advance over earlier criticism which, if it did not regard the comic scenes entirely superficially,[213] was content to point out their origins in popular narrative and custom.[214] Modern critics, however, have fallen into the other extreme. If they are right to criticize the generation of Chambers and Young for mechanically transferring the categories of biological evolution theory to the history of literature, they must also face the charge that they are studying isolated cells from the living organism of drama under the microscope without paying due heed to the genetic and ecological conditions under which these organisms exist. Since they entirely neglect the 'reception situation' of the medieval audience, the reader of these very subtle analyses often feels uncomfortable: one is impressed by their wealth of detailed observation and theological learning, nor does one dare deny their theological relevance; but it is equally hard to believe that the audiences in Yorkshire or Cheshire should have been composed of that mixture of theologians, Scholastics, and New Critics who alone would be capable of appreciating all those minutiae of design and correspondence. This discomfort could be alleviated if the many correspondences became recognizable as elements of larger, homomorphous structures. For as integrated components of complexes they would be relevant even for the not-so-subtle spectator. Margery M. Morgan occasionally suggests such an idea, for instance when she interprets the secular action of our three plays as an antithesis and burlesque of the religious one.[215] But she overlooks the fact that analogous-religious and burlesque-perverting correspondences fulfil different dramaturgic functions and, because of different origins, create different aesthetic effects. Robert Weimann is more successful in that he follows up the meshing of pre-Christian-popular and biblical-liturgical elements in the reality of the dramatic process.[216] He also makes the important point that the analogues which link the Mak story with events in Bethlehem are not to be found in the Wakefield Master's probable source and may therefore be assumed to be his own contribution. Taking his ideas a step further, we recognize that many of those correspondences which at first appear over-subtle, are in fact aesthetically effective because they belong to contrasting but comparable structures. The pagan rites, pushed aside into unofficial usage since the advent of Christianity, and the Christian liturgy, which had appropriated the forms and often the times and places of the former, were able to form an aesthetic unity because both, despite their development from totally conflicting social positions, went back to ritualistic origins. This creates correspondences which will strike the modern reader as parodistic, but the parodistic intent is incapable of conclusive proof. The un-Christian elements of the folk customs need not be anti-Christian, and consciously they are certainly not so. The value of the burlesque in the religious drama can be determined exactly only when the social and historical ground on which popular and liturgical elements come into contact and realize the aesthetic unity which we have observed, has been studied more accurately.

Whatever the specific circumstances of these contacts in the various countries and cities may have been like – a few general facts of Western art and aesthetics which are immediately relevant to our discussion can be stated: the evil, the ugly and the grotesque, whose place in the arts and the aesthetic theory of the Middle Ages had always been assured, though marginal – a passing mention of misericords and gargoyles must suffice here[217] –, gain importance with the influx of popular elements into the religious drama.

On turning now to the quarrel in the Chester Shepherds Play, it may be useful to give a brief account of how such quarrels usually arise. Before the quarrel can begin, one may assume, the parties have to meet. They will greet each other, they exchange a few words, an incidental remark made by the one irritates the other, the dispute gradually becomes more heated. If we approach the Chester Shepherds Play with this quite unreflected 'normal notion', we will note at once that here the quarrel flares up in quite a different way. Trowle, the servant tending the sheep of his three masters, is called over by the First Shepherd so that he may take part in the common meal. Prior to this, the calling of Trowle is discussed by the Three Shepherds rather elaborately and is approved by all (lines 149–60). In this discussion the feelings voiced by the Shepherds are full of kindness and praise for their excellent servant. Trowle enters when the First Shepherd has blown his horn (SD 164+). However, instead of immediately joining the others, he delivers a long and sullen speech, the tenor of which is highly surprising after the conversation of the three. He describes himself as a friendless loner. His speech is thinly disguised as a prayer, but in reality it is directed at the spectators. This becomes apparent in its second stanza, when Trowle promises the audience:

> you shall here sone in sight,
> of small hannes[218] that to me neden.
> (lines 183f in DM, after the line corresponding to line 175 in LM)

These lines, curiously absent from MS Huntington 2 which Lumiansky and Mills chose as a base for their edition, indicate what the coming quarrel is in truth: not a change in previously existing interpersonal relations, but a demonstration before the spectators which Trowle himself feels as a 'need'. We can assume for certain that the wrestling bouts which Trowle is soon to provoke are traditional popular pastimes of which the Church was highly critical.[219] Whether they preserve the victory of the new year over the old or not, they resemble liturgical representations in that they do not rest on a substratum of interpersonal relationships. They thus oblige the two parties to become completely submerged in the rôles prescribed by the ritual. In the liturgical representations we called these rôles 'Revealers' and 'Recipients';[220] now they are those of attacker and attacked. That Trowle is the servant and thus a good acquaintance of the other three is irrelevant during the course of the flyting.

Trowle's further speeches are equally 'ritualistic' in the sense that they merely accompany, rather than interlock with, the action:

> Nowe wyll I sitt here adowne
> and pippe at this pott like a pope.
> Would God that I were downe
> harmeles, as I hastelye hope. (lines 188–91)

Even the self-introduction and the flyting speeches sound like inverted songs of praise. Just as the Shepherds at the Manger often produce only a series of praising epithets, Trowle enumerates objects which belong to his masters and which he makes sound most horrible by such devices as alliteration and consonance:

> Fye on your loynes and your liverye,
> your liverastes, livers, and longes,
> your sose, your sowse, your saverraye,
> your sittinge withowt any songes! (lines 202–5)

The rather thick alliteration of these lines makes us suspect later revision. Nevertheless, the diction still suggests the tone of the traditional flytings, even though it has here been transposed to a grossly rustic level, finding its crowning conclusion in a crude obscenity, which characteristically is purely scatological:

> The better in the bore, [*arsehole*
> as I had before
> of this bovearte,[221]
> yea, hope I more.
> Keepe well thy score
> for feare of a farte. (lines 274–9)

Even during the wrestling proper the change of speakers remains regular, stanza-by-stanza. The uniform tempo is not varied under the influence of the physical action: one Shepherd replies to Trowle's challenge, Trowle abuses him once more, and subsequently throws him to the ground. The measured, pounding rhythm of the last-quoted lines is a palpable expression of this state of affairs. Even the crudest swearword is not the symptom of agitated emotion, which would inform speech and action equally, but the fulfilment of a necessity prescribed by the ritual. The stage directions (*Tunc primus* [2.*us*, 3.*us*] *projicitur*: lines 268, 276, 290[222]) leave no doubt that speech precedes action and that the two do not interlock.

In the entire flyting episode the representational function of language dominates over the appellative; in this the episode resembles the dialogue in liturgical offices. We have reason to believe that the flyting is not a late addition inserted for the sake of 'comic relief', but an original constituent part of the play. It is, as it were, a palpable and realistic version of the *Magnificat*,[223] a burlesque antithesis to the biblical events.[224] F.M. Salter has demonstrated how strong the influence of the Church was on the Chester Plays until 1531,[225] and a detailed study of the compositional history of the Shepherds Play shows the effects of this influence on the form of this play.[226] In the Shepherds Plays we can observe that Trowle's rude and uncouth behaviour was increasingly surrounded and 'soft-cushioned' by moralising and didactic passages. Rather than entirely suppressing the burlesque scene, the Church appears to have preferred to neutralize its irreverent tone of the flyting-and-wrestling episode by other scenes.[227]

As far as the use of dramatic language is concerned, the Shepherds Plays by the Wakefield Master are the exact opposite of Ch VII. The quarrels are more numerous and more diverse, they are expressions of real social relations, and they are embedded in specific physical and spatial situations. Robert Weimann has demonstrated how the *Secunda Pastorum* passes from conventional audience-address to dramatic, situationally embedded dialogue.[228] A similar process is to be observed in the *Prima Pastorum*: after the Second Shepherd has finished addressing the audience he turns to the First. This is done in a highly realistic manner and under due consideration of the actual distance between the two: since the First has already started walking towards the town,[229] he must now be at some distance from the Second and can be recalled only by loud, repeated shouts (T XII, 82f). After this we become, as in the *Secunda Pastorum*, witnesses of a goodneighbourly salutation. But the dramatist is not content merely to depict social customs; the characterization of his Shepherds is astonishingly consistent and resourceful. It begins in the monologues and is continued in the dialogue, and it is achieved by indirect, stylistic means.[230] The serious, introvert *Primus Pastor* who laments the loss of his sheep is contrasted with a rather aggressive, extrovert *Secundus Pastor*. The conventional quarrel, familiar already from Chester, now finds motivation in the Second Shepherd's character. And characterization is not an end in itself, but serves the purposes of social satire and criticism: 'This absurd quarrel has a realistic background in the endless disputes over rights of common that we find recorded in the manor-court rolls of the period.'[231] The quarrel over grazing rights, which is borrowed from a popular tale,[232] is thus grounded in contemporary reality.

The dramatic form of the quarrel is highly different from the Trowle episode, too. The spoken word does not merely accompany the fighting, it is itself a weapon in the fight and a direct expression of psychological agitation. Irony ('A, good syr, ho!', T XII, 103) soon becomes defiance:

> 1 PASTOR: I wyll pasture my fe
> Wheresoeuer lykys me;
> Here shall thou theym se.
> 2 PASTOR: Not so hardy!
> Not oone shepe-tayll shall thou bryng hedyr.
> 1 PASTOR: I shall bryng, no fayll, a hundreth togedyr.
> 2 PASTOR: What, art thou in ayll? Longys thou oght-whedir?
> 1 PASTOR: Thay shall go, saunce fayll. Go now, bell-whedir
> [*Urges forward his imaginary sheep.* (lines 105–12)[233]

The language, rich in exclamations, appears as a direct reflexion of the antagonists' movements ('ho' 103, 'what' 111, 'whop' 119, 'lo' 121). Quarrelsomeness and stubbornness escalate one against the other. Both are verbalized most consistently and at the same time with great variety. Each of the Shepherds is a party to destroying the goodneighbourly mood of the first salutation: the Second Shepherd begins the quarrel by stickling for his baseless claim, but the First takes the decisive step from reality to foolish delusion. To strengthen his claim he acts as if he were the owner of new sheep and finally believes in his own fancy.

The utopian abundance of the feast is represented with a similarly insistent realism. One of the Shepherds grabs the other's cup (lines 249ff), they tease each other about their speech (lines 206f, 276f):[234] in brief, the Shepherds show signs of quarrelsomeness even in this new abundance. They are better off now, and this prevents their peace from being disturbed too seriously. But it is made quite clear that this is not the peace which the Angel is to announce some time later.

To characterize the Wakefield Master merely as a lovable humorist or as a social critic of the 'gentlery-men' (T XIII, 18) is to overlook the fact that like all great humorists he is also a moralist and that the truly honest social critic will not close his eyes to the fact that social injustice affects not only men's well-being but also their character.

In the Second Shepherds' Play we find the same warm-hearted love of people without false idealization which characterizes the First. But here it finds expression in a fable which is unique in the English mystery cycles. The story of Mak the sheep-stealer differs from all non-biblical episodes in that it creates suspense and leads towards a solution which is unknown and – theoretically at least – impossible to guess at. All other *intermezzi*[235] remain episodic, their outcome is determined beforehand by the surrounding biblical action: Noah's wife may offer as much resistance as she likes – in the end she has to board the Ark since the story of the Flood demands it. Even the quarrels of the *Prima Pastorum* make no progress, if we regard them as dramatic conflicts. By contrast, the Mak story is sufficiently independent of the following biblical events as to be uncertain in its outcome: Mak's success would increase the poverty of the Shepherds, but it would not make them less suitable as first recipients of the Good News.

But if the singularity of the Mak story were only a matter of its content, the episode would merely be an interesting special case. What surpasses all other dramatic art of the English Middle Ages is its dialogue technique. This technique, which continues the earlier realistic tendencies we have observed, is now being put in the service of the new content. Until now the only legitimate question we were able to ask was: how are the utterances of the speakers embedded in the physical reality and in the relationships between the interlocutors? Now we can ask a different and much more far-reaching question: how does dramatic speech change the situation? And we can even ask: how does a speaker mean to change the situation by his utterance? This is an important difference between the quarrel in the *Prima Pastorum* and the Mak episode: there, the changes merely occurred; here, they are planned, first by Mak, then by the Third Shepherd. Quoting Hegel may sound pretentious in this context. But his definition of the drama as an

action [which] originates in the minds of the characters who bring it about, but at the same time its outcome is decided by the really substantive nature of the aims, individuals and collisions involved[236]

is thoroughly applicable to the Mak episode.

The Wakefield Master's solid grip on the new problems becomes evident in a comparison between the entry of Daw, the Third Shepherd, and that of Mak. The encounter between Daw and the two older Shepherds is still in the old 'quarrel' style which, for all its aggressiveness, is not directed at a solution and for that reason is fundamentally undynamic. Mak's entry, by contrast, produces at once an atmosphere of suspense: the purpose of the dialogue is no longer simply to communicate and to state, but to find out and to conceal:

> 2 PASTOR: Mak, where has thou gone? Tell vs tythyng. (line 199)
> 1 PASTOR: Why make ye it so qwaynt? Mak, ye do wrang. (line 208)

Even the smallest detail is subordinated to the goals of the action as a whole. This becomes particularly clear in Mak's far-reaching intrigue. On the question of how his wife is doing he replies, 'Lyys walteryng' (line 236), and goes on to give a vivid picture of the bewildering and costly frequency of her pregnancies. By this he prepares the ground for his later withdrawal: next morning, having stolen a sheep in the night and hidden it in his wife's cradle, he will take leave with the excuse that he has dreamt of his wife giving birth again (lines 386ff).

After the clever engineering of his plan Mak's performance vis-à-vis his wife is rather less impressive. With the stolen sheep under his arm he appears outside the cottage, telling her to make light and to open the door (line 296). She grumbles in reply that she is still spinning at this late hour to earn a little money, but she will hardly make a penny if she is constantly interrupted (lines 297–304). Mak finds a sophistical excuse – he is worth his meat since even in a tight corner he gets more than others who swink and sweat all day (lines 309–13) – but the picture of the good-for-nothing who ruins his wife with child-bearing and nightwork is firmly established, especially since it is his wife who has the saving idea: 'A good bowrde have I spied, syn thou can none' (line 332). But skilful characterization and vivid dialogue are here not ends in themselves. Even the physical environment which is suggested apparently without intention – light has to be made (line 296), Gyll has to go to the door (lines 297–304), which at first stays open on Mak's entry (lines 327f) – testifies not merely to the dramatist's (no doubt very lively) delight in details. All this conspires to give a picture of the conditions of that life which is in need of salvation. This places the Wakefield Master in a tradition which we have encountered already in some of the earlier Towneley plays, i.e. T IV (*Abraham*) and T X (*Annunciacio*). The methods of presentation have become more mature and complex; but the fearless eye, which recognizes and presents the harshness and godlessness of the world, is the same.

That Mak and Gyll do not fulfil the ideal of a Christian marriage is made clear by yet another episode. From the Joseph plays, every medieval playgoer was cheerfully familiar with the dialogue between the wife and the returning husband. In all the cycles, even in N-Town, the homecoming of Joseph and his discovery of Mary's pregnancy was a prominent scene which was often enriched with incidental comic detail. Scholars have been so busy discovering holy and unholy trinities, 'patterns' and 'designs' to establish correspondences between the Mak episode and the events in Bethlehem,[237] that this obvious and scenically most effective analogy has been all but overlooked.[238] This neglect is surprising since the grotesquely distorting correspondences are particularly obvious and are by no means limited to the comedy of the homecoming: Mak's alleged dream concerning the birth of his new child (lines 386ff) is usually interpreted as a parallel to the dream of the Shepherds. But it also suggests the Angel appearing to Joseph and explaining to him the true cause of Mary's pregnancy. The analogy is the more convincing as in both instances the dream concerns the dreamer's own wife. The contrast between Mary and Gyll, Joseph and Mak, however, could not be greater: there, the virgin; here, the woman who gives birth every year; there, Joseph who exercises restraint regarding his wife and cares for her lovingly;[239] here, the irresponsible rascal who begets more children than he can feed.

But while these comparisons are hardly flattering to Mak, they are intensely amusing to the audience, and they certainly do not detract from their sheer delight in Mak's rascally nature. Mak represents not only natural man's sinfulness and need of redemption, but also his vitality and his wealth of ideas,[240] and these latter celebrate their greatest, albeit last, triumph when the Shepherds enter Mak's cottage to seek the lost sheep which they suspect he has hidden there. Mak is capable of thinking of a thousand different things to dispel the Shepherds' already awakened suspicion. He pretends to be worried about their wet clothes and offers to light a fire (lines 494f). The lines that follow are characterized by a truly breath-taking impudence, transforming the cat-and-mouse game which now begins into an acrobatic dance on the brink of an abyss. For it is Mak himself who draws the Shepherds' attention to that embarrassing piece of furniture, the cradle: acting the part of the excited parent, he begins to talk about the child. He plans to hire a nurse. His wages – meaning of course the annual child that he had dreamt of – have been paid. But nothing can be done against this annual blessing, everyone has to drink as he brews! But surely the guests will stay for supper (lines 496–503)? This verbal cataract, which constantly changes the topic and is effectively underlined by the moaning of the woman who has allegedly just given birth, contrasts beautifully with the cool and distant tone of the rather monosyllabic Shepherds. A dramatist capable of writing such parts must have been able to rely on the mimetic skill of his actors.[241]

The absurd climax of this farce is reached with Mak and Gyll defending their 'child' even after the Shepherds have discovered its true identity. The 'long snout' spotted by Daw, the youngest of the Shepherds, is now attributed to the child's having been bewitched by an elf (lines 613ff). There certainly is an element of popular superstition here, especially since the face of the wether resembles that of the Devil,[242] and the oft-noted contrast to the Lamb of God is undeniable. But reference to these superstitious and religious notions should not let us overlook the fact that they are uncommonly frequent just in this scene, thus helping to underline the desperateness of Mak's and Gyll's situation. It is hardly accidental that it should be the deceivers who invoke such pre- and anti-Christian heresies. For all the a-moral and purely aesthetic fun which we are certainly meant to enjoy vis-à-vis this thieves' comedy, we should not forget that the position which the dramatist has assigned his unholy family is absolutely unambiguous, both in ideological and in dramatic terms. Mak always remains the Anti-Joseph, the bringer of strife who precedes the heavenly messenger of peace (in this respect resembling Trowle in Ch VII and the scoffer Iak Garcio in the *Prima Pastorum*), just as the Antichrist precedes Christ's Second Coming. This becomes apparent already in the polarity of the stage.[243] The Mak story is much more than a mirthful, secularized version of the Nativity; it stands at a highly interesting turning point in the history of the drama: the polarity of myth and mime which juxtaposes Trowle and Mak with Christ, enchantment with disenchantment, is still to be felt; the plot, however, is no longer determined by ritualistic folk *custom*, but by the fabliau-like realistic folk *tale*.[244] This brings about an important change in the relationship between the religious and the secular. The juxtaposition of the two is no longer 'immiscible'.[245] The story of the myth is now integrated in the mode of everyday experience, but this latter is also patterned by the myth. Lawrence J. Ross has pointed out that Mak appears precisely at the moment when the audience expected the Angel announcing the birth of the Saviour, and that consequently the unholy events of the Mak story were seen against the foil of the holy events of the Nativity.[246] The story of the false birth must have instilled in the audience an impatience for the true birth which is hard for a modern audience to imagine. At the same time the ending of the Mak story makes the moral point that the Good News of Christ's birth is indeed first imparted to men of good will: the Shepherds discover the sheep only after they have remembered to give a present to what by then they are forced to accept (though probably still against their real conviction) as a new-born babe.[247] And they do not put Mak to death as would be legal by the standards of the time,[248] they merely toss him in a blanket. In the Adoration scene the agonistic dialogue of the Mak episode with its constant forward thrust is replaced by a 'celebratory mode'.[249] The Mak story and the Nativity are thus related to each other not merely in static symmetry, but as suspense and resolution.[250] The brilliant integration of dialogue and stage action is much more than the masterpiece of an experienced craftsman. It shows a deep love for the world of everyday experience, which however never loses sight of the fact that this world is in need of salvation. In contrast to other cycle plays the *Secunda Pastorum* 'narrows [the] gap ... between the everyday world and its God, step by step.'[251]

9 Conclusions

Inevitably, the factors investigated in this study differ in their relevance for the Corpus Christi play as a dramatic genre. We have seen, for instance, that the plays are quite capable of representing emotions, but they mostly do this by generalizing personal experience by way of the audience-address. It is only in a few, presumably late plays that we find direct expression of emotions, such as the non-cycle Abraham plays or Mary's Lament at the Cross in LC XXXII, 810ff (p. 300). Especially remarkable in this respect is the Joseph of the York Plays. While the Joseph of the Towneley Plays generalizes the plight of his supposed cuckoldom in an audience-address, his York counterpart breaks forth in a personal complaint which centres not on the fate of old men in general but on his specific, momentary calamity and which therefore does not depend on the audience as an addressee. The influence of school rhetoric, which is still more in evidence with characters like Abraham and Adam and Eve, is to be felt even here.[1] The greater the literary and rhetorical ambition of the playwrights, the less are emotions represented by specifically dramatic means.

Even dialogue, which truly is the core of drama, hardly shows signs of continuous development. Truly dramatic dialogue, which makes the spoken word an instrument of interaction, is by and large the property of the two dramatists who stand out as clearly delineated personalities from the mass of anonymous writers: the York Realist and the Wakefield Master. A third playwright with a similar talent for dialogue may be identifiable in the author of the short octaves of the N-Town cycle. But to him our selection of aspects has done insufficient justice.

The York Realist's dialogue style is perhaps best characterized as 'ceremonious showing'. With him, even the scourging of Christ becomes a ceremony in which action and speech parallel, rather than interlock with, each other. In this he continues a style which must have been known far beyond York, as the Chester scenes witness. But he extends and adapts this style to the representation of court ceremonial, as in the Pilate and Herod scenes where it serves to set off the true majesty of Jesus against that merely assumed by Pilate and Herod. In Lukács' terms, this type of dialogue constitutes a world which is independent of the beholder but whose internal relationships are comparatively undeveloped. In this respect the Wakefield Master goes further. Especially in the *Coliphizacio* (T XXI) he weaves a tight web between the speech and the action of the Torturers without losing sight of the pain they inflict on Jesus. A similarly tight web is woven in the short octave plays of the N-Town cycle, especially 'Lazarus' and 'The Woman Taken in Adultery'.

But these factors, important as they are, are less central to the genre than two others, which are determined by the physical conditions of the performance itself. These are the structure of the stage with its two poles of *locus* and *platea* and the constant interaction of play-sphere and audience-sphere. These two factors, which make themselves felt whenever a practical theatrical problem has to be solved, mark the intermediate position of the vernacular medieval drama between the liturgical ceremony and the post-medieval drama.

The mystery plays (together with other types of medieval drama) differ from the liturgical ceremony in that they are performed before an onlooking audience, not a potentially participating congregation. In contrast to most post-medieval drama, on the other hand, they do not pretend to ignore that audience. Nevertheless, we have been able to observe a variety of attempts to increase the distance between audience-sphere and play-sphere. Here belong the Chester and N-Town cycles with the Expositor and Contemplacio, the Digby *Herod's Killing of the Children* and *Conversion of Saint Paul* with their *Poetae*, as well as the Brome *Abraham* with its *Doctor*. But the tendency is also present in the expository dialogues of the Chester Ministry plays and in the St John the Baptist of the York cycle (Y XXI) who substitutes his opening prayer for an audience-address, in the plays of the York Realist which reduce audience rapport even in their bragging speeches and which, like the N-Town Passion plays, strive for isolated show effects. In York this tendency is associated with a preference for unity of place. The influences which modify the original play-type require further study, although it seems possible that classical learning is among them.

But the mainstream of the genre is represented by those plays which preserve the contrast between the two spheres. The greatest variety in this respect is achieved by the Wakefield Master, who uses the *ad spectatores* not only at the beginning of his plays but also in the middle, who psychologizes the Shepherds' speeches which in other cycles would be quite frankly addressed to the audience, who has Noah's audience-address followed by Mrs Noah's, and who is perhaps also responsible for the social satire in the Towneley Pilate (T XX, XXII). The variety in his speeches is so great that it is hard to avoid the conclusion that he is consciously and artistically playing with the convention.

Whenever we can isolate texts that show clear evidence of late revision, we find a characteristic way of shaping the relationship between playworld and audience world. This is as true of the Chester Expositor as it is of the York Realist and of the Wakefield Master. It may also be true of the playwright to whom we owe the Contemplacio group in the N-Town cycle. This suggests that the relationship was of central concern to the medieval dramatists.

Notes

INTRODUCTION

1 Cf. *REED Newsletter* 1 (1976), pp. 1–2.
2 Craig, *ERD*, pp. 4–6.
3 Prosser, *Drama and Religion*, p. 85.
4 For a useful list of this and similar expressions see James, 'Ritual', note 40.
5 Kolve, *Corpus Christi*.
6 Rossiter, *English Drama*, and Weimann, *Shakespeare and the Popular Tradition*.
7 A few years later a similar continuity was postulated by Warning, *Funktion und Struktur*. The findings of Warning's book are summarized in his 'Alterity'.
8 Lukács, *Ästhetik*, Part I, 1st semivolume, p. 446.
9 de Boor, *Textgeschichte*. Stemmler, *LFGS*. Stemmler takes his categories from Szondi, *Theorie des Dramas*, who is strongly influenced by Hegel and Lukács. Szondi's book is now available in English as *Theory of the Modern Drama*. The German terms 'Spiel' and 'Feier' are also used in English; see Flanigan, 'Liturgical Drama', pp. 96ff.
10 The conventions governing the relationship between actor and audience have also been used by Axton to distinguish between 'popular' and liturgical plays: 'Popular Modes', pp. 13–40, esp. p. 15.
11 That cycle must have been very different from the text which appears in the manuscript (British Library Vespasian D.viii) and which can hardly have been played at all in its extant form. See Meredith, ed., *Mary Play*, esp. p. 4, and Meredith, ed., *Passion Play*, pp. 2f.

LITURGY AND THE DRAMA

1 Bentley, *Life of the Drama*, p. 150. See also Diller, 'Erste und Zweite Welt'.
2 Elam, *Semiotics*.
3 The criterion of self-containedness is used by Theo Stemmler to distinguish between 'religious play' and 'liturgical office'. Cf. Stemmler, *LFGS*. But the self-containedness of the 'religious play' is at best a relative one when compared with the liturgical office.
4 Cf. Pfister's extensive discussion of 'sending and receiving information' in his *Drama*.
5 The literature on the signifying modes of the liturgy and the church year is

Notes to pages 10–12

too vast to be done justice to here. On allegoreses of the Mass in general see Franz, *Messe*. On symbolic places within the church see Sauer, *Symbolik des Kirchengebäudes*.

6 Young, *DMC*, vol. 1, p. 242 *et passim*.
7 German ethnologists distinguish rather carefully between *Darstellung* ('representation') and *Verkörperung* ('embodiment'), as opposed to the one English word 'impersonation'. Cf. Stumpfl, *Kultspiele der Germanen*, p. 33, and Höfler, *Geheimbünde der Germanen*, vol. 1, p. 288. More recently Benjamin Hunningher has tried to refute the ecclesiastical origins of the drama with a similar pair of terms: *Origins*, p. 51: ' the celebrating priest in the Church did not *portray* but *represented*: his medium was not creative acting but commemorative symbolism. The effectiveness of the symbolism depended upon acceptance of the doctrine it accompanied, which clearly indicates its difference from creative acting.'
8 It should be noted in passing that speculation on intentions must always be unsatisfactory. It supposes that the performers of those early ceremonies already had a clearly defined idea of the fundamental novelty of what they were doing. The insufficiency of impersonation as a distinguisher between 'liturgical' and 'liturgico-dramatic' actions has been underlined by Wolff, 'Terminologie des mittelalterlichen Dramas', p. 16.
9 On this problem cf. Stemmler, *LFGS*, pp. 18f and *passim*. The frequency of these 'ineptitudes' has caused Stemmler to refer not to liturgical dramas but to 'quasi-dramatic liturgical offices' and to reserve the term 'religious play' for some few texts which are largely independent of the liturgy and free of 'ineptitudes'. These are the Benediktbeuern Easter Play, the four Latin Passion Plays that have come down to us and a small number of Magi Plays. I have only two reservations concerning Stemmler's terminology: often it is not entire plays but individual scenes which avoid 'ineptitudes' (e.g. many *Hortulanus* scenes within the Easter offices), and independence from the liturgy is often difficult to assess. To retain the traditional terminology does no harm as long as we remember that it is the combination of dramatic and non-dramatic elements which is characteristic of the genre. Where we find Stemmler's categories useful we shall use them without hesitation (cf. p. 75).
10 This is not to deny that Young points out, e.g., that the different parties of the dialogue are distinguished by liturgical vestments. But he does not draw the appropriate genre-theoretical conclusions from this observation.
11 E.g., by Williams, *Drama*, p. 11. Stemmler (*LFGS*, p. 61) rightly points out that the censing is not integrated into the dialogue and for that very reason is a 'non-dramatic' feature (with reference to the Zwiefalten office, Young, *DMC*, vol. 1, pp. 266f).
12 Cf. Amalarius, 'Libri', cols. 1057d-58a, English translation in Hardison, *Christian Rite*, p. 163.
13 *LThK*, 1st edn, vol. 10, *s.v.* 'Typologie'.
14 Auerbach, 'Figura', p. 50. Significantly, most of the biblical instances of typological thinking are to be found in the Epistles and in the Gospel according to St John. On the most important passages see *LThK*, 'Typologie'.
15 Auerbach, 'Figura', p. 53; Kolve, *Corpus Christi*, p. 65.

16 Cf. Franz, *Messe*; also Hardison, *Christian Rite*, ch. 2.
17 Flanigan, 'Roman Rite', p. 264: 'Genuine ritual is more than a performance in which a few act while others watch, listen, and are instructed.'
18 The following analysis should be compared with Mathieu, 'Distanciation et émotion'. Although working within an entirely different conceptual framework, Mathieu's goal in identifying 'dramatic' and 'liturgical' features in Æthelwold's *Visitatio* is similar to our own.
19 Symons, ed., *Regularis Concordia*, pp. 50–2. Insertions in brackets after Bevington, ed., *Medieval Drama*, pp. 27ff. Compare also facsimiles no. 3 and 4 in Sheingorn, *The Easter Sepulchre*.
20 For an analysis along similar lines but reaching somewhat different conclusions see McDonald, 'Drama in the Church', pp. 93f.
21 Adam, *Wo sich Gottes Volk versammelt*, pp. 93, 96.
22 Peter McDonald, however, makes the important point that these vestments were not worn at Matins and that they were 'worn to "distinguish" – not to deceive' ('Drama in the Church', p. 94).
23 Lesage, *Vestments*, p. 102.
24 On the cultic use of incense in Christianity and other religions cf. Lesage, *Vestments*, pp. 59ff.
25 Symons, ed., *Regularis Concordia*, p. 44.
26 Covers on the altar come into use in the third century (Adam, *Wo sich Gottes Volk versammelt*, p. 97).
27 Cf. Fischer-Lichte, *Semiotik des Theaters*, vol. 1, p. 28.
28 Cf. Stemmler, *LFGS*, pp. 23f.
29 On this cf. the extensive discussion in Stemmler, *LFGS*, pp. 47ff, esp. p. 58.
30 The relationship between this part of the 'stage action' and the verb *quaerere* comes interestingly close to what in modern semantics would be called a 'prototype'. Strangely, the purely conceptual, non-mimetic character of this 'seeking' appears to have escaped previous critics. Cf. the otherwise valuable study by Mathieu, 'Distanciation et émotion'.
31 The pairwise grouping of actions has been studied above all in conversation analysis, where it appears usually as the result of the interaction of several participants. Cf. above all the works of Schegloff and Sacks; a very clear and succinct exposition is to be found in Edmondson, *Spoken Discourse*, pp. 46–9. As our examples show, pairwise grouping is not tied to interaction.
32 Elam, *Semiotics*, p. 103. He adopts the question from Rescher, *Possibility*, p. 93.
33 Cf. Flanigan, 'Roman Rite', p. 264.
34 The term 'world-containing' is a translation from the German 'welthaltig'. A scene is said to contain a 'world' if the events portrayed in it can exist by themselves, without regard to potential onlookers. Cf., above all, Lukács, *Ästhetik*, and Szondi, *Theory*.
35 Jantzen, *Ottonische Kunst*, p. 73: 'nach irgendeiner anderen Seite hin als der durch die Gebärde versinnbildlichten aufgefaßt, als so oder so sich verhaltende, in anderer Lage möglicherweise anders empfindende, innerlich bewegte Wesen bewertet zu werden'.
36 Messerer, 'Darstellungsprinzipien', p. 177: 'um den in der Gebärde vollzogenen und neu geschehenden Sinn zu vernehmen'.

37 Panofsky, 'Imago Pietatis', p. 265: '[gedrängt] in die Stellung eines bloß Verehrenden'.
38 'Imago Pietatis', p. 265: 'nicht das Hineinnehmen der Gegenständlichkeit in unseren subjektiven Erlebniszusammenhang, sondern umgekehrt ein Hinausprojizieren des subjektiven Erlebnisses in die Gegenstandssphäre, weniger eine Assimilation des Dargestellten an das Bewußtsein, als die Assimilation des Bewußtseins an das Dargestellte'.
39 Quoted from Hardison, *Christian Rite*, p. 171.
40 Text of stanzas 4–6 according to Young, *DMC*, vol. 1, p. 273, quoted there from Dreves and Blume, eds., *Analecta Hymnica*, vol. 54, pp. 12–13. Helmut de Boor has recognized the end position of the sequence as a feature of the widespread 'Passau type', while the more 'logical' reverse order is prevalent only in a comparatively limited area, i.e. Prague and St Lambrecht (Styria). Cf. de Boor, *Textgeschichte*, pp. 181–5.
41 Cf. de Boor, *Textgeschichte*, pp. 180f.
42 Young, *DMC*, vol. 2. p. 47; cf. also Anz, *Die lateinischen Magierspiele*, p. 16.
43 Young, *DMC*, vol. 2, pp. 61, 65, 71, 88, 96, 188, 449.
44 Anz, *Die lateinischen Magierspiele*, pp. 90ff. The encounter is mentioned, however, by John of Hildesheim (1310x20–1375) in his *Historia de translatione beatissimorum trium regum* [Cologne, 1486], cap. xviii (first published Mainz, 1477, as *Liber de Trium regum corporibus Coloniam translatis*). But the first dramatic representations of this encounter are to be dated c.1200.
45 Young, *DMC*, vol. 2, p. 59. Also Böhme, *Das lateinische Weihnachtsspiel*, p. 99.
46 Young, *DMC*, vol. 2, p. 20.
47 Young, *DMC*, vol. 2, pp. 21, 22, 61, 71, 188, 429. In some plays it is shortened to *Pastores, dicite quidnam vidistis?* (pp. 65, 96).
48 On presentation (*Darstellung*), expression (*Ausdruck*), and appeal (*Appell* or *Auslösung*) as linguistic functions see Bühler, 'Axiomatik', esp. pp.74–90.
49 On the important step which this sentence marks in the dramatization of the Easter events cf. Hardison, *Christian Rite*, pp. 232f. After Hardison's convincing interpretation of the Aquileia Resurrection play (Young, *DMC*, vol. 1, p. 628) Wilhelm Meyer's view has to be rejected. Meyer saw the purpose of the new version merely in rectifying the rhyme, which was faulty when one Angel (*caelicola*) faced two or three Marys (*Christicolae*). Cf. W. Meyer, 'Fragmenta Burana', p. 84, also de Boor's remarks on 'Typus II' (de Boor, *Textgeschichte*, esp. p. 148).
50 Cf. the chapter on the *planctus*.
51 On this important point cf. again Pfister, *Drama*, ch. 3.
52 There is still no agreement on where the *Visitatio Sepulcri* was performed in the church building. While Konigson favours the westwork, Pamela Sheingorn believes that in England more evidence argues for the choir. (Konigson, *L'Espace*, pp. 24–5; Sheingorn, *The Easter Sepulchre*, p. 24.)
53 This is radically different from the situation in the mystery plays. When Noah, for instance, shows and names his tools, his axe is an axe even if he doesn't call it one. His naming it merely facilitates its identification, it does not establish its identity. But the altar became the 'dramatic' Sepulchre only when it was thus called in the dialogue.

54 These terms are from Jakobson, 'Linguistics and Poetics'. Jakobson owes his conceptual framework to Bühler, 'Axiomatik', but his terminology is better known in the English-speaking world. Jakobson's referential function corresponds to Bühler's *Darstellungsfunktion*, his conative function to the latter's *Appellfunktion*.

55 Young, *DMC*, vol. 1, p. 247; cf. also the repetition of this criticism in connection with the same arrangement in *Regularis Concordia*, p. 250.

56 'It is as though the women at first think only of their own joy, forgetting their duty of announcing, indeed of proving to the world, the marvelous event of which they are witnesses' (Williams, *Drama*, p. 11). The inadequacy of this explanation has been pointed out by Stemmler, *LFGS*, p. 59. Stemmler, however, does not really get beyond Young in attributing the arrangement to a 'liturgical mode of thought' ['liturgische Denkweise'] which 'leaves the core of the traditional liturgical piece untouched' ['bleibt der Kern des traditionellen liturgischen Stücks unangetastet']. This does not explain the function which the liturgical text assumes in the new 'quasi-dramatic' environment. That function is the 'Revealing gesture'.

57 Owing to this isolation the speeches and actions can fluctuate between the two planes of cultic representation and cultic reality with comparative ease: the showing of the linen, addressed as it is to the choir, is already part of the First World, and in many plays (Young, *DMC*, vol. 1, pp. 249, 251, 263, 266f, 313, 328, 362) *Venite* triggers off a purely liturgical act: the Marys cense the empty Sepulchre. The thuribles thus show the same dualism which we have repeatedly observed on other occasions: they 'mean' (or 'suggest') the ointments brought by the biblical Marys, but they do not cease to 'be' liturgical objects. Cf. on this Diller,'Erste und Zweite Welt'.

LITURGICAL POINT OF VIEW SURROUNDING THE DRAMATIC CORE DIALOGUE

1 Young, *DMC*, vol. 1, p. 240, n. 4, and p. 576, can give only one dubious example of a 'pure' dialogue.

2 On the geographical distribution of these antiphons see de Boor, *Textgeschichte*, pp. 56–67.

3 Young, *DMC*, vol. 1, p. 240.

4 Bjork, 'Dissemination', p. 11.

5 This is also the opinion of de Boor after a thorough discussion of the relevant texts (*Textgeschichte*, pp. 50–2).

6 Cf. p. 22 of this study.

7 For references cf. ch. 1, n. 57, of this study.

8 Young, *DMC*, vol. 1, p. 257.

9 Young, *DMC*, vol. 2, p. 85.

10 John 20.6–10 reports that, on the contrary, John and Peter saw the 'linen clothes lying'.

11 Cf. Lange, *Osterfeiern*, p. 31.

12 E.g. Young, *DMC*, vol. 1, pp. 255, 267, 297 (the Marys); 295, 298, 303f, 318, 330, 341 (choir or the like); 357 (Peter and John). De Boor has pointed out that this antiphon was used even in different phases of the story (*Textgeschichte*, pp. 113–18).

13 E.g. Young, *DMC*, vol. 1, pp. 256, 265, 268.
14 There seems to be only one exception: in the late Constance text (Young, *DMC*, vol. 1, pp. 301f).
15 Cf. de Boor, *Textgeschichte*, p. 101.
16 Young, *DMC*, vol. 1, p. 277.
17 Young, *DMC*, vol. 1, pp. 285, 291f, 293, 294f. The different character of the *Hortulanus*, which I have called 'world-containing', is made evident by the fact that there only one character is left for the encounter with the risen Christ.
18 Cf. p. 23f. of this study.
19 On the liturgical word as 'quotation' cf. Albert, *Stilcharakter*, p. 7.
20 Cf. pp. 37f and the statistical tables in Anz, *Die lateinischen Magierspiele*, p. 112.
21 These will be treated more extensively pp. 46f.
22 Young (*DMC*, vol. 1, p. 601) doubts that it is a genuine antiphon, although it is called one in many texts. It is based on Matt. 28.1 and runs: 'Maria Magdalena et alia Maria ferebant diluculo aromata' (Young, *DMC*, vol. 1, p. 314).
23 Young, *DMC*, vol. 2, p. 34 (Limoges, date uncertain); also pp. 39 and 434 (Besançon, seventeenth century).
24 Especially clear in St Florian, Young, *DMC*, vol. 1, pp. 365–7 (cf. Lange, *Osterfeiern*, Nr. 203, pp. 127–9).
25 *Et dicebant ad invicem: Quis revolvet...* (Young, *DMC*, vol.p. 259); *Pastores loquebantur ad inuicem*, (Young, *DMC*, vol. 2, p. 65).
26 Cf. Glunz, *Literarästhetik*, pp. 38ff. This point has been made more specifically with reference to the liturgy by Flanigan, who, following Eliade, interprets the 'individual ritual act' as the 'image of the [platonic] archetype' ('Roman Rite', p. 265).
27 Cf. Isidore's warning against pictures which, instead of recalling the real model, try to produce its illusion (Lindsay, ed., *Isidori Hispalensis episcopi*, Etymologiarum Liber XIX, cap. xvi). Cf. also de Bruyne, *Études d'esthétique médiévale*, vol. 1, pp. 92f. See also Tertullian's well-known polemic against the deceptions of actors. On the small esteem of specific detail also Gardiner, *Mysteries' End*, p. 24; and H. Brinkmann, *Dichtkunst*, pp. 81ff.
28 Cf. Albert, *Stilcharakter*, p. 10.
29 Young, *DMC*, vol. 2, p. 39. The time in which this ceremony originated is unknown. In its recorded form it is presumably late medieval (cf. Young, '*La Procession des Trois Rois*', pp. 76–83). According to Anz (*Die lateinischen Magierspiele*, p. 45, n. 3), the quoted passage is from a hymn which is first attested as a trope in the *Benedicamus* of Epiphany in the twelfth century.
30 Young, *DMC*, vol. 2, p. 54 *et passim*.
31 Cf. ch. 1, n. 43, with references.
32 On this cf. p. 65f.
33 Young, *DMC*, vol. 2, p. 34 (probably after 1100, cf. Meyer in 'Fragmenta Burana', p. 38). This introital anthem, too, originated outside the liturgical drama.
34 Young, *DMC*, vol. 2, p. 36.
35 Cf. Petsch, *Wesen und Formen*, esp. pp. 10–20, 353–78.
36 In other places, such as before the Easter mass, the *Quem quaeritis* was

normally used as a processional hymn, which apparently allowed only for scant mimesis; cf. Hardison, *Christian Rite*, p. 199.

37 The exception is: *Et recordatae sunt*...

'WORLD-CONTAINING' SITUATIONS

1 For the dating cf. Anz, *Die lateinischen Magierspiele*, pp. 122ff. But Young quotes a fragment (Paris, Bibl. Nat., MS lat. 1152) which may go back to the tenth century (Young, *DMC*, vol. 2, p. 443).
2 Cf. Young, *DMC*, vol. 2, pp. 43f, after *Antiphonale du B. Hartker*, Facsimile edn in *Paléographie*, 2nd series, vol. 1 (Solesmes, 1900), pp. 73f.
3 Young, *DMC*, vol. 2, pp. 43, 435ff; also *MP* 6 (1908–9), 201, 224–7.
4 Young, *DMC*, vol. 2, pp. 69, 85. The first of these texts is kept in a library in Montpellier but seems to be related to Rouen, the second is from the famous Fleury Playbook.
5 It is called an antiphon in the text, but Young was unable to provide liturgical attestation for it (Young, *DMC*, vol. 2, p. 69).
6 Because of this fact Stemmler excludes the *Officia Stellae* (apparently with the exception of Limoges and Besançon) from the class of 'quasi-liturgical ceremonies' (*LFGS*, p. 84). Such a decision, however, obscures the fact that these *Officia* still combine dramatic and liturgical elements. It is only the ratio of the mixture which has changed.
7 Cf. Albert, *Stilcharakter*, p. 18.
8 Apart from summary remarks in the well-known surveys the following should be mentioned: Anz, *Die lateinischen Magierspiele*; Sondheimer, *Die Herodes-Partien*; Böhme, *Das lateinische Weihnachtsspiel*, pp. 69ff; Tomlinson, *Der Herodes-Charakter*; Parker, 'The Reputation of Herod'. David Staines gives a fine analysis of the portrayal of Herod from the Bible and early biblical commentators to the English cycle plays, pursuing his progeny even further to the braggarts of the Elizabethan stage (Staines, 'To Out-Herod Herod').
9 An extreme example is Böhme, *Das lateinische Weihnachtsspiel*, p. 70: 'Die Magier waren Typen, Herodes ist der *erste Charakter auf der mittelalterlichen Bühne* [emphasis in the original].' ('The Magi were types, Herod is the first character on the medieval stage.') To appreciate this quotation, one has to keep in mind the rather emphatic meaning of the German 'Charakter', which comes close to E. M. Forster's 'round character'.
10 Bühler, 'Axiomatik', esp. pp. 74–90.
11 Quoted from Young, *DMC*, vol. 2, p. 54. The same syntactic incompleteness appears in the oblation of the Kings at the Manger.
12 Young, *DMC*, vol. 2, pp. 37–40, e.g.:

> Cantores: Gauisi sunt gaudio magno valde.
> 1. Rex: Et intrantes domum inuenerunt puerum cum Maria matre eius
> 2. Rex: Et procedentes adorauerunt eum.
> 3. Rex: Et apertis thesauris suis.
> Cantores: Obtulerunt ei munera.
> 1. Rex: Aurum.
> 2. Rex: Thus.
> 3. Rex: Et myrrham.

Notes to pages 37–40   261

13 Young, *DMC*, vol. 2, p. 70.
14 Cf. the statistics in Anz, *Die lateinischen Magierspiele*, p. 112.
15 Young, *DMC*, vol. 2, p. 70. Young regards this text as part of the Rouen tradition. The 'gibberish' has been identified by Anton Schall as corrupt Aethiopian; cf. Stemmler, *LFGS*, p. 86.
16 Young, *DMC*, vol. 2, pp. 78 and 95, already quoted p. 34.
17 Cf. Albert, *Stilcharakter*, p. 7.
18 *Protevangelium Jacobi* 21.$_2$ (*Evangelia apocrypha*, ed. Tischendorf); cf. Anz, *Die lateinischen Magierspiele*, p. 63. Böhme (*Das lateinische Weihnachtsspiel*, p. 78) suggests classical sources for the messenger. Although he is apparently overlooking the servants mentioned in this passage when he claims that the messenger is absent from the Apocrypha, his suggestion is attractive in view of the strong classical overtones of the Herod scenes. And it can be said in Böhme's favour that the similarities between the liturgical play and the *Protevangelium* are weak: while in the *Protevangelium* the Magi go straight to Bethlehem and have to be fetched by Herod, no such necessity exists in the liturgical drama where the Magi, in accordance with Matt. 2.1ff, first go to Jerusalem.
19 This position has been argued most extensively by Sondheimer, *Die Herodes-Partien*, pp. 39ff; but see also Anz, *Die lateinischen Magierspiele*, pp. 89f, Young, *DMC*, vol. 2, *passim*.
20 Anz, *Die lateinischen Magierspiele*, p. 117. Cf. also Sondheimer's reference to his 'turgid' and 'domineering' tone (*Die Herodes-Partien*, pp. 44f: 'schwülstig' and 'herrisch'.)
21 Young, *DMC*, vol. 2, pp. 93, 183.
22 In Fleury, Young, *DMC*, vol. 2, p. 85, the same request appears without causing a messenger to inform Herod of their arrival. Rather, Herod himself reacts 'quibus uisis', sending an *armiger* to question the Magi about their intentions.
23 Bilsen, Young, *DMC*, vol. 2, p. 76. Young (*DMC*, p.82) interprets these questions as a means to demonstrate the dignified, self-assured behaviour of the Magi.
24 Young, *DMC*, vol. 2, p. 64.
25 Ibid., pp. 93ff.
26 Ibid., p. 76.
27 Ibid., p. 76.
28 Ibid., pp. 85f.
29 Ibid., p. 69 (Montpellier MS).
30 This scene has been interpreted rather one-sidedly under the aspect of realism by Böhme, *Das lateinische Weihnachtsspiel*, p. 71, and Sondheimer, *Die Herodes-Partien*, p. 39.
31 Young, *DMC*, vol. 2, p. 76.
32 Stemmler, *LFGS*, p. 84, on the *Officia Stellae* in general: 'Es handelt sich durchweg um logisch aufgebaute Kompositionen, nicht um liturgische Montagen.'
33 It occurs also in Young, *DMC*, vol. 2, pp. 54, 60, 64, 69, 94. Bilsen is probably a degenerate version of the earlier Freising play (Young, *DMC*, pp. 92–7), since a number of scenes are exclusive to these two plays, with their cohesion being disrupted in Bilsen by expansion and displacement.

34 Something similar occurs in a play from Strassburg (*c*. 1200, Young, *DMC*, vol. 2, pp. 64ff) where the *symmistae*, subordinate priests at Herod's court who call on the Scribes for an interpretation of the relevant biblical passages, announce the Christian truth: 'Si scripta illum [namely puerum] probauerint, solus regnabit, nostraque lex coram illo silebit.' This passage has received two comments which are particularly apt to illustrate the naïve application of naturalistically psychological standards to the liturgical drama: Anz (*Die lateinischen Magierspiele*, p. 62) calls the phrase 'simply meaningless' (*sinnlos*). Young (*DMC*, vol. 2, p. 67) is more concerned about a sympathetic understanding, but he too fails to recognize its 'supra-personal' Revelation character when he suspects that it 'may have been motivated... by frightened whisperings between Herod and his attendants'. Although such stage action is quite conceivable, Young's interpretation neglects the fact that the words immediately before those quoted, which certainly were a clearly audible command, give no sign that the speakers do not identify themselves with the Christian message which they imply:

> O principes sacerdotum, et o uos scribe populorum,
> pertractate dicta magorum,
> et dicite nobis tanti pueri ortum.

35 Anz, *Die lateinischen Magierspiele*, p. 59, sees correctly that the passage thus becomes 'more effective', but he says nothing about the kind of effect that is intended.
36 Sondheimer, *Die Herodes-Partien*, pp. 18, 65; Young, *DMC*, vol. 2, p. 58.
37 Young, *DMC*, vol. 2, pp. 184f (lines 398–429).
38 This combination, however, seems to be confined to late plays which may already be under the influence of classical drama, e.g. Y XVI, 193ff, and Marguerite de Navarre, *La comédie de l'adoration des Trois Rois*.
39 Young, *DMC*, vol. 2, pp. 78, 95, 87f. Sondheimer's opinion that in Bilsen it is the Scribes who advise Herod to let the Magi go to Bethlehem and to question them on their return journey (*Die Herodes-Partien*, p. 71), is hardly tenable. The rubrics, though incomplete, are unambiguous (Young, *DMC*, vol. 2, p. 78).
40 In Bilsen the conversation with *Armiger* follows, in Freising it precedes, the second interrogation of the Magi. The dialogue between Herod and his son (Fleury) appears in the Norman play (Young, *DMC*, vol. 2, p. 72) at its logical place after the return of the Magi to their respective countries.
41 Especially Sondheimer, *Die Herodes-Partien*, p. 10 and *passim*. Craig and his pupil Kretzmann also believe that the vernacular plays evolved directly from their counterparts in liturgy and liturgical drama.
42 Especially on Herod see Creizenach, *Geschichte*, vol. 1, p. 58; Sondheimer, *Die Herodes-Partien*, pp. 93ff; Young, *DMC*, vol. 2, *passim*; further Tomlinson, *Der Herodes-Charakter*; Roscoe E. Parker, 'The Reputation of Herod'; Staines, 'To Out-Herod Herod'; Skey, 'Iconography of Herod'. On the stage presentation of emotions William Archer has important things to say, in spite of his narrow naturalistic bias. But he deals only with the drama from the seventeenth to the nineteenth century (*Drama*).
43 Young, *DMC*, vol. 2, pp. 72, 77.
44 Ibid., pp. 87, 95.

45 Anz, *Die lateinischen Magierspiele*, pp. 53f.
46 Young, *DMC*, vol. 2, p. 77.
47 Ibid., pp. 95, 71.
48 Cf. the reaction of the judge in the Rebdorf version of the legend of St Margaret; Wolpers, *Heiligenlegende*, p. 106.
49 The one emotion of wrath revealed the entire Herod already to the Church Fathers. Cf. Anz, *Die lateinischen Magierspiele*, pp. 51f.
50 Protevangelium Jacobi, 21.2 (ed. Tischendorf). The Protevangelium here follows Matthew closely: Herod, hearing of the arrival of the Magi, was troubled (Matt. 2.3, Prot. J. 21.2: ἐταράχθη). When he realizes that he was mocked of the wise men' (Matt. 2.16), he becomes 'exceeding wroth' (Matt. 2.16: ἐθυμώθη λίαν, Prot. J. 22.1: ὀργισθείς). On the legend in general cf. Kehrer, *Die Heiligen Drei Könige*, vol. 1. For a condensed synopsis of the motifs of the legend see Waetzoldt, 'Drei Könige', col. 480.
51 Cf. Réau, *Iconographie*, vol. 2, part 2, p. 245.
52 Cf. Künstle, *Ikonographie*, vol. 1, p. 357.
53 Vezin, *L'adoration*, p. 98.
54 H. von Einem, 'Das Problem des Mythischen', p. 270: 'innerhalb einer Gestalt die Darstellung zweier Verrichtungen, die, organisch gedacht, so nicht zusammen möglich sind'. To state these similarities between art and drama does not presuppose that one medium had influenced the other. The relationship between early art and drama is still far from clear. Art historians who have studied the problem usually regard the drama as the more original part, but their statements usually concern the period from the twelfth century onward and plays of a pronounced narrative character, such as the Emmaus play or the mystery cycles. Otto Pächt, however, has plausibly argued for an influence of the liturgical *Interfectio Innocentium* on the Albani psalter (*The Rise of Pictorial Narrative*, p. 53). But Pächt also demonstrates (pp. 48f) that during the tenth century, i.e. during the period which saw the birth of the liturgical drama, the liturgical text was influenced by iconographic conventions, whereas in the twelfth century the direction of the influence was reversed.
55 Chambers, *Stage*, vol. 1, pp. 336–7. The *Festum Innocentium*, which was led by the Boy Bishop, is attested from the tenth century onward (p. 338). On the close relationship between the ceremony of the Boy Bishop and the presentation of Herod see Young, *DMC*, vol. 1, pp. 106ff, and vol. 2, pp. 99f. But the documents from Padua which Young prints are only from the thirteenth century.
56 On the use of minor characters as 'attributes' see Messerer, 'Darstellungsprinzipien', p. 160.
57 Anz, *Die lateinischen Magierspiele*, p. 96, claims that in Bilsen and Freising the courtiers scatter in a hurry after they have heard the prophecies, but this is not supported by the texts.
58 Young, *DMC*, vol. 2, pp. 72, 87. This scene is rightly praised by Böhme (*Das lateinische Weihnachtsspiel*, p. 83), who, however, overlooks its thoroughly exceptional character.
59 MS No. 201 of the municipal library of Orléans is catalogued as thirteenth century. This view is shared by Père Lin Donnat, quoted in Campbell and Davidson, eds., *Fleury Playbook*, p. 162, though Albrecht and Collins argue

in favour of the twelfth century; cf. Albrecht, ed., *Four Latin Plays*, pp. 3f, 90, and Collins, 'Home of the Fleury *Playbook*', p. 28.
60 Young, *DMC*, vol. 2, p. 88.
61 On the history of Fleury see Chenesseau, *L'Abbaye de Fleury*, and Collins, 'Home of the Fleury *Playbook*'.
62 Young, *DMC*, vol. 2, p. 119.
63 Ibid., p. 105.
64 As was done, e.g., by Böhme (*Das lateinische Weihnachtsspiel*, p. 70). H. Brinkmann is more cautious: 'Comparatively unified from early times is the figure of Herod, whose speech, gesture and action show him as a tyrant.' ('Verhältnismäßig geschlossen ist seit früher Zeit die Gestalt des Herodes, der in Wort, Gebärde und Handlung als Tyrann sich zeigt.') Brinkmann recognizes that 'in the Middle Ages we must not expect any *psychological motivation*'. ('daß wir vom Mittelalter keine *psychologische Motivierung* [emphasis in the original] erwarten dürfen'. ('Eigenform des mittelalterlichen Dramas', p. 82f)
65 On attribution see Messerer, 'Darstellungsprinzipien'.
66 Earlier scholarship believed that the Passion play had originated from the *planctus*. This opinion, still held by Young (*DMC*, vol. 1, pp. 493, 538) is no longer tenable since D. M. Inguanez discovered a highly developed Latin Passion play with a rudimentary Italian *planctus*. Cf. Inguanez, 'Un dramma della passione'; Sticca, 'The Planctus Mariae'. Inguanez' second publication prints, in addition to the complete drama, a fragment which is largely identical with it, the so-called Sulmona Fragment.
67 Young, *DMC*, vol. 2, pp. 103ff, and, more extensively, Young, *Ordo Rachelis*.
68 Young, *DMC*, vol. 2, pp. 123f.
69 'Fragmenta Burana', pp. 106ff.
70 Marian laments and the laments of the *Visitatio* are often lumped together as symptoms of a general tendency to 'lyricize' the drama. E. K. Chambers for instance (*Stage*, vol. 2, p. 32) expressly calls the *Visitatio* laments *planctus*, crediting them with outstanding liveliness.
71 See Sticca, *Planctus Mariae*, p. 120
72 *Planctus ante nescia* by Geoffrey of St Victor (died 1194), both printed in Young, *DMC*, vol. 1, pp. 496–9.
73 Werner, *Studien*, pp. 94ff. For an English summary of Werner see Flanigan, 'Liturgical Drama', pp. 100–2.
74 Young, *DMC*, vol. 1, pp. 504ff, 507ff.
75 This is emphasized, in a polemic against Young, by Craig (*English Religious Drama*, p. 47).
76 Stanzas 5a and 5b of *Planctus ante nescia* (quoted from Young, *DMC*, vol. 1, p. 497). We shall use Young's numbering of the stanzas because it brings out the symmetry between pairs of stanzas better than *Analecta Hymnica*. (Cf. Dreves, ed., *Analecta Hymnica*, vol. 20, pp. 156–8).
77 Cf. E. Panofsky, 'Imago pietatis'. It can hardly be accidental that the emotionalization which in the arts leads to the devotional picture is above all to be observed in the images of the lamenting Mary and the crucified Jesus.
78 Stanzas 2 and 2a of *Flete fideles animae*, quoted from *AH*, vol. 20, p. 155.
79 Forcellini, *Lexicon Totius Latinitatis*, s.v. 'profluvium'. In the Vulgate the word appears twice, both times in its gynaecological sense (Lev. 12.7; Mark

5.25). On the typological significance of Christ's lateral wound as a source of life see Auerbach, 'Typologische Motive', p. 19.
80 Printed in Young, *DMC*, vol. 1, pp. 498f. On the motif of joining the lament cf. Wechssler, *Marienklagen*, p. 16.
81 Cf. Wolpers, 'Marienlyrik', p. 15; see also Grieshammer, *Sprachgestaltende Kräfte*, p. 86.
82 T. Meier, *Die Gestalt Marias*, p. 59; Wolpers, 'Marienlyrik'; on Mary in general: Beissel, *Geschichte der Verehrung Marias*.
83 Werner, *Studien*, p. 106.
84 For this cf. generally Righter, *Shakespeare*, pp. 21f, and, more extensively, pp. 169–80 [orig.] of this study.
85 On didacticism in the English mystery cycles cf. Diller, 'Theological doctrine'.

THE DRAMATIZATION OF NARRATIVE SOURCES

1 On the origin and date of this scene see Meyer, 'Fragmenta Burana', pp. 88f; de Boor, *Textgeschichte*, pp. 299ff.
2 Coffman, *A New Theory*, p. 66; see also pp. 79f. For a similar definition see Brockett, '*Persona* in *Cantilena*', p. 123
3 Petsch, *Wesen und Formen des Dramas*, p. 83.
4 This distinction seems to us more important than the purely genetic question whether the *Hortulanus* originated directly from the Vulgate or via liturgical antiphons. Craig, who believes, against Young, in a liturgical origin of the scene (*ERD*, p. 35), ignores this distinction, as does Young, who pronounces in favour of the Vulgate. (Though the peculiar quality of the scene is certainly explained more naturally by a narrative source.) Stemmler (*LFGS*) overlooks the special nature of the *Hortulanus* scene because he is concerned only with the 'dramatic' or 'liturgical' nature of entire plays (or offices [Feiern]). In fact a 'dramatic' *Hortulanus* can perfectly well be attached to a 'quasi-dramatic' *Visitatio*.
5 As for instance in Young, *DMC*, vol. 1, pp. 371 ('pedibus eius *citissime* sese offerat'), 383, 409, 418, 428 ('Eaque uolente iam tangere pedes eius').
6 De Boor, *Textgeschichte*, p. 9: 'Schreiten, Knien, sich Erheben, sich Trennen und Vereinigen, Beräuchern, verehrungsvoll Küssen'.
7 See Young, *DMC*, vol. 1, p. 383. This is the well-known Easter play from the nunnery of Barking near London which is connected with the name of Katherine of Sutton (abbess 1363–76).
8 E.g. Young, *DMC*, vol. 1, pp. 387, 391, 399. Young (*DMC*, vol. 1., p. 401) seems to regard such passages as scribal errors. Against this compare the Engelberg Easter play, where a later hand has actually added the words 'quod dicitur magister'. (Young, *DMC*, vol. 1., p. 376, n. 3).
9 Young, *DMC*, vol. 2, pp. 267–74.
10 Similar examples in the *Daniel* by Hilarius (Young, *DMC*, vol. 2, pp. 283, 285).
11 Young, *DMC*, vol. 2, p. 273 (lines 223–6); similarly Young, *DMC*, vol. 2, p. 267 (lines 31–6).
12 For a succinct biography of Hilarius see Fuller, *Hilarii Versus et Ludi*, pp. 7–16. See also Häring, 'Hilarius'.

13 *Historia de Daniel Representanda*, lines 238+, Young, *DMC*, vol. 2, p. 283. Similar examples lines 286+ and 312+ (Young, *DMC*, vol. 2, p. 285).
14 MS 201, *olim* 178, Miscellanea Floriacensia saec. xiii, Bibl., Orléans; MS lat. 4660 and 4660a, Carmina Burana saec. xiii, Bayerische Staatsbibliothek, München; MS lat. 11331, Bibliothèque Nationale, Paris.
15 Fleury, 'Conversio Beati Pauli', Young, *DMC*, vol. 2, pp. 221, 220.
16 Young, *DMC*, vol. 1, p. 165.
17 Ibid.
18 It is classified as such by Coffman, *A New Theory*, pp. 67–71. On the justness of this classification cf. next section.
19 Young, *DMC*, vol. 2, pp. 259–64.
20 On the contrast between *Andachtsbild* (devotional image) and 'historical' image see Pickering, *Literature and Art*, p. 54. The German word is also used in English. See also Marrow, '*Circumdederunt me canes*', p. 167.
21 Weydig rightly emphasizes that the miracle play comes closer to the modern notion of drama than the liturgical offices and the later mystery plays. But the criteria which he uses are comparatively superficial, such as manageable length, small cast, closely knit structure, etc. He is also right to observe that the miracle play is the first religous drama to appeal to 'human' emotions such as passion and sympathy, but he does not say which elements were selected for scenic presentation, and it is certainly those elements which made the effects described possible (*Beiträge*, p. 11).
22 Cf. Coffman, *A New Theory*, pp. 35–8, who is here following Bédier, *Les légendes épiques*.
23 Knowledge of Latin was not a matter of course in the thirteenth century, even among educated laymen (J. W. Thompson, *Literacy*, p. 133).
24 On the extension of this group cf. p. 56 of this study. Sometimes the influence of wandering scholars has been assumed for these plays (cf. Coffman, *A New Theory*, p. 40), but apart from Hilarius clear proof is not forthcoming. And there is Otto Schumann's useful reminder that the way and the feeling of life of resident clerics in monastery schools hardly differed from that of the wandering scholars. Schumann accordingly suggests the term 'secular clerical poetry' (*weltliche Klerikerlyrik*) (Hilka and Schumann, eds., *Carmina Burana*, Vol. 2: *Kommentar*, p. 87*).
25 Tack, *Überrollenmäßige Sprachgestaltung*, p. 3.
26 Ott, *Personengestaltung*, pp. 55ff.
27 Young, *DMC*, vol. 2, p. 184 (lines 390f).
28 Ibid., p. 185 (lines 408f).
29 Matt. 2 describes Herod merely as 'troubled', not as of a violent temper.
30 Even without being very observant it is possible to discover implausibilities in the characterization. When the messengers, for instance, believe that Herod will be glad to hear of the new king's birth, one may well doubt that the servants should know their master so little. But even this is a point which gives at least a foothold to criticism in terms of character; and that is more than was possible in the traditional liturgical drama.
31 Quoted from Young, *DMC*, vol. 2, p. 338.
32 Text Young, *DMC*, vol. 2, pp. 344f; see also Young's comment *DMC*, vol. 2, p. 349.

33 This difference between the two plays has been noted by Weydig, who however regards Hilarius' accurate point-by-point treatment as psychologically more profound (*Beiträge*, p. 86).
34 This idea was first put forth by Sepet, *Les origines*, p. 169, and again by Albrecht, ed., *Four Latin Plays*. As the monastery school at Orléans was famous for cultivating *auctores*, such influence is by no means impossible. The metre, too, points to classical Latin influence. The theory gains further support by the well-known fact that Plautinian themes found a strong echo in the *comoediae elegiacae* of the Loire region; cf. de Ghellinck, *L'essor*, vol. 2, pp. 254ff.
35 Leo, ed., *Plauti comoediae*, vol. 1, p. 121.
36 Young, *DMC*, vol. 1, pp. 421f and 433.
37 Ibid., p. 262.
38 On Jacob cf. Gen. 27.11f; on Pilate: Williams, *Characterization*, ch. I: 'Pilate in Medieval Literature'.
39 Printed in the Mombritius version by Young, *DMC*, vol. 2, pp. 488–90. This version of the legend has probably served as the immediate source of the play (cf. Albrecht, *Four Latin Plays*, p. 20).
40 The earliest MS (from Hildesheim) is dated eleventh/twelfth century (Young, *DMC*, vol. 2, p. 311, n. 6), but an earlier version is preserved in twelfth and thirteenth century MSS (from Regensburg and Villers, Belgium, respectively); cf. Schumann, 'Urfassung', pp. 386–90.
41 Young, *DMC*, vol. 2, p. 488.
42 Schumann, 'Urfassung'.
43 Young, *DMC*, vol. 2, pp. 325ff, 330ff, 344ff.
44 Ibid., p. 350.
45 Cf. Diller, 'Craftsmanship', pp. 254–8.
46 Young, *DMC*, vol. 2, pp. 330ff; see also Young's observations *DMC*, vol. 2, pp. 333, 336f.
47 Ibid., pp. 325ff.
48 This episode is lacking from the Einsiedeln fragment.
49 pp. 13ff.
50 For the Sepulchre see Young, *DMC*, vol. 2, pp. 510 and *passim*, Brooks, *Sepulchre*, pp. 54f, 59–61, 89; Sheingorn, *The Easter Sepulchre*, pp. 22f. For the Manger see Young, *DMC*, vol. 2, pp. 8, 22, 27, 36, 47. A good summary is to be found in Michael, *Frühformen*, pp. 11f, and Stemmler, *LFGS*, pp. 31–3.
51 But see Bryan, *Ethelwold*, pp. 93 and 119, who adduces some archaeological evidence for a very large Sepulchre in Winchester. Bevington also assumes, for the Fleury *Visitatio*, a Sepulchre which can be entered ('Staging', p. 68).
52 Young, *DMC*, vol. 2, p. 85. Incidentally, the Fleury play resembles in this the apocryphal *Protevangelium Jacobi*, cap. XXI, V.2, where the servants are also sent by Herod. But in the Protevangelium Herod had not sighted the Magi, he had merely heard of their arrival in Bethlehem (not Jerusalem!). The influence of the Protevangelium is thus far from proved. Cf. ch. 3, fn. 18.
53 The play's failure to distinguish between play-sphere and stage-sphere is further demonstrated by the fact that those addressed by the Magi are called *astantes*, which probably refers to members of the congregation. This

interpretation gains support from the fact that the *astantes* do not answer the Magi's question. Before this encounter the *Pastores* had addressed the congregation, as they do in many Christmas plays: *inuitent populum circumstantem adorandum Infantem*. But Michael's conjecture that the people join in the Angel's song (*Frühformen*, p. 19) is surely a misinterpretation of *multitudo*, which explicitly refers to those standing with the Angel on the choir-loft (Young, *DMC*, vol. 2, p. 84). It seems to be a characteristic of 'world-containing' situations that they have use only for the *silent* onlooker.

54 On the influence of clerical poetry on the Star procession see Albert, *Stilcharakter*, pp. 66f. Albert's emphasis, however, is too exclusively on the linguistic and stylistic aspects of the text. While he is right to insist on the 'half naïve, half learned' character of the 'astrological argument', he neglects the new relationship between representing and represented reality emerging in Benediktbeuern.

55 Young, *DMC*, vol. 2, pp. 43, 53f, 68, 85.

56 Ibid., p. 191.

57 The learned origins of this allusion have often been noted. Cf. Young, *DMC*, vol. 2, p. 334, n. 3, for references.

58 A very similar development in the selection of moments for representation is to be observed in medieval art: 'So ist in Bildern von Martyrien das Anordnen des Richters, das Zuschlagen des Henkers, der Sturz des Opfers zu sehen,... – lauter Akte im Vollzug – nicht wie in späteren Darstellungen der gleichen Szenen das Ausholen zum Schlag, die gefaßte Erwartung,... – also lauter Verhaltensweisen, in denen sich ein Zustand des Menschen in Spannung zum äußeren Vorgang zeigt.' (Representations of martyrdoms show the judge's decision, the executioner's stroke, the victim's fall (i.e. acts and processes in completion), not as in later renderings of the same scenes the lifting of the arm, the martyr's composed waiting (i.e. moments which show the person in a state of tension with the external process). (Messerer, 'Darstellungsprinzipien', p. 178).

THE ORIGINS OF THE CREATION TO DOOM CYCLE AND ITS STAGE

1 Craig, *ERD*, p. 88.

2 Anti-evolutionism has become the new orthodoxy since Hardison, *Christian Rite*, but the most concise criticism of such biological analogies has been put forward by Coffman: 'literature is not an organism but a product and has no power within itself to reproduce. A product which meets popular approval becomes a fashion, and thus a new type is established. Its origin is the result of some new factors, of forces within the period in which it first makes its appearance.' (*New Theory*, pp. 10f) This criticism has the additional advantage of steering clear of all irrationalist speculation on the autonomy of the work of art.

3 Datings according to Stemmler, *LFGS*, pp. 170f, who corrects Craig, *ERD*, pp. 100f.

4 Chambers' view (*Stage*, vol. 2, p. 77) that laymen took part in these productions has been refuted by Wickham, *Early English Stages*, vol. 1, pp.

140f. Wickham believes that even the clergy of smaller towns, such as Chester, had sufficient manpower to stage a cycle by themselves (*Early English Stages*, p. 140). Theo Stemmler's minute analysis of the relevant documents supports the view that there is no direct line of development from these productions: 'Fronleichnamszyklen', pp. 393–405.
5 Young, *DMC*, vol. 1, pp. 518, 413; vol. 2, p. 362.
6 Creizenach, *Drama*, vol. 1, pp. 100–60, *passim*; Chambers, *Stage*, vol. 2, pp. 88–90; Young, *DMC*, vol. 2, p. 423; somewhat different: Frank, *Medieval French Drama* (quoted by Wickham, p. 144).
7 Craig, *ERD*, p. 96.
8 Davis, *Non-Cycle Plays*, p. xiv; Craig, *ERD*, p. 103; Creizenach, *Drama*, vol. 1, pp. 112–14; Froning, *Drama des Mittelalters*, pp. 15f.
9 Brinkmann, *Liturgische Formen*, esp. the introduction; Werner, *Studien*, p. 10.
10 Printed, with reference to earlier editions and commentaries, by Young, *DMC*, vol. 2, pp. 362–4; subsequently by Rauhut, 'Der Sponsus'. Rauhut is of the opinion that the Latin text originally stood by itself and that the Romance interpolations represent didactic glosses and illustrations; cf. esp. p. 45. Similarly Thomas, *Le 'Sponsus'*, pp. 136ff. On the dating (end of eleventh century) cf. Thomas, pp. 15f.
11 Axton, *European Drama*, p. 112. See also Hardison, *Christian Rite*, p. 271. Editions: *Le Mystère d'Adam*, ed. Studer; *Le jeu d'Adam*, ed. Noomen. *La Seinte Resureccion* exists in two versions: the earlier one in the Paris MS (late thirteenth/early fourteenth century) and the more recent one in the Canterbury MS (late thirteenth century) which is separated from the original by several revisions. The text has been edited twice: The Paris MS as *Résurrection du Sauveur*, ed. Wright, both MSS together as *La Seinte Resureccion*, ed. Wright et al. The French originals of both the *Jeu d'Adam* and the *Résurrection* have been published together with English translations by Bevington, ed., *Medieval Drama*. On the staging of *Adam* cf. Frank, 'Genesis and Staging'. On the relation of the *Adam* to the liturgy see especially Muir, *Liturgy and Drama*.
12 Edition with commentary by Meyer, ed., *'Les Trois Maries'*.
13 Hardison, *Christian Rite*, pp. 272f.
14 Recently Lynette Muir has pointed out a few similarities between the *Resureccion* and the N-Town cycle, but these do not concern the staging: 'Medieval English Drama: The French Connection', in Briscoe and Coldewey, *Contexts*, pp. 63–6.
15 Hardison, *Christian Rite*, p. 270.
16 Wright, ed., *Résurrection du Sauveur*, p. VI; Wright et al., eds., *La Seinte Resureccion*, p. CXV.
17 Cf. the present writer's 'Erste und Zweite Welt'.
18 Hardison, *Christian Rite*, pp. 259f; cf. 'Liber Responsalis', *PL*, vol. 78, cols. 748–9. See also Noomen, ed., *Jeu d'Adam*, p. 7.
19 Cf. at length Stemmler, *LFGS*, pp. 200–8.
20 But see Stemmler, 'Entstehung und Wesen', and Travis, *Dramatic Design*, pp. 19–29.
21 Clopper, 'Chester Cycle'.

22 Palmer, '"Towneley Plays"'. See also Mills, '"The Towneley Plays"', where the 'cycle' status of Towneley is questioned. Wakefield as the home of Towneley is defended by Stevens, *Mystery Cycles*.
23 For Towneley see previous note. For N-Town cf. Meredith, ed., *The Mary Play*, esp. p. 4.
24 Witness frequently recurring phrases like 'for the honour of God, and worship of the City'. Cf. James, 'Ritual', esp. note 40.
25 Clopper, 'Lay and Clerical Impact', pp. 111f.
26 Cf. Diller, 'Composition'; Axton, *European Drama*, p. 184; Travis, *Dramatic Design*, pp. 41f.
27 Cf., e.g., Palmer, '"Towneley Plays"', p. 318.
28 Lancashire, *Dramatic Texts*, p.xv.
29 This is emphasized also by Werner, *Studien*, pp. 23, 41, and *passim*. But Werner does not discuss the various forms which the rapport with the audience assumes in German medieval drama. On the liturgical office cf. also H. Brinkmann: 'Not a spectacle for a festive crowd of children of the world, but a religious office where celebrants and bystanders share in the elevation to God.' ('Kein Schauspiel für eine festlich gestimmte Schar von Weltkindern, sondern religiöse Feier, in der Mitwirkende und Anwesende als eine Gemeinschaft der Gläubigen die Erhebung zu Gott begehen.') ('Eigenform des mittelalterlichen Dramas', p. 19.)
30 On the 'inclusion of the congregation as audience' see now Tydeman, *Theatre*, pp. 55–6, and, specifically for the Fleury Plays, Bevington, 'Staging', p. 64.
31 Chambers, *Stage*, vol. 2, p. 82; Wright, ed., *La Seinte Resureccion*, p. cxix; Hardison, *Christian Rite*, p. 266.; Bevington, ed., *Medieval Drama*, p. 122.
32 Cf. James, 'Ritual'. James sees the Corpus Christi procession and the plays as two complementary functions 'to express the social bond and to contribute to social integration' (p. 4).
33 On *locus* and *platea* cf. Weimann, '*Platea* und *locus*'; Weimann, *Shakespeare and the Popular Tradition*, pp. 73–85; also Diller, 'Wakefield Master', pp. 24ff.
34 Weimann, '*Platea* und *locus*', p. 350; *Shakespeare and the Popular Tradition*, p. 63; Stevens, *Mystery Cycles*, the first chapter of which is significantly titled 'The York Cycle: City as Stage'.
35 Weimann, *Shakespeare and the Popular Tradition*, p. 58.
36 Weimann, '*Platea* und locus', p. 345; *Shakespeare and the Popular Tradition*, p. 82: 'a comic challenge to the biblical myth'.
37 As such they often appear in the criticism of the 'revaluers' who accordingly undervalue these passages. Cf. the discussion of Craig and Prosser in the introduction to this study. That 'realism' in medieval art and drama means the close study of reality not for its own sake but as a revelation of divine order has recently been emphasized by Sheingorn, 'Visual Language'.
38 Southern, *Medieval Theatre*. Objections have been raised by many scholars, notably by Schmitt, 'Medieval Theatre'.
39 A. Nelson, *Medieval English Stage*, pp. 15–81. This view, though perhaps the most strongly argued in Nelson's book, has met with universal disagreement. The *opinio communis* is represented most succinctly by Beadle, ed., *The York*

Plays, pp. 30–7. For a careful weighing of Nelson's evidence see Cawley, 'Staging', p. 59. For an attractive though speculative 'compromise' position, see Kahrl, *Traditions*, pp. 45f.

40 For obiter references to this state of affairs see now Meredith, ed., *Passion Play*, esp. pp. 7ff. See also Cameron and Kahrl, 'Staging the N-Town Cycle', esp. p. 123. On the composition of N-Town in general see Spector, *Genesis*, and Spector, 'Composition'.

41 See again Cawley, 'Staging', pp. 58ff.

42 Weimann, '*Platea* und locus', p. 344; *Shakespeare and the Popular Tradition*, pp. 74, 81f.

43 This description is a gross simplification. For the extremely complex textual situation see now Meredith, ed., *Passion Play*, esp. pp. 8f and 245–7.

THE REPRESENTATION OF TIME AND SPACE IN THE CYCLES

1 On what is here called 'continuous correspondence' cf. Petit de Julleville, who calls it 'l'un des inconvénients du procédé dramatique du moyen-âge'. But at the same time Petit ignores the existence of the 'cutting technique': 'Comme l'action n'est jamais censée s'interrompre dans aucun des divers lieux où elle se poursuit simultanément, il devient nécessaire d'exposer ... les périodes intermédiaires, quoique insignifiantes, qui séparent celles où le sujet se développe.' (*Histoire du théâtre en France: les mystères*, vol. 2., p. 456). Cf. also Diller, 'Representation of space'.

2 Bradbrook, *Themes and Conventions*, pp. 9f; Bradbrook's famous example – 'Well, this is the forest of Arden' (*AYL*, II, iv, 15) – is, however, much more strongly embedded in the situation than is usual in medieval plays.

3 Graesse, *Legenda Aurea*, p. 89.

4 Similarly Ch IV, lines 37–40.

5 Chester is unique among the English cycles in giving the Melchisedek episode.

6 Salter, ('Banns', p. 445) attributes this speech to the author of the late Banns which he dates 1575.

7 Contrast this with another passage which is not content with an impersonal description but gives a lively, momentary reaction:

> Nowe blessed be hee us hither brought;
> in land lyves non so bright.
> See where hee sittes thatt wee have sought
> amonge yonder maisters micle of might. (Ch XI, 303–6)

But this text is an import from York (Y XX, 219–22). The parallel was first discovered by Hohlfeld, 'kollektivmisterien', p. 260.

8 It may be noted in passing that the fact that Maria Salome corrects Maria Jacobi does not find expression in either's speech. In everyday speech Maria Salome would probably say something like 'No, it's two men, not one!' and Maria Jacobi would answer with an equivalent of 'Yes, you are right.' The 'interpersonal' function of language, so important in normal dialogue, finds no expression here. The interpersonal function of language has been emphasized above all by the British linguist Michael Halliday and his school;

see, e.g., Halliday, 'Functions and Universals', and *Learning how to mean*, passim.
9 On the appropriateness of the term 'realism' cf. Diller, 'Craftsmanship', and Munson, 'Audience and Meaning'.
10 Ch VII ll. 47f, 59f, 161ff.
11 Foster, ed., *Stanzaic Life*.
12 Graesse, ed., *Legenda Aurea*, ch. XIV:'De epiphania domini', p. 89.
13 In MS Harley 2124, which served as the basis for Deimling's edition, the animals are even called horses (eques)!
14 Wilson. 'Stanzaic Life', p. 430. For the *Passion de Saumur* see Roy, ed., *Mystère*, esp.: *La Passion Nostre Seigneur Jhesu Christ, copiée à Saumur*, lines 2900–3009. For the question of French influence on the Chester cycle cf. Baugh, 'Chester Plays'. The Octavian-Sibyl episode, unknown elsewhere in England, was very popular in France. It is to be found, *inter alia*, in the *Passion de Saumur*, in the *Mystère du Viel Testament*, the *Passion d'Arras*, and in the Rouen *Nativité*.
15 Very often – and this includes the Chester *Nativity* (lines 564–643, 699–722) – he is content to leave stageworthy episodes to the Expositor's narrative, apparently without any concern for dramatic effect.
16 Even Alan Nelson has to admit it for 'part of the sixteenth century', though he believes without support that they were played indoors during the reign of Elizabeth (*Medieval Stage*, pp. 158–62). A stationary out-of-doors performance until 1521 is assumed by Clopper, 'History', p. 222. No scholar doubts that the plays in their preserved form are suitable only for processional staging.
17 If change of place and cutting technique are more wide-spread in the French drama than in the English, this is probably owing to the size of the French stages and to the scenic possibilities opened thereby. A particularly impressive example, which is quite unthinkable on the English pageant-waggon, is the *Mystère de la Passion d'Arnoul Greban*, which has the Shepherds appear no fewer than three times before they embark, in a fourth scene, on their journey to Bethlehem (Paris and Raynaud, eds., *Arnoul Greban*, lines 4638–4854, 4967–4978, 5171–5235, 5476–5751). These scenes are punctuated by others which show Mary and Joseph in Bethlehem, the angels in heaven, or the Three Kings on their way to Jerusalem.
18 Apart from the four great cycles the Slaughter is preserved in the *Shearmen and Tailors Pageant* from the fragmentary Coventry cycle and in the Candlemas play of MS Digby 133 (Baker, Murphy, and Hall, eds., *Late Medieval Plays*). This play may well be a product of the early sixteenth century: cf. Baker and Murphy, 'Late Medieval Plays', p. 163.
19 Moreover, we know of two lost plays – Beverley and Newcastle upon Tyne – which, like York and Towneley, gave the Flight a separate play. Cf. Davis, ed., *Non-Cycle Plays*, p. xliii; Lancashire, *Dramatic Texts*, pp. 83, 230; Anderson, ed., *REED: Newcastle upon Tyne*, p.6.
20 Matt. 2.13f; Young, *DMC*, vol. 2, pp. 111, 118.
21 Graesse, ed., *Legenda Aurea*, pp. 63f. The *Legenda aurea* is also the source of the *Stanzaic Life* at this point.
22 Salter, *Medieval Drama*, p. 90.

23 Cf. ten Brink, *History*, pp. 244f.
24 This is the position taken by Schmidt, *Kunst des Dialogs*, pp. 139f. His criticism has, I hope, caused me to word this passage more carefully than in the German original.
25 Eliade, *The Sacred*, pp. 20ff.
26 This is the form of the name in the Vulgate. The Authorized Version has Peniel and Pe-nuel.
27 Auerbach, *Mimesis*, pp. 7–10.
28 This section, written in couplets, is probably the oldest part of this very heterogeneous play; cf. Lyle, *Original Identity*, pp. 75ff.
29 *Uersus de Resuscitatione Lazari* from Fleury (Young, *DMC*, vol. 2, pp. 199ff); *Suscitatio Lazari* by Hilarius, Young, *DMC*, vol. 2., pp. 212ff.
30 Fleury, lines 88ff, 208ff; Hilarius, lines 17ff.
31 Fleury, lines 122ff; Hilarius, lines 29ff.
32 In this respect T XXXI resembles Hilarius, lines 120f, though it differs from Fleury, lines 208–13.
33 Bradbrook, *Themes and Conventions*, pp. 9f; Doran, *Endeavors*, pp. 279ff.
34 The division of earlier plays was frequently practised in York in order to accommodate the wishes of guilds that had become independent or had come into wealth. The inverse process, however, is also to be found: plays were joined together in order to relieve the burden on impoverished guilds. But a unified episode like the Flood, for which the Building of the Ark is a mere preparation, has in all likelihood begun as one play. The arguments regarding metre and content which Greg and Chambers adduce for the high age of the Building of the Ark are not compelling (Greg, *Miracle Cycles*, pp. 78f; Chambers, *Close*, pp. 29f). But the play must have come into being before 1415, since it appears already in the first Burton List (*York Plays*, p. xx).
35 Cf. Morris, ed., *Cursor Mundi*, p.106, where the one hundred years of the building of the Ark are meant to give humanity an opportunity for repentance. The *Cursor* contains no reference to Noah becoming tired.
36 E.g. *Nuncius*' journey to Sirinus T IX or Joseph's walk to the midwives Y XIV.
37 'There is abundant evidence that the late York school was writing about 1420.' (Frampton, 'Date', p. 109.) On the York Realist see Robinson, 'York Realist'. Also Davidson, *From Creation to Doom*, p. 210 who dates him *c.* 1422–32.
38 Hulme, ed., *Harrowing of Hell*, pp. 26ff.
39 Creizenach, *Drama*, vol. 1, p. 291.
40 See Cawley, ed., *Wakefield Pageants*, p. 86, and note to lines 298f (p. 121). Cf. also the present writer's 'Craftsmanship', p. 253 (with further examples).
41 Rose, ed., *The Wakefield Mystery Plays*, pp. 26–42; A. Nelson, *Medieval English Stage*.
42 The standard edition is still Block, ed., *Ludus Coventriæ, or The Plaie Called Corpus Christi*. Facsimile edition: Meredith and Kahrl, eds., *The N-Town Plays*. Spector's new EETS edition had not appeared when this book went to press. For arguments linking the cycle with Lincoln see: Cameron and Kahrl, 'N-Town Plays at Lincoln', pp. 61–9; see also: Cameron and Kahrl, 'Staging the N-Town Cycle', pp. 122–38, 152–65, with further literature. Linguistic

evidence points to Norfolk: cf. Eccles, 'Ludus Coventriae'; Spector, Genesis, pp. 148–52, and Meredith, ed., Passion Play, p. 9. The latest editor of parts of the cycle calls its cyclical character into question, regarding its composition as purely scribal: Meredith, ed., The Mary Play; and Meredith, ed., Passion Play.
43 Block, ed. Ludus Coventriae, p. lv; see further Prosser, Drama and Religion, pp. 196f, with numerous references to earlier assessments.
44 Block, ed., Ludus Coventriae, pp. 1–16.
45 For the Proclamation stanza: Greg, Miracle Cycles, p. 141; Gayley, Plays, p. 139; Swenson, Inquiry, pp. 5f; Craig, ERD, pp. 247ff, and Spector, Genesis, pp. 28–67. For the Chester stanza: Craig, ERD, p. 248. For a more recent theory of the composition of the N-Town manuscript see Meredith, ed., The Mary Play.
46 This play is clearly revised, since the Proclamation distributes its contents over two pageants; it is also metrically heterogeneous. But the beginning of the play corresponds exactly with the Proclamation and is entirely in regular thirteen-line stanzas. It seems therefore justified to regard this part of the play at least as early.
47 This, too, appears to be the original part of a revised play. Cf. pp. 213f of this study.
48 E.g. Passion Play II, lines 1059–1063 (p. 308), 1496ff (p. 323); LC XXXVIII (Appearance to Cleophas and Luke), line 275 (p. 345).
49 Craig, ERD, p. 247.
50 Greg, Miracle Cycles, p. 141; Swenson, Inquiry, pp. 32f, 36f. This is largely confirmed by Spector, Genesis, pp. 69f.
51 Cf. Cameron and Kahrl, 'Staging the N-Town Cycle', p. 126. Judging from his experience with a modern production, Cameron is convinced that 'The Temptation' (LC XXIII) and 'The Woman Taken in Adultery' (LC XXIV) 'suggest individual pageants,... and they would probably gain greatly from being staged in the highly focused environment of a single pageant' ('Lincoln Plays, p. 148).
52 See, e.g. :

> But ȝit sum mede and ȝe me take
> I wyl with-drawe my gret rough toth
> gold or sylvyr I wol not for-sake
> but evyn as all somnorys doth.   (LC XIV, 125–8 (p. 128))

53 See above, p. 96.
54 Gayley, Plays, pp. 191f.
55 Prosser, Drama and Religion, pp. 107f.
56 E.g.:

> Shall we lete here go qwyte agayn
> or to hire deth xal she be brought.   (lines 207f, p. 207)

Similarly: lines 222f, 227f.
57 Swenson, Inquiry, p. 38, praises this play for its 'rapid shifting of scene' without, however, going into details.
58 Young, DMC, vol. 2, pp. 199ff.
59 Cf. Greg, Miracle Cycles, p. 142. Spector ('Genesis', p. 146) also sees evidence that the 'short octave plays' were written for 'theater in the round

production', but from the printed version this statement seems to have been omitted.
60 The first expression is used by Saintsbury (*English Prosody*), Swenson (*Inquiry*), and Craig (*ERD*); the latter by Greg (*Miracle Cycles*). The fullest study of the metres of N-Town is now Spector, *Genesis*.
61 Gen. 4.23f describes Lamech as a revenger, but the identification of the victim as Cain is pure legend. In Gen 5.28 Lamech is Noah's father, i.e. a descendant of Seth, not of Cain.
62 Gayley, *Plays*, p. 151.
63 E.g. the *Detractores* in LC XIV ('The Trial of Joseph and Mary'; see next chapter), or the *Accusatores* in LC XXIV ('The Woman Taken in Adultery'); they belong to Spector's 'short octaves'.
64 Cf. Block, ed., *Ludus Coventriae*, p. xxxii. Block believes that they were independent before they were adapted for the cycle. Cameron and Kahrl, on the other hand, conclude that an earlier version of them had originally been part of the cycle and were *subsequently* made into self-contained units. (Cameron and Kahrl, 'Staging the N-Town Cycle', p. 128). Spector's account is more complex, but permits the same conclusion ('Composition', pp. 75f). Meredith stresses the 'independence' of the Passion Plays, but he, too, recognizes 'old pageant material' in both of them (*Passion Play*, pp. 7f). Our observation of 'earlier' techniques would favour such a view.
65 See next chapter for a more extensive treatment of the problem.
66 LC VIII ('The Conception of Mary'), IX ('Mary in the Temple'), XIII ('The Visit to Elizabeth'), and parts of X ('The Betrothal of Mary') and XI ('The Parliament of Heaven'). Cf. Craig, *ERD*, p. 249. These plays are regarded by Peter Meredith as belonging to the 'Mary Play from the N.Town Manuscript' (*Mary Play*). Spector groups them as 'long octave' plays (*Genesis*, p. 77).
67 Block, ed. *Ludus Coventriae*, p. xlvii. Cameron and Kahrl, 'Staging the N-Town Cycle' regard the St Anne's play as a later revision which was made into a self-contained play in the process of that revision. They assume that beginning in the 1470s the play saw independent production.
68 Cf. Graesse, ed., *Legenda Aurea*, ch. 86 ('De nativitate Johannis baptistae'), p. 357: 'David enim rex...XXIV summos sacerdotes instituit, quorum tamen unus major erat qui princeps sacerdotum dicebatur.'
69 Graesse, ed., *Legenda Aurea*, ch. 131: 'De nativitate beatae Mariae virginis', p. 587.

ADDRESS TO THE AUDIENCE

1 Venzmer, *Chöre*, p. 17; Young, *DMC*, vol. 2, pp. 403f.
2 Cf. Pascal, 'Origins', p. 378.
3 E.g. the Doctor's speech in Ch V, lines 388ff (only in 3 MSS); Ch VI, 699ff. But compare Contemplacio's divergent, narrative speech in LC XIII, 23ff (see above, p. 107).
4 This thesis finds support not only in the fact that the choir sings utterances whose point of view fits into the represented situation. Converse proof is also possible. The Magi, for instance, take over a choral antiphon which assumes the point of view of the celebrating congregation (*Pastores dicite, quidnam*

vidistis, et annunciate Christi nativitatem). Cf. the extensive analysis on pp. 29f.

5 This fundamental difference between 'ritual' and 'drama' has been pointed out by Speirs ('Mystery Cycle', p. 312). Speirs, however, is concerned to demonstrate pagan-ritualistic features in the mystery plays. We believe that it is precisely there that important differences between 'ritual' and 'drama' are overlooked. On the autonomy of the mystery play see Hardison, Essay VII. When Hardison calls the Mass a 'sacred drama' he is not overlooking this difference; he is merely using the term 'drama' in a sense which ignores the aspect of representation (Hardison, *Christian Rite*, p. 30). For some slight qualification of the sweeping statement that the liturgical drama knows no audience see now Tydeman, *Theatre*, p. 57, and Bevington, 'Staging'.

6 On the decline of the liturgy as a communal act of worship during the Middle Ages cf. McDonald, 'Drama in the Church', pp. 116–18.

7 Young, *DMC*, vol. 2, pp. 259ff, 267ff.

8 Ibid., vol. 2, p. 267.

9 The quotations are from Symons, ed., *Regularis Concordia*, pp. 50 (lines 1f), 43 (line 4), 44 (lines 9 and 10), 50 (lines 23f).

10 Cf. Brecht, 'Short Organon', section 50; see also section 49 on 'the showman Laughton' and 'the Galileo whom he is showing'. Similarities and differences between the medieval theatre and his own are pointed out by Brecht himself ('Short Organon', section 42). That the actor's task was seen as 'telling' also in the Middle Ages, is borne out by Ch IV, 6–8, where it is said of Abraham that 'he is comen into this place...to tell you of storye'.

11 On the highly complex relations between illusion and reality on the medieval stage see Weimann, '*Platea* und *locus*', *Shakespeare and the Popular Tradition*, pp. 73–85.

12 This problem has been discussed more extensively in Diller, 'Theatrical Pragmatics'.

13 This is the most important feature which the medieval audience-address has in common with the popular 'aside' of the Shakespearean stage; cf.Weimann, '*Platea* und *locus*'; 'Shakespeare und das Volkstheater', esp. p. 123 and p. 129; *Shakespeare and the Popular Tradition*, p. 226.

14 E.g. in LC, p. 238, lines 221–2, where speeches of the disciples Peter and John are explicitly called 'prechyng'.

15 Such characters are more popular in Continental, especially in German plays than they are in the English ones; cf. Creizenach, *Drama*, vol. 1, p. 296, and the synopsis in Heinzel, *Beschreibung des geistlichen Schauspiels*, pp. 63–7, together with brief comments on their functions ibid., pp. 256–8. It is at least remarkable that Continental influences should have been suspected again and again for Ch and LC, even though definitive proof is not forthcoming; cf. Ungemach, *Quellen*; Utesch, *Quellen der Chester Plays*, Falke, *Quellen*. For criticism of Ungemach see Baugh, 'Chester Plays', pp. 35–6. A comparison between Continental and English audience-addresses would certainly not decide this question, but it might throw new light on it. For an important study of Latin, German, and English plays see Fichte, *Expository Voices*.

16 Quotations will usually be from the latest edition by Lumiansky and Mills. The base text of this edition is MS Hm (Huntington 2, called D by Deimling and Matthews). Since the spelling of this MS is often erratic and even

misleading, it is sometimes necessary to quote from the older edition by Deimling and Matthews. In those cases the references are marked '(DM)'.
17 See above all the opening monologues in Ch V, XIII, XIV, XV, XVIII, XX, XXI.
18 Ch X, XVIII, XXIII. The people addressed by Herod and Pilate are hardly of a type to be found in a medieval English town: *Princes, prelates of price,/ barons in blamner and byse* (Ch X, 1f); *You kemps, you knowne knightes of kynde* (Ch XVIII, 10). Furthermore, Pilate refers to Jerusalem as 'this cyttye' (line 29). We may assume, therefore, that the potentates are in fact addressing their own courts rather than the audience.
19 Ch VIII, IX, XI.
20 In the Huntington MS, which forms the base text for Lumiansky and Mills' edition, Nuntius is called *Preco* in Ch IV, the Expositor is *Doctor* in Ch V and XII.
21 This fact hardly allows us to assume that *Nuntius* and *Expositor* were originally the same character, as Chambers would have it (*Close*, p. 26). Moreover, *Nuntius*' speeches are purely concerned with the technicalities of the performance, while *Expositor's* are didactic and homiletic in content.
22 But see now Axton's suggestion that Nuntius' 'appearances and disappearances have an air of formulaic magic' and may well be remnants of older, popular dramatic practices (*European Drama*, p. 185).
23 This tone will be found in the speech of other figures, cf. pp. 119–21.
24 Ch XXII, 29. Similarly IV, 468; V (App. IB), 307f, 322, 353; VI, 568; XXII, 85, 90, 96, 105, 107, 114, 157, 161, 170.
25 Ch V (App. IB), 340. Similarly V (App. IB), 355; VI, 601; XXII, 243, 273, 277, 285, 289.
26 Ch V (App. IB), 371, 389; VI, 633; XXII, 86, 106, 159, 333. Cf. also 'I saye veramente' (IV, 117), 'leeve ye me' (V (App. IB), 81).
27 Ch IV, 130, 207, 471; VI, 572.
28 Ch IV, 121; more emphatically XII, 282: 'the great goodnes of Godes deede'.
29 Ch IV, 119, 193; V (App. IB), 67f.
30 E.g. Ch IV, 130, 468ff; VI, 572; also all of the Prophets' proclamations in Ch V (App. IB) and XXII.
31 This observation neglects Expositor's narrative passages, which are largely taken over from *St. L* (Ch VI, XII). Cf. on this Wilson, '"Life of Christ" and the Chester Plays', esp. pp. 414, 431.
32 Cf. Ch IV, 115f: 'that unlearned standinge herebye / may knowe what this may bee' with *St. L*, line 7152: 'for lewet men that her ben by'. Cf. also the emphasis on 'usefulness' in Ch XXII, 28 (quoted above) and Ch IV, 463 with *St. L* 1415. Like Expositor, the narrator of *St. L* 'expounds' (Ch IV, 114, *St. L* 2403).
33 Extensive verbal echoes in Ch VI and XII, 'possible influence' (Foster, ed., *Life of Christ*, p. xlii) in Ch IV and V. For a full list of the borrowings see Wilson, '"Life of Christ" and the Chester Plays', p. 413. Of the plays in which Expositor appears, only Ch XXII is uninfluenced by *St. L*. But this play, too, clearly exhibits the influence of a non-dramatic, homiletic source. The enumeration of the Fifteen Signs before Doom (Ch XXII, 261–340) corresponds closely to that in a poem ascribed to Lydgate, 'The Fifftene Tokyns aforn the Doom' (Brown and Robbins, *Index*, No. 408; MacCracken,

ed., *John Lydgate*, vol. 1, pp. 117–20) and the first sermon in *Mirk's Festial* (cf. Mirk, *Mirk's Festial*, ed. Th. Erbe, pp. 2f). Like the passages shared by Expositor and *St. L.*, the description of the Fifteen Signs goes back to the *Legenda Aurea*. Cf. Sandison, 'Quindecim signa', pp. 80f.

34 This view is now supported by Fichte, *Expository Voices*, p. 102, and more forcefully by Travis, *Dramatic Design*, pp. 47ff.

35 The dramatic function of salutations and blessings is emphasized by Robinson, 'Late Medieval Cult', p. 513.

36 E.g. Jesus' parting words to Lazarus' sisters:

> Haue good day, my Deghter deer!
> wherever you goe, farr or neer,
> my blessinge I geue you here.
> to Ierusalem I take the way.   (Ch XIII, 486–9[DM])

37 Cf. Hohlfeld, 'Kollektivmisterien', p. 260; Greg, *Miracle Cycles*, 89.

38 In the liturgical drama, too, the Shepherds had more contact with the congregation than other dramatic characters: They are the only ones regularly to take the lead in the mass that followed their office; cf. Young, *DMC*, vol. 2, pp. 20 *et passim*.

39 Chambers, *Close*, p. 28, describes the play as 'largely rewritten'; similarly Craig, *ERD*, pp. 187f. See also Diller, 'Composition', for a fuller discussion.

40 Carey, *Wakefield Group*, p. 92, note 63; Brownstein, 'Revision', pp. 55–65, esp. 58.

41 This type of the audience-address has been discussed by Weimann (*'Platea und locus'*, pp. 343–5, where the N-Town Joseph is used to illustrate the type). On the progeny of this and similar speech-types see the same author's 'Shakespeare und das Volkstheater', pp. 119ff and *Shakespeare and the Popular Tradition*, pp. 224ff.

42 Lines 3f of the interpolation. On the late date of the passage cf. Deimling, ed., *Chester Plays*, p. xx.

43 A crooked staff as used in folk-games (*MED*).

44 The same cry is used by the *Tortores* in the Towneley *Processus Talentorum* (T XXIV, 73, 113, 145). These and similar cries seem especially to accompany entries not from one of the stations but from outside the stage; e.g. Tytivillus in *Mankind*, line 467 and – in the form of the Latin Caveatis' – line 469. Such entries, which are the norm in the folk-play, are exceptional in the mystery plays.

45 Cf., e.g., the Mummers' Play from Camborne, Cornwall (Tiddy, *Mummers' Play*, p. 146):

> Here comes I old Bealzibub,
> On my shoulders I carry my club...
> I have a fire that is long lighted.

with Ch X, 437f(DM):

> And with this Croked Cambrock your backs shall I cloe,
> and all falce beleuers I burne in a low.

46 This version of the play is printed as Appendix IB by Lumiansky and Mills. Deimling, *The Chester Plays*, p. xxi, believes that the lines in question were not part of the original play.

47 Craig, *ERD*, p. 193, believes that Ch XXII-XXIV were originally one eschatological play, to which Ch XXII formed the 'introduction'.
48 Ott, 'Personengestaltung', pp. 26f, 29, 31.
49 See, e.g., 'shall no man..., may no man...' etc. (Ch. V, 317, 366), 'man', 'mankind' (lines 367, 379, 394, 399).
50 And, *mutatis mutandis*: Ch V (App. IB), 297, 361, 393ff.
51 Ch XXII, 1, 49, 53. The *you* in line 208 (*forsooth as I you tell*) is not as unambiguously identifiable, but on balance it is more likely that it is also addressed at humanity at large rather than at the actual audience.
52 For references see previous footnote.
53 Ch XXII, 4, 51, 59, 126.
54 Craig, *ERD*, p. 193.
55 Travis, *Dramatic Design*, pp. 47–58; Clopper, 'Chester Cycle'.
56 Cf., above all, Weimann, *Shakespeare and the Popular Tradition*, and Righter, *Shakespeare*, esp. pp. 21f. Characteristically, Righter's examples of medieval dramaturgy are exclusively from Towneley.
57 Cf. the attempts by Pollard ('Introduction'), Hohlfeld ('kollektivmisterien'), Gayley (*Plays*), Charles Davidson (*English Mystery Plays*), Greg (*Miracle Cycles*), Chambers (*Close*), Reese ('Alliterative Verse'), Williams (*Characterization*), Stevens ('Towneley Plays'), Beadle (ed., *York Plays*, pp. 19–29).
58 Cf. especially the farewells in York.
59 See below, pp. 154f.
60 Cf. Pollard, 'Introduction', p. xxvii. On the minstrel-like or even lyrical quality of these lines see Pearson, 'Isolable Lyrics', p. 237; Dunn, 'Lyrical Form', pp. 83f.
61 The statement in the German original was too sweeping. The mistake was brought to my notice by Schmidt, *Kunst des Dialogs*, p. 30.
62 Conceivably we are here dealing with a general feature of Northern English medieval religious poetry. As is well known, one of the earliest religious poems of Northern England, the *Cursor Mundi*, was written with the intention of exploiting the popularity of secular fiction (i.e. romances) for religious purposes; a strong influence of secular narrative forms on Northern legends was discovered by Wolpers (*Heiligenlegende*, esp. pp. 274f).
63 Y X, 1ff (Abraham) and XI, 85ff (Moses). Also Y IX, 1ff (Noah) and the Abraham of the Towneley cycle (T IV) and the Wakefield Master's Noah (T III).
64 Chambers (*Close*, p. 33) assigns this play to his 'middle period'. The *terminus ante quem* is Burton's 1415 list, which already contains the play. (Johnston and Rogerson, eds., *REED: York*, p. 18.)
65 More on the 'tone' of these prayers in the chapter on the opening prayer.
66 Y VIII, 150f, XI, 379f, XVI, 391f, XX, 51, 74, 288; XXIV, 208f, XLII, 176(?), 275f, XLIII, 225f; T XI, 89f; T XXVI, 633f, XXVII, 379f. T XXVI was borrowed from Y and is largely identical with Y XXXVIII. The ending (Mary Magdalene's encounter with the risen Christ), of which the lines given form a part, has been replaced in Y by a new play (Y XXXIX). T XXVII, which is in the same stanza as T XXVI ('Burns measure') and whose opposite number in Y is presumably a late play (Y XL), may well be an early York play; cf. Lyle, *Original Identity*, pp. 47, 53.

67 Rare exceptions: Y VIII, 150f, T XI, 89f.
68 Cf. p. 15.
69 See Hemingway, ed., *English Nativity Plays*, p. xlvii.
70 Since what matters is the awareness of there being an audience, we disregard for the moment the fact that the audience is not overtly addressed. We will see later that this little difference may also be significant.
71 Cf. on this Wickham's polemic in *Early English Stages*, vol. 1, p. 119.
72 See above, p. 74, and note 24.
73 Weimann, *Shakespeare und die Tradition des Volkstheaters*, p. 91. The sentence does not appear in the translation (p. 45).
74 The relevant passages are T XXVI 633f and XXVII end. On the relationship see Pollard, 'Introduction', p. xxvi; Lyle, *Original Identity*, pp.85ff; Craig, *ERD*, p. 216.
75 On alliteration as a criterion for dating the York plays see Reese, 'Alliterative Verse', Craig, *ERD*, p. 225.
76 Cf. Stevens, 'Dramatic Setting', p. 196.
77 Weimann, *Shakespeare and the Popular Tradition*, p. 80; on Apemantus see pp. 224–7.
78 To reduce the Shakespearean aside to a single type is of course an oversimplification which is merely to highlight the basic difference between the genres. On the extremely varied use of the aside in Shakespeare see Riehle, *Das Beiseitesprechen bei Shakespeare*.
79 Quoted from Alexander, ed., *Shakespeare*.
80 On the close kinship of this *argumentum ad hominem* with the medieval sermon cf. Owst, *Literature and Pulpit*, p. 492 *et passim*.
81 T XIII, 91f, T XV, 149f.
82 This satiric moralizing also finds parallels in the sermon; cf. Owst, *Literature and Pulpit*, p. 521. Eckhardt has discovered the same trait in the later moralities and interludes, without however mentioning its presence in the mystery plays (*Die lustige Person*, p. 209).
83 Cf. the bibliography in Cawley, ed., *Wakefield Pageants*, pp. xxxvf.
84 Weimann, *Shakespeare and the Popular Tradition*, p.139.
85 Cf. p. 125.
86 On the same speech-type in connection with potentates see next section.
87 This type of entry from the audience probably appears as early as the thirteenth century; cf. the earliest preserved fragment of an English drama, the 'Cambridge Prologue': 'And sittet rume and wel atwo / þat men moȝt among ev go.' (Davis, ed., *Non-Cycle Plays*, p. 115, lines 3f). R.H. Robbins, the Prologue's first editor, concluded from this that the actors 'would be moving among the audience, either to present crowd scenes or to make an entrance or exit'. At any rate, the same close contact existed between audience and actors as in the Towneley scenes under discussion. Cf. Robbins, 'English Mystery Play Fragment', p. 33.
88 *Canterbury Tales*, line A 3124 ('The Miller's Prologue'), Benson, ed., *The Riverside Chaucer*, p. 67.
89 The *terminus ante quem* for this play is the 1415 Burton list, where it appears with its cast.
90 Stevens, 'Towneley Plays'.
91 Lyle, *Original Identity*, p. 98.

92 Dated by Alfred Harbage as 'late fourteenth cent.' (*Annals of English Drama*, p. 8); Davis, ed., *Non-Cycle Plays*, p. c, opts for mid-fourteenth century.
93 His wording betrays occasional blasphemous echoes of the Bible, thus creating an explicit antithesis to divine or apostolic power: 'ffor I may bynd and lowse of band' (T IX, 16) and 'whether I wyll saue or spyll.' (T IX, 30).
94 Frampton, 'Date'.
95 The parts common to both plays, however, appear only in Smith's No. XVII (*The York Plays*).
96 Beadle, ed., *York Plays*, p. 429.
97 Hohlfeld, 'kollektivmisterien', p. 293; Frampton, 'Date', p. 91; J. H. Smith, 'Wakefield Borrowings', p. 599. But see Lyle, *Original Identity*, p. 60, who regards T XIV as the York play mentioned by Burton in 1415. But this is unlikely, since the *Nuncius*, so important in the Towneley play, appears in the list only as a later insertion, which may suggest a revision in York after 1415. (Johnston and Rogerson, eds., *REED: York*, p. 19).
98 Chambers, *Close*, pp. 31f; and Reese, 'Alliterative Verse', pp. 959ff.
99 Frampton, 'Towneley XX'. Possibly this play was still two plays in the copy from which the scribe worked: its heading is 'Incipit Conspiracio' and it ends 'Explicit Capcio Ihesu'. Frampton, 'Processus Talentorum', would like to regard T XXIV as a lost play from York mentioned in Burton's second list. This is contradicted by Stevens ('Composition'), who finds no Northern dialect features in T XXIV as one would expect in a York play. The dialect is Northeast Midlands and thus does not fit York (Stevens, 'Composition', p. 432).
100 A complete list of all 'Wakefield stanzas' in Cawley, ed., *Wakefield Pageants*, p. xviii. Frampton ('Date', p. 114) and Carey, (*Wakefield Group*, p. 223), believe these stanzas to be early work by the Master. In this view the Wakefield Master would have begun as a reviser before he turned to writing entire plays.
101 Gayley (*Plays*, p. 162) thinks he is the author of both speeches. Frampton ('Date', p. 113) and Carey (*Wakefield Group*, pp. 220–22) credit him at least with T XXII. A. Williams (*Characterization*, p. 64) would deny him even this speech. Martin Stevens, who has demonstrated that the so-called nine-line stanza is less distinctive than is usually thought, accepts the opening of T XXII as the Master's and would probably accept T XXIII as well ('Nine-Line Stanza', esp. p. 115). Stevens also considers the Wakefield Master 'the primary reviser of the Towneley cycle as a whole' ('Nine-Line Stanza', note 31).
102 Such amalgamations led, e.g., to the composition of Y XXIV and XXXIII. Cf. L.T. Smith, ed., *The York Plays*, pp. xxiv-xxv; Frampton, 'Date', p. 103, note 79; Beadle, ed., *York Plays*, pp. 441, 450.
103 T XIV, 3:'who that makys noyse *whyls I am here*'; T XX, 10:'ye wote not wel, I weyn / what wat is commen to the towne'; T XXIII, 3: 'Whyls ye ar present in my sight'.
104 T IX, 10: 'if ye knew me oght'; T XXII, 5: 'Say, wote ye not that I am pylate, perles to behold?' See also T XX, 10, quoted in previous footnote.
105 On social criticism in the portraits of Herod see Owst, *Literature and Pulpit*, pp. 493f, who sees its origins in sermons critical of the age.
106 This opening speech shows the Wakefield Master's stanza. That writer also

shows elsewhere his awareness of the non-identity of the two dramatic Worlds and exploits it for comic effect: he names, for instance Kemptown and Surrey as Herod's dominions in direct juxtaposition with Egypt and India, exploiting even the rhyme to highlight the incongruity. (T XVI, 44, 47), and the First Shepherd in *Secunda Pastorum* dreams to his evident discomfort that he has fallen asleep in England (T XIII, 353)!

107 This is probably an interpolation, as we saw p. 134.
108 On Jesus as a personification of the common man see A. Williams, *Characterization*, p. 40; on social criticism in the Pilate scenes see A. Williams, *Characterization*, and Owst, *Literature and Pulpit*, pp. 495f; on parallels in the medieval sermon ibid., p. 339. This picture of Jesus was presented already in the Pseudo-Bonaventuran *Meditationes Vitae Christi*: 'as another comune man of the peple' (Love, *Mirrour of the Blessed Lyf*, p. 219, ch. xl: 'Of the passioun of oure lorde Jesu criste [and first of his prayer and takynge at matyn tyme]').
109 Robert Mannyng's English translation, *Meditations on the Supper of Our Lord and the Hours of the Passion*, had an important influence on the tone of the English Passion plays. Cf. McNeir, 'Dramatic Art', p. 608; Prosser, *Drama and Religion*, p. 41.
110 More about this pp. 237f.
111 Stevens, 'Nine-Line Stanza', p. 115, however, would claim it for the Master.
112 The words 'As malleatoris' are probably a corruption of 'os malleatotis' – the hammerer's mouth (which is a mask of the Devil). This interpretation of Pilate's name goes as far back as Isidore of Seville. Hrabanus Maurus uses it to identify Pilate typologically with the Devil. Cf. Maltman, 'Pilate'.
113 The character of the Vice (as opposed to the word) is thus considerably older than the sixteenth century. Cf. above all pp. 149f.
114 cf. pp. 143f.
115 For more detail cf. Diller, 'Craftsmanship', esp. pp. 255f.
116 A. Hohlfeld, who coined this term ('kollektivmisterien', esp. pp. 283–5), uses it above all to describe those features which arouse awe and fear rather than laughter. The term is a happy one in that it touches on that concept of tragedy which the Middle Ages shared with the Renaissance; cf. Farnham, *Medieval Heritage*, esp. chs. III and IV: 'Falls of Princes'.
117 The distinction between the two terms, which seem to be practically synonymous in English, is an attempt to render Schadewaldt's useful distinction between *Monolog* and *Selbstgespräch*. Cf. Schadewaldt, *Monolog und Selbstgespräch*.
118 On the necessity of considering the native tradition along with classical influences cf. Sehrt, *Der dramatische Auftakt*, pp. 66, 70. Sehrt, however, considers only the entry speeches of the moralities among native influences.
119 On the York Realist cf. pp. 142ff.
120 Cf. Graf, *Miles Gloriosus*. Graf, however, derives all the braggarts of the Middle English drama from the Germanic tradition of self-glorification and regards the Unferth of *Beowulf* as their ancestor. The style of Herod in York (or in Coventry), which clearly differs from the bragging speeches of earlier dramas, is not discussed by Graf.

Notes to pages 142–5   283

121 'Jupiter' and 'Jouis' (line 2) appear as two distinct planets, Venus (line 10) is of the masculine gender. On similar gaffes among late medieval Humanists in France cf. Huizinga, *Waning*, pp. 326f.
122 On the influence of rhetoric and theological, especially Scotist, learning on the York cycle cf. Laut, *Drama Illustrating Dogma*, pp. 224ff. Laut believes that the author of the later plays was a Franciscan educated at Oxford. This is of course bound to remain speculative. But since in the fourteenth century York was one of the most important centres of learning in England and since the house of the Augustinian Hermits possessed one of the best-furnished libraries of the period, the assumption of learned influence can claim a high degree of probability. Cf. William A. Pantin, *English Church*, p. 119.
123 For a comprehensive evaluation cf. Robinson, 'York Realist'. Robinson's concern is to distinguish between 'conventional' and 'original' features in the work of the realist, without, however, discussing the 'conventions' in the light of their staging conditions. This leads him to seeing 'progress' only where the Realist approaches the modern notions of dramatic art, and he underestimates the significance of those conventions which were sacrificed to that progress. On the work of the Realist as 'affective art' see now Clifford Davidson, *From Creation to Doom*, ch. VII, esp. p. 118. On dates see ibid; p. 120.
124 Y XXXI ('Christ before Herod') 19; XXXII ('The Remorse of Judas') 14; XXXIII ('Christ before Pilate') 13; XXXIV ('The Road to Calvary') 9.
125 Robinson, 'York Realist', pp. 247f.
126 Robinson, 'York Realist', p. 246. *The Pride of Life*, which uses the same device in lines 303f, precedes the Realist by perhaps seventy years (cf. Harbage, *Annals*, p. 8, and Davis, ed., *Non-Cycle Plays*, p. c). McNeir, who sees in these scenes a portrayal of 'the self-indulgence of the upper class', attaches probably too much importance to a peripheral aspect ('Dramatic Art', p. 611). Towneley shows much more social criticism than York, but it lacks the dramaturgical necessity of this type of scene. Another aspect, namely that of characterization, is singled out by Wells: 'Caiphas, Pilate, and Herod are all of a stamp, each eating, drinking, and retiring to slumber.' ('Style', p. 369). Neither of these interpretations lacks justification; but they cannot explain why social criticism takes the form it does. This fact is best explained by the over-all stylistic tendencies of the Realist.
127 LC XXIX, 66ff, p. 273. For the poor motivation of this scene-ending cf. Weimann, 'Platea und locus', p. 335; *Shakespeare and the Popular Tradition*, p. 75.
128 Among these the most important is the well-known scene with Pilate's wife in Y XXX, which is most likely an addition by the York Realist.
129 Robinson, 'York Realist', p. 248.
130 See pp. 233ff for more extensive discussion.
131 The MS shows the date 1468 on fo. 100v at the close of the 'Purification' play, an interpolation (Block, ed., *Ludus Coventriæ*, p. xv). This possibly is the date of the last revisions, to which we owe, above all, the *Contemplacio* group about which more will have to be said later (Chambers, *Close*, p. 48). Cameron and Kahrl prefer to apply the date only to the Marian part of the

cycle. According to them, the revision of the *Passion Plays* took place in the 1470s (Cameron and Kahrl, 'Staging the N-Town Cycle', p. 128). Spector's conclusions (*Genesis*, p. 25) are similar.
132 On the metres of N-Town see now Spector, *Genesis*, with a succinct survey of earlier research (ibid., pp. 270–9).
133 Cf. Swenson, *Inquiry*; Craig, *ERD*, pp. 247–59; Cameron and Kahrl, 'N-Town Plays at Lincoln', 'Staging the N-Town Cycle'; Spector, *Genesis*, pp. 69f, 141.
134 Cf. Swenson, *Inquiry*, p. 16.
135 For the term cf. Ott, 'Personengestaltung', pp. 25ff; see above, p. 120.
136 After his prayer Noah says, clearly turning toward the audience: 'Noe serys my name is knowe' (LC IV, 1, p. 35). Similarly Abraham: 'Abraham my name is kydde' (LC V, 9, p. 43).
137 Greg, *Miracle Cycles*, p. 141, believes that they were taken over from another cycle. See also Spector, *Genesis*, p. 69.
138 For a list of these plays see Spector, 'Composition', n. 11, and *Genesis*, p. 29.
139 Cf. Righter, *Shakespeare*, pp. 21f.
140 Swenson, *Inquiry*, pp. 32f, calls it 'late but not ecclesiastical'. This, though rather vague, seems acceptable.
141 *Allegory of Evil*, pp. 180f. See now also Kahrl, *Traditions*, p. 78.
142 On an extensive analysis of this speech form cf. Spivack, *Allegory of Evil*, *passim*, who however puts more emphasis on the psychological basis than on the linguistic form of the Vices' speeches. For this see now Hentschel, *Die Gestalt des Vice*. Most valuable is Happé, 'The Vice'.
143 Cf. Happé, 'The Vice', p. 19. Happé mentions 'the devils and villains of the Mystery Cycles' as forerunners of the Vice (p. 17) but does not specifically refer to LC XIV in his checklist.
144 Eccles, ed., p. xxxviii.
145 Eckhardt, *Die lustige Person*, pp. 102, 116; Weimann, 'Rede-Konventionen', esp. pp. 120–30.
146 Cf. the references in Habicht, *Studien* ('Einleitung').
147 Smart, 'The *Castle of Perseverance*'; Harbage, *Annals*, p. 8: 1405–25. Eccles, ed., *The Macro Plays*, p. xi: 1400–25. According to Jacob Bennett the largest part of the play, including the passages which will be quoted in the text, was written before 1398 ('The "Castle of Perseverance"'; 'Linguistic Study').
148 Bloomfield, *Seven Deadly Sins*, p. 231.
149 The following excerpt may serve for comparison with the quotations from LC XIV:

> ʒa, lowde lesyngys lacchyd in les,
> Of talys vntrewe is al my mende.
>   Mannys bane abowtyn I bere.
> I wyl þat ʒe wetyn, all þo þat ben here,
> For I am knowyn, fer and nere,
> I am þe Werldys meesengere,
>   My name is Bacbytere.
>
> (*Castle*, lines 653–9, quoted from Eccles, ed., *The Macro Plays*)

150 Cf. Owst, *Literature and Pulpit*, pp. 450–8, esp. 452. Especially interesting among the rich literature quoted there is *Ancrene Riwle*, whose depiction of the backbiter could almost be used as a blueprint for the greatest of them all,

Iago: 'Ac þe latere [bacbitare] cumeð forð al an oþer wise. and is wurse ueond þen ðe oþer. auh under ureondes huckel. weorpeð adun þet heaued. and foð on uor te siken er he owiht sigge. and makeð drupie chere. bisaumpleð longe abuten uor te beon þe betere ileued.' (Day, ed., *Ancrene Riwle*, p. 38. The tironic note has been expanded into 'and'.)

151 Cf. e.g. Envy in *Piers Plowman*, B-Text, Passus V, lines 84ff (ed. A. V. C. Schmidt, London: Dent, 1978, pp. 44–6).
152 Cf. Bryant, 'Function', p. 341, see also Greg, *Miracle Cycles*, p. 130 n. Spector, *Genesis*, p. 122, is slightly more cautious.
153 The lines of the prologue are counted separately by Block (*Ludus Coventriae*).
154 E.g. *Hyckescorner*, lines 309ff, 333ff; *Kynge Johan*, lines 439ff, 1212ff (Manly, ed., *Pre-Shakespearean Drama*, vol. 1); *Lusty Juventus* (Dodsley, ed., *Old English Plays*, pp. 65f); *Appius and Virginia* (Dodsley, ed., *Old English Plays*, p. 118).
155 More on this in the sections on 'The Assumption of the Virgin' and Contemplacio, below.
156 On this horse's significance for the staging of the cycle cf. the introduction to Rose, ed. and trans., *The Wakefield Mystery Plays*, p. 36.
157 A comparable example occurs in T XXII, 40ff, in a passage which is perhaps still later than the work of the Wakefield Master; cf. p. 137 of this book.
158 See esp. Chambers, *Close*, p. 51.
159 Cf. Owst, *Literature and Pulpit, passim*.
160 On the dramaturgical function and the theological contents of this prologue cf. Benkovitz, 'Notes'.
161 LC VIII (pp. 62f, 'The Conception of Mary'), IX (p. 71, 'Mary in the Temple'), XI (pp. 97f, 'The Parliament of Heaven'), XIII (pp. 117f, 121f, 'The Visit to Elizabeth'), XXIX (p. 271, 'The Passion Play II'). Plays VIII-XIII form a unit which is often called 'the *Contemplacio* group' or 'the Marian plays' (Swenson, *Inquiry*, p. 26; Block, ed., *Ludus Coventriae*, p. xx; Chambers, *Close*, p. 48) and which has been edited as *The Mary Play from the N-town Manuscript* by Peter Meredith. Swenson (*Inquiry*, p. 26, note 1, and p. 51) doubts the common origin of Contemplacio in LC XXIX with the '*Contemplacio* group'. This view is strongly supported by Meredith's analysis of the manuscript; cf. Meredith, ed., *Passion Play*, pp. 1–2. For differences in audience-address see below.
162 For this episode cf. Traver, *Four Daughters*. For more recent literature on this episode, especially in Continental drama, cf. Wright, *Vengeance*, p. 175, n. 47.
163 Greg, *Miracle Cycles*, p. 125. Greg's harsh judgment is implicitly rejected also by Forrest, 'Role of the Expositor Contemplacio', pp. 60–76.
164 Cf. Hardison, *Christian Rite*, Essay II.
165 LC XIII, 23–42 (pp. 116f).
166 See Fichte, *Expository Voices*, pp. 112–17. Fichte, however, distinguishes insufficiently between the two figures going by the name of Contemplacio.
167 Forrest, 'Role of the Expositor Contemplacio', p. 65, describes his attitude toward the public as one of 'benevolent authority'.
168 This is overlooked by Forrest, who emphasizes too exclusively the homiletic character of Contemplacio's part.

169 Cf. also the opening LC VIII, 3–8, 14f (p. 62).
170 For these devices cf. Tilgner, *Die 'aureate terms'*.
171 This view is reported though not shared by Chambers, *Stage*, vol. 2, p. 145, and *Close*, p. 49.
172 Swenson, *Inquiry*, p. 26, note 1, and p. 51.
173 Greg, *Miracle Cycles*, p. 142.
174 E.g. *compiled breffly* (line 11, p. 62), *in fewe wordys talkyd þat it xulde nat be tedyous* (line 14, p. 62), *breffnes of tyme consyderynge* (line 4, p. 71), *Eche on wolde suffyce ffor An hool day* (line 8, p. 81).
175 Cf. Craig, *ERD*, p. 259; juxtaposition of the two texts in Falke, 'Quellen', p. 93.
176 As far as they occur at all, they appear to be a kind of religious *termini technici* which belong to the person or object so described as of right: *gloryous* (line 2), *seynt* (line 3), *holy* (line 16), *devouthly* (line 17).
177 On a possible relationship between N-town and the Digby Plays see Patch, 'Ludus Coventriae'. That the Contemplacio group and the Digby *Massacre* originally belonged together is an attractive proposition, but hardly capable of proof. To explain the similarities between the plays it is sufficient to point to their common East Midland origin.
178 Both plays quoted from the edition by Baker, Murphy, and Hall, eds., *Late Medieval Plays*.
179 Cf. the quotation given in p. 156.

INTRA-DRAMATIC SPEECHES

1 In Daneš's typology this is a 'text with constant theme' ('Typus mit einem durchlaufenden Thema'). Cf. Daneš, 'Textstruktur', p. 76.
2 Mohr, 'Einfache Formen', vol. 1, p. 323, right column.
3 For the following observations I am indebted to Daneš, 'Textstruktur'. I have endeavoured to keep the linguistic terminology to a minimum.
4 þerfore me rewis þat I þe worlde began.   (Y XLVII, 8)
   þerfore no lenger, sekirlye,
   Thole will I þare wikkidnesse.   (Y XLVII, 47f)
5 It appears in 'most fifteenth-century literature' (Fry, 'Unity', p. 569).
6 Craig, *ERD*, p. 225, and Lyle, *Original Identity*, pp. 53, 68ff, believe that T I is the original first play of York. Beadle is moved by the 'archaic flavour' of Y I to place it at 'the turn of the fourteenth century, making it one of the oldest parts of the York cycle' ('Poetry, Theology and Drama', p. 213).
7 On *repetitio* cf. Laut, 'Drama Illustrating Dogma', p. 224 and *passim*.
8 Smith's reading seems preferable to Beadle's 'þis warke his to my pay / Righit will, withoutyn wyne' (lines 49f). But since *wyne* rhymes with *clene*, *sene* and *mene*, it should probably read *wene* ('doubt'). The expression *withowten wene* occurs, e.g., Y XI, 104.
9 Cf. Cl. Davidson, *From Creation to Doom*.
10 On Lydgate cf. Tilgner, *Die 'aureate terms'*.
11 In a more general context this has already been observed by Wells, 'Style'.
12 This should not be taken to detract from the religious content of the play; cf. Schless, 'The Comic Element'. In contrast to the York plays, *Processus Noe* relies for its religious impact not on theological didaxis, but on the

presentation of a reality in which human disorder and divine order correspond with each other in highly complex ways. Cf. also Nelson, 'Currents', and Gardner, 'Imagery and Allusion'.
13 In other cycles He avoids this by sending an angel: LC IV, 118ff (p. 39) and Newcastle, lines 39ff.
14 Cf. Diller, 'Craftsmanship', pp. 247f. Clopper has established beyond reasonable doubt that Ch I did not enter the cycle before 1505, the most likely date being between 1521 and 1532: 'Chester Cycle', pp. 228, 231, 243; see also Travis, *Dramatic Design*, pp. 45f.
15 Craig, *ERD*, p. 183.
16 Traditionally the first person of the Trinity is identified as God's power, the second as his wisdom, the third as his love. Cf. Pseudo-Bonaventura, 'Meditationes Vitae Christi', p. 512.
17 Cf. the stage direction at the beginning of Ch III: 'And firste in some high place – or in the clowdes, if it may be – God speaketh unto Noe'. The same SD appears in Latin in MS H (cf. Lumiansky and Mills, p. 42).
18 This is also true of the bragging speeches which in Towneley reflect the character rather than the rank of the tyrant; in this they differ from the 'Trauerspielelemente' (Hohlfeld, 'kollektivmisterien') in the York Plays.
19 The only (apparent) exception is the Harrowing of Hell, which allows prayer-like speeches, although Christ is the only person of the Trinity to put in an apearance. But here he has already given up his human shape and can thus be prayed to.
20 Ch IV, 17ff; Ch VIII, 1ff; Ch XI, 1ff. All three plays were written under the influence of the *Stanzaic Life of Christ*. Cf. Foster, ed., *Life of Christ*, pp. xxviii–xliii; also Wilson, '"Life of Christ" and the Chester Plays'. Foster's opinion that the *Stanzaic Life* was familiar already to the author of the original Chester cycle (p. xlii), has been convincingly refuted by Wilson.
21 Cf., in the above quotation, line 426. Furthermore Ch IV, 18 ('that endinge ne begininge hase'); VIII, 2 ('that rules the people of Judee'); IX, 2 ('to honour thee wee may bee fayne') and 6 ('that for mankynde would suffer payne'); XVII, 2 ('our comfort and our counselour').
22 Cf. also Ch IV, 21–4: VIII, 7–12: XVII, 9–16.
23 Ch II, 437; IV, 29: VIII, 13; XI, 19.
24 Ten Brink, *English Literature*, vol. 2, p. 244: 'In *Jacob and Esau* the dramatic art is still of a low standard.' As was shown pp. 88f, this 'low standard' is largely due to the treatment of time and space.
25 Cf. references in notes 22 and 23.
26 It is true, however, that Isaac never learns that the command comes from God (cf. Woolf, 'Effect of Typology', p. 806). But since the Towneley Abraham play is about Abraham's obedience, not Isaac's, this flaw is perhaps less serious than Woolf thinks.
27 On the relationship between the two plays see above, pp. 134f.
28 We call them opening prayers although they begin 'scenes' rather than plays (T XVI, 85ff; Y XVI, 57). In the case of Y XVI it is virtually certain that the prayer originally stood at the beginning of the Goldsmiths' pageant (Beadle, ed., *York Plays*, p. 429). See Beadle for justification of the 'convenient though anachronistic' term 'scene'.
29 'I loue þe' (Y XVI, 57): 'I worshippe þe' (Y XVI, 70).

30 The First King begins with almost the same words as Noah:
   That lord þat leves ay-lastand lyff,
   I loue þe euer with hart and hande,   (Y IX, 1f)
   A, lorde that levis, euerelastande light,
   I loue þe evir with harte and hande,   (Y XVI, 57f)
31 Craig, ed., *Coventry Plays*, p. 87. The Magi play is lines 475–900 of the *Shearmen and Taylors' Pageant*.
32 Cf. Horstmann, ed., *The Three Kings of Cologne*, p. 38.
33 Craig, ed., *Coventry Plays*, p. xxv.
34 Craig, *ERD*, p. 295.
35 Craig, *ERD*, p. 295.
36 For the 'Schaubild' in late medieval narrative cf. Wolpers, *Heiligenlegende*, p. 33.
37 Lyle assumes that these two plays are related (*Original Identity*, pp. 74f). On the audience-address in T XIX cf. p. 122.
38 The validity of our comparison does not – as it also did not in the case of the Magi plays – depend on the two plays being genetically related. We are not concerned with the pre-history of a specific York play, but with the respective solutions that were found for the same dramaturgical task, once in the prayer, once in the audience-address.
39 Cf. p. 173.
40 Smith's edition had even enclosed lines 29–49 in quotation marks.
41 In the manuscript, this prayer is prefaced, perhaps characteristically, 'Introitus abrahe'.
42 Similarly LC IV, 5f; VI, 9–16.
43 The literature on this field is very rich. Let it suffice therefore to quote only three studies: Habicht, *Die Gebärde*; Blaicher, *Das Weinen*; Roeder, *Die Gebärde*.
44 Compare H. Brinkmann, *Wesen und Formen*, pp. 81ff. But see Panofsky's ground-breaking discovery of a 'naturalism not as yet wholly secular' (*Early Netherlandish Painting*, vol. 1, p. 142) which has inspired, *inter alios*, the drama criticism of L.J. Ross and Clifford Davidson. Davidson in particular stresses the importance of nominalism for late-medieval affective piety (*From Creation to Doom*, ch. 7).
45 E.g. Chambers, *Close*, p. 32; Waterhouse, *Non-Cycle Plays*, pp. liiif.
46 Among others: Salzer, *Beiworte und Sinnbilder Mariens*; Thien, *Marienklagen*; Mueller, *Mittelenglische*; Patterson, *Penitential Lyric*; Wolpers, On *planctus* and drama see especially Sticca, 'Literary Genesis', *Planctus Mariae*; Taylor, 'The "Mariae"'; Taylor, 'Relation'; Thien, *passim*.
   Thien, 'Marienklagen', *passim*.
47 Prosser, *Drama and Religion*.
48 Ibid., p. 58; cf. p. 2 of this book.
49 Cf. Hardin Craig's review in *Spec.* 37 (1962), 295–8.
50 Zappert, *Ausdruck des geistigen Schmerzes*, pp. 94ff.
51 The importance of the emotional, as distinct from the typological, impact is emphasized by Munson, 'Typology'.
52 Cf. the very succinct survey of Marian piety in Meier, *Die Gestalt Marias*, esp. pp. 147ff.

53 This is true in particular of T XXII and XXIII; cf. G.C. Taylor, 'The Planctus Mariae"', p. 625.
54 The shared lines are (Y XXXIV before the slash, T XXII after): 106–15/260–7, 126–35/268–75, 190–9/348–55, 216–19/356–7, 226–9/358–9, 230–49/360–75, 260–99/376–407. Cf. *in extenso* Frampton, 'York Play XXXIV'.
55 Frampton, 'York Play XXXIV', believes that Y XXXIV, sts. 1–9 (= lines 16–105), which contain the dialogue between the *milites*, are later than the rest of the play.
56 The 'profound humanity of this simple question' has been justly praised by McNeir ('Dramatic Art', p. 617). But unfortunately McNeir recognizes here only an isolated 'moment of pathos', thus failing to see the dialogic-dramatic embedding of the question.
57 He is speaking to the three Marys.
58 For arguments that would extend the Master's canon to such deviant forms see Stevens, 'Nine-Line Stanza', esp. pp. 114ff.
59 Carey, *Wakefield Group*, p. 239: 'One is tempted to conclude that the Wakefield Author was experimenting here with his stanza.' This hypothesis is weakened by the strongly Northern colouring of these stanzas, which contrasts with the more Midlands forms of the Wakefield Master. Cf. Trusler, 'Wakefield Playwright', esp. p. 19; Stevens, 'Towneley Plays', *passim*.
60 Gayley, *Plays*, p. 165.
61 Cf. Davidson, *From Creation to Doom*, pp. 127f, and Woolf, 'Effect of Typology', p. 265.
62 See esp. pp. 143f.
63 Line references in this discussion will be to Deimling/Matthews before, to Lumiansky/Mills after the slash. To preserve uniformity, quotations will be from Deimling/Matthews throughout.
64 Greg, *Miracle Cycles*, pp. 34ff. Travis, *Dramatic Design*, pp. 186–91, quotes from H, but ignores the difference between the versions.
65 For instance, Joseph of Arimathia's and Nicodemus' journey from Golgotha to Pilate is introduced more carefully in H (Ch XVI, 817–36(DM)/Ch XVIA, 412–23(LM)). Cf. Deimling, Introduction, p. xxv.
66 G.C. Taylor, 'The "Planctus Mariae"', p. 625.
67 On the further distribution of the second scene cf. Meier, *Die Gestalt Marias*, pp. 207ff.
68 In contrast to the tradition of the Apocrypha, which we find in York and Towneley; cf. p. 183. On the unusual character of this encounter between Mary Magdalene and the Mother of Jesus see Vriend, *Blessed Virgin Mary*, p. 126, and G.C. Taylor, 'The "Planctus Mariae"', p. 624, n.2.
69 On the motif of Mary rebuking Jesus and its origins in medieval preaching cf. now Briscoe, 'Preaching', pp. 165ff. The same motif was identified by Briscoe in T XXIII (p. 165).
70 Furnivall, ed., *The Digby Plays*, pp. 169ff.
71 Craig, *ERD*, p. 331. For extensive discussion see Baker and Murphy, 'Digby Plays'. See also Baker and Murphy, eds., *Digby Facsimiles*, p. xvi; and Baker, Murphy and Hall, eds., *Late Medieval Plays*, p. lxxv.
72 Baker, Murphy and Hall, eds., *Late Medieval Plays*, p. lxxv. Our line

numbering will follow this edition, with CB for the *Burial* and CR for the *Resurrection*.
73 See Baker, Murphy and Hall, eds., *Late Medieval Plays*, pp. lxxvii–lxxxviii, esp. lxxxviii.
74 Chambers, *Stage*, Vol. 2, p. 129.
75 Taylor, 'The "Planctus Mariae"', p. 636.
76 Baker, Murphy and Hall, eds., *Late Medieval Plays*, p. lxxxix, n.2, quote two versions of this planctus, with further references.
77 Emphasis added.
78 On the somewhat homespun middle-class character of many Marian laments of the fifteenth century see Wolpers, 'Marienlyrik', p. 39.
79 Chambers, *Close*, p. 37; Pollard, 'Introduction', p. xxix; Prosser, *Drama and Religion*, pp. 92ff; Hemingway, ed., *English Nativity Plays*, pp. xviii and xlvii.
80 Cf. especially Woolf, 'Effect of Typology', p. 816, who calls this play 'in every way inferior to the others'. Against this position see Munson, 'Typology'.
81 The former existence of this convention in York may be inferred. The second part of T X has frequently been regarded as the original version of Y XIII: Hohlfeld, 'kollektivmisterien', pp. 219f; Cl. Davidson, *From Creation to Doom*, p. 156; Lyle, *Original Identity*, pp. 2, 34f; Craig, *ERD*, p. 216. Even Chambers, a decided opponent of the theory of the common origin of the two cycles, has to admit the similarities between the two plays (*Close*, p. 36). Against these see Hemingway, ed., *English Nativity Plays*, pp. xliif, and Prosser, *Drama and Religion*, p. 92, who regard Y XIII as the original. For a discussion of Prosser see notes 88 and 92.
82 Prosser, *Drama and Religion*, p. 93.
83 Cf. pp. 77f of this book.
84 This aspect is elaborated by Weimann, '*Platea* und *locus*', pp. 344f; Weimann, *Shakespeare and the Popular Tradition*, pp. 81f (with reference to the corresponding scene in the N-Town cycle).
85 Chambers, *Close*, p. 27.
86 Cf. n. 81.
87 Pollard, 'Introduction', p. xxvi; Lyle, *Original Identity*, p. 96f; Gayley, *Plays*, p. 134, n.1; Charles Davidson, *Studies*, p. 130. Davidson (*Studies*, p. 261), Gayley (*Plays*, pp. 153ff), Greg (*Miracle Cycles*, pp. 7f) and Chambers (*Close*, pp. 29f) regard, however, the York *Abraham* as part of the oldest stratum of that cycle, but with the exception of Greg they use metrical arguments which have been refuted by Lyle, *Original Identity*, pp. 30–46. Greg, according to his own words, bases his judgment on 'literary' arguments. At the beginning (*c.* 1350 in his opinion!) he sees 'a simple didactic cycle, carefully composed in elaborate stanzas and withal rather dull'. He thus presupposes what needs to be proved: that the earliest stage of the cycle was marked by didacticism.
88 In contrast to Prosser (*Drama and Religion*, p. 93, cf. p. 195 of this study) we believe that York grounds the telling of the pre-history more firmly in Joseph's present emotion than does Towneley.
89 Lyle, *Original Identity*, pp. 96f; similarly, although with the opposite value judgment: Woolf, 'Effect of Typology', esp. pp. 806, 816.
90 He is, for instance, slightly more than thirty years old (Y X, 82). That Isaac's fear of death should be limited to his 'flesh' is also reminiscent of Christ (e.g.

Y XXVIII, 2). On typology in general: Woolf, 'Effect of Typology'; Williams, 'Typology'; Th. Stemmler, *LFGS*, *passim*, and 'Typological Transfer'; Munson, 'Typology'. See now also Diller, 'Typologie'.
91 Kolve, in a very careful analysis (p.74), points out that the sacrifice of Isaac will effect the salvation of mankind only indirectly, that it is above all the prerequisite and not merely the *figura* of Christ's death. Note in passing the remarkable coherence of soteriological thinking in this cycle: Abraham's sacrifice is still remembered by God in the prologue to the *Annunciacio*: 'To abraham I am in dett/To safe hym and his gett' (T X, 41f).
92 Prosser rightly points out the inconsistencies and redundancies in the York *Joseph's Trouble about Mary* (*Drama and Religion*, p. 92). But these are explained more naturally by York being a derivative from Towneley than by the reverse relationship which she supposes.
93 Robinson, 'York Realist', p. 250; Weimann, 'Realismus', p. 112, n. 4; Weimann, *Shakespeare and the Popular Tradition*, p. 276, n. 70.
94 On the realism and present relevance of the medieval sermon cf. Owst, *Literature and Pulpit*, ch. I, esp. pp. 24ff.
95 This may be influenced by legendary traditions concerning the curse on Judas' begetting and birth. What characterizes the dramatist's art is that he does not pedantically enumerate these details but makes Judas merely allude to them.
96 Cf. Reese, 'Alliterative Verse', p. 660.
97 Cf. Laut, 'Drama Illustrating Dogma', p. 165, on figures of *sermo sublimis* in this monologue.
98 Cf. Chambers, *Close*, p. 27: 'The dramatic action is generally simple and straightforward, without much attempt to exploit the psychological possibilities of the themes dealt with.'
99 For the refutation of these theses cf. Salter, *Medieval Drama*, pp. 32–42; Stemmler, 'Datierung', and especially Clopper, 'Chester Cycle'.
100 E.g. Chambers, *Close*, p. 27; Craig, *ERD*, pp. 168, 180, 195. Heavy didacticism is also considered a sign of early composition by Harper, *Comparison*, p. 65. Cf. the contrary opinion of Severs, 'Relationship'.
101 Craig, *ERD*, p. 195.
102 Authoritative edition: Davis, ed., *Non-Cycle Plays*, pp. 43–57. Discussion of the manuscript ibid., pp. lviii–lxiii. The Brome commonplace book has been edited by Smith, ed., *Commonplace Book*. The manuscript of the commonplace book is now in the Yale University Library; see Davis, ed., *Non-Cycle Plays*, p. lix.
103 Smith, ed., 'Abraham and Isaac'.
104 Harper, *Comparison*, esp. p. 65.
105 Severs, 'Relationship'. The article contains an extensive survey of previous studies of the question. Davis, ed., *Non-Cycle Plays*, p. lxiv, emphatically agrees with Severs.
106 Severs, 'Relationship', p. 140.
107 A good example of such preconceived notions is Craig, *ERD*, p. 309, who without mentioning Severs decrees: 'The Brome Abraham and Isaac is obviously a skilfully developed version of the Chester Abraham and Isaac. The matter would never have been in doubt if scholars had been willing to allow for the continual revisions of mystery plays that went on throughout

their career.' Craig is here practising an 'evolutionism' which he pretends to fight in the introduction to his book.

108 Latest edition in Davis, ed., *Non-Cycle Plays*, pp. 32–42. Since the play was discovered in a manuscript of Trinity College, Dublin, it is sometimes referred to as the 'Dublin' Abraham play. But the manuscript belongs clearly to Northampton. This was recognized already by the first editor, Rudolf Brotanek, 'Abraham und Isaak'. Davis, ed., *Non-Cycle Plays*, pp. xlvii–lvii, refers to the 'Northampton Abraham'. For both plays cf. Woolf, 'Effect of Typology'.

109 It is a measure of the Chester reviser's underdeveloped sense of drama that this passage (lines 258–85 in Ch IV) should be particularly rich in corruptions (cf. Severs, 'Relationship', p. 147). Instead of a gradual rise we get a repetition of effective details without regard for the context. E.g. Isaac inquires twice about the purpose of the drawn sword (Ch IV, lines 265ff, 277ff).

110 Brotanek, ed., 'Abraham und Isaak'; Craig, *ERD*, pp. 308f.

111 Waterhouse, ed., *Non-Cycle Plays*, p. lii.

112 Rothschild, ed., *Mistère*, 9, II, pp. 7ff (lines 9516ff). Cf. also Davis, ed., *Non-Cycle Plays*, p. liii.

113 There is only one exception: the *Famuli* in Y X. This play shows first beginnings of an emotional atmosphere (cf. p. 95), which however does not attain to the level of Nh. On the lack of concreteness in the narrative style of the Bible see E. Auerbach's excursus on Abraham and Isaac in *Mimesis*, pp. 7–13.

114 Cf. Craig, *ERD*, p. 308. There is no indication of craft performances in Northampton (Brotanek, ed., 'Abraham und Isaak', p. 25; Chambers, *Stage*, II, p. 386; Craig, *ERD*, p. 308.)

115 See above, n. 102.

116 Chambers, *Stage*, II, pp. 255f; Baskervill, 'Dramatic Aspects', p. 83. Kahrl is too categorical: 'It is thus extremely unlikely that the text of the [Brome] play of Abraham and Isaac as we have it was copied out for someone intending to stage the play.'(*Traditions*, p. 158).

117 On this see now Donald C. Baker: 'Reflections'.

118 Jean Fouquet's miniature of the martyrium of St Apollonia, which is contained in that book, has been thoroughly analysed by Southern, *Medieval Theatre*, pp. 91–107.

119 Cf. esp. the chapter on Joseph, Prosser, *Drama and Religion*, pp. 96–102. But compare also our criticism pp. 213 and 216.

120 Cf. also lines 92 and 95 quoted above.

121 It is of course true that the age ("Thyrty ʒere and more sum dele') fulfils primarily a typological function (cf. Woolf, 'Effect of Typology'), but it is peculiar for York to establish the typology not merely by the bald juxtaposition of the two father–son relationships but by adding such specific details, which are avoided in a severer play like LC V. For a fuller discussion see Diller, 'Typologie'.

122 This is a particularly clear example of the tendency of medieval poetry to regard the generic as more 'real' than the specific (Brinkmann, *Dichtkunst*, pp. 81ff).

123 Spector, 'Composition', p. 65 and n. 11; cf. Craig, *ERD*, p. 250, and, with a few minor modifications which can be neglected here, Cameron and Kahrl, 'Staging the N-Town Cycle', p. 155.
124 Block, ed., *Ludus Coventriae*, p. 6, lines 170–82.
125 Block, ed., *Ludus Coventriae*, pp. xxi and 82, lines 14–17. This fact has caused Meredith to excise the Joseph play from his reconstruction of the Mary play and to relegate it to an Appendix. See Meredith, ed., *The Mary Play*, p. 124, for further details.
126 Block, ed., *Ludus Coventriae*, p. 108, n. 4. See also p. xxi.
127 For the blanks cf. Block, ed., *Ludus Coventriae*, pp. 108 and 155. See also Block's note 4, p. 115, which suggests that the scribe had estimated the space required for LC XII: 'The writing on Ff. 71, 71v, and 72 [of the following play, LC XIII] is slightly less cramped.' It seems that the scribe was particularly anxious to fit LC XII into the space available. Cameron and Kahrl, 'Staging the N-Town Cycle', p. 155, following Hemingway, ed., *English Nativity Plays*, p. xxxv, believe that LC XII was at first left out on purpose. It is difficult to see why in that case the scribe should have left one page and four folios blank, starting his next play in the midst of a quire.
128 Greg, *Miracle Cycles*, p. 126.
129 Ibid., p. 129.
130 Outside LC XII it occurs only in the 'Purification' (LC XIX), which like our play is indebted to Love's *Mirrour* and which bears the date 1468. On the metre cf. Swenson, *Inquiry*, p. 4; Greg, *Miracle Cycles*, p. 129, and Spector, *Genesis*, p. 104; on the source Block, ed., *Ludus Coventriae*, p. xxx and *passim*.
131 Prosser, *Drama and Religion*, pp. 96–102; Weimann, '*Platea* und *locus*', pp. 342–6; Weimann, *Shakespeare and the Popular Tradition*, pp. 81–3.
132 Weimann, '*Platea* und *locus*', p. 344; *Shakespeare and the Popular Tradition*, p. 81.
133 Prosser, who concludes from this passage that the N-Town Joseph is being depicted as particularly repulsive (*Drama and Religion*, p. 98: 'a cantankerous lout, now wallowing in self-pity'), overlooks the fact that the Joseph of Y XIII (lines 248f, 253ff) reacts quite similarly. But the York Joseph, according to Prosser, is not as subtly characterized.
134 E.g. T X, 344: 'I rewe full sore.'
135 Cf., above all: 'The playwright wished to establish in the most vivid manner possible the grace of Mary and the divine power of repentance. The more sinful Joseph is made, the greater the miracle.' (Prosser, *Drama and Religion*, p. 102.)
136 Prosser, *Drama and Religion*, pp. 100f.
137 Cf. p. 18 of this study for this and for a similar relationship in high medieval painting. Cf. further the literature given there. In the schema R = represented figure ('dramatis persona'), S = spectator.
138 But cf. also the section on the *Stella* procession, pp. 28f.
139 Young, *DMC*, vol. 1, pp. 385f (MS thirteenth century). This hymn is the most widely used of all *Visitatio* laments. The same tripartite division appears in many other plays.
140 This refers to the choral antiphon *Maria Magdalena*.

141 Young, *DMC*, vol. 1, pp. 381f.
142 Ibid., pp. 375, 386, 390.
143 Wells finds that the Three Marys scenes have always preserved their 'liturgical' style ('Style', p. 505). This statement is acceptable if it means simply that there are liturgical reminiscences in these scenes which are absent from others; but our analysis also shows how utterly limited the analogies between the two genres must of necessity remain.
144 Only the Latin-English Shrewsbury Fragment retains the first person plural (see Davis, ed., *Non-Cycle Plays*, pp. 3f; Young, *DMC*, vol. 2, 517f).
145 On this technique of the 'trialogue' in Ch cf. Haller, *Technik des Dialogs*, p. 13.
146 On the exception of the so-called *Digby Resurrection* see p. 224.
147 Wilson, '"Life of Christ" and the Chester Plays', p. 421; Foster, ed., *Stanzaic Life*, pp. xl-xlii.
148 Cf. Kretzmann, *Liturgical Element*, p. 148.
149 Matt. 28.2ff and Mark 16.5 have one angel or young man, whereas Luke 24.4. mentions two persons.
150 The following rephrases a too sweeping statement of the original, thanks to criticism by Schmidt, *Kunst des Dialogs*, p. 66.
151 In line 523 the speaker's name ('primus rex') has been omitted, clearly by scribal error.
152 For the concept of 'andachtsbildartig', cf. Wolpers, *Heiligenlegende*, pp. 30ff. Wolpers also discusses the justification of transferring this term from the history of art to the narrative style of high and late medieval legends.
153 This is the literal translation of one of Weimann's chapter headings (*Shakespeare und die Tradition des Volkstheaters*). In the English translation it has become 'flexible dramaturgy' (*Shakespeare and the Popular Tradition*).
154 See especially the work of Gayley.
155 Compare the excellent survey in Prosser, *Drama and Religion*, pp. 3–12.
156 McNeir, 'Dramatic Art', pp. 614, 623.
157 Craig, *ERD*, p. 6.
158 Prosser, *Drama and Religion*, esp. p. 85.
159 Craig, Review of Prosser, *Drama and Religion*, pp. 295–8.
160 Rossiter, *English Drama*, pp. 73f and *passim*.
161 See, above all, Warning, *Funktion und Struktur*; Weimann, *Shakespeare and the Popular Tradition*, esp. pp. 62f. For an attempt to refute Rossiter by close textual analysis see Diller, 'Medium', and 'Torturers'.
162 Watt, 'Dramatic Unity'; F.J. Thompson, 'Unity'; Lumiansky, 'Comedy and Theme'; Schless, 'The Comic Element'; W.M. Manly, 'Shepherds and Prophets'; Morgan, '"High Fraud"'; A.H. Nelson, 'Currents'; Gardner, 'Theme and Irony'; Davidson, 'Unity'. Ross, 'Symbol and Structure', p. 203. Cf. Mack, 'Reconsideration', p. 81: 'What penetrates the deception is an overflowing kindness.'
163 Curtius, *European Literature*, pp. 417–35; White, 'Medieval Mirth'. Cf. the latter author's subsequent study, 'Elusive Boundaries'.
164 Young, *DMC*, vol. 2, p. 238; cf. also n. 175.
165 Eckhardt, *Die lustige Person*, pp. 53–6; Rudwin, *Der Teufel*, pp. 7–11. A lack of understanding for this kind of laughter may have misled Cushman into

Notes to pages 225–30

denying any comic feature to the mystery devils: *The Devil and the Vice*, pp. 16f.
166 Kolve, *Corpus Christi*, pp. 137f, 180ff.
167 Janicka, *Comic Elements*, p. 13.
168 Warning, 'Ritus', 96: 'eine Antwort auf das von der je bestimmenden Lebens- und Daseinsverfassung als das Entgegenstehende Ausgegrenzte, und zwar genauer: eine positive Antwort, d.h. eine solche, durch welche dieses Ausgegrenzte in seiner positiven Zugehörigkeit zum Lebensganzen ergriffen, bestätigt und gegen das ausgrenzende Prinzip ausgespielt wird.'
169 Rossiter, *passim*; Janicka, *Comic Elements*, pp. 50ff; Weimann, *Shakespeare and the Popular Tradition*, p. 62.
170 In a production by the Lincoln Players which the author saw in the summer of 1986 this line (with the accompanying noise) was repeated at least on two more occasions. Needless to say, the tone of the play was altered considerably.
171 The mystery devils (apart from Tutivillus and his companions in those parts of the Towneley Judgment Play which were interpolated by the Wakefield Master) thus behave very much like those of many martyrs' legends when they have to recognize that their efforts at seducing the saint have failed; cf. Wolpers, *Heiligenlegende*, pp. 25, 114, 122 *et passim*.
172 *Paradise Lost*, I, 263 (*The Works of John Milton*, New York: Columbia University Press 1931, Vol. II, Part i, p. 17).
173 Eckardt, *Die lustige Person*, pp. 137f.
174 Kolve, *Corpus Christi*, p. 137f.
175 The liturgical drama contains an important example of this pious *Schadenfreude*: In the *Presentatio Mariae* by Philippe de Mézières Synagoga flees in tears and is scoffed by the people after Mary has been received into the temple (Young, *DMC*, vol. 2, 238). Immediately after Lucifer enters howling (*ululantem*) and *finget se timorosum et trementem*. This suggests that the quarrelling of the mystery devils is merely the dialogical representation of that wretchedness which de Mézières represents only in gesture.
176 Cf. above all Zutt, 'Rede bei Hartmann', p. 69; see also Faral, *Les arts poétiques*, p. 97, p. 236 n. 13, p. 63 n. 13.
177 For Cain's self-righteousness cf. Ch II, 549–52, and Prosser, *Drama and Religion*, pp. 72f. In her anxiousness to claim a high degree of homiletic efficacy for the Chester Cain, Prosser fails to see that his singularly arrogant 'prayer' hardly allows the audience to recognize themselves in him. No medieval Christian would ever have dreamt of uttering such a prayer, although there must have been many whose prayers, judged from the objective point of view of the homilist, amounted to such arrogance.
178 With his arguments, which may appeal to natural reason, Cain does, however, deny the basis of medieval social thinking: he replaces the 'law of love' which ought to govern all relationships between master and servant, God and man, by the 'law of debt and obligation'. Cf. Gardner, 'Theme and Irony', esp. p. 516.
179 Weimann, *Shakespeare and the Popular Tradition*, pp. 139f.
180 *The Mummers' Play*, p. 111. See also Cawley, ed., *Wakefield Pageants*, p. 91, note to T II, 25ff.

181 See Cawley, ed., *Wakefield Pageants*, p. 91 (note on lines 25ff). Axton, *European Drama*, pp.177f, counts nine, rejecting Cawley's identification of Donnyng (line 32) as a diminutive of Down (line 29); see his note 15 on p. 215. Axton, too, doubts that there were eight (or nine) animals on stage, and at least considers the possibility of their representation by boys.
182 Rose, ed., *The Wakefield Mystery Plays*, p. 31.
183 Cf. Baskervill, 'Dramatic Aspects', pp. 33f.
184 'Hexaemeron', *PL*, vol. 91, col. 63; cf. Dürrschmidt, *Sage von Kain*, pp. 33–7.
185 *Historia Scholastica*, 'Liber Genesis', ch. 27, *PL*, vol. 198, col.1078; cf. Dürrschmidt, *Sage von Kain*, pp. 29–32, 42–50, esp. 45.
186 On *avaritia* as the root of all sins in late medieval thought cf. Gardner, 'Theme and Irony'; Bloomfield, *Seven Deadly Sins*, pp. 72–4.
187 See also Creizenach, *Drama*, vol. 1, p. 295, where Cain is seen as a deterring exemplar of the mean tight-fisted farmer.
188 Frampton, 'Brewbarret Interpolation', p. 900.
189 For such a tropological interpretation of Cain cf. Maltman, 'Evil Characters', p. 80. See also Davidson, 'Unity', p. 500: 'The world...could never be excluded from this drama.'
190 This chapter has been strongly revised. A close study of the relationship between speech and action has convinced me that the 'ecstatic' and 'Dionysiac' quality which the German version postulated for the torturing scenes of York and Chester was an illusion. The bulk of the chapter is contained in a paper read at the 6th Congress of the Société Internationale du Théâtre médiéval in Lancaster in July 1989, and was published in *Medieval English Theatre*, 1991 ('Torturers'). I thank the editors of *METh* for permission to re-use the material here.
191 The following quotation is symptomatic of a still prevailing incomprehension: 'their audiences may be presumed to have enjoyed it, though modern sensibilities are unable to explain or understand it'. (Longsworth, *Cornish Ordinalia*, p. 68). Cf. also Longsworth's helplessness vis-à-vis these scenes p. 98.
192 See especially Bernd Neumann, *Geistliches Schauspiel im Zeugnis der Zeit*, esp. Parts 4 and 5. The best-known example from England is the Fergus episode in the lost York play of the Assumption of the Virgin; cf. Johnston and Rogerson, eds., *REED: York*, pp. 47f.
193 Rossiter, *English Drama*, p. 70.
194 Weimann, *Shakespeare and the Popular Tradition*, p. 62.
195 Weimann, *Shakespeare und die Tradition*, p. 119. From the English translation this phrase has been omitted. For Wycliffite criticism of the 'miracle plays' cf. *A Middle English Treatise*, ed. Davidson. For the charge of 'expresse maumetrye' (i.e. paganism) cf. ibid., p. 52.
196 A very similar method was used by the Poculi Ludique players of Toronto. (Oral communication by Alexandra Johnston, SITM Congress, Lancaster, July 1989.)
197 Travis, *Dramatic Design*, pp. 184f.
198 I.e. fasten the cloth which is to blindfold Christ.
199 The importance of 'game' in this play has been studied in particular by Sanders, 'Who's Afraid?'

200 Stanley Kahrl's comment is most apposite: 'Christ's suffering is not...a remote contemplation... It is part of a world we have recently been brought to see again in all too horrifying clarity; a world where man's inhumanity to man is a constant' (Kahrl, *Traditions*, p. 89).
201 Sanders, 'Who's Afraid?'
202 Salter, '"Trial and Flagellation"', p. 7. For the relevant document see now Clopper, ed., *REED: Chester*, pp. 6f (translation pp. 493f).
203 Cf. Craig, *ERD*, p. 192. Craig believes both plays to have had the same metre, which he loosely describes as 'three-foot ballad-stanza'. The metre is not easy to characterize, but it is probably nearer the truth to call it two-beats with irregular slacks and almost regular alliteration. The rhyme-scheme in Ch XVI and XVIA remains the one usual in the cycle: aaabcccb; in Ch VII, by contrast, part of the shorter lines are grouped in simple tail-rhyme stanzas: aabccb. In the case of Ch VII Craig, too, believes that the short lines form the oldest stratum of the play (p. 188). In Ch XVI (and XVIA) he has no explanation for the deviation (p. 192). For Ch VII cf. Diller, 'Composition'. See now also Travis, *Dramatic Design*, pp. 42ff.
204 Foster, ed, *The Northern Passion*, lines 1599–1620, pp. 186–91.
205 E.g. by Morgan, '"High Fraud"'; Weimann, *Shakespeare and the Popular Tradition*, pp. 85–97; Mack, 'Reconsideration'.
206 Diller, 'Craftsmanship'. See also Munson, 'Audience and Meaning'.
207 Weimann, '*Platea* und *locus*'; 'Realismus'; *Shakespeare and the Popular Tradition*, pp. 73–97.
208 Weimann, 'Realismus', p. 134; Weimann, *Shakespeare und die Tradition des Volkstheaters*, p. 157. The passage has been omitted from the English translation.
209 Morgan, '"High Fraud"', pp. 684–6; Kolve, *Corpus Christi*, pp. 156ff, also recognizes the ritualistic origins of this episode 'of youth overcoming age, of the servant overcoming the master'.
210 Cf. Diller, 'Composition'.
211 For a deepened understanding of this much used term see Rossiter, *Angel*, pp. 274–92.
212 References see note 162.
213 Moore, *Comic*; Wood, 'Comic Elements'.
214 Especially Speirs, 'Mystery Cycle'. See also Speirs' contributions on the cycles (especially the Towneley Shepherds Plays) in the first volumes of, respectively, *The Pelican Guide to English Literature* (Harmondsworth: Penguin Books, 1954) and *The New Pelican Guide to English Literature* (Harmondsworth: Penguin Books, 1982). The latter should be read together with Derek Pearsall's 'Postscript: Changing Perspectives' in the same volume.
215 Morgan, '"High Fraud"', p. 686.
216 Weimann, 'Realismus', esp. pp. 113, 116–20; *Shakespeare and the Popular Tradition*, pp. 91f.
217 In medieval aesthetics, which had always been a theory of beauty rather than of art, ugliness had an assured position – pretty much as evil had an assured position in medieval ethics. Cf. Mroczkowski, 'Mediaeval Art', pp. 204–21, esp. p. 200; de Bruyne, *Etudes d'esthétique médiévale*, vol. 2, pp. 215f.
218 Not otherwise known as a noun; *hannen* occurs in Laȝamon's *Brut* 31676, as

'to fight, to struggle with sb.' (*MED*). Perhaps also cognate with *to hanny* (obs., Lancs.) = 'to dispute, argue (in a pub)', *hannier* (obs., Yks.) = 'a cross, teasing person' (Wright, *EDD*). *Hannes* presumably = 'fights, quarrels'.

219 'wrastlynges' are among those pastimes against which the *Handlyng Synne* warns (*Robert [Mannyng] of Brunne's 'Handlyng Synne'*, ed. Frederick J. Furnivall, Part II, London 1903, EETS, OS, 123, p. 263, l. 8987). Wrestling bouts between shepherds are attested in Scotland as late as the eighteenth century. For these fights special 'castles' were erected, which reappear in the Shepherds Plays as 'looe' or 'lowe' (STCo 214, 218; Ch VII, 46), 'height' (Ch VII, 94), 'hill' (Ch VII, 206) or 'balk' (T XIII, 49). The attestations in STCo are particularly interesting, since this play does not contain a wrestling bout. Possibly they are the remainder of a fight which formed part of an earlier version. On the 'hill' as a stage *locus* cf. Southern, *Medieval Theatre*, p. 130. On wrestlings, especially among shepherds, cf. Baskervill, 'Dramatic Aspects', pp. 54, 59.

220 Cf. pp. 17f.

221 I.e. 'bullock, used as a jocular term of abuse' (*MED*).

222 Line references are to Deimling/Matthews, which is here based on MS H. Stage directions in the other MSS are less complete.

223 Cf. Luke 1.52: *Deposuit potentes de sede, et exaltavit humiles*, with Ch VII, 237: *put him forth that is moste of might* (Trowle speaking).

224 Cf. Morgan, '"High Fraud"', p. 686.

225 Salter, *Medieval Drama*, pp. 43f.

226 Cf. Diller, 'Composition'.

227 In support of this conjecture see now Axton, *European Drama*, pp. 182–90, and Travis, *Dramatic Design*, pp. 41–3.

228 Weimann, *Shakespeare and the Popular Tradition*, pp. 86f.

229 'To the fare [fair] will I me,/ To by shepe, perdé' (T XII, 42f).

230 Cf. Diller, 'Craftsmanship', pp. 255f.

231 Cawley, ed., *Wakefield Pageants*, p. 100, note on T XII, 101ff.

232 Eaton, 'Source'.

233 Stage direction added by the editor.

234 Weimann's interpretation of lines 206f ('Slowpace, cursed by the First Shepherd, returns only kind words', *Shakespeare and the Popular Tradition*, p. 94) seems a little forced. More likely the reply is a way of returning the insult. Cf. also Froward's similar reply in the *Coliphizacio* (T XXI, 380), which is not peaceful at all. On the parallel see Cawley, ed., *Wakefield Pageants*, p. xix.

235 The term is used merely for the sake of brevity. Schless's interpetation of the Wakefield *Noah* and our own analysis of the Trowle episode will have shown that these 'intermezzi' are highly significant integral parts of the plays ('The Comic Element').

236 Hegel, *Aesthetics*, vol. 2, p. 1158.

237 See the references in n. 162.

238 Jerome Taylor at least hints at the correspondence: 'the ludicrous recalcitrance of Noah's wife, prefigured in Eve's conduct toward Adam, extended in the relationship of a Towneley Mak and Gyll, and contradicted

in the docility of Mary toward Joseph' ('Dramatic Structure', p. 185, repr. in Taylor and Nelson, eds. *Medieval English Drama*, p. 155). Cf. now Gibson, '"Porta haec clausa erit"', pp. 152f, with further supporting details.
239 Cf. Ch VII, 506f: 'Why, with his berde though it be rough,/right well to heere he hydes' [other MSS: heedes].
240 On natural man's vitality cf. Kolve, *Corpus Christi*, pp. 210–14, who, however, does not use Mak to illustrate these qualities.
241 On the dramatic precision demanded by many parts written by the Wakefield Master cf. Diller, 'Craftsmanship', pp. 252f.
242 Cf., e.g., the Devil's 'crooked snout' in the Newcastle Noah Play, line 125 (Davis, ed., *Non-Cycle Plays*, p. 29).
243 Weimann has repeatedly recorded his opinion that Mak's cottage and the Stable in Bethlehem were represented by the same stage *locus* (*'Platea* and *locus'*, p. 116; *Shakespeare and the Popular Tradition*, p. 90). But apart from an *obiter dictum* in Rossiter's *English Drama* (p. 72) and somewhat more pronounced conjectures by Speirs (*Medieval English Poetry*, p. 339) and Salter (*Medieval Drama*, p. 103) I can discover nothing to support this belief. Our knowledge of the medieval pageant-waggon (Cawley, ed., *Wakefield Pageants*, p. xxvi) leads us rather to expect a polar stage structure which symbolizes the contrast between good and evil. If, as seems now more likely, the Towneley Plays have been performed on a scaffold stage, all considerations of the size of the pageant-waggon that might justify the double use of the hut would be without foundation.
244 Cf. the bibliography in Cawley, ed., *Wakefield Pageants*, pp. xxxvf, esp. Cosbey, 'The Mak Story'. The terms 'enchantment' and 'disenchantment' are Weimann's and translate the German 'verzaubern' and 'entzaubern' (*Shakespeare und die Tradition des Volkstheaters*, p. 48 *et passim*, and *Shakespeare and the Popular Tradition*, p. 12 *et passim*).
245 Rossiter, *English Drama*, p. 72.
246 Ross, 'Symbol and Structure', p. 203.
247 Cf. Mack, 'Reconsideration', p. 81: 'What penetrates the deception is an overflowing kindness.'
248 Chidamian, 'Mak and the Tossing'.
249 Mack, 'Reconsideration', p. 78.
250 On this point cf. Diller, 'The Wakefield Master', esp. pp. 34–8.
251 Mack, 'Reconsideration', p. 78.

CONCLUSIONS

1 Cf. Wells, 'Style', esp. pp. 509–14.

Bibliography

BIBLIOGRAPHIES AND RESEARCH REPORTS

Harbage, Alfred. *Annals of English Drama, 975–1700*. Revised by S. Schoenbaum. London: Methuen, 1965

Henshaw, Millet. 'Survey of Studies in Medieval Drama'. *Progress of Medieval and Renaissance Studies in the United States and Canada*, Bulletin No. 21. Boulder, Colorado: University of Colorado Press, 1951

Severs, J. Burke. *A Manual of the Writings in Middle English, 1050–1500*. New Haven: Connecticut Academy of Arts and Sciences, 1967–

Stratman, Carl J. *Bibliography of Medieval Drama*. Berkeley: University of California Press, 1954

Bibliography of Medieval Drama. 2nd edn, revised and enlarged, 2 vols. New York: Ungar, 1972

Watson, George. *The New Cambridge Bibliography of English Literature*. 5 vols. Cambridge: Cambridge University Press, 1974–7

Wells, John Edwin. *A Manual of Writings in Middle English, 1050–1400*. 9 supplements. New Haven: Yale University Press, 1916–51

Further the periodical bibliographies in *ABELL, EDAM Newsletter, PMLA, REED Newsletter, Spec., YWeSt*

EDITIONS CITED

Abraham and Isaac. See Brotanek, Davis, Smith, Waterhouse

Adam. See Noomen, Studer

Aethelwold. *Regularis Concordia*. See Symons

Albrecht, Otto E., ed. *Four Latin Plays of Saint Nicholas from the 12th Century Fleury Play-Book*. London: Oxford University Press, 1935

Alexander, Peter, ed. *William Shakespeare. Complete Works*. 4 vols. London: Collins, 1951–8

Amalarius of Metz. 'De Ecclesiasticis Officiis Libri Quatuor'. *Patrologiae Cursus Completus. Patrologia Latina*. Vol. 105. Ed. J.-P. Migne. Paris: Migne, 1855, 985–1244

Anderson, J. J., ed. *Records of Early English Drama: Newcastle upon Tyne*. Toronto: University of Toronto Press, 1982

Apokryphen. See Tischendorf

Baker, Donald C. and John L. Murphy, eds. *The Digby Plays. Facsimiles of the*

plays in Bodley MSS Digby 133 and e Museo 160. Medieval Drama Facsimiles 3. Leeds: The University of Leeds School of English, 1976
Baker, Donald C., John L. Murphy and Louis B. Hall, Jr, eds. *The Late Medieval Religious Plays of Bodleian MSS Digby 133 and e Museo 160.* EETS, OS 283. Oxford: Oxford University Press, 1982
Beadle, Richard, ed. *The York Plays.* London: Edward Arnold, 1982
Beadle, Richard and Pamela M. King, eds. *York Mystery Plays. A Selection in Modern Spelling.* Oxford: Clarendon Press, 1984
Beadle, Richard and Peter Meredith, eds. *The York Play. A facsimile of British Library MS Additional 35290, together with a facsimile of the Ordo Paginarum section of the A/Y Memorandum Book.* Medieval Drama Facsimiles 7. Leeds: The University of Leeds School of English, 1983
Bede, The Venerable. 'Hexaemeron'. *Patrologiae Cursus Completus. Patrologia Latina.* Vol. 91. Ed. J.-P. Migne. Paris: Migne, 1862, 9–190
Benson, Larry D., general ed. *The Riverside Chaucer.* Based on *The Works of Geoffrey Chaucer.* Ed. F. N. Robinson. Oxford: Oxford University Press, 1987
Bevington, David, ed. *Medieval Drama.* Boston: Houghton Mifflin, 1975
Bible. See Colunga, Weber
Block, K. S., ed. *Ludus Coventriae, or The Plaie called Corpus Christi.* EETS, ES 120. London: Oxford University Press, 1922
Bonaventura. See Pseudo-Bonaventura
Brandl, Alois, ed. *Quellen des weltlichen Dramas in England vor Shakespeare.* Quellen und Forschungen zur Sprach- und Culturgeschichte der germanischen Völker 80. Strassburg: Trübner, 1889
Brotanek, Rudolf, ed. 'Abraham und Isaak; ein mittelenglisches Misterium aus einer Dubliner Handschrift'. *Anglia* 21 (1899): 21–55
Brown, Carleton and Rossel Hope Robbins, comp. *The Index of Middle English Verse.* New York: Columbia University Press, 1943 (See also Robbins.)
Carmina Burana. See Hilka
Cawley, A. C., ed. *The Wakefield Pageants in the Towneley Cycle.* Old and Middle English Texts. Manchester: Manchester University Press, 1958
Cawley, A. C. and Martin Stevens, eds. *The Towneley Cycle. A facsimile of Huntington MS HM 1.* Medieval Drama Facsimiles 2. Leeds: The University of Leeds School of English, 1976.
Chaucer. See Benson
Chester Plays. See Deimling, Matthews, Lumiansky
Clopper, Lawrence M., ed. *Records of Early English Drama: Chester.* Toronto: University of Toronto Press, 1979
Colunga, Alberto and Lorenzo Turrado, eds. *Biblia Sacra iuxta Vulgatam Clementinam.* 3rd edn. Madrid: La Editorial Católica, 1959
Coventry Corpus Christi Plays. See Craig
Craig, Hardin, ed. *Two Coventry Corpus Christi Plays.* 2nd edn. EETS, ES 87. London: Oxford University Press, 1957
Davidson, Clifford, ed. *A Middle English Treatise on the Playing of Miracles.* Washington DC: University Press of America, 1981
Davis, Norman, ed. *Non-Cycle Plays and Fragments.* EETS, SS 1. London: Oxford University Press, 1970

Day, Mabel, ed. *The English Text of the Ancrene Riwle* EETS, OS 225. London: Oxford University Press, 1952

Deimling, Hermann, ed. *The Chester Plays*. Part I. EETS, ES 62. London: Oxford University Press, 1892

Digby Plays. See Baker, Furnivall

Dodsley, Robert, ed. *A Select Collection of Old English Plays*. 4th edn, revised and enlarged by W. Carew Hazlitt. London: Reeves and Turner, 1874

Dreves, Guido Maria and Clemens M. Blume, eds. *Analecta Hymnica Medii Aevi*. 55 vols. Leipzig: Reisland, 1886 ff

Eccles, Mark, ed. *The Macro Plays*. EETS, OS 262. London: Oxford University Press, 1969

England, George, ed. *The Towneley Plays*. Introduced by A. W. Pollard. EETS, ES 71. London: Paul, Trench, Trübner & Co., 1897

Fleury. See Albrecht

Foster, Frances A., ed. *The Northern Passion*. EETS, OS 145 and 147. London: Paul, Trench, Trübner & Co., 1913 and Oxford University Press, 1916

A Stanzaic Life of Christ. EETS, OS 166. London: Oxford University Press, 1926

Froning, Richard, ed. *Das Drama des Mittelalters*. 3 vols. Stuttgart: Union Deutsche Verlagsgesellschaft, 1891–3

Fuller, John Bernard, ed. *Hilarii Versus et Ludi*. New York: Holt, 1929

Furnivall, Frederick J., ed. *The Digby Plays*. EETS, ES 70. London: Paul, Trench, Trübner & Co., 1896

Robert [Mannyng] of Brunne's 'Handlyng Synne'. Part II. EETS, OS 123. London: Paul, Trench, Trübner & Co., 1903

Gospel of Nicodemus. See Hulme

Graesse, T., ed. *Jacobi a Voragine Legenda aurea vulgo Historia Lombardica dicta*. Dresden: Arnold, 1846

Greban, Arnoul. See Paris

Greene, Richard Leighton, ed. *The Early English Carols*. Oxford: Clarendon Press, 1935

Harrowing of Hell. See Hulme

Hemingway, Samuel B., ed. *English Nativity Plays*. Yale Studies in English 38. New York: Holt & Co., 1909

Hilarii Versus et Ludi. See Fuller

Hilka, Alfons and Otto Schumann, eds. *Carmina Burana*. 2 vols. Heidelberg: Winter, 1930

Horstmann, Carl, ed. *The Three Kings of Cologne*. EETS, OS 85. London: Trübner, 1986

Hulme, W. H., ed. *The Middle English Harrowing of Hell and Gospel of Nicodemus*. EETS, ES 100. London: Paul, Trench, Trübner & Co., 1907

Inguanez, D. M., ed. *Un Dramma della Passione del secolo XII*. 2nd edn. Miscellanea Cassinese 17. Monte Cassino: Badia de Montecassino, 1939

John of Hildesheim. See Horstmann

Johnston, Alexandra F. and Margaret Rogerson, eds. *Records of Early English Drama: York*. 2 vols. Toronto: University of Toronto Press, 1979

Leo, Friedrich, ed. *Plauti comoediae*. 2 vols. Berlin: Weidmann, 1958, reprinted 1985

Lindsay, W. M., ed. *Isidori Hispalensis episcopi etymologiarum sive originum libri 20*. 2 vols. Oxford: Clarendon Press, 1962
Love, Nicholas. *The Mirrour of the Blessed Lyf of Jesu Christ*. Ed. Lawrence F. Powell. Oxford: Clarendon Press, 1908
Ludus Coventriae. See Block, Meredith
Lumiansky, R. M. and David Mills, eds. *The Chester Mystery Cycle. A facsimile of MS Bodley 175*. Medieval Drama Facsimiles 1. Leeds: The University of Leeds School of English, 1973.
The Chester Mystery Cycle. Vol. 1: *Text*. EETS, SS 3. London: Oxford University Press, 1974
The Chester Mystery Cycle. Vol. 2: *Commentary and Glossary*. EETS, SS 9. London: Oxford University Press, 1986
MacCracken, H. N., ed. *The Minor Poems of John Lydgate*. 2 vols. EETS, ES 107. London: Oxford University Press, 1911
Macro Plays. See Eccles
Manly, J. M., ed. *Specimens of the Pre-Shakespearean Drama*. 2 vols. Boston: Ginn, 1897
Mannyng, Robert, of Brunne. *Meditations on the Supper of Our Lord, and the Hours of the Passion*. Ed. J. Meadows Cowper. EETS, OS 60. London: Trübner & Co., 1875
Marguerite de Navarre. *La comédie de l'adoration des Trois Rois*, in *Les Marguerites de la Marguerite des Princesses, très illustre Royne de Navarre*. Lyon: Pierre de Tours, 1549
Matthews, J., ed. *The Chester Plays*. Part II. EETS, ES 115. London: Oxford University Press, 1916
Meredith, Peter, ed. *The Mary Play. From the N.Town Manuscript*. London: Longman, 1987
The Passion Play from the N.Town Manuscript. London: Longman, 1990
Meredith, Peter and Stanley J. Kahrl, eds. *The N-Town Plays. A facsimile of BL MS Cotton Vespasian D VIII*. Medieval Drama Facsimiles 4. Leeds: The University of Leeds School of English, 1977
Meyer, Paul, ed. 'Les Trois Maries, mystère liturgique de Reims'. *Romania* 33 (1904): 239–45
Mirk, John. *Mirk's Festial*. Ed. T. Erbe. EETS, ES 96. London: Paul, Trench, Trübner & Co., 1905
Montecassino Passion Play. See Inguanez
Morris, Richard, ed. *Cursor Mundi*. Part I. EETS, OS 57. London: Oxford University Press, 1874
Nativity Plays. See Hemingway
Newcastle, Records of Early English Drama. See Anderson
Nicodemus, Gospel of. See Hulme, Tischendorf
Non-Cycle Mystery Plays. See Waterhouse
Non-Cycle Plays and Fragments. See Davis
Noomen, Willem, ed. *Le jeu d'Adam*. Paris: Classiques Français du Moyen Age, 1971
Northern Passion. See Foster
N-Town. See Block, Meredith

Paris, Gaston and Gaston Raynaud, eds. *Mystère de la Passion d'Arnoul Greban.* Paris: Vieweg, 1878
Passion. See Roy
Petrus Comestor. 'Historia Scholastica'. *Patrologiae Cursus Completus. Patrologia Latina.* Ed. J.-P. Migne. Vol. 198. Paris: Migne, 1855, 1045–1722
Pollard, A. W., ed. *English Miracle Plays, Moralities and Interludes.* 8th edn, revised. Oxford: Clarendon Press, 1947 (See also England.)
Pseudo-Bonaventura. 'Meditationes Vitae Christi'. *Opera Omnia Sancti Bonaventurae.* Ed. A. C. Peltier. Vol. 12. Paris: Vives, 1868, 509–630
Purvis, Canon J. S., ed. and trans. *The York Cycle of Mystery Plays.* London: SPCK, 1957
REED: Chester. See Clopper
REED: Newcastle-upon-Tyne. See Anderson
REED: York. See Johnston
Regularis Concordia. See Symons
Robbins, Rossel Hope and John L. Cutler, comp. *Supplement to the Index of Middle English Verse.* Lexington, Kentucky: University of Kentucky Press, 1965 (See also Brown)
Rose, Martial, ed. and trans. *The Wakefield Mystery Plays.* London: Evans Bros, 1961
Rothschild, James, Baron de, ed. *Le Mistère du Viel Testament.* Société des Anciens Textes Français 9. 6 vols. Paris: Rothschild, 1887–91
Roy, Emile, ed. *Le Mystère de la Passion en France.* Dijon: Damidot, 1903
Schumann, Otto. See Hilka
Seinte Resureccion. See Wright
Smith, Lucy Toulmin, ed. 'Abraham and Isaac, a Mystery Play; from a Private Manuscript of the 15th Century' ['Brome Abraham']. *Anglia* 7 (1884): 316–37
  The York Plays. London: Clarendon Press, 1885
  A Common-place Book of the Fifteenth Century. Norwich: privately printed, 1886
Stanzaic Life. See Foster
Studer, Paul, ed. *Le Mystère d'Adam.* Manchester: Manchester University Press, 1917
Symons, D. T., ed. *Regularis Concordia.* Medieval Classics. London: Nelson, 1953
Thomas, Lucien-Paul, ed. *Le 'Sponsus' (Mystère des Vierges folles), suivi des trois poèmes limousins et farcis du même manuscrit.* Université Libre de Bruxelles, Travaux de la Faculté de Philosophie et Lettres 12. Paris: Presses Universitaires de France, 1951
Tischendorf, Constantin v., ed. *Evangelia apocrypha.* 2nd edn. Leipzig: Mendelssohn, 1876
Towneley Plays. See Cawley, England, Rose
Trois Maries. See Meyer
Viel Testament. See Rothschild
Vulgata. See Colunga, Weber
Wakefield Plays. See Cawley, England, Rose
Waterhouse, Osborn, ed. *The Non-Cycle Mystery Plays.* EETS, ES 104. London: Paul, Trench, Tübner & Co., 1909

Weber, Robert, ed. *Biblia Sacra juxta Vulgatam versionem*. 2 vols. 2nd edn. Stuttgart: Württembergische Bibelanstalt, 1975
Wright, Jean, ed. *La Résurrection du Sauveur. Fragment de jeu*. Les Classiques Français du Moyen Age 69. Paris: Champion, 1931
Wright, Jean et al., eds. *La Seinte Resureccion*. Anglo-Norman Text Society 4. Oxford: Blackwell, 1943
York Plays. See Beadle, Smith

CRITICAL WORKS

Adam, Adolf. *Wo sich Gottes Volk versammelt. Gestalt und Symbolik des Kirchenbaus*. Freiburg: Herder, 1984
Albert, Heinrich. *Der Stilcharakter des mittellateinischen Dramas*. Diss. Munich University, 1927
Altieri, Joanne S. 'The Ironic Structure of the Towneley "Fflagellacio"'. *Drama Survey* 7 (1968/9): 104–12
Anz, Heinrich. *Die lateinischen Magierspiele*. Leipzig: Hinrichs, 1905
Archer, William. *The Old Drama and the New*. London: Heinemann, 1923
Assunto, Rosario. *Die Theorie des Schönen im Mittelalter*. Trans. Christa Baumgarth. Cologne: DuMont Schauburg, 1963
Auerbach, Erich. *Mimesis. The representation of reality in Western Literature*. Trans. Willard R. Trask. Princeton: Princeton University Press, 1953
 Typologische Motive in der mittelalterlichen Literatur. Schriften und Vorträge des Petrarca-Instituts Köln 2. Krefeld: Scherpe, 1964
 'Figura'. *Scenes from the Drama of European Literature*. Gloucester, Mass.: Peter Smith, 1973, 11–76
Axton, Richard. 'Popular Modes in the Earliest Plays'. *Medieval Drama*. Ed. Neville Denny. Stratford-upon-Avon Studies 16. London: Arnold, 1973, 13–40
 European Drama of the Early Middle Ages. London: Hutchinson, 1974
Baker, D. C. 'The Bodleian MS *e Mus*. 160 *Burial and Resurrection* and the Digby Plays'. *RES*, NS 19 (1968): 290–3
 'When Is a Text a Play? Reflections upon What Certain Late Medieval Dramatic Texts Can Tell Us'. *Contexts for Early English Drama*. Ed. Marianne C. Briscoe and John C. Coldewey. Bloomington: Indiana University Press, 1989, 20–40
Baker, D. C. and J. L. Murphy. 'The Late Medieval Plays of MS. Digby 133: Scribes, Dates, and Early History'. *RORD* 10 (1967): 153–66
Baskervill, Charles R. 'Dramatic Aspects of Mediæval Folk Festivals in England'. *SP* 17 (1920): 19–87
Baugh, A. C. 'The Chester Plays and French Influence'. *Schelling Anniversary Papers*. New York: Century, 1923, 35–63
Beadle, Richard. 'Poetry, Theology and Drama in the York *Creation and Fall of Lucifer*'. *Religion in the Poetry and Drama of the Late Middle Ages in England. Sixth J. A. W. Bennett Memorial Lectures, Perugia, 1988*. Ed. Anna Torti and Piero Boitani. Cambridge: D.S. Brewer, 1990, 213–27
Bédier, Joseph. *Les légendes épiques*. Paris: Champion, 1908
Beissel, Stephan. *Geschichte der Verehrung Marias in Deutschland während des Mittelalters*. Freiburg: Herder, 1909

Benkovitz, Miriam J. 'Some Notes on the "Prologue of Demon" of "Ludus Coventriae"'. *MLN* 60 (1945): 78–85

Bennett, Jacob. 'A Linguistic Study of "The Castle of Perseverance"'. Diss. Boston University, 1960

'The "Castle of Perseverance": Redactions, Place, and Date'. *MS* 24 (1962): 141–52

Bentley, Eric. *The Life of the Drama*. New York: Atheneum, 1965

Bernbrock, John A. 'Notes on the Towneley Cycle "Slaying of Abel"'. *JEGP* 62 (1963): 317–22

Bevington, David M. *From Mankind to Marlowe*. Cambridge, Mass.: Harvard University Press, 1962

Review of *Christian Rite and Christian Drama in the Middle Ages* by O. B. Hardison. *English Language Notes* 4 (1967): 211–14

'The Staging of Twelfth-Century Liturgical Drama in the Fleury *Playbook*'. *The Fleury* Playbook. *Essays and Studies*. Ed. Thomas P. Campbell and Clifford Davidson. Early Drama, Art, and Music Monograph Series 7. Kalamazoo, Michigan: Medieval Institute Publications, 1985, 62–81

Bjork, David A. 'On the Dissemination of *Quem quaeritis* and the *Visitatio sepulchri* and the Chronology of Their Early Sources'. *Drama in the Middle Ages. Comparative and Critical Essays*. Ed. Clifford Davidson, C. J. Gianakaris, and John H. Stroupe. Introduction by Clifford Davidson. New York: AMS Press, 1982

Bläser, P. 'Typos in der Schrift'. *LThK*. Vol. 10. 2nd edn. Freiburg: Herder, 1965, 422–3

Blaicher, Günther. *Das Weinen in mittelenglischer Zeit. Studien zur Gebärde des Weinens in historischen Quellen und literarischen Texten*. Diss. Saarbrücken University, 1966

Bloomfield, Morton. *The Seven Deadly Sins*. East Lansing, Michigan: Michigan State College Press, 1952

Böhme, Martin. *Das lateinische Weihnachtsspiel (Grundzüge seiner Entwicklung)*. Beiträge zur Kultur- und Universalgeschichte 40. Leipzig: Voigtländer, 1917

Boor, Helmut de. *Die Textgeschichte der lateinischen Osterfeiern*. Hermaea. Germanistische Forschungen, NF 22. Tübingen: Niemeyer, 1967

Bradbrook, Muriel C. *Themes and Conventions in Elizabethan Tragedy*. Cambridge: Cambridge University Press, 1935

Brandl, Alois. 'Das Bibelstück-Fragment von Rickinghall Manor'. *Archiv* 144 (1922): 255–6

Braun, Margareta. *Symbolismus und Illusionismus im englischen Drama vor 1620. Eine Untersuchung illusionsfördernder und illusionszerstörender Tendenzen, vor allem in den frühen Historien, unter besonderer Berücksichtigung des Monologs und des Aside*. Diss. Munich University, 1962

Brecht, Bertolt. 'A Short Organon for the Theatre'. *Brecht on Theatre. The Development of an Aesthetic*. Trans. John Willett. London: Methuen, 1964, 179–205

Brink, Bernhard ten. *History of English Literature*. Trans. W. Clarke Robinson. Vol. 2. London: Bell, 1893

Brinkmann, Alfons. *Liturgische und volkstümliche Formen im geistlichen Spiel des*

deutschen Mittelalters. Diss. Munich University, 1930. Mülheim-Ruhr: Kopineck, 1932
Brinkmann, Hennig. *Zu Wesen und Formen mittelalterlicher Dichtkunst*. Halle: Niemeyer, 1928
'Zum Ursprung des liturgischen Spieles'. *Xenia Bonnensia*. Bonn: Cohen, 1929
'Die Eigenform des mittelalterlichen Dramas in Deutschland'. *GRM* 18 (1930): 16–37, 81–98
Briscoe, Marianne G. 'Preaching and Medieval English Drama'. *Contexts for Early English Drama*. Ed. Marianne G. Briscoe and John C. Coldewey. Bloomington: Indiana University Press, 1989, 151–72
Briscoe, Marianne G. and John C. Coldewey, eds. *Contexts for Early English Drama*. Bloomington: Indiana University Press, 1989
Brockett, Clyde W. '*Persona* in *Cantilena*: St. Nicholas in Music in Medieval Drama'. *The Saint Play in Medieval Europe*. Ed. Clifford Davidson. Early Drama, Art, and Music Monograph Series 8. Kalamazoo, Michigan: Medieval Institute Publications, 1986, 11–29
Brooks, Neil C. *The Sepulchre of Christ in Art and Liturgy*. University of Illinois Studies in Language and Literature 7, 2. Urbana: University of Illinois, 1921
Brown, Arthur. 'Folklore Elements in Medieval Drama'. *Folk-Lore* 63 (1952): 65–78
'York and its Plays in the Middle Ages'. *Chaucer und seine Zeit: Symposion für Walter F. Schirmer*. Ed. Arno Esch. Buchreihe der *Anglia* 14. Tübingen: Niemeyer, 1968, 407–18
Brownstein, Oscar L. 'Revision in the "Deluge" of the Chester Cycle'. *Speech Monographs* 36 (1969): 55–65
Bruyne, Edgar de. *Etudes d'esthétique médiévale*. 3 vols. Rijksuniversiteit te Gent. Werken uitgegeven door de Faculteit van de Wijsbegeerte en Letteren. Vols. 97–9. Bruges, 1946
L'esthétique du moyen âge. Louvain: Editions de l'Institut supérieur de philosophie, 1947
Bryan, George B. *Ethelwold and Medieval Music-Drama at Winchester*. Berne: Lang, 1981
Bryant, J. A. 'The Function of *Ludus Coventriae* 14'. *JEGP* 52 (1953): 340–5
Bühler, Karl. 'Die Axiomatik der Sprachwissenschaften'. *Kantstudien* 38 (1933): 19–90
Cady, Frank W. 'The Couplets and Quatrains in the Towneley Mystery Plays'. *JEGP* 10 (1911): 572–84
Cameron, Kenneth. 'The Lincoln Plays at Grantham'. *RORD* 10 (1967): 141–51
Cameron, Kenneth and Stanley J. Kahrl. 'The N-Town Plays at Lincoln'. *TN* 20 (1965/6): 61–9
'Staging the N-Town Cycle'. *TN* 21 (1967): 122–38, 152–65
Campbell, Thomas P. 'Why Do the Shepherds Prophesy?'.*Comparative Drama* 12 (1978): 137–50
Campbell, Thomas P. and Clifford Davidson, eds. *The Fleury Playbook. Essays and Studies*. Early Drama, Art, and Music Monograph Series 7. Kalamazoo, Michigan: Medieval Institute Publications, 1985

Carey, Millicent. *The Wakefield Group in the Towneley Cycle*. Hesperia Ergänzungsreihe 11. Göttingen: Vandenhoeck & Ruprecht, 1930
Cargill, Oscar. 'The Authorship of the *Secunda Pastorum*'. *PMLA* 41 (1926): 810–31
Drama and Liturgy. New York: Columbia University Press, 1930
Cawley, A. C. 'The Staging of Medieval Drama'. The Revels *History of Drama in English*. Vol. 1. Ed. A. C. Cawley *et al*. London: Methuen, 1983, 1–66
Chambers, Edmund K. *The Mediaeval Stage*. 2 vols. London: Clarendon Press, 1903
The English Folk-Play. Oxford: Clarendon Press, 1933
English Literature at the Close of the Middle Ages. Vol. 2, part 2 of *Oxford History of English Literature*. 2nd edn. Oxford: Clarendon Press, 1947
Chenesseau, G. *L'Abbaye de Fleury à Saint-Benoît-sur-Loire*. Paris: Van Oest, 1931
Clopper, Lawrence M. 'The History and Development of the Chester Cycle'. *MP* 75 (1978): 219–46
'Lay and Clerical Impact on Civic Religious Drama and Ceremony'. *Contexts for Early English Drama*. Ed. Marianne G. Briscoe and John C. Coldewey. Bloomington: Indiana University Press, 1989, 103–36
Coffman, George Raleigh. *A New Theory Concerning the Origin of the Miracle Play*. Diss. Chicago University. Menasha, Wisconsin: Banta, 1914
'The Miracle Play in England – Nomenclature'. *PLMA* 31 (1916): 448–65
'The Miracle Play in England: Some Records of Presentation and Notes on Preserved Plays'. *SP* 16 (1919): 57–66
'A New Approach to Medieval Latin Drama'. *MP* 31 (1924/5): 239–71
'A Plea for the Study of the Corpus Christi Plays as Drama'. *SP* 26 (1929): 411–24
Collins, Fletcher. 'The Home of the Fleury *Playbook*'. *The Fleury* Playbook. *Essays and Studies*. Ed. Thomas P. Campbell and Clifford Davidson. Early Drama, Art, and Music Monograph Series 7. Kalamazoo, Michigan: Medieval Institute Publications, 1985, 26–34
Cosbey, Robert C. 'The Mak Story and its Folklore Analogues'. *Spec.* 20 (1945): 310–17
Craig, Hardin. 'The Origin of the Old Testament Plays'. *MP* 10 (1912/3): 473–87
English Religious Drama of the Middle Ages. Oxford: Clarendon Press, 1955
Review of *Drama and Religion in the English Mystery Plays* by E. Prosser. *Spec.* 37 (1962): 295–8
Craigie, W. H. 'The Gospel of Nicodemus and the York Mystery Plays'. *An English Miscellany*. Presented to Dr Furnivall in Honour of His Seventy-Fifth Birthday. Oxford: Clarendon Press, 1901
Creizenach, Wilhelm. *Geschichte des neueren Dramas*. 2 vols. 2nd edn. Halle: Niemeyer, 1911
Curtius, Ernst R. *European Literature and the Latin Middle Ages*. Trans. Willard R. Trask. London: Routledge and Kegan Paul, 1953
Cushman, Lysander W. *The Devil and the Vice in the English Dramatic Literature before Shakespeare*. Studien zur englischen Philologie 6. Halle: Niemeyer, 1900

Daneš, František. 'Zur linguistischen Analyse der Textstruktur'. *Folia Linguistica* 4 (1970): 72–8

Davidson, Charles. *Studies in the English Mystery Plays*. Transactions of the Connecticut Academy of Arts and Sciences 9. New Haven, 1892. Reprinted New York: Haskell House, 1965

Davidson, Clifford. 'The Unity of the Wakefield "Mactacio Abel"'. *Traditio* 23 (1967): 495–500

From Creation to Doom. The York Cycle of Mystery Plays. New York: AMS Press, 1984

Diller, Hans-Jürgen. 'The Craftsmanship of the "Wakefield Master"'. *Anglia* 83 (1965): 271–88. Reprinted in *Medieval English Drama: Essays Critical and Contextual*. Ed. Jerome Taylor and Alan H. Nelson. Chicago: University of Chicago Press, 1972, 245–59 (References are to the reprint.)

'The Wakefield Master. Secunda Pastorum'. *Das englische Drama vom Mittelalter bis zur Gegenwart*. Ed. Dieter Mehl. Vol. 1. Düsseldorf: Bagel, 1970, 21–38

'The Composition of the Chester "Adoration of the Shepherds"'. *Anglia* 89 (1971): 178–98

'The representation of space in the English mystery plays'. *Le Théâtre et la Cité dans l'Europe médiévale. Actes du Vème Colloque International de la Société pour l'étude du Théâtre Médiéval. (Perpignan, Juillet 1986)*. Ed. Jean-Claude Aubailly and Edelgard E. DuBruck. *Fifteenth-Century Studies* 13. Stuttgart: Heinz, 1988. 177–93

'Erste und Zweite Welt im geistlichen Spiel des Mittelalters'. *Meaning and Beyond. Ernst Leisi zum 70. Geburtstag*. Ed. Udo Fries and Martin Heusser. Tübingen: Narr, 1989, 3–19

'Theatrical Pragmatics: The Actor–Audience Relationship from the Mystery Cycles to the Early Tudor Comedies'. *Comparative Drama* 23 (1989): 156–65

'Typologie in den englischen Fronleichnamsspielen: wann liegt sie vor und was bewirkt sie?'. *Paradeigmata. Litarische Typologie des Alten Testaments*. Ed. Franz Link. Schriften zur Literaturwissenschaft im Auftrag der Görres-Gesellschaft. 5/1. Berlin: Duncker & Humblot, 1989, 103–14

'The Medium is Half the Message: The Isolation of Christ in Medieval Drama, Art, and Devotional Writing'. Paper read at the 2nd Congress of the Sociedad Española de Lengua e Literatura Inglesas Medievales. Cordoba: 30 September 1989. To appear in *Acta del Segundo Congreso de SELIM*

'Theological Doctrine and Popular Religion in the Mystery Plays'. *Religion in the Poetry and Drama of the Late Middle Ages in England. Sixth J. A. W. Bennett Memorial Lectures, Perugia, 1988*. Ed. Anna Torti and Piero Boitani. Cambridge: D.S. Brewer, 1990, 199–212.

'The Torturers in the English Mystery Plays', *METh* (1991)

Doran, Madeleine. *Endeavors of Art*. Madison, Wisconsin: University of Wisconsin Press, 1954

Dunn, E. Catherine. 'Lyrical Form and the Prophetic Principle in the Towneley Plays'. *MS* 23 (1961): 80–90

Dürrschmidt, Hans. *Die Sage von Kain in der mittelalterlichen Literatur Englands*. Diss. Munich University, 1918. Bayreuth: Ellwanger, 1919

Eaton, H. A. 'A Source for the Towneley "Prima Pastorum"'. *MLN* 14 (1899): 265–8
Eccles, Mark. '*Ludus Coventriae*: Lincoln or Norfolk?', *MÆ* 40 (1971): 135–41
Eckhardt, Eduard. *Die lustige Person im älteren englischen Drama (bis 1642)*. Palaestra 17. Berlin: Mayer und Müller, 1902
Edmondson, Willis. *Spoken Discourse. A Model for Analysis*. Longman Linguistic Library 27. London: Longman, 1981
Edwards, Robert. *The Montecassino Passion and the Poetics of Medieval Drama*. Berkeley: University of California Press, 1977
Einem, Herbert von. 'Das Problem des Mythischen in der christlichen Kunst'. *DVjs* 13 (1935): 260–79
Elam, Keir. *The Semiotics of Theatre and Drama*. London: Methuen, 1980
Eliade, Mircea. *The Sacred and the Profane. The Nature of Religion*. Trans. Willard R. Trask. New York: Harcourt, 1959
Falke, E. *Die Quellen des sog. "Ludus Coventriae"*. Diss. Kiel University, 1908
Faral, Edmond. *Les arts poétiques du XIIe et du XIIIe siècle. Recherches et documents sur la technique littéraire du moyen âge*. Bibliothèque de l'école des hautes études, Sciences historiques et philologiques 238. Paris: Champion, 1924
Farnham, Willard. *The Medieval Heritage of Elizabethan Tragedy*. Oxford: Blackwell, 1956 (corrected reprint)
Fehsenfeld, Erdmut. 'Der Dialog in den englischen Moralitäten bis zur Mitte des 16. Jahrhunderts'. Diss. Göttingen University, 1956
Fichte, Jörg O. *Expository Voices. Essays on the Mode and Function of Dramatic Exposition*. Erlanger Beiträge zur Sprach- und Kunstwissenschaft 53. Nürnberg: Carl, 1975
Fischer-Lichte, Erika. *Semiotik des Theaters*. 3 vols. Tübingen: Narr, 1983
Flanigan, C. Clifford. 'The Roman Rite and the Origins of the Liturgical Drama'. *UTQ* 43 (1973/4): 263–84
  'The Liturgical Drama and Its Tradition: A Review of Scholarship'. *RORD* 18 (1975): 100–2
Ford, Boris, ed. *The Pelican Guide to English Literature*. Harmondsworth: Penguin Books, 1954
  The New Pelican Guide to English Literature. Harmondsworth: Penguin Books, 1982
Forrest, Sister M. Patricia. 'The Role of the Expositor Contemplacio in the St. Anne's Day Plays of the Hegge Cycle'. *MS* 28 (1966): 60–76
Foster, Frances A. 'Was Gilbert Pilkington Author of the Secunda Pastorum?'. *PMLA* 43 (1928): 124–36
Frampton, Mendal G. 'The Brewbarret Interpolation in the York Play, the "Sacrificium Cayme and Abel"'. *PMLA* 52 (1937): 895–900
  'The Date of the "Wakefield Master": Bibliographical Evidence'. *PMLA* 53 (1938): 86–117
  'The Towneley "Harrowing of Hell"'. *PMLA* 56 (1941): 105–19
  'The York Play of *Christ Led Up to Calvary* (Play XXXIV)'. *PQ* 20 (1941): 198–204
  'Towneley XX: The *Conspiracio (et Capcio)*'. *PMLA* 58 (1943): 920–37
  'The Processus Talentorum (T XXIV)'. *PMLA* 59 (1944): 483–91, 646–54

Frank, Grace. 'Revisions in the English Mystery Plays'. *MP* 15 (1917/8): 565–72
Review of *The Original Identity* by M. C. Lyle. *MLN* 35 (1920): 45–8
'The York Plays and the *Gospel of Nicodemus*', *PMLA* 43 (1928): 153–65
'Genesis and Staging of the *Jeu d'Adam*'. *PMLA* 59 (1944): 7–17
The Medieval French Drama. Oxford: Oxford University Press, 1954
Franz, Adolph. *Die Messe im deutschen Mittelalter*. Freiburg: Herder, 1902
Freundorfer, J. 'Typus'. *LThK*. Vol. 10. 1st edn. Freiburg: Herder, 1938
Fry, Timothy. 'The Unity of the *Ludus Coventriae*'. *SP* 48 (1951): 527–70
Gamer, H. M. 'Mimes, Musicians and the Origin of the Mediaeval Religious Play'. *Deutsche Beiträge zur geistigen Überlieferung* 5 (1965): 9–28
Gardiner, Harold C. *Mysteries' End: An Investigation of the Last Days of the Medieval Stage*. Yale Studies in English 103. New Haven: Yale University Press, 1946
Gardner, John. 'Theme and Irony in the Wakefield *Mactacio Abel*'. *PMLA* 80 (1965): 515–21
'Imagery and Allusion in the Wakefield Noah Play'. *Papers on Language and Literature* 4 (1968): 3–12
Gautier, Léon. *Les Tropes*. Vol. 1 of *Histoire de la poésie liturgique au Moyen Age*. Paris: Palmé, 1886
Gayley, Charles Mills. *Plays of Our Forefathers*. New York: Duffield, 1907
Ghellinck, J. de. *L'essor de la littérature latine au XIIe siècle*. 2 vols. Brussels: Edition universelle, 1946
Gibson, Gail McMurray. '"Porta haec clausa erit": Comedy, Conception, and Ezekiel's Closed Door in the *Ludus Coventriae* Play of "Joseph's Return"'. *Journal of Medieval and Renaissance Studies* 8 (1978): 137–56
Glunz, Hans H. *Die Literaturästhetik des europäischen Mittelalters*. 2nd edn. Frankfurt/Main: Klostermann, 1963
Goppelt, Leonhard. *Typos. Die typologische Deutung des alten Testaments im Neuen*. Gütersloh: Bertelsmann, 1939
Graf, Hermann. *Der Miles Gloriosus im englischen Drama bis zur Zeit des Bürgerkrieges*. Diss. Rostock University, 1891
Greg, W. W. *Bibliographical and Textual Problems of the English Miracle Cycles*. London: Moring, 1914
Grieshammer, Rudolph. *Sprachgestaltende Kräfte im geistlichen Schauspiel des deutschen Mittelalters*. Jenaer Germanistische Forschungen 16. Jena: Frommann, 1930
Grundmann, Herbert. 'Das Mittelalter-Problem'. *Jahrbuch der Akademie der Wissenschaften in Göttingen für das Jahr 1967*. Göttingen: Vandenhoeck & Ruprecht, 1968, 40–54
Guardini, Romano. *Vom Geist der Liturgie*. 6th edn. Freiburg: Herder, 1962
Habicht, Werner. *Die Gebärde in englischen Dichtungen des Mittelalters*. Abhandlungen der Bayerischen Akademie der Wissenschaften, philosophisch-historische Klasse, NF 46. Munich: Beck, 1959
Studien zur Dramenform vor Shakespeare. Moralität, Interlude, romaneskes Drama. Anglistische Forschungen 96. Heidelberg: Winter, 1968
Häring, Nikolaus M. 'Die Gedichte und Mysterienspiele des Hilarius von Orléans'. *Studi Medievali*, Seria Terza 17 (1976): 915–68

Haller, Julius. *Die Technik des Dialogs im mittelalterlichen Drama Englands*. Diss. Gießen University, 1916

Halliday, Michael A. K. *Learning How to Mean. Explorations in the Development of Language*. London: Edward Arnold, 1975

'Functions and Universals'. *System and Function in Language. Selected Papers*. Ed. Gunther Kress. London: Oxford University Press, 1976, 26–35

Happé, Peter. 'The Vice: A Checklist and an Annotated Bibliography'. *RORD* 12 (1979): 137–56

Harbage, Alfred. *Annals of English Drama*. Revised edn. by S. Schoenbaum. London: Methuen, 1964; 3rd edn, rev. by Sylvia S. Wagonheim. London: Routledge, 1990

Hardison, O. B., Jr. *Christian Rite and Christian Drama in the Middle Ages*. Baltimore: Johns Hopkins Press, 1965

Harper, Carrie A. *A Comparison between the Brome and Chester Plays of 'Abraham and Isaac'*. Radcliffe College Monographs 15. Boston, 1910, 51–73

Hartl, Eduard. 'Das Drama des Mittelalters'. *Deutsche Philologie im Aufriß*. Ed. Wolfgang Stammler. Vol. 2. 2nd edn. Berlin: Schmidt, 1960, 1,949–96

Hegel, Georg Wilhelm Friedrich. *Aesthetics. Lectures on Fine Art*. 2 vols. Trans. T. M. Knox. Oxford: Clarendon Press, 1975

Heinzel, Richard. *Beschreibung des geistlichen Schauspiels im deutschen Mittelalter*. Beiträge zur Ästhetik 4. Hamburg: Voss, 1898

Helterman, Jeffrey. *Symbolic Action in the Plays of the Wakefield Master*. Athens, Georgia: University of Georgia Press, 1981

Hentschel, H. J. *Die Gestalt des Vice und seine Redekonventionen im Wandel und Niedergang der Moralität. Ein Beitrag zur Dramaturgie des Moralitäten-Theaters*. Diss. Munich University, 1974

Herttrich, Oswald. *Studien zu den York Plays*. Diss. Breslau University, 1886

Hinnebusch, William A. *The Early English Friars Preachers*. Rome, Vatican: Santa Salina, 1951

Höfler, Otto. *Kultische Geheimbünde der Germanen*. Vol. 1. Frankfurt/Main: Diesterweg, 1934

Hohlfeld, Alexander. 'Die altenglischen kollektivmisterien, unter besonderer berücksichtigung des verhältnisses der York- und Towneleyspiele'. *Anglia* 11 (1889): 219–310

Huizinga, Johan. *The Waning of the Middle Ages*. Garden City, New York: Doubleday, 1954. (First published 1924)

Hunningher, Benjamin. *The Origin of the Theatre*. The Hague: Querido, 1955

Hussey, S. S. 'How Many Herods in the Middle English Drama?'. *Neophilologus* 48 (1964): 252–9

Iannarelli, Catherine Topper. 'Marian Lyrics in Middle English'. Diss. Pennsylvania University, 1957, Mic. 20–794

Jakobson, Roman. 'Linguistics and Poetics'. *Style in Language*. Ed. Thomas A. Sebeok. New York: John Wiley, 1960, 350–77

James, Mervyn. 'Ritual, Drama and Social Body'. *Past and Present* 98 (1983): 3–29

Janicka, Irena. *The Comic Elements in the English Mystery Plays against the Cultural Background (Particularly Art)*. Poznańskie Towarzystwo Przyja-

ciół Nauk, Wydział Filologiczno-Filozoficzny, Prace Komisji Filologicznej, Tom XVI, Zeszyt 6. Poznań: Państwowe Wydawnictwo Naukowe, 1962
Jantzen, Hans. *Ottonische Kunst*. 2nd edn. Hamburg: Rowohlt, 1959
John of Hildesheim. *Historia de translatione beatissimorum trium regum*. Cologne: Guldenschaff, 1486
Kahrl, Stanley J. *Traditions of Medieval English Drama*. London: Hutchinson University Library, 1974
Kamann, Paul Julius Gustav. *Über Quellen und Sprache der York Plays*. Diss. Halle University, 1887
Kehrer, Hugo. *Die Heiligen Drei Könige in Literatur und Kunst*. 2 vols. Leipzig: Seemann, 1909
Kingdon, A. M. *Medieval Drama*. Literature in Perspective. London: Evans Bros., 1968
Kolve, V. A. *The Play Called Corpus Christi*. Stanford, California: Stanford University Press, 1966
Konigson, Elie. *L'Espace théâtral médiéval*. Paris: CNRS, 1975
Kretzmann, Paul Edward. *The Liturgical Element in the Earliest Forms of the Medieval Drama, with Special Reference to the English and German Plays*. University of Minnesota Studies in Language and Literature 4. Minneapolis, 1916
Künstle, Karl. *Ikonographie der christlichen Kunst*. 2 vols. Freiburg: Herder, 1928
Lancashire, Ian. *Dramatic Texts and Records of Britain: A Chronological Topography to 1558*. Cambridge: Cambridge University Press, 1984
Lange, Carl. *Die lateinischen Osterfeiern*. Munich: Stahl, 1887
Laut, Stephen Joseph. 'Drama Illustrating Dogma: A Study of the York Cycle'. Diss. University of North Carolina, 1960, Mic. 60–4,855
Leach, Arthur F. 'Some English Plays and Players, 1220–1548'. *An English Miscellany Presented to Dr. Furnivall in Honour of His Seventy-Fifth Birthday*. Ed. W. P. Ker et al. Oxford: Clarendon Press, 1901, 205–34
Lesage, Robert. *Vestments and Church Furniture*. Trans. Fergus Murphy. Faith and Fast Book 113. London: Burns & Oates, 1960
Lexikon für Theologie und Kirche. 2nd edn. Ed. Josef Höfer and Karl Rahner. Freiburg: Herder, 1957–67. (1st edn. Ed. M. Buchberger. Freiburg: Herder, 1930–8)
Lipphardt, W. 'Studien zu den Marienklagen'. *PBB* 58 (1934): 390–444
Lipson, Ephraim. *The Economic History of England*. 3 vols. 12th edn. London: Black, 1959
Longsworth, Robert. *The Cornish Ordinalia: Religion and Dramaturgy*. Cambridge, Mass.: Harvard University Press, 1967
Lott, Bernhard. *Der Monolog im englischen Drama vor Shakespeare*. Diss. Greifswald University, 1909
Lukács, Georg. *Ästhetik. Teil I*. 2 semivols. Georg Lukács Werke 11, 12. Neuwied: Luchterhand, 1963
Ästhetik (abridged). 4 vols. Neuwied: Luchterhand, 1972
Lumiansky, R. M. 'Comedy and Theme in the Chester "Harrowing of Hell"'. *Tulane Studies in English* 10 (1960): 5–12

Lumiansky, R. M. and David Mills. *The Chester Mystery Cycle. Essays and Documents*. Chapel Hill: University of North Carolina Press, 1983
Lyle, Marie C. *The Original Identity of the York and Towneley Cycles*. University of Minnesota Studies in Language and Literature 6. Minneapolis, 1919
'The Original Identity of the York and Towneley Cycles – a Rejoinder'. *PMLA* 44 (1929): 319–28
McDonald, Peter F. 'Drama in the Church'. *Medieval Drama*. Vol. 1 of *The Revels History of Drama in English*. Ed. A. C. Cawley *et al.*, General ed. Lois Potter. London: Methuen, 1983, 92–121
McKinnon, Effie. 'Notes on the Dramatic Structure of the York Cycle'. *SP* 28 (1931): 433–49
McNeir, Waldo F. 'The Corpus Christi Passion Plays As Dramatic Art'. *SP* 48 (1951): 601–28
Mack, Maynard Jr. 'The *Second Shepherd's Play*: A Reconsideration'. *PLMA* 93 (1978): 78–85
Maltman, Sister Nicholas. 'A Study of the Evil Characters in the English Corpus Christi Cycles'. Diss. University of California, Berkeley, 1957
'Pilate – *os malleatoris*'. *Spec* 36 (1961): 308–11
Manly, J. M. 'Literary Forms and the New Theory of the Origin of Species'. *MP* 4 (1906/7): 577–95
Manly, William M. 'Shepherds and Prophets: Religious Unity in the Towneley *Secunda Pastorum*'. *PMLA* 78 (1963): 151–5
Marrow, James. '*Circumdederunt me canes multi*: Christ's Tormentors in Northern European Art of the Late Middle Ages and Early Renaissance'. *Art Bulletin* 59 (1977): 167–81
Marshall, Mary H. 'The Dramatic Tradition Established by the Liturgical Play'. *PMLA* 56 (1941): 962–91
'Aesthetic Values of the Liturgical Drama'. *English Institute Essays*, 1950. New York: Columbia University Press, 1951, 89–115
Marshall, Robert Doyle. 'Dogmatic Formalism to Practical Humanism – Changing Attitudes towards the Passion of Christ in Medieval English Literature'. Diss. Wisconsin University, 1965, Mic. 65–4,819.
Mathieu, Michel. 'Distanciation et émotion dans le théâtre liturgique du moyen âge'. *Revue d'histoire du théâtre* 21 (1969): 95–117
Meier, Hermann. *Die Strophenformen in den englischen Misterienspielen*. Diss. Freiburg University, 1921
Meier, Theo. *Die Gestalt Marias im geistlichen Schauspiel des deutschen Mittelalters*. Philologische Studien und Quellen. Berlin: Schmidt, 1959
Messerer, Wilhelm. 'Einige Darstellungsprinzipien der Kunst im Mittelalter'. *DVjs* 36 (1962): 157–78.
Meyer, Wilhelm. 'Fragmenta Burana'. *Festschrift zur Feier des hundertfünfzigjährigen Bestehens der Königlichen Gesellschaft der Wissenschaften zu Göttingen: Abhandlungen der philologisch-historischen Klasse*. Berlin: Weidmann, 1901, 1–190
Michael, Wolfgang F. *Frühformen der deutschen Bühne*. Schriften der Gesellschaft für Theatergeschichte 62. Berlin: Gesellschaft für Theatergeschichte, 1963
Mills, David. '"The Towneley Plays" or "The Towneley Cycle"?'. *Leeds Studies in English* NS 17 (1958): 95–104

Mohr, Wolfgang. 'Einfache Formen'. *Reallexikon der deutschen Literaturgeschichte*. 2nd edn. Ed. W. Kohlschmidt and W. Mohr. Berlin: de Gruyter, 1958, 321–8

Moore, John Brooks. *The Comic and the Realistic in English Drama Before Shakespeare*. Chicago: University of Chicago Press, 1925

Morgan, Margery M. '"High Fraud": Paradox and Double-plot in the English Shepherds' Plays'. *Spec.* 39 (1964): 676–89

Mroczkowski, Przemysław. 'Mediaeval Art and Aesthetics in *The Canterbury Tales*'. *Spec.* 33 (1958): 204–21

Mueller, A. *Mittelenglische geistliche und weltliche Lyrik des 13. Jahrhunderts*. Studien zur englischen Philologie 44. Halle: Niemeyer, 1911

Muir, Lynette. *Liturgy and Drama in the Anglo-Norman Adam*. Medium Ævum Monographs NS 3. Oxford: Blackwell, 1973

'Medieval English Drama: The French Connection'. *Contexts for Early English Drama*. Ed. Marianne G. Briscoe and John C. Coldewey. Bloomington: Indiana University Press, 1989, 57–76

Munson, William F. 'Typology and the Towneley Isaac'. *RORD* 11 (1968): 129–37

'Audience and Meaning in two Medieval Dramatic Realisms'. *The Drama of the Middle Ages. Comparative and Critical Essays*. Ed. Clifford Davidson et al. New York: AMS Press, 1982, 183–206

Nelson, Alan H. '"Sacred" and "Secular" Currents in the Towneley Play of "Noah"'. *Drama Survey* 3, 1964, 393–401

The Medieval English Stage. Corpus Christi Pageants and Plays. Chicago: University of Chicago Press, 1974

Neumann, Bernd. *Geistliches Schauspiel im Zeugnis der Zeit. Zur Aufführung mittelalterlicher religiöser Dramen im deutschen Sprachgebiet*. Münchner Texte und Untersuchungen zur deutschen Literatur des Mittelalters 84–5. Munich: Artemis, 1987

Nicoll, Allardyce. *Masks, Mimes, and Miracles*. New York: Harrap, 1931

Ogilvy, J. D. A. '*Mimi, Scurrae, Histriones*: Entertainers of the Early Middle Ages'. *Spec.* 38 (1963): 603–19

Ott, Hanns. *Die Personengestaltung im geistlichen Drama des Mittelalters*. Diss. Bonn University, 1939

Owst, G. R. *Literature and Pulpit in Medieval England*. 2nd revised edn. Oxford: Blackwell, 1961

Pächt, Otto. *The Rise of Pictorial Narrative in Twelfth-Century England*. Oxford: Clarendon Press, 1962

Palmer, Barbara. '"Towneley Plays" or "Wakefield Cycle" Revisited'. *Comparative Drama* 21 (1987): 318–48

Panofsky, Erwin. 'Imago Pietatis', *Festschrift für Max Friedländer*. Berlin: Seemann, 1927, 261–308

Pantin, William A. *The English Church in the Fourteenth Century*. Cambridge: Cambridge University Press, 1955

Parker, Roscoe E. 'The Reputation of Herod in Early English Literature'. *Spec.* 8 (1933): 59–67

Pascal, Roy. 'On the Origins of Liturgical Drama in the Middle Ages'. *MLR* 36 (1941): 369–87

Patch, Howard R. 'The *Ludus Coventriae* and the Digby *Massacre*'. *PMLA* 35 (1920): 324–432
Patterson, F. A. *The Middle English Penitential Lyric*. New York: Columbia University Press, 1911
Pearson, Lu Emily. 'Isolable Lyrics of the Mystery Plays'. *ELH* 3 (1936): 228–52
Pelican Guide. See Ford.
Petit de Julleville, [Louis]. *Histoire du théâtre en France: les mystères*. 2 vols. Paris, 1880 (reprint: Geneva: Slatkine, 1968)
Petsch, Robert. *Wesen und Formen des Dramas*. Halle: Niemeyer, 1945
Pfister, Manfred. *The Theory and Analysis of Drama*. Trans. J. Halliday. Cambridge: Cambridge University Press, 1988.
Pickering, F. P. *Literature and Art in the Middle Ages*. London: Macmillan, 1970
Pollard, A. W. 'Introduction'. *The Towneley Plays*. Ed. George England. EETS, ES 71. London: Paul, Trench, Trübner & Co., 1897
Prosser, Eleanor. *Drama and Religion in the English Mystery Plays: A Reevaluation*. Stanford Studies in Language and Literature 23. Stanford, California: Stanford University Press, 1961
Rauhut, Franz. 'Der Sponsus'. *Romanische Forschungen* 50 (1936): 21–50
Reallexikon zur deutschen Kunstgeschichte. Ed. Otto Schmitt et al. Vols. 1–8. Stuttgart: Metzler; Stuttgart: Druckenmüller; Munich: Beck, 1937ff
Réau, Louis. *Iconographie de l'art chrétien*. 3 vols. Paris: Presses universitaires de France, 1959
Reese, Jesse Byers. 'Alliterative Verse in the York Cycle'. *SP* 48 (1951): 639–68
Rescher, Nicholas. *A Theory of Possibility*. Pittsburgh: Pittsburgh University Press, 1975
Riehle, Wolfgang. *Das Beiseitesprechen bei Shakespeare. Ein Beitrag zur Dramaturgie des elisabethanischen Dramas*. Diss. Munich University, 1964
Righter, Anne. *Shakespeare and the Idea of the Play*. London: Chatto & Windus, 1962
Robbins, R. H. 'An English Mystery Play Fragment *ante* 1300'. *MLN* 65 (1950): 30–5
'Middle English Carols as Processional Hymns' *SP* 56 (1959): 559–82
Robinson, J. W. 'Medieval English Acting'. *Theatre Notebook* 13 (1959): 83–8
'The Art of the York Realist'. *MP* 60 (1962/3): 241–51. Reprinted in: *Medieval English Drama : Essays Critical and Contextual*. Ed. Jerome Taylor and Alan H. Nelson. Chicago: University of Chicago Press, 1972, 230–44 (References are to the original article)
'The Late Medieval Cult of Jesus and the Mystery Play'. *PMLA* 80 (1965): 508–14
Roeder, Anke. *Die Gebärde im Drama des Mittelalters*. Munich: Beck, 1974
Ross, Lawrence J. 'Symbol and Structure in the *Secunda Pastorum*'. *Comparative Drama* 1 (1967/68): 122–43. Reprinted in: *Medieval English Drama : Essays Critical and Contextual*. Ed. Jerome Taylor and Alan H. Nelson. Chicago: University of Chicago Press, 1972: 177–211 (References are to the reprint.)
Rossiter, A. P. *English Drama from Early Times to the Elizabethans*. London: Hutchinson, 1950
Angel with Horns. London: Longman, 1961
Rudwin, Maximilian Josef. *Der Teufel in den deutschen geistlichen Spielen des*

Mittelalters und der Reformationszeit. Hesperia 6. Göttingen: Vandenhoeck & Ruprecht, 1915

Saintsbury, George. *A History of English Prosody*. 3 vols. London: Macmillan, 1906–10

Historical Manual of English Prosody. London: Macmillan, 1910

Salter, Frederick M. 'The "Trial and Flagellation": A New Manuscript'. *The Trial and Flagellation with Other Studies in the Chester Cycle*. Malone Society Studies. Oxford: Oxford University Press, 1935, 1–73

'The Banns of the Chester Plays'. *RES* 15 (1939); 432–57: *RES* 16 (1940): 1–17, 137–47

Medieval Drama in Chester. Toronto: University of Toronto Press, 1955

Salzer, A. *Die Beiworte und Sinnbilder Mariens in der deutschen Literatur und lateinischen Hymnpoesie des Mittelalters*. Programmschrift des Gymnasiums zu Seitenstetten. Linz, 1893

Sanders, Barry. 'Who's Afraid of Jesus Christ?: Games in the *Coliphizacio*'. *Comparative Drama* 2 (1968): 94–9

Sandison, H. E. 'Quindecim signa ante iudicium. A Contribution to the History of the Latin Version of the Legend'. *Archiv* 124 (1910): 73–82

Sauer, Joseph. *Die Symbolik des Kirchengebäudes und seiner Ausstattung in der Auffassung des Mittelalters*. Freiburg: Herder, 1924

Schadewaldt, Wolfgang. *Monolog und Selbstgespräch. Untersuchungen zur Formgeschichte der griechischen Tragödie*. Neue Philologische Untersuchungen 2. Berlin: Weidmann, 1926

Schegloff, E. A. 'Notes on a Conversational Practice: Formulating Place'. *Studies in Social Interaction*. Ed. D. Sudnow. New York: Free Press, 1972, 75–119

Schegloff, E. A. and H. Sacks. 'Opening up Closings'. *Semiotica* 8 (1973): 289–328

Scheltema, F. Adama van. *Die Kunst des Mittelalters*. Stuttgart: Kohlhammer, 1953

Schirmer, Walter F. *John Lydgate. Ein Kulturbild aus dem 15. Jahrhundert*. Buchreihe der *Anglia* 1. Tübingen: Niemeyer, 1952

Schless, Howard H. 'The Comic Element in the Wakefield *Noah*'. *Studies in Medieval Literature in Honor of A. C. Baugh*. Ed. MacEdward Leach. Philadelphia: University of Pennsylvania Press, 1961, 229–43

Schmidt, Dieter M. *Die Kunst des Dialogs in den Wakefield-Spielen*. European University Studies, Series XIV: Anglo-Saxon Language and Literature. Vol. 82. Frankfurt/Main: Lang, 1980

Schmitt, Natalie Crohn. 'Was there a Medieval Theatre in the Round?'. *TN* 23 (1969): 130–43; *TN* 24 (1970): 18–25

Schumann, Otto. 'Die Urfassung des Nikolausspiels von den drei Jungfrauen'. *ZRPh* 62 (1942): 386–90

Schwietering, Julius. 'Über den liturgischen ursprung des mittelalterlichen geistlichen spiels'. *ZfdA* 62 (1925): 1–20

Seewald, Gerd. 'Die Marienklage im mittellateinischen Schrifttum und in den germanischen Literaturen des Mittelalters'. Diss. Hamburg University, 1952

Sehrt, Ernst Theodor. *Der dramatische Auftakt in der elisabethanischen Tragödie*.

Abhandlungen der Akademie der Wissenschaften in Göttingen. Philosophisch-historische Klasse 3. Folge 46. Göttingen: Vandenhoeck & Ruprecht, 1960

Sepet, Marius. *Les origines catholiques du théâtre moderne*. Paris: Lethielleux, 1901

Severs, J. Burke. 'The Relationship between the Brome and Chester Plays of "Abraham and Isaac"'. *MP* 42 (1944/5): 137–51

Sheingorn, Pamela. *The Easter Sepulchre in England*. Early Drama, Art, and Music Reference Series 5. Kalamazoo, Michigan: Medieval Institute Publications, 1987.

'The Visual Language of Drama: Principles of Composition'. *Contexts for Early English Drama*. Ed. Marianne G. Briscoe and John C. Coldewey. Bloomington: Indiana University Press, 1989, 173–91

Shull, Virginia. 'Clerical Drama in Lincoln Cathedral, 1318–1561'. *PMLA* 52 (1937): 946–66

Skey, Miriam Anne. 'The Iconography of Herod in the Fleury Playbook and the Visual Arts'. *Comparative Drama* 17 (1983): 55–78

Smart, Walter K. 'Some Notes on *Mankind*'. *MP* 14 (1916/7): 45–58, 293–313

'The *Castle of Perseverance*: Place, Date and a Source'. *The Manly Anniversary Studies in Language and Literature*. Chicago: University of Chicago Press, 1923: 42–53

Smith, John Harrington. 'The Date of Some Wakefield Borrowings from York'. *PMLA* 53 (1938): 595–600

Sondheimer, Isaak. *Die Herodes-Partien im lateinischen liturgischen Drama und in den französischen Mysterien*. Beiträge zur Geschichte der romanischen Sprachen und Literaturen 3. Halle: Karras, 1912

Southern, Richard. *The Medieval Theatre in the Round*. London: Faber and Faber, 1957

Spector, Stephen. 'The Genesis of the N-Town cycle'. Diss. Yale University, 1973

'The Composition and Development of an Eclectic Manuscript: Cotton Vespasian D VIII'. *Leeds Studies in English* 9 (1977): 62–83

The Genesis of the N-Town Cycle. New York: Garland, 1988.

Speirs, John. 'The Mystery Cycle: Some Towneley Cycle Plays'. *Scrutiny* 18 (1951/2): 86–117, 246–65

Medieval English Poetry. The Non-Chaucerian Tradition. London: Faber and Faber, 1957

Spivack, Bernard. *Shakespeare and the Allegory of Evil*. New York: Columbia University Press, 1958

Staines, David. 'To Out-Herod Herod: The Development of a Dramatic Character'. *Drama in the Middle Ages. Comparative and Critical Essays*. Ed. Clifford Davidson, C. J. Gianakaris, and John H. Stroupe. Introduction by Clifford Davidson. New York: AMS Press, 1982, 207–31

Stamm, Rudolf. *Geschichte des englischen Theaters*. Bern: Francke, 1951

Stemmler, Theo. 'Entstehung und Wesen der englischen Fronleichnamszyklen'. *Chaucer und seine Zeit. Symposion für Walter F. Schirmer*. Buchreihe der *Anglia* 14. Ed. Arno Esch. Tübingen: Niemeyer, 1968, 393–405

'Zur Datierung der Chester Plays'. *GRM*, NF 18 (1968): 308–13

Liturgische Feiern und geistliche Spiele. Studien zu Erscheinungsformen des

Dramatischen im Mittelalter. Buchreihe der *Anglia* 15. Tübingen: Niemeyer, 1970
'Typological Transfer in Liturgical Offices and Religious Plays of the Middle Ages'. *Studies in the Literary Imagination* 8 (1975): 123–43
Stevens, Martin. 'The Language of the Towneley Plays'. Doctoral Dissertation Series 16754, Michigan State University, 1956
'The Composition of the Towneley *Talents Play*: A Linguistic Examination'. *JEGP* 58 (1959): 423–33
'The Dramatic Setting of the Wakefield *Annunciation*'. *PMLA* 81 (1966): 193–8
'Did the Wakefield Master Write a Nine-Line Stanza?'. *Comparative Drama* 15 (1981): 99–119
Four English Mystery Cycles. Textual, Contextual, and Critical Interpretations. Princeton: Princeton University Press, 1987
Sticca, Sandro. 'The Planctus Mariae and the Passion Plays'. *Symposion* 15 (1961): 41–8
'The Literary Genesis of the Latin Passion Play and the *Planctus Mariae*: A New Christocentric and Marian Theology'. *The Medieval Drama*. Ed. Sandro Sticca. Albany: State University of New York Press, 1972, 39–68
The Planctus Mariae in the Dramatic Tradition of the Middle Ages. Trans. Joseph R. Berrigan. Athens, Georgia: University of Georgia Press, 1988
Sticca, Sandro, ed. *The Medieval Drama*. Albany: State University of New York Press, 1972
Stumpfl, Robert. *Kultspiele der Germanen als Ursprung des mittelalterlichen Dramas*. Berlin: Juncker & Dünnhaupt, 1936
Swenson, Esther L. *An Inquiry into the Composition and Structure of 'Ludus Coventriae'*. University of Minnesota Studies in Language and Literature 1. Minneapolis, 1914
Szondi, Peter. *Theory of the Modern Drama*. Trans. Michael Hays. Cambridge: Polity Press, 1987
Tack, P. *Überrollenmäßige Sprachgestaltung in der Tragödie*. Munich: Hueber, 1931
Taylor, Geoffrey Coffin. 'The English "Planctus Mariae"'. *MP* 4 (1907): 605–37
'The Relation of the English Corpus Christi Play to the Middle English Religious Lyric'. *MP* 5 (1907): 1–38
Taylor, Jerome. 'The Dramatic Structure of the Middle English Corpus Christi, or Cycle, Plays'. *Literature and Society*. Ed. Bernice Slote. Lincoln, Nebraska: University of Nebraska Press, 1964: 175–86
Taylor, Jerome and Alan H. Nelson, eds. *Medieval English Drama. Essays Critical and Contextual*. Chicago: University of Chicago Press, 1972
Thien, Hermann. *Über die englischen Marienklagen*. Diss. Kiel University, 1906
Thompson, F. J. 'Unity in the "Second Shepherds' Tale"' [sic]. *MLN* 64 (1949): 302–9
Thompson, James Westfall. *The Literacy of the Laity in the Middle Ages*. University of California Publications in Education. Berkeley: University of California Press, 1939
Thrupps, Silvia L. 'The Gilds'. *Cambridge Economic History of Europe*. Ed. M. M. Postan *et al.* Vol. 3. Cambridge: Cambridge University Press, 1963
Tiddy, R. J. E. *The Mummers' Play*. Oxford: Clarendon Press, 1923

Tilgner, Elfriede. *Die 'aureate terms' als Stilelemente bei Lydgate.* Germanische Studien 182. Berlin: Ebering, 1936
Tomlinson, Warren Everett. *Der Herodes-Charakter im englischen Drama.* Palaestra 195. Leipzig: Mayer & Müller, 1934
Traver, Hope. *The Four Daughters of God.* Bryn Mawr Monographs 6. Philadelphia: Bryn Mawr College, 1907
Travis, Peter W. *Dramatic Design in the Chester Cycle.* Chicago: University of Chicago Press, 1982
Trusler, M. 'The Language of the Wakefield Playwright'. *SP* 33 (1936): 15–39
Tydeman, William. *The Theatre in the Middle Ages. Western European Stage Conditions c. 800–1576.* Cambridge: Cambridge University Press, 1978
English Medieval Theatre, 1400–1500. London: Routledge & Kegan Paul, 1986
Ungemach, H. G. *Die Quellen der fünf ersten Chester Plays.* Leipzig: Deichert, 1890
Utesch, Hans. *Die Quellen der Chester Plays.* Diss. Kiel University, 1909
Venezky, Alice S. *Pageantry on the Shakespearean Stage.* New York: Twayne, 1951
Venzmer, Berthold. *Die Chöre im Drama des deutschen Mittelalters.* Diss. Rostock University, 1897
Vezin, Gilberte. *L'adoration et le cycle des Mages dans l'art chrétien primitif. Etude des influences orientales et grecques sur l'art chrétien.* Paris: Presses universitaires de France, 1950
Vriend, Johannes. *The Blessed Virgin Mary in the Medieval Drama of England.* Diss. Amsterdam University, 1928
Vries, K. de. 'De Mariaklachten'. Diss. Nijmegen University, 1964
Waetzoldt, Stephan. 'Drei Könige'. *RDK.* Vol. 4. Stuttgart: Metzler, 1937ff, 476–501
Walsh, Sister Mary Margaret. 'The Judgment Plays of the English Cycles'. *American Benedictine Review* 20 (1969): 378–94
Warning, Rainer. 'Ritus, Mythos und geistliches Spiel'. *Poetica* 3 (1970): 83–114
Funktion und Struktur. Die Ambivalenzen des geistlichen Spiels. Theorie und Geschichte der Literatur und der schönen Künste 35. Munich: Fink, 1974
'On the Alterity of Medieval Religious Drama'. *NLH* 10 (1978/79): 265–92
Watt, Homer A. 'The Dramatic Unity of the *Secunda Pastorum*'. *Essays and Studies in Honor of Carleton Brown.* New York: New York University Press, 1940, 158–66
Wechssler, E. *Die romanischen Marienklagen.* Halle: Niemeyer, 1893
Weimann, Robert. 'Shakespeare und das Volkstheater seiner Zeit'. *Sh.-Jb.* 100/101. Weimar: Böhlau, 1964/5. 72–134
'*Platea* und *locus* im Misterienspiel: zu einem Grundprinzip vorshakespearescher Dramaturgie'. *Anglia* 84 (1966): 330–52
'Realismus und Simultankonvention im Misteriendrama. Mimesis, Parodie und Utopie in den Towneley-Hirtenszenen'. *Sh.-Jb.* 103. Weimar: Böhlau, 1967, 108–35
'Rede-Konventionen des Vice von *Mankind* bis *Hamlet*'. *ZAA* 15 (1967): 117–51
Shakespeare und die Tradition des Volkstheaters. Berlin: Henschel, 1967

Shakespeare and the Popular Tradition in the Theater. Trans. Robert Schwartz. Baltimore: Johns Hopkins University Press, 1978

Wellek, René. 'The Concept of Evolution in Literary History'. *Concepts of Criticism.* Ed. Stephen J. Nichols. New Haven: Yale University Press, 1963

Wells, Henry W. 'Style in the English Mystery Plays'. *JEGP* 38 (1939): 360–81, 496–524

Werner, Wilfried. *Studien zu den Oster- und Passionsspielen des deutschen Mittelalters in ihrem Übergang vom Lateinischen zur Volkssprache.* Philologische Studien und Quellen 18. Berlin: Schmidt, 1963

Weydig, Otto. *Beiträge zur Geschichte des Mirakelspiels in Frankreich. Das Nikolausmirakel.* Diss. Jena University, 1910. Erfurt: Hahne, 1910

White, Beatrice. 'Medieval Mirth'. *Anglia* 78 (1960): 284–301

'The Elusive Boundaries of *Terra Ridentium*'. *Chaucer und seine Zeit. Symposion für Walter F. Schirmer.* Ed. Arno Esch. Buchreihe der *Anglia* 14. Tübingen: Niemeyer, 1968, 35–45

Wickham, Glynne. *Early English Stages. 1300 to 1660.* 2 vols. London: Routledge & Kegan Paul, 1959

'Drama and Religion in the Middle Ages'. *FMLS* 3 (1967): 319–33

Review of *Christian Rite and Christian Drama in the Middle Ages* by O. B. Hardison. *RES*, NS 18 (1967): 300–3

Williams, Arnold. *The Characterization of Pilate in the Towneley Plays.* East Lansing, Michigan: Michigan State College Press, 1950

The Drama of Medieval England. East Lansing, Michigan: Michigan State College Press, 1961

'Typology and the Cycle Plays: Some Criteria'. *Spec.* 43 (1968): 677–84

Wilson, R. H. 'The "Stanzaic Life of Christ" and the Chester Plays'. *SP* 28 (1931): 413–32

Winslow, Ola Elizabeth. 'Low Comedy as a Structural Element in English Drama, from the beginnings to 1642'. Diss. Chicago University, 1926

Withington, Robert. *English Pageantry.* Cambridge, Mass.: Harvard University Press, 1918

'The Ancestry of the Vice'. *Spec.* 7 (1932): 522–29

Wolff, Erwin. 'Die Terminologie des mittelalterlichen Dramas in bedeutungsgeschichtlicher Sicht'. *Anglia* 78 (1960): 1–27

Wolpers, Theodor. 'Geschichte der englischen Marienlyrik im Mittelalter'. *Anglia* 69 (1950): 3–88

Die englische Heiligenlegende des Mittelalters. Buchreihe der *Anglia* 10. Tübingen: Niemeyer, 1964

Wood, F. T. 'The Comic Elements in the English Mystery Plays'. *Neophilologus* 25 (1939): 39–48, 194–206

Woolf, Rosemary. 'The Effect of Typology on the English Mediaeval Plays of Abraham and Isaac'. *Spec.* 32 (1957): 805–25

Wright, Stephen K. *The Vengeance of our Lord.* Toronto: Pontifical Institute of Medieval Studies, 1989

Young, Karl. 'A Contribution to the History of Liturgical Drama at Rouen'. *MP* 6 (1908/9): 201–27

The Harrowing of Hell in Liturgical Drama. Transactions of the Wisconsin Academy of Sciences, Arts, and Letters 16.2. Madison, 1909, 889–947

Officium Pastorum: A Study of the Dramatic Developments Within the Liturgy of Christmas. Transactions of the Wisconsin Academy of Sciences, Arts, and Letters 17. 1. Madison, 1912, 229–390

'*La Procession des Trois Rois* at Besançon'. *The Romanic Review* 4 (1913): 76–83

'The Origin of the Easter Play', *PMLA* 29 (1914): 1–58

Ordo Rachelis. University of Wisconsin Studies in Language and Literature 4. Madison, 1919

The Dramatic Associations of the Easter Sepulchre. University of Wisconsin Studies in Language and Literature 10. Madison, 1920

'Concerning the Origin of the Miracle Play'. *The Manly Anniversary Studies in Language and Literature*. Chicago: University of Chicago Press, 1923, 254–68

The Drama of the Medieval Church. 2 vols. Oxford: Clarendon Press, 1933

Zappert, G. *Über den Ausdruck des geistigen Schmerzes im Mittelalter*. Denkschrift der Wiener Akademie, Historisch-philologische Klasse 5. Wien: Gerold, 1854

Zumwalt, Eugene E. 'Irony in the Towneley *Shepherds' Plays*'. *Research Studies of the State College of Washington* 26 (1958): 37–53

Zutt, Herta: 'Die Rede bei Hartmann von Aue'. *Der Deutschunterricht* 14. 6 (1962): 67–79

Indexes

I Cited passages

Plays in Index IA are given with their place of origin and with references in Young, *DMC*. Because of the shortness of the plays, line references were not felt to be necessary. Index IB, on the other hand, contains line references wherever appropriate. References to the pages in this book are in bold print.

IA Latin plays and offices

Easter plays and offices
Angers (I,251)   **258**
Aquileia (I,251)   **257**
Barking (I,381–4)   **56, 57, 58, 265**
Benediktbeuern (I,432–7)   **62, 255**
Chiemsee (I,327–8)   **258**
Cividale (I,268)   **259**
Constance (I,301–2)   **259**
Coutances (I,408–10)   **265**
Einsiedeln (I,390–2)   **265, 294**
Engelberg (I,375–7)   **265, 294**
Fleury (I,393–7)   **267**
Fritzlar (I,257)   **26**
Halle (I,340–2)   **258**
Klosterneuburg (I,317–18)   **258**
Klosterneuburg (I,421–9)   **62, 265**
Moosburg (I,361–3)   **258**
Narbonne (I,284–6)   **46, 259**
Nuremberg (I,398–401)   **265**
Origny (I,413–19)   **72, 265**
Padua (I,294–5)   **258f**
Regensburg (I,256)   **259**
Regensburg (I,295–7)   **258**
Reichenau (I,259–60)   **259**
Rheinau (I,385–9)   **46, 218, 265**
Shrewsbury (I,516–20)   **72, 294**
St Florian (I,366–7)   **259**
Strassburg (I,255–6)   **258**
Toul (I,265–6)   **259**
Trier **72**
Troyes (I,291–2)   **259**
Udine (I,298–9)   **258**
Winchester [*Regularis Concordia*] (I,249–50)   **13–15, 17f, 112, 256, 258, 267, 276**
Zurich (I,314–15)   **259**
Zwiefalten (I,266–7)   **255, 258**
n.p., France (I,293)   **259**
n.p., Germany (I,263)   **258**
n.p., Germany (I,312–13)   **258**

Passion play
Benediktbeuern (I,518–33)   **47, 51ff, 72**

Shepherds' play
Shrewsbury (II,514–16)   **72**

Magi plays
Besançon (II,37–40)   **37, 259f**
Bilsen (II,75–80)   **38f, 41f, 59, 65, 261–3**
Compiègne (II,53–6)   **39, 259f, 268**
Fleury (II,84–9)   **26, 33, 39, 41–3, 65f, 257f, 260–4, 267f**
Freising (II,92–7)   **33f, 38f, 41f, 59, 65, 261–3**
Freising (II,117–20)   **44**
Laon (II,103–6)   **44, 264**
Limoges (II,34–5)   **30, 259f**
Padua (II,99–100)   **263**
Rouen (II,43–5)   **33, 260, 268, 272**
Rouen [Ms Montpellier] (II,68–72)   **34, 37f, 42f, 257, 260–3**
Sicily (II,59–62)   **257**
Strassburg (II,64–6)   **39, 257, 259, 261f**
n.p., Germany (II,447–9)   **257**

Christmas play
Benediktbeuern (II,172–90)   **39f, 54, 59, 62, 66f, 257, 261f, 266, 268**

St Nicholas plays
Iconia, Fleury (II,344–51)   **61, 63f, 68**
Iconia, Hilarius (II,338–41)   **56, 60f, 63, 72**
Tres Clerici, Einsiedeln (II,335–6)   **63f, 68, 267**
Tres Clerici, Fleury (II,330–2)   **63f, 67**
Tres Clerici, Hildesheim (II,325–7)   **63f**
Tres Filiae, Fleury (II,316–23)   **63**

Tres Filiae, Hildesheim (II,311–14) **62f**

Others
Conversio Beati Pauli, Fleury (II,219–22) **56f, 266**
Daniel, Beauvais (II,290–306) **35, 41**
Daniel, Hilarius (II,276–86) **35, 41, 56, 265f**
Lazarus, Fleury (II,199–208) **90, 103, 273**
Lazarus, Hilarius (II,212–18) **90, 103, 273**
Ordo de Ysaac et Rebecca, Vorau (II,259–64) **57, 62, 111**
Ordo Ioseph, Laon (II,267–74) **55–7, 111**
Praesentatio Mariae (II,227–42) **225, 294f**
Sponsus (II,362–4) **72, 269**

IB English plays

Br **191, 204, 206, 207–9, 252, 291**
  67–9 **207**
  79f, 93, 135–67 **208**

Castle of Perseverance **77f, 150f**
  653–9 **284**
  1823–30 **151**

Ch I **120**
  1–51, 7–12 **167**
  8, 11f, 16, 19 **168**
  20–3 **167**
  27, 36f **168**
  36–41 **167**
  251 **227**

Ch II **120, 167, 228**
  57–60 **167**
  345 **205**
  345–52 **204**
  350, 353–8, 360 **205**
  425–32 **170**
  426, 437 **287**
  549–52 **295**
  601–16 **228**

Ch III **119f, 169**
  stage direction **287**
  97–112 **119**

Ch IV **115, 204, 206f, 209, 277, 291**
  1ff **115**
  6–8 **276**
  17ff **170, 287**
  18, 21–4, 29 **287**
  29–32 **81**
  37–40 **271**
  114 **277**
  115 **115**
  115f, 117, 121, 130, 207 **277**
  217ff **207**
  228 **80**
  258–85 **292**
  463 **277**
  464 (DM) **116**
  468ff, 471 **277**

Ch V **115, 119–21, 277**
  1ff, 67f, 81 **277**
  124–63 **119**
  297 **279**
  297–432 **120**
  307f **277**
  317 **279**
  322, 340, 353, 355 **277**
  361, 366f **279**
  371 **277**
  377 **120**
  379 **279**
  388ff **275**
  389 **277**
  393ff, 399 **279**

Ch VI **85f, 96, 115, 205, 277**
  123ff **205**
  124–52 **206**
  153–60 **205**
  177ff **115**
  177–296 **86**
  296 **85**
  297–372 **86**
  372 **85**
  373–643 **86**
  457–60 **96**
  564–643 **272**
  568, 572, 601, 633 **277**
  644–714 **86**
  699ff **275**
  699–722 **272**

Ch VII **83, 96, 239–41, 243, 245, 250, 297**
  17f, 25–8, 33f **118**
  46 **298**
  47f, 59f, 161ff **272**
  86 **118**
  94 **298**

149–60, SD 164+ **243**
165 **241**
183f **243**
188–91, 202–5 **244**
206 **298**
268, 274–9, 276, 290 **244**
506f **299**
693–6 **117**

Ch VIII **84, 173, 219, 221, 277**
1ff **170, 287**
7–12, 13 **287**
13f **81**
15f **82**
101–8 **84**
110 **85**

Ch IX **219, 221, 277**
2, 6 **287**
71, 73, 80, 86 **221**
128–31 **83**
162 **221**

Ch X **87, 130**
1ff **277**
434–57 **119**
437f **278**

Ch XI **277**
1ff **170, 287**
19 **287**
303–6 **271**
327ff **117**

Ch XII **115f, 277**
282 **277**

Ch XIII **82f**
1ff **277**
15f **82**
315 **80**
486–9 **278**

Ch XIV **82f**
1ff **277**
1–8 **82**

Ch XV **82f**
1ff **277**
3f **82**

Ch XVI **297**
49–120 **239**
70–109, 307–54 **235**
313–84, 457–600 **239**
625–64, 626–32 **187**

630f, 633–6 **188**
641–56 **187–9**
643f **189**
645 **188**
649–56 **189**
657–60 **188f**
657–64 **187, 189**
733–6 **187**
817–36 **289**

Ch XVII **120**
1ff **170**
2, 9–16 **287**
162, 130 **227**

Ch XVIII
1ff, 10, 29 **277**
309–32 **220**
333–41 **83**
339–44 **220**

Ch XIX **115**
273 **117**

Ch XX
1ff **277**

Ch XXI
1ff **277**

Ch XXII **115, 120f, 277, 279**
1, 4 **279**
25–8 **116**
28f **277**
49, 51, 53, 59 **279**
76 **115**
85f, 90, 96, 105–7, 114 **277**
126 **179**
131f **121**
157, 159, 161, 170 **277**
179f **121**
208 **278**
243, 261–340, 273, 277, 285, 289, 333 **277**
333–40 **116**

Ch XXIII **279**
1ff **277**

Ch XXIV **120, 279**

'*Digby*' Plays

Burial and Resurrection **191, 209, 223, 294**
CB
459, 467, 473f **192**

526–8, 532–43 **193**
550, 564 **192**
565, 567 **193**
600–2, 608 **192**
918–24 **223**

CR
55ff, 107ff, 141ff, 168ff **224**

Conversion of Saint Paul **158, 252**
7–9, 656–62 **158**

Herod's Killing of the Children **158, 252**
19–24 **158**
551–8 **158f**

LC, *Proclamation* **100f, 149**
170–82 **293**
183–6 **149**
397–8, 462–5, 589ff **106**

LC I **168**
2–6, 12–15 **168**
81 **226**

LC II **168**
83–6 **169**
365ff, 374–7, 380–4, 391–403 **210**

LC III **228**
144–56 **228**

LC IV **104–6, 145f, 179**
1 **284**
1–4 **179**
5f **288**
11f, 14ff **146**
118 **104**
118ff **287**
140, 198, 206, 242 **105**

LC V **145f, 179, 211, 292**
1–3 **179**
5f **146**
5–8 **180**
9 **284**
10, 13f, 17 **146**
89–93 **211**
91 **212**
95–7 **211**
149–55, 179ff **212**

LC VI **145f, 179**
1–8 **145**
9–16 **288**
187ff, 193f **147**

LC VII **145f**
131ff **147**

LC VIII **107, 149, 157, 275, 285**
Prologue of Contemplacio **213**
Prol. 1 **156**
Prol. 3–8 **286**
Prol. 4 **156**
Prol. 14f **286**
Prol. 14–17 **293**
73–83 **107**

LC IX **149, 157, 275, 285**
84ff **107**

LC X **154, 157, 275, 285**
27 **99**

LC XI **123, 154f, 157, 213, 275, 285**

LC XII **78, 154, 205, 212f, 285, 293**
1–8, 21–47, 44, 48 **214**
49 **206, 215**
49ff **148, 214**
49–51 **206**
49–61 **214**
54–6, 60 **215**
62–87 **214**
81–3 **206**
84–7 **213–15**
88ff **215**
88–117 **214**
101–3 **216**
101–5, 118 **215**
118–26 **213f**
127ff **215**
127–79 **214**
130, 149f, 163–5 **215**
171f **216**
180–3 **99**
180–5 **215**
180–224 **214**

LC XIII **107, 149, 213, 275, 285, 293**
23 **155**
23ff **275**
23–7 **107**
23–42 **285**

Epilogue of Contemplacio
29–34 **156**

Prologue of Summoner **151**
9–12 **152**

LC XIV **100, 148, 150f, 154, 275, 284**

Indexes

1–8 **149**
3f **150**
17–26 **149**
29f, 33 **150**
73 **100**
105 **149**
121–8 **151**
125–8, 207f, 222f, 227f **274**

LC XV **147**
57, 65–8, 97–102, 137f **101**
313f **147**

LC XVI **99**
89 **100**
90 **99**

LC XVIII **100, 152**
1ff **152**
7–9 **153**
9f, 12, 14 **152**
15 **153**
16f, 69f **152**
71f **153**
95ff, 103–12 **100**

LC XIX **293**

LC XXI **103f, 149**
201–32 **103**
287f **147**

Johannes Baptysta **148**

LC XXIII **274**

LC XXIV **101, 103, 107, 149, 274f**
113f, 117f, 121f **102**
124f **101**
174ff **102**
229–32 **103**
293–6 **148**

LC XXV **90, 103–5, 147, 149, 179f**
1f, 3, 6ff **180**
10, 14, 100–212 **104**
449ff **147**

LC XXVI–XXVIII **78, 104, 107, 153f, 190**

Prologue of Demon
4f **154**

LC XXVI–XXVIII
221f **276**
SD 397+, 462–5 **105**

589–93 **106**
1041f, 1063, 1077–9, 1083f **190**

LC XXIX–XXXV **78, 153f, 157f, 189f, 285**

Prologue of Contemplacio
7 **157**
7f **156**
10–12 **157**

LC XXIX–XXXV
1ff **152**
1–4, 11, 14, 17f **153**
66ff **283**
SD 160+, 165–7 **234**
446 **233**
SD 675+, SD 677+, 682 **234**
SD 769+, SD 777+, 808f **190**
810ff **251**
811–13, 830f, 836f, 842ff, 845 **191**
1059–63, 1496ff **274**

LC XXXVI **220**

LC XXXVIII
275 **274**

LC XLI
2–4, 8, 11, 14, 16f **286**

Prologue of Doctor **157**
1 **158**
3 **157**
26 **158**

LC XLII **168**

Mankind **150, 230**
467, 469 **278**

Mummer's Play **127, 131, 278, 295**

Newcastle, Noah-Play
39ff **287**
125 **299**

Nh **206–9**
68ff **207**
90f, 109ff, 134f **208**

Pride of Life **132**
STCo
214, 218 **298**
540–3, 560f **174**
562ff **175**
580f **174**

582–9 175
584f 174
586ff 175
594–602, 671–81 222
689–98 223

T I 162–5, 167
1–6 162
4 163
7–12 164
21, 37 163
137, 150 227
162ff 164

T II 140, 228
5 131
15 140, 231
20 130
25ff 231
29, 32 296
48ff 231
62, 85, 91–6 229
96 228
97 230
99f 229
104 228
130, 167 230
202 231
239–42 228
387ff 231
405, 419–38 228

T III 129, 279
73–117, 84–6 165
94f, 100–2 166
109f 98, 166
445 98

T IV 194, 207f, 248, 279
4 172
9ff 195
12, 33–6 172
49–56, 65–73 199
79 196, 211
81–8 196
82 197
105ff 195
110 197
113–16 195
177–212 200
214, 225–9 195

T VI 88–91, 171
1–4 171
1–6 91
6 172

SD 58+ 88
110 89

T VII 123f, 145
1 123
26, 58 124
87, 90 123
100, 110, 118, 160–2, 167 124

T VIII 93, 122, 132

T IX 85, 93, 132
10 281
13f 133
16, 30 281
37, 40 133

T X 194, 198, 248, 290
15 198
41f 291
155, 158 194
161 194, 197
165–70 196
187, 195, 204 195
227ff 129, 195
344 293

T XI
89f 127, 279f

T XII 139, 240f, 245–7, 250
42f 298
82f 245
101ff 298
103, 105–12, 119, 121 246
206f 298
249ff, 276f 246
452 98

T XIII 106, 129, 131, 197, 240f, 245–7, 250
18 246
49 298
91f 280
199, 208, 236 247
296–304, 309–13, 327f, 332 248
353 282
386ff 247f
494f, 496–503, 613ff 249

T XIV 134–6, 140, 173f, 177, 221, 281
3 281
104 173
149, 152f, 169f 221
193–6, 493–558 222
505–40 223
523 294

T XV
44ff, 92ff **177**
149f **129, 280**

T XVI **140**
4, 10–13 **140**
21 **141**
44, 47 **282**
80ff **140**
85ff **287**

T XIX **122, 148, 175f, 288**
9, 13–16 **122**
21f, 35f, 37, 41f, 47, 51–64 **123**

T XX **135, 252, 281**
10 **131, 281**
19–23 **136**

T XXI **99, 236, 240, 252**
2f, 43, 299 **98**
380 **298**
364–6, 394f, 397–405, 430 **238**

T XXII **130, 135, 137, 183–5, 236, 252, 281, 289**
5 **281**
10–13 **137**
23f **138**
23ff **130**
31–5, 36 **137**
36ff **130**
36–9 **138**
40ff **285**
44–52 **137**
53–249 **184**
58f, 72 **237**
74f, 135f **236**
136, 139–42, 148f **237**
260–75 **289**
283, 292–4, 312–15 **184**
322 **237**
332f **184**
341 **237**
348–407 **289**

T XXIII **135, 138f, 185, 203, 281, 289**
1 **139**
1–28 **138**
3 **281**
309, 313–60, 321f **185**
325f **186**
329f **185**
335, 350ff **186**
361f, 372–81, 383f **185**

T XXIV **135, 252, 281**
73 **278**
73–176 **99**
113, 145 **278**
146 **99**
157 **98**

T XXV **162, 252**

T XXVI **279**
334ff **221**
623–34 **126**
633f **279f**

T XXVII **279f**
379f **128, 279**

T XXX **130, 295**
349ff **130**

T XXXI **90f, 104**
38ff **90**
39f **91**
63–7 **90**
66 **91**

Y I **162**
1f, 4f, 7–11 **164**
9–16 **163**
20ff **164**
100 **227**
108, 115, 117 **226**

Y II **162, 164, 167**
25f, 34, 47 **164**
49f **286**

Y III **162, 164**

Y VI
1–24 **201**
30ff, 34ff **200**
36, 41–52 **201**
42–5 **198**
46f **197**
61–9 **201**
65–8 **198**
77–122 **198, 201**
82 **197**
88, 93 **210**
123–34, 144 **201**
144–55 **200**
155 **201**

Y VII   228, 230
   34–72   229
   60ff   228

Y VIII   92f
   112–17   92
   150f   279f

Y IX   92, 119, 125
   1f   288
   1ff   279
   1–8   162
   3   172
   15ff   146
   191ff   128

Y X   292
   1ff   279
   79–82   211
   82   290
   115f   95
   201–94   200
   210, 223–94   199
   239   197
   243–5   199

Y XI   93, 97, 132
   1ff, 14, 18   122
   85ff   279
   104   286
   289–98, 311f   94
   379f   279

Y XIII   205, 290
   1   197
   1–20   199
   43   198
   248f, 253ff   293

Y XIV
   1ff, 15f   177
   15–21   96, 101
   25–8   177
   41–4   96
   78–82   97

Y XV   95
   86–95   96

Y XVI   134f, 141–3, 173, 175–8, 222, 287
   2, 10   283
   21   141
   57   287
   57f   288
   59–65   173
   70   287

   81–4   174
   103ff, 109, 113–16   222
   185–96   223
   193ff   262
   277–84, 297–308   223
   317–20, 330–2, 341–4   174
   391f   279

Y XVIII   177
   1ff, 15–18   177

Y XX
   51, 74   279
   219–22   271
   288   279

Y XXI   148, 175f, 252
   2, 6f   176
   29–49   176, 288

Y XXIV   104, 281
   208f   127, 279

Y XXVIII
   2   291

Y XXIX   143
   10–13   143
   353–79   235

Y XXX   95, 142, 283
   20–4   142
   236ff   144
   318, 320   95

Y XXXI
   19   283
   59ff   144

Y XXXII
   14   283
   129–52   202

Y XXXIII   281
   13   283
   140ff, 216ff   95
   349–426   235
   431   236

Y XXXIV   183, 185, 289
   9   283
   16–115, 126–35   289
   136f   184
   150–3, 180–2   183
   190–9, 216–19, 226–49, 260–99   289

Y XXXV
1ff, 100, 105–16 239

Y XXXVI 186
118–54 186
261–4 187

Y XXXVII 162
5–12 162f
13–16 163
99 226

Y XXXVIII 279
187ff, 204f, 210f, 217–22 221

Y XXXIX 279
1–22 199
148f 128

Y XL 128, 279
191ff 128

Y XLII
176, 275f 279

Y XLIII 97
126, 175ff 97
225f 279

Y XLVII 162
8 286
21, 27, 39 164
47f 286

II *Dramatis personae*

(Biblical names are usually given in the Vulgate spelling)

Abel 226–31
Abisacher 100, 154
Abraham 80–2, 89, 125, 133, 145f, 170, 172f, 179, 194–7, 199, 207f, 210–12, 251, 276, 279, 284, 287, 291f
Accusator 101f
Adam 170, 197f, 200f, 204f, 210, 251, 298
Adulteress 101–3
Angels 10, 13, 15–17, 20f, 23f, 26f, 54, 63, 65, 87–9, 96, 104, 117, 196, 200f, 207f, 210f, 214–16, 218, 224, 246, 248, 250, 257, 268, 272, 287, 294, 297
Anna 99
Annas 98, 237
Antichrist 114, 250
Apemantus 129, 280
Apostles 19f, 34, 38, 155, *see also* Disciples
Archpriest 107
Armiger 39, 41, 43, 65, 261, 262
Augustus, *see* Caesar Augustus

Backbiter(s) 137f, 150f, 227, 284, *see also* Detractor
Barbarus 60f
Beelzebub 131
Benjamin 55
Boy Bishop 43, 263
Brewbarret 296

Caesar Augustus 85–7, 93, 132f, 142, 272
Caiaphas 98, 143, 237, 283
Cain 3, 104, 130f, 140, 226–31, 275, 295f
Christ, *see* Jesus Christ
Civis 101
Cleophas 115, 274
Clerici 64, 67f
Consolatores, Consolatrix 46, 104
Contemplacio 107, 123, 154–8, 168, 213, 252f, 275, 283, 285f
Cyrenius 85, 93, 273

Daniel 56, 121
Darius 56
Daw 247, 249
Demons 119, 130
Den 149, 151
Detractor 149, 151
Deus, *see* God
Devil 153f, 205, 225f, 282, 295, 299
Disciples 10, 13, 15f, 20, 23, 26–8, 82, 90, 97, 104, 110, 123, 176, 276, *see also* Apostles
Doctor 155, 157f, 252, 275, 277, *see also* Expositor
Doctors [in the Temple] 103, 147

Egyptians 94
Elizabeth 107, 127, 155
Esau 88
Eve 197f, 200f, 210, 251, 298
Expositor 86, 109–11, 115–16, 118, 121,

123, 126, 154f, 157, 171, 189, 238, 252f, 272, 277f, 285

Flesh 151
Froward 237f, 298

Garcio, Gartius 117, 131, *see also* Iak Garcio
Gluttony 151
God (*also* Deus) 80f, 89, 93f, 97, 120, 160–9, 171, 173, 195f, 198, 207f, 211, 231, 287, 291
Gyll 248f, 298

Hamlet 129, 194
Herod 13, 17, 33–45, 52, 57, 59, 65f, 75, 85, 87, 100, 114, 119, 132, 134, 136, 140–2, 144, 152f, 158, 222, 233, 236, 251f, 260–4, 266f, 277, 281–3
High Priests 98, 237f
Holy Family 87
Holy Spirit 97

Iak Garcio 250
Isaac 62, 173, 195, 199f, 206, 208, 211f, 287, 290–2
Iuvenis 101

Jack Finney 131, 230
Jacob 88f, 91, 171f, 267
Jesus Christ 15, 47–50, 53–5, 80–2, 90, 95, 98f, 102–5, 117, 126f, 129, 136f, 147f, 161–3, 170, 183–91, 202, 212, 221, 223f, 226f, 232–9, 250–2, 259, 264f, 278f, 282, 287, 289–91, 296f
Jew [in anonymous *Iconia* play] 61, 63, 68
Jews [in Passion and Crucifixion] 48, 50, 62, 95, 97, 102, 106, 142, 187, 190, 233f, 239, *see also* Torturers
Joachim 99, 107
John the Baptist, Saint 52, 122f, 148, 175f, 252
John the Evangelist, Saint 19, 28, 107, 121, 155, 183f, 186, 191f, 258, 276
Joseph, husband of Mary 3, 53, 78, 86f, 96, 99, 101, 103, 107, 128–30, 133, 147f, 154f, 177f, 194–8, 200, 205f, 210, 213–16, 223, 248f, 251, 272f, 278, 290–3, 299
Joseph of Arimathia 192f, 289
Joseph, son of Jacob 55
Judas 105f, 193f, 202f, 291

Kings, *see* Magi
Kings [in *Radix Jesse*] 146f

Lamech 104f, 275
Lazarus 81, 90, 103f, 179f
Lechery 151
Lucifer 154, 226f, 295
Luke 115, 274

Magdalene 55, 218
Magi (*also* Kings) 17, 21f, 28–30, 33f, 36–45, 59, 65–7, 76, 83–5, 87, 89, 100, 110, 134, 136, 141, 145, 170, 173–5, 177f, 217, 219, 221–3, 255, 260–3, 267f, 272, 275
Mak 131, 203, 242–50, 298f
Maria Cleophas 223
Maria Iacobi 83, 184, 220, 271
Maria Salome 83, 220f, 271
Martha 80–2, 90, 103f, 278
Mary 37, 45, 47–53, 86, 96, 99–101, 103, 107, 147f, 155, 158, 182–96, 198, 205, 213–16, 248, 251, 264f, 272, 289, 291, 293, 295, 299
Mary of Bethany 82, 91, 103f, 278
Mary Magdalene 19f, 27, 46f, 54f, 83, 105, 110, 126, 184, 190–2, 219, 221, 223f, 259, 279, 289, 293
Marys 10f, 13–20, 22–8, 31, 37f, 46f, 49, 54–7, 63, 65, 83, 107, 110, 126, 183f, 190, 217–20, 234, 257–60, 289, 294
Melchisedech 81, 170, 271
Midwives 21, 33, 101, 147, 273
Moses 94, 123f, 145–7, 179, 279
Myscheff 150

New-guyse 150
Nicholas, Saint 62, 68
Noah 89, 92f, 98, 104f, 110, 119, 125f, 129f, 133, 145f, 162, 165f, 170, 173, 179, 223, 252, 257, 273, 275, 279, 284, 288, 298
Noah's wife 93, 165, 246, 252, 298
Nought 150
Now-a-days 150
Nuntius 39, 93, 115, 134, 136, 140, 273, 277, 281, *see also* Preco

Paul, Saint 56f, 158
Peter, Saint 19, 28, 97, 107, 155, 235, 258, 276
Pharao 94, 122, 132
Phariseus 102
Pikeharness 130, 230f
Pilate 62f, 95, 99, 114, 130f, 137–9, 142, 183, 187, 223, 233–6, 251f, 267, 277, 282f, 289
Poeta 158, 252
Potiphar's wife 55, 57

Indexes

Preco 85f, 277, see also Nuntius
Prophets 120f, 145f, 277, 294

Rachel 45f
Raiseslander 150
Recipients 17–20, 33, 243
Revealers 17–19, 31, 33f, 110, 243
Rex vivus 132

Sara 195, 208, 209
Satan 115, 154, 163, 227
Scribes 38, 40f, 262
Senescallus 100
Sephor (Mary's maid) 214
Shepherds 17, 21, 26, 30, 34, 37, 76, 83, 89, 95f, 98–100, 110, 117f, 129f, 139, 217, 223, 226f, 238, 239–50, 252, 257, 259, 268, 272, 275, 278, 282, 294, 297f
Sibyl 85–7, 124, 272
Simeon [Presentation in the Temple] 170

Simon the Leper 82, 105
Sirinus, see Cyrenius
Sloth 151
Soldiers 142, 144, 235f, 239, 282, 289, see also Torturers, Jews

Thief 63
Thomas, Saint 90
Timon 129f
Torturers 53, 98f, 131, 137, 144, 185, 225, 227, 236–40, 252, 296
Trowle 241, 243–5, 250, 298
Tutivillus 130, 295, 279

Vetula 64
Vice(s) 102, 106, 137, 148f, 150f, 227, 230, 282, 284, 295

Women at the Sepulchre, see Marys

Zachary 107

III Authors and anonymous works

Adam 256
Adam, jeu d', see *Ordo repraesentationis Adae*
Albert 259–61, 268
Albrecht 263f
Amalarius 255
Ancrene Riwle 284f
Anderson 272
Anz 21, 39, 42, 257, 259–63
Apocrypha see Tischendorf
Appius and Virginia 285
Archer 262
Æthelwold 14, 256
Auerbach 89, 255f, 273, 292
Axton 254, 269f, 277, 296, 298

Baker 272, 289f, 292
Bale 285
Baskervill 292, 296, 298
Baugh 272, 276
Beadle 134, 141, 270, 279, 281, 286f
Bede, Venerable 230f
Bédier 266
Beissel 265
Benkovitz 285
Bennett 284
Bentley 9f, 254
Bevington 256f, 269f, 276
Bjork 25, 258
Blaicher 288
Block 216, 273–5, 283, 285, 293

Bloomfield 284, 296
Böhme 257, 260f, 263f
de Boor 3, 54, 254, 257–9, 265
Bradbrook 81, 271, 273
Brecht 276
ten Brink 273, 287
Brinkmann, Alfons 72, 269
Brinkmann, Hennig 259, 264, 270, 288, 292
Briscoe 289
Brockett 265
Brotanek 209, 292
Brown 277
Brownstein 278
de Bruyne 259, 297
Bryan 267
Bryant 285
Bühler 22, 35, 257f, 260

Cameron 271, 273–5, 283f, 293
Campbell 263
Carey 278, 281, 289
Carmina Burana 266
Cawley 271, 273, 280f, 295f, 298f
Chambers 1, 4f, 71, 191, 203, 241, 263f, 268f, 270, 273, 277–9, 281, 283, 285f, 288, 290–2
Chaucer 132, 280
Chenesseau 264
Chidamian 299
Clopper 74, 121, 269f, 272, 279, 287, 291, 297

Coffman 54, 265f, 268
Collins 263f
Cosbey 299
Craig 1–4, 71f, 100, 107, 121, 167, 175, 203, 225, 254, 262, 264f, 268–70, 274f, 278–80, 284, 286–94, 297
Creizenach 71, 97, 262, 269, 273, 276, 296
Cursor Mundi 273, 279
Curtius 225, 294
Cushman 294

Danes 286
Davidson, Charles 279, 290
Davidson, Clifford 263, 273, 283, 286, 288–90, 294, 296
Deimling 188, 278
Diller 240, 254, 258, 265, 267, 269–73, 276, 278, 282, 287, 291f, 294, 297–9
Doran 273
Dreves 257, 264
Dunn 279
Dürrschmidt 296

Eaton 298
Eccles 274, 284
Eckhardt 150, 227, 280, 284, 294
Edmondson 256
von Einem 263
Elam 9, 11, 17, 254, 256
Eliade 13, 89, 259, 273

Falke 276, 286
Faral 295
Farnham 282
Fichte 276, 278, 285
Fischer-Lichte 256
Flanigan 13, 254, 256, 259, 264
Forrest 285
Foster 272, 277, 287, 294
Frampton 134, 273, 281, 289, 296
Frank 269
Franz 255
Froning 269
Fry 286
Furnivall 191, 289

Gardiner 259
Gardner 287, 294, 295f
Gayley 101, 103f, 274f, 279, 281, 289f, 294
de Ghellinck 267
Gibson 299
Glunz 259
Gospel of Nicodemus 95, 144, 183
Graf 282
Greban 272

Greg 4f, 148, 155, 157, 188, 213, 216, 273–5, 278f, 284–6, 289f, 293
Grieshammer 265

Habicht 284, 288
Hall 289f
Haller 294
Halliday 271f
Happé 284
Harbage 281, 283f
Hardison 72, 255–7, 260, 268–70, 276, 285
Harper 207, 291
Harrowing of Hell 273
Hegel 247, 254, 298
Heinzel 276
Hemingway 280, 290, 293
Hentschel 284
Hilarius 55f, 60f, 63, 72, 265–7, 273
Höfler 255
Hohlfeld 271, 278f, 281f, 287, 290
Huizinga 283
Hunningher 255
Hyckescorner 285

Inguanez 264
Isidore of Seville 259, 282

Jakobson 258
James 254, 270
Janicka 225, 295
Jantzen 18, 256
Johannes a Voragine, see *Legenda aurea*
John of Hildesheim (*see also Three Kings of Cologne*) 175, 257
John the Deacon 62
Johnston 279, 281, 296

Kahrl 271, 273–5, 283f, 292f, 297
Kehrer 263
Kolve 1f, 225, 227, 254f, 291, 295, 297, 299
Konigson 257
Kretzmann 262, 294
Künstle 263
Lancashire 270, 272
Lange 258f
Langland, see *Piers Plowman*
Laut 283, 286, 291
Legenda aurea 81, 84, 87, 107, 271f, 275, 278
Lesage 256
Longsworth 296
Love 216, 282, 293
Lukács 3, 73, 252, 254, 256
Lumiansky 243, 276–8, 287, 294
Lusty Juventus 285

Lydgate 156, 165, 277f, 286
Lyle 273, 279–81, 286, 288, 290

Mack 294, 297, 299
Maltman 282, 296
Manly, 294
Mannyng 298
Marguerite de Navarre 262
Marrow 266
Mathieu 256
Matthews 188, 276f
McDonald 256, 276
McNeir 282f, 289, 294
Meier, Theo 265, 288f
Mercadé, see Passion d'Arras
Meredith 107, 213, 254, 270f, 273–5, 285, 293
Messerer 18, 256, 263f, 268
Meyer, Paul 269
Meyer, Wilhelm 46, 257, 259, 265
Michael 267f
Mills 243, 270, 276–8, 287
Milton 227, 295
Mirk 278
Mohr 161, 286
Moore 297
Morgan 242, 294, 297f
Mroczkowski 297
Mueller 288
Muir 269
Munson 272, 288, 290f, 297
Murphy 272, 289f

Nelson 98, 270–3, 287, 294, 299
Neumann 296
Northern Passion 144, 239, 297

Ordo repraesentationis Adae 269
Ott 59, 120, 266, 279, 284
Owst 280–2, 284f, 291

Pächt 263
Palmer 270
Panofsky 18f, 257, 264, 288
Pantin 283
Parker 260, 262
Pascal 275
Passion d'Arras 272
Patch 286
Patterson 288
Pearsall 297
Pearson 279
Petit de Julleville 271
Petsch 259, 265
Pfister 254, 257
Pickering 266

Piers Plowman 285
Plautus 61, 267
Pollard 279f, 290
Prosser 1f, 102f, 181f, 209, 213, 216, 225, 254, 270, 274, 282, 288, 290–5
Pseudo-Bonaventura 137, 287

Rauhut 269
Réau 263
Reese 279–81, 291
Rescher 256
Resureccion, La Seinte 72–5, 269f
Riehle 280
Righter 265, 279, 284
Robbins 277, 280
Robinson 201, 273, 278, 283, 291
Roeder 288
Rose 98, 273, 285, 296
Ross 250, 288, 294, 299
Rossiter 2f, 225, 232, 237, 254, 294–7, 299
Roy 272
Rudwin 294

Saintsbury 275
Salter 87, 245, 271f, 291, 297–9
Salzer 288
Sanders 296f
Sandison 278
Sauer 255
Schadewaldt 282
Schegloff and Sacks 256
Schless 286, 294, 298
Schmidt 273, 279, 294
Schmitt 270
Schumann 267
Sehrt 282
Sepet 267
Severs 207, 291f
Shakespeare 92, 129, 280
Sheingorn 256f, 267, 270
Skey 262
Smart 284
Smith, John Harrington 281
Smith, Lucy T. 134, 281, 286, 288
Sondheimer 40, 260–2
Southern 77, 270, 292, 298
Spector 104, 148, 271–5, 284f, 293
Speirs 276, 297, 299
Spivack 150, 284
Staines 260, 262
Stanzaic Life of Christ 84–7, 116, 171, 189, 204, 219, 238, 272, 277f, 287, 294
Stemmler 3, 254–6, 258, 260f, 265, 267–9, 291
Stevens 76, 132, 270, 279–82, 289

Sticca 264, 288
Stumpfl 255
Swenson 157, 274f, 284–6, 293
Szondi 254, 256

Tack 58, 266
Taylor, Geoffrey C. 191, 288–90
Taylor, Jerome 298f
Thien 288
Thompson, F.J. 294
Thompson, James Westfall 266
Three Kings of Cologne 288
Tiddy 230, 278
Tilgner 286
Tischendorf 261, 263
Tomlinson 260, 262
Traver 285
Travis 121, 235, 269f, 278f, 287, 289, 296–8
Trusler 289
Tydeman 270, 276

Ungemach 276
Utesch 276

Venzmer 109, 275
Vezin 263
Viel Testament, Mistère du 209, 272, 292
Vriend 289

Waetzoldt 263
Wakefield Master 98, 102, 118, 129, 131, 134f, 137, 139f, 165f, 184f, 194, 203, 225, 231, 236, 240–2, 245–8, 251–3, 270, 279, 281f, 285, 289, 295, 299
Warning 226, 254, 294f
Waterhouse 209, 288, 292
Watt 294
Wechssler 265
Weimann 2f, 76–8, 129, 131, 199, 201, 230, 232, 240–2, 245, 254, 270f, 276, 278–80, 283f, 290f, 293–9
Wells 283, 286, 294, 299
Werner 47f, 51f, 72, 264f, 269f
Weydig 266f
White 225, 294
Wickham 268f, 280
Williams 24, 255, 258, 267, 279, 281f, 291
Wilson 87, 272, 277, 287, 294
Wolff 255
Wolpers 263, 265, 279, 288, 290, 294f
Wood 297
Woolf 287, 289–92
Wright, Jean 269f
Wright, Stephen K. 285

York Realist 95, 134f, 140f, 143f, 145, 183, 186f, 201f, 236, 251–3, 273, 282f, 291
Young 10–13, 21, 24–31, 33, 40, 46f, 52, 61, 63, 67, 109, 241, 255, 257–69, 272–6, 278, 293–5

Zappert 288
Zutt 295